History and Spirit

History and Spirit

AN INQUIRY INTO THE PHILOSOPHY OF LIBERATION

Joel Kovel

BEACON PRESS • BOSTON

BEACON PRESS
25 Beacon Street
Boston, Massachusetts 02108

*Beacon Press books
are published under the auspices of
the Unitarian Universalist Association of Congregations.*

98 97 96 95 94 93 92 91   8 7 6 5 4 3 2 1

Text design by Mike Fender

Library of Congress Cataloging-in-Publication Data

Kovel, Joel, 1936–
    History and spirit : an inquiry into the philosophy of liberation
    Joel Kovel.
        p.   cm.
    Includes bibliographical references and index.
    ISBN 0-8070-2916-5
    1. Spirit.   2. Spirituality.   3. Civilization, Modern—1950–
I. Title.
BL624.K68   1991
128′.1—dc20   90-22937
                                                    CIP

To Padre Trinidad de Jesus Nieto
and all who struggle for justice in Central America

Contents

Acknowledgments

A fellowship from the John Simon Guggenheim Foundation for 1987 gave me essential time to explore and reflect. John Clark and David Michael Levin read an early draft of the manuscript and made many valuable suggestions. Robert M. Young did likewise, and gave much support besides. Stanley Diamond read and commented at a later stage of the project, though my intellectual indebtedness to him long precedes it. Paul Buhle, an inspirited man, has been a fruitful source of dialogue. So too has Julio Torres, who also introduced me to the liberation church of El Salvador. Deborah Johnson and Lauren Bryant of Beacon Press have given superb editorial input, as has Joy Sobeck for copyediting. Mildred Marmur connected me to reality. Alex Kovel and Steve Roeder provided valuable help in the preparation of the manuscript. Other help was given by Jim Hamilton, Ynestra King, Donald Nonini, Tanya Coiner, Nancy Galvin, Eric Putzig and Dan Hallin. Finally, Dee Dee Halleck, critic and soul mate, has been at my side.

But God hath chosen the foolish things of the world to confound the wise; and God hath chosen the weak things of the world to confound the things which are mighty;

And base things of the world, and things which are despised hath God chosen, yea, and things which are not, to bring to nought things that are.

1 Corinthians 1:27–28 (KJ)

Introduction

Now two men remained in the camp, one named Eldad, and the other named Medad, and the spirit rested upon them; they were among those registered, but they had not gone out to the tent, and so they prophesied in the camp. And a young man ran and told Moses, "Eldad and Medad are prophesying in the camp." And Joshua, the son of Nun, the minister of Moses, one of his chosen men, said, "My lord Moses, forbid them." But Moses said to him, "Are you jealous for my sake? Would that all the LORD'S people were prophets, that the LORD would put his spirit upon them!"

Numbers 11:26–29 (RSV)

THE GENEALOGY of the present work is long, but its most notable recent ancestors are Herbert Marcuse's *Eros and Civilization* and Norman O. Brown's *Life Against Death*.[1] I encountered these books, products of the fifties and harbingers of the sixties, at a moment when medical-psychoanalytic ambitions and hopes for an emancipated politics were confusedly clashing in me. The place of Marcuse and Brown in history may be uncertain, but as catalysts of my own development they have always been in the first rank. Marcuse and Brown gave me the idea, and above all, the hope, that psychoanalytic thought could be turned toward emancipatory purposes rather than toward the narrow clinical orthodoxy in which I was being indoctrinated. I think, too, that from the first reading of *Eros and Civilization* and *Life Against Death* I conceived an ambition of one day writing a speculative work along the same lines. Much has happened to me since then—including becoming a psychoanalyst and then lapsing in that profession—but the ambition remained, and *History and Spirit* is its expression.

History and Spirit is not about psychoanalysis, but about the "spirit" of its title; that is, *what happens to us as the boundaries of the self give way*. Or we could say that it is about the "soul," by which we shall mean *the form of 'being' taken by the spiritual self*. And it is about "spirituality," which we may define as *the ways people seek to*

1

realize spirit and soul in their lives. Eros and Civilization and *Life Against Death* drew psychoanalysis away from the clinic because Marcuse (from the Frankfurt School perspective of Hegelian Marxism), and Brown (from a background of religious Puritanism) saw an emancipatory potential in Freud's discoveries.[2] In *History and Spirit,* however, the emancipatory potential is seen in what psychoanalysis has superseded, namely, spirituality; and Freud's discoveries are "analyzed" into their prepsychological core in the dynamics of human ontology. Thus psychoanalysis is seen as that "ego" which emerges from and represses its "id" in the human spirit. As such it is part of a project of *despiritualization*—Max Weber's "disenchantment of the world"—the essence of which is to unburden us of the implications of spirit, and not incidentally, to foster resignation to the conditions of modern society.[3] Despiritualization occurs at the arrival of technocracy, the deadening of nature and the loss of the sacred, and the breaking up of organic wholes into isolated fragments.

Like the psychological ego which it represents, psychoanalysis is adapted to reality and accepts society as it is; while spirit breaks loose from reality and, we shall argue, transforms society. Spirit emancipates not in some otherworld, but within society and history. Thus if spirit is like Freud's id in being outside the established reality, it is not mute and unconquered nature but the product of history and nature. Spirit does pertain to nature, and we should not hesitate to engage in radical speculation to try and understand how this may be so; but spirit enters human existence only through history, and we must also try to understand why this may be. Here I take the view that history entails an unending dialectic of splitting and the overcoming of splitting. These splits are created in domination and overcome in liberation. We know them as the categories of class, gender, and race—grand abstractions all, yet they define the concrete fracture lines according to which history and every particular life are played out. The domination of workers creates the splitting of class and becomes the condition of workers' movements up to and including the now-eclipsed hope of proletarian revolution. The male domination of women leads to the split between the genders and sexual war, eventuating in the rise of women's movements. The domination of blacks by whites leads to the splits of racism and the rise of black consciousness. The domination of nationalities leads to other racisms and other national liberation movements. Finally—both in sequence and significance, for nature enters into all these relations—the domination of nature erupts in the ecological crisis. All these dialectics interpenetrate, ebb and flow in their time, and cascade endlessly into each individual life. All this is well known. What is less well known, and what this work will argue, is that what we call "spirit" occurs in the motion of the dialectic, as splitting is overcome, and in relation to the liberation of nature. Spirit is not opposed to matter, or the flesh; rather it is revealed, indeed created, in the freeing of matter and flesh; that is, in the overcoming of splitting. And spirit is not a by-product, or an indicator, of this overcoming; it is the lived process itself. Thus liberation is a spiritual project, and spirituality is emancipatory. *History and Spirit* may be read, therefore, as a this-worldly appropriation of liberation theology, as a "liberation spirituality."

And yet we cannot simply draw an equation between what is spiritual and what is good. Nazism, after all, transformed society, and had definite spiritual ambitions. It is not enough to dismiss evils of this kind—and they are legion—by saying that the spirituality in question was false or bad, unless we know just what false or bad spirituality is. This is a job for the text to come. In any case, I contend only that the *repression* of spirit in the modern tradition is wrong—not that modernity per se is evil. In fact, the values advanced here—emancipation, critique, respect for science, the happiness of the body—are quintessentially modern; and *History and Spirit* contends only that there exists a rational basis for spirituality which respects them.

Note that I speak of spirituality and not religion. There is of course a great deal about religion in this book. This is because religion is the principle manifestation taken by spirit, however, and not because I am a religious person. At times deeply moved by religion, I would draw close to a faith, only to discover gross institutional defects which I could not stomach. In my younger days I was decidedly anticlerical; however, a recent involvement with religious pacifism and, especially, liberation theology in Central America taught me that religion could be a powerfully progressive as well as a reactionary force. Indeed, it was these experiences which made me "feel the spirit" and sharpened my disaffection with psychoanalysis. But while they heightened my interest in spirituality, and played a considerable role in motivating this study, they did not bring me into any church.[4]

And so this is a study from the outside, by one who has felt spirit but has never been able to situate it in any religion. Though religious tradition (mostly Judeo-Christianity, with less of Buddhism and Hinduism, and, because of regrettable ignorance, very little of Islam[5] or other religions) figures prominently in *History and Spirit*, the work focuses on the texture and forms taken by spirituality, and their values for human existence. Religion is the most prominent of these forms, because in religion spirit emerges from the whole of existence and is woven into history. Yet religion can no longer be taken as the automatic end of spirituality. Some may wonder what right an unbeliever has to speak of spiritual matters, as if a person who has never eaten good food could write of cooking. On the other hand, there is some benefit to be drawn from my lack of religious partiality or sectarianism—and from the consonance of my irreligion with the times. The modern crisis of faith has driven many to redefine their relation to the place in culture traditionally occupied by religion. Indeed, the modern tradition may be seen essentially in this light. Hegel, Marx, Nietzsche, Freud, Kafka, Heidegger: was not the work of each defined by the effort to restate the question of spirituality outside a religious framework, like Prometheus stealing spiritual fire from dying gods?

In any case, I take the position that there is much more to spirituality than religion, and that not all religious practices are equally spiritual. Religion always engages spirit, but in different degrees, which reflect the fact that religions are particular historical ways of binding spirit and socially expressing it. As we shall try to understand it, spirit breaks loose from the given world; but all religions have to live in the world if they are to make an impact on human events. Therefore each religion compromises. Each religion is an institutionalization of spirit, which means that it is less than fully spiritual. This casts no disgrace upon religion. All spirituality is less than fully spiritual, because all manifestations of spirituality are historically bound. The quality of spirituality, religious or not, depends not on the fact of its being limited, but on the concrete social relations it advances. There may or may not be an absolute Spirit, or God; in fact, I argue in Chapter Five of this work for some such concept, which I call Ultimate Being. But human spirituality is always concrete and limited, which means that it can be described, delimited, and evaluated critically.

Once we disengage the notion of spirit from religion, we can see spiritual possibilities in every sphere of existence: in sexuality, in politics, and in the humble activities of everyday life. This omnipresence of spirit poses an acute problem for our study, which can offer no more than cursory treatment for many major topics and is in no sense a comprehensive "survey" of the spirit. My goal rather is to draw attention to basic themes which are overlooked or diluted in the despiritualization of the modern age. But what is basic to the spirit is also old, and has been perpetually rediscovered through the centuries. In following the track of spirit, I encountered insights which had been made long before my arrival. If *History and Spirit* is an original work, then, it is original in the sense of "going back to origins." That is essentially what I try to do here: to recover, from under the cloud of despiritualization, something of a suppressed language of being, and apply this to various things. It may seem odd to invoke so conservative a message in a work whose political stance is frankly to the left. There is, however, no contradiction, for the suppression of spirit has the ideological function of reinforcing the existing order. Spirituality has a kind of resonance with nature, but it is also basically critical of power and domination.

History and Spirit consists of five interwoven meditations on spirit followed by a concluding chapter which expounds the nature of soul. The five chapters together comprise a kind of extended definition of the notion of spirit. They view spirit from the standpoint of power (as in being "full of spirit"); as an indwelling being (as in the "spirits of ancestors"); as authentic meaning ("the spirit of '76"); in relation to desire (the opposition of spirit to flesh[6]); and as ultimate being (the problem of godhead). Each meditation incorporates and expands upon the previous one. I see these as five different perspectives, each of which grasps something of spirit along an axis, or plane, and gives dimensionality to all the others. As for the whole of spirit, I do not think it can be grasped in any language. Yet we work with words. Given the fact that the word "spirit" can be used in all these senses, and that these meanings are both distinct from one another yet emanate from a deeper unity, it would seem that this approach is best suited to do justice to the notion of spirit. No one perspective is adequate, perhaps all taken together are not adequate; yet taken together they may define a "polyhedral" sense of spirit within the broader framework of human history and nature.

In a sense, this study resumes the philosophical project most famously addressed by Hegel, the philosopher of Spirit as such. And it tracks contours defined by a number of the traditions which germinated from his work: Marxism, existentialism, Nietzsche's thought, Heidegger's philosophy, and on into post-structuralism and the philosophies of deconstruction. (Freud may be also seen as a post-Hegelian thinker, though he undoubtedly would have denied the association.[7]) Many issues raised here demand additional and more concrete exploration; for example, fascism, Marxism, nonviolent direct action, feminist spirituality, liberation theology, religious fundamentalism, "New Age" spirituality, Jungian psychoanalysis, and ecological politics. These are all "spiritual pathways," a term both clumsy and somewhat clichéd, but necessary to signify the fact that spirit works through history in many ways, which cannot be understood in spiritual terms alone, but must also be grasped in moral and political terms. It should be observed that a number of endnotes have been composed with an eye turned toward a fuller explication of these varied matters; they may help in situating the present work on the spectrum of current discourse.

History and Spirit is written not simply to advance a philosophy of spirit but in response to a profound spiritual crisis. Spirit reaches beyond the material, historical world of economy and technology, yet it is deeply affected by the time and place at which it arises. Thus spirit stands outside history, acts within history, and is acted upon by history. There is always something of the "beyond" in history with respect to spirit, and there is always something "underneath" in spirit with respect to history. It is this very tension which causes the two to act upon each other. And in our time, history has been very hard on spirit.

We have already begun to speak of this effect as a process of "despiritualization." Let us define this as the pressure or tendency in social institutions to devalue the spiritual dimension, render it irrational, or even suppress its expression altogether. From work to lovemaking, from the rearing of children to the pastimes of adults, spirituality seems decreasingly an element of modern experience than in so-called traditional society—by which I mean a precapitalist society, albeit one organized into social classes and nation-states. The transition from traditional to modern society was not something that happened all at once, at some point when capitalism was, so to speak, switched on. In reality, capitalism is not merely an economic arrangement but something which keeps on happening, and traditional society is that which is continually transformed as capitalism keeps on happening. In traditional society—and the reader may reflect for a moment on what society was like for grandparents and great-grandparents—the communal basis of life was relatively secure, and values were relatively stable and taken for granted. The change from traditional to modern society—characterized by a breakdown in the sense of values and the communal life underlying those values—is one entailing despiritualization, among other things. Its most remarkable feature from our standpoint has been the loss of the great world religions of traditional society as the principle vehicles for spiritual life.

Traditional society, however, is not the original society, and even traditional spirituality contains seeds from an earlier transformation.

There was a first great revolution in spirituality, which accompanied the emergence of social classes and the state from the earliest form of society. These earliest societies have been called "primitive," a term that should signify "original" rather than "backward."[8] Unfortunately, the term "primitive" has come to designate a kind of homogeneous essence, a blank to be filled with the preoccupations of the observer. It has acquired in this way so much unwanted conceptual baggage—a childlike simplicity, a savage instinctuality, or a romantic projection of imagined purity—as to require scrapping, at least for this work. I have chosen instead to use "tribal," "original," or some other circumlocution. Often I use the clumsy term, "state-free people," which at least has the merit of indicating what it is about "primitives" which deserves emphasis. I might add that my beliefs in this matter began to take shape in 1961, when I spent some time in the jungles of Suriname studying tropical medicine and was sufficiently struck by the character of the people I met there to want to account for what seemed a genuine state of grace.

The hallmark of this kind of original society—which today survives only as a dimly approximated ideal type—is an organic sense of unity between human beings and nature, related to an absence of social class and the state. Accordingly, the spirituality of state-free people is also marked by an organic unity, despite its profuse forms. In the transformation from original to state society—a process which moved across an immense frontier of time and space, often coerced with bloody and genocidal consequences—the organic spiritualities of state-free societies were uprooted and changed into the religious institutions which provided the cultural glue and legitimating framework of the traditional statist society. The history of the world religions was written during this epoch, which has now been overturned by modernity.

There was no single pattern to the change. In some instances original spiritual views were more or less agglomerated, for example, the polytheistic religions of Rome. In other cases, such as those of Hinduism or Christianity, the earlier beliefs were synthesized into a new unity which was then further adapted when it became a state religion. In yet other situations, as in the impact of Christianity on the Indian cultures of Latin America, a syncretism occurred in which the native faith altered the metropolitan religion (e.g., in various cults of the Virgin). Finally, there were occasions, such as the persecution of witches, when the state religion violently suppressed a spiritual predecessor.[9]

Through all the changes from the dawn of society through the origins of the modern nation-state, however, one persistent theme was woven into the immensely complex fabric: an axiomatic belief in spirituality's central place in human existence. Undoubtedly official religion alienated the essence of spirituality as a way of enforcing subservience to temporal power. But something had to be there in order to be alienated: not just the presence of spirituality, but the conviction that spirituality really mattered and had the power to define the terms of existence. Premodern society, in both its primitive and traditional forms, achieved its very identity on the basis of spirituality: this tribe's belief in the spirits of the waters or the ancestors differed from that tribe's, and thereby defined the difference between the tribes, just as the religion of Christendom differentiated the nations of Europe from the nations of North Africa and Western Asia. As nation-states arose, they were often accompanied by religious differentiation; for example, when Henry VIII instituted the Church of England as a way of proclaiming England's emergence as a world power. These religious changes were not mere indicators of an independent political process, like tags attached to suitcases: they were part of the process, and their spiritualities became signifiers of the whole.

Indeed, history details a perpetual struggle to the death between competing spiritual systems and doctrines, because spirituality was a matter of life and death, the mythopoetic framework which made existence intelligible. It is striking how the spiritualities occupied a kind of defining place before the modern age, and how that place is missing today, leaving spiritualities scattered about the cultural landscape. This is a mark of despiritualization. Though we have an increasingly unified world system, bound together by a technology unthinkable in former times, and presided over by global capitalism, we do not have within that system anything like a single spirituality, nor do the spiritualities that we have tend to serve as coherent signifiers. There are obvious, even gross exceptions. But these are the proverbial exceptions which prove the rule, for they occur in often conscious reaction to the despiritualizing tide of modernity. Think only of Iran under Khomeini—a consciously spiritual regime defined by hostility to modernity, as signified by the "Great Satan" of America. Or the reactionary spirituality of the religious right in America, which opposes the effects of modernity on personal and family life.

Though these major political forms of spirituality are defensive, this does not mean that their source is drying up. As I shall argue below, spirituality is inherent to human beings, and arises wherever there is human existence. There is today certainly no dearth of spiritual movement. Nor is it obvious that a plurality of weak or reactive spiritualities is a bad thing, given the many horrors associated with dominant traditional spiritualities. But in any case, the conditions of modern society are such that spirituality must always contend with the pressure of despiritualization.

It is time to look a bit more closely at the source of this pressure, and to evaluate it. People have variously referred to the dynamism underlying modernity as "science," "individualism," or "loss of community." Undoubtedly, all these are present in modernism with its pressure toward despiritualization. But they do not constitute its essence, or allow us to get a handle on the phenomenon. Science in itself cannot be the antithesis to spirituality for the simple yet compelling reason that great scientists—one need only think of Einstein, but there are many others—have often been deeply spiritual persons who not only found no contradiction, but actually saw science and spirit in the same light. No doubt a certain form of science has been antispiritual; but this observation leads us to criticize these kinds of science rather than oppose science to spirituality.

Individualism and loss of community, on the other hand, are indeed antithetical to spirit and have played a role in despiritualization. But are these self-actuating causes, or symptoms of a deeper and more pervasive condition? Individualism, after all, is but one possibility open to human beings. For individualism to be rampant in a society such as ours, there must be systematic forces at work selecting for ruthlessness, greed, and self-aggrandizement. And as for loss of community, I have not met many people who did not regret this absence, or bitterly resent the forces in society which have worked to destroy communal bonds.

We are led, therefore, to look at the dynamism of society as a whole if we are to understand what has created an antispiritual science, fostered ruthless individualism, or broken community into bits. And since the masters of our society and their propaganda mills have no difficulty in triumphally shouting the name of this dynamism as *capitalism,* I see no reason why we should not follow suit. For it is capitalism which has created modernity in such a way that traditional spirituality has been eroded. And it is capitalism which remains spirit's greatest antagonist.

A word of definition is in order here, because capitalism is too vast an entity, and too caught up in ideology, for any simple formulation. Today, amidst an orgy of capitalist triumphalism and self-congratulation, it is all the more important to be clear as to what capitalism really is. Thus when I speak of capitalism I do not mean only a "market" society, for markets can simply mean the principle of rational exchange and regulation. Nor do I mean only a society in which people are free to start their own enterprises—a society of mom-and-pop candy stores, truck gardens and backyard innovators. There are many such ventures in our society, and they are by and large one of its virtues, but they surely do not characterize the society as a whole, or capitalism in its essence. For what do these features tell us about the reality of capitalism—its iron tendency toward corporate gigantism, its staggering concentration of power and wealth in the hands of a few, its global reach and the systematic impoverishment of masses of people around the globe to aggrandize these few, penetration and colonization of all spheres of life, its insensate plundering of the earth, its fantastic creation of waste and toxins? Capitalism is a system, and anyone interested in a realistic portrait would have to explain these characteristics first of all. And to do so we have to go deeper than "markets" or "free enterprise." We have to consider, rather, the way wealth is produced and wage labor is constituted as a form of domination, the way social classes arise on this basis, the role played by technology. And this level of analysis leads to even more elementary things: basic relations between people, relations between humanity and nature, a fundamental orientation to reality, notions of power, and the drive toward power. And all these levels sustain one another. In short, capitalism is a fundamental *way of being* first of all, and then a society built around and perpetuating that way of being. Here the capitalist economic system comes into view, organizes and runs the society, allowing some mom-and-pop stores, but driving masses into poverty and raping the earth. We cannot offer a full portrait of the system in the confines of this work, to be sure—though a number of features will be developed as we proceed—but we must keep the perspective in mind.

Although medieval thinkers warned against its coming, the danger posed by capitalism to spirituality was masked in its early years when the new economic system was instrumental in propelling the Protestant Reformation.[10] It has since remained obscured by the pious posturing of bourgeois state leaders, who never tire of proclaiming their love for God (often linked with anticommunist tirades about attacks by Marxism-Leninism against religion). But capitalism's threat to spirituality is real, and integral to capitalist production itself. While it is impossible to establish this point before we have defined the notion of spirit, a few observations may be helpful here.

It does not take a Karl Marx to conclude that something is awry in a society which grossly worships commodities and money. Marx, however, pinpointed this phenomenon under the rubric of the "fetishism of commodities."[11] He realized that under capitalism, value is detached from human activity and placed onto the object made to be sold. This is not incidental; indeed, it is the very essence of capitalism. Without it, there would be no capital to accumulate, and of course, no capitalists to get rich and powerful. But it is a devastating situation for spirit. For it means that the capitalist mode of production displaces the core of human activity from human beings to things. If spirit is somehow a function of what it means to be a human being—and I do not see how this conclusion can be escaped—then it follows that under capitalism, spirit is bound to be thwarted, or as Marx (following Hegel) would have said, alienated.

The story does not end here of course; indeed it barely begins. The rest of its plot, some of which will unfold in the following pages, starts from the point at which people try to rescue their spirituality from the trap set by capitalism, and dissociate or *split* themselves in order to retain a spiritual core. This spares the individual spirit, but at the cost of fragmenting reality and dehumanizing social production. More than spared, the individual is released from the communal bonds of precapitalist production, and becomes free to aggrandize the self. Thus the epoch of individualism emerges, in a social order which alienates spirit as it destroys the community. In the same process, spirituality becomes part of the "otherworld," and loses relevance to the economy and politics.[12] Since the economic sphere is the domain of what is rational, rationality in capitalism belongs with the despiritualized economy and polity; that is to say, reason becomes narrow and technical, losing sight of the whole. And this becomes the pattern of an antispiritual science, a science of pure technique and compartmentalization.

In such an atmosphere, spirit becomes residual, and spirituality becomes irrational and irrelevant. Everyone is free to pursue spirituality under capitalism, and almost everybody does. But none of it matters to the order of things. The true religion of modern society is to be found on the television set on Super Bowl Sunday, where one can watch the cult of macho militarism and the worship of commodities. By contrast, piety becomes an anachronistic gesture even though the great world leaders regularly display it.[13]

Though spirituality no longer matters to the power structure, it still matters greatly to individuals, who pursue it with a fierce and even desperate energy. The result is a great plethora of spiritualities, a pattern characteristic of the United States from the beginning of our history, for this was the first society to be consciously designed along the lines of capitalist modernity.[14] At the beginning of our history as a nation, as at the beginning of capitalism itself, spirituality could be linked to a coherent worldview and a hope of substantial participation in society. For all but a few, that hope has faded under the domination of colossal corporations and an all-pervasive apparatus of mass culture. In reaction, people have turned inward, away from an increasingly insane world, to find personal spiritual rationality. As Louis Dupré has written,[15] under modern conditions authentic spirituality has come more and more to mean pure inwardness. People go their own way, seeking spirit in the dark.

But a spirituality which is dissociated and purely internal drifts toward disaster, as does the society from which it has split off. Franz Kafka, who though irreligious was a great spiritual genius, detailed some implications of this destinationless voyage. Kafka's protagonists typically engaged in doomed, endless spiritual quests depicting the intrinsic unreason of contemporary spirituality. Kafka's famous evocation of horror consists of his ability to render precisely existence stripped down to an elementary spiritual drive, across a landscape whose only realization of that drive is annihilation. Each of his main tales—*The Metamorphosis, The Trial, The Castle,* even *In the Penal Colony*—documents an instance in which the self is dissolved in a hopeless spiritual voyage, and soul is gained at the price of its destruction. The absence of a coherent framework of spiritual practice leaves the soul no place of fulfillment but hell.

Kafka is a prelude, and his hell is real. The Kafkaesque vision is doubly precise: in its depiction of inner states of soul-annihilation, and in its anticipation of mass horror. Genius is prophetic; it does not so much re-present as pre-figure. The pits and the garbage into which Kafka's immolated heros are tossed[16] anticipate the contours of a society given over to pure instrumentality and accumulation—total war, the Holocaust, Hiroshima, Cambodia, Chernobyl, toxic waste dumps, Bantustans, nuclear processing plants, melting ice caps, uprooted and burned forests, and the slums which overwhelm the cities of debt-ridden Third World nations while bankers intone the virtues of economic discipline. Such is the heritage of an enlightened reason split from spirit.

A world order that commits planetary suicide in the search for profit while driving the majority of human beings into despair and poverty is a killing/producing machine without spiritual center. Theodor Adorno once suggested that after the Holocaust there could be no poetry. The same might be said for spirituality. If the universal condition of the despiritualized world is a kind of bland numbness,[17] this is in some measure due to the need to ward off the omnipresence of horror. Faced with the holocausts regularly prescribed in the name of efficiency, order, and profit, the soul takes refuge in inwardness, or is simply turned off.

This work disputes Adorno's pessimism, though not his sense of crisis. It is written in the belief that spiritual possibilities exist which neither avoid nor resign themselves to the actual state of things. It does not try to precisely detail these spiritualities, for spirituality cannot be chosen from a catalog. It tries to show, rather, the nature of the ground on which they may be built. This ground lies in a rejection of the world as thoroughgoing as the most esoteric mysticism, yet deeply committed to struggling in the here and now for partial, prefigurative gains. This is paradoxical, perhaps impossible, but it is also necessary. Something of the attitude may be summed up in the reply of an old Spanish anarchist, when confronted with the fact that his ideals were beautiful but unrealizable: "Of course it is impossible to realize them. But don't you see that everything that is possible today, is worthless?"[18] Sensible people might see this as evidence of quixotism, but they would be wrong. For a radically spiritual attitude, though it may have no immediate possibility of realization, is, when turned outward, the most practical thing in the world. The reason we should fight for spirit is the here and now, because spirit creates a new sense of the possible, and the belief that the possible is worth striving for. Thus the impossible must be imagined if it is to be realized, and it is true sanity to do so.

Before we bring this introduction to its close, it would be well to draw attention to some of the limits of *History and Spirit*. The most daunting is the sharp contrast between the scope of human spirituality and the limited perspective I can bring to it. It is less a matter of my ignorance than of the immense scale of spiritual phenomena over the ages and in all parts of the world. The problem is particularly troubling because the study demands as a starting point acceptance of the idea that there universally exists a spiritual dimension in human beings. This, however, is an abstraction I am unequipped to make given the whole range of spiritual phenomena. I am convinced that there is a quality, best called spiritual, which characterizes human beings and cannot be explained away psychologically; that is, there is a spiritual component to human nature. To account for this, I derive a set of terms which serve to describe spiritual life, words like *being, soul, Ego, Other, desire,* and so forth. It would be absurd to think, however, that my use of these terms, and the relations drawn between them, are free of cultural and gender bias, and that they are as useful in accounting for, say, the spirituality of Sioux Indians in the nineteenth century, or Mahayana Buddhism of fifth-century India, as they may be for the current-day spiritual politics of the Western world. I am certain also that the concepts are less serviceable for the description of the spirituality of the Wife of Bath, or King Henry V, or Thomas Jefferson, or Sojourner Truth than of a citizen of the technocratic age. Indeed, in reviewing the manuscript for this book, I have been repeatedly struck by how much, despite all its claims for inclusivity and all my efforts to expand its scope, the spiritual frame of reference remains that of a white male.

The problem is fundamentally the same as that faced by Freud when he pronounced on the universal qualities of the psyche from his perch in fin de siècle Vienna. The limitation belongs to every work which proposes to say something valid about humanity. For the mere fact of *saying* something puts one in the peculiar yet near-universal dilemma posed by our dependence upon language and ordered discourse. The point may seem not to require emphasis, since it is perfectly obvious that a book such as this is dependent, like any written text, on the linear sequence of word-symbols. And yet the implications need to be drawn. We love language and are made human by it; but our narcissism should never fool us into thinking that language is, or can be, a wholly adequate window on reality. Language is, rather, as much a part of our reality as it is a medium for conveying reality, and we can no more use language to fully describe the world than we can stand outside of our own thinking. In the present case we have an additional level of bias to contend with as well, for the limits of language become especially acute in the zone of spirit. It will not spoil our journey, I hope, to be reminded again that the whole of spirit cannot be expressed in speech of any kind, and certainly not in prose. <u>Poetry does a better job, because in it the word and the thing are brought together; but poetry sacrifices the lucidity and range necessary to express the manifold relations of spirit and history. And so we will have to accept the limits of approaching spirit in discursive, linear prose.</u>

Even so, it would be well to keep in mind that plain prose can never be kept fully plain if it is to say anything about spirit. All use of language touches upon the potential power announced at the beginning of the Johannine Gospel—"in the beginning was the Word, and the Word was God." No doubt for John, the Word, or *logos,* is a long way from the discursive prose which centuries later ends up electronically transmitted onto the pages of books. The intellectual lineage of *logos* descended from the Heraclitean fire until it became the fusion point of Hellenic and Hebrew cultures, and later the power of God made into flesh in the form of Jesus. The Greek term derives from the Indo-European root, *leg-*, meaning "to collect," and later, "to speak." In Greek, *logos* comes to mean "speech," "word," and "reason." The Latin carries the root forward into *legere*, with its associations of reading ("legible," "legend") and choosing ("intelligent," "collect"). However, the power adhering to *logos* derives from the Hellenic identity between the power of the mind, i.e., reason, and the product of the mind—speech, or the word spoken and written down. Thus Western culture passed, as Walter Ong has described, from the oral to the literate mode, sweeping away and burying from view the tremendous power of speech, which still maintains hidden power over what has been written.[19] The power of speech and language in human experience cannot be overestimated; and what ancient philosophers and the Bible viewed as transcendent still stalks among us, and is relevant in many ways to this study.

No student of spirituality or religious movements can fail to be impressed by the widespread influence of sectarianism and cultism. Each sect or cult orders itself about certain "sacred texts" in which the "Word" is given. A peerless, usually male leader is given the power to enunciate the logos of the sect. It matters little what claptrap or nonsense he enunciates: what counts is that the leader is authorized to speak logos; he becomes logos personified. The divine force which comes out of his mouth is the essence of the elusive quality called charisma. Peerless or charismatic leaders can range from geniuses like Freud, Marx, or Mao Zedong, to dubious characters like Lyndon LaRouche or Jimmy Swaggart. An associated phenomenon is the extraordinary role played by fundamentalist interpretations of sacred texts in modern religious movements, a tendency which emerged in the Protestant Reformation[20] and now reaches ridiculous heights with modern televangelism.

Such uses of logos are directly, if problematically, "spiritual." But the power of the word persists in the despiritualized world as well. Here the effect is much more subtle, and mediated through the institutionalized power of professional bodies. In the splitting up of knowledge into specialized technical compartments, the trace of logos is felt as a suffix granting the magical power of Science. We say "bio-*logy*," for example, or "theo-*logy*," where despiritualized logos is to be read as the "science of" life or God. In other instances we shall have to attend to psycho-*logy*, the science of mental processes and behavior; or onto-*logy*, the division of philosophy concerned with being (for spirit is a function of that elusive but essential concept). In all cases we tend to forget that a science is first of all a statement, and only secondarily a description of its domain. Thus biology is a set of constructions about something called "life," and it reflects not only life but the worldview of those who make and respond to the statement. If this worldview is a despiritualized one, then the perimeters of biology will be drawn so as to exclude any participation of spirit in nature.

Each of these instances is ambiguous, because the claims of logos—to synthesize reason, knowledge, and discourse—overlap with and can be substituted for the claims of science: the collective and patient accumulation of objective knowledge about the world. And there is a hidden, third term as well—worldly power—which binds together the first two. Coordinated with the march of despiritualization, then, is the rise of technocratic power.

Why mention this now? Because in trying to make our way through the labyrinth of spirit we will encounter some of these "ologies" and their claims to universal knowledge. Psychoanalysis has become such an "ology," as has Marxism. Undoubtedly *History and Spirit* is brushed too, because this work, too, is definitely a kind of "ology." Even if it stands outside professional discourse, it remains subject to all the hazards of logos. To the degree that this book escapes these hazards it will signify that perhaps as a result of the spiritual crisis itself, a mutation of logos is possible for us now. Perhaps there could arise a kind of "critical logos," which reflects upon and transcends itself, and so comes closer to spirit. I have tried to grope in this direction.

Prelude

In Search of Spirit

THE *OXFORD ENGLISH DICTIONARY* contains five large pages of tiny type which describe the various meanings of the word *spirit*. I will not burden the reader by going through them all. Let me turn instead to a simpler dictionary definition. The *American Heritage Dictionary* lists the following meanings under *spirit*:

1. That which is traditionally believed to be the vital principle or animating force within living beings. 2. *Capital* S. The Holy Ghost . . . 3. *Capital* S. *Christian Science.* God. 4. Any supernatural being, such as a ghost. 5. a. That which constitutes one's unseen, intangible being. b. The essential and activating principle of a person; the will. 6. A person as characterized by some stated quality: *He is a proud spirit.* 7. An inclination or tendency of a specified kind. 8. *Plural.* One's mood or emotional state. 9. A particular kind of emotional state characterized by vigor and animation. 10. Strong loyalty or dedication. 11. The predominant mood of an occasion or period: *"The Spirit of 1776 is not dead."* (Jefferson). The real sense or significance of something: *The spirit of the law* . . .—tr.v. **spirited, -ing, -its.** 1. To carry off mysteriously or secretly . . . 2. To impart courage, animation or determination to; stimulate; encourage. [Middle English, from Norman French, from Latin *spiritus*, breath, breath of a god, inspiration, from *spirare*, to breathe. See **spirare** in Appendix.]

Whence we learn that *spirare* is linked to, besides *spirit: spiracle, as-pirate, cesspool, conspire, expire, respire, suspire, transpire*—and of course *inspire* and *aspire*.

It is hard to make much sense out of this. From the breath of a god, to an animating principle, to the real significance of something, to an unseen other, to what is immaterial and opposed to flesh, to the divine itself—the term *spirit* seems at first to have as its only coherent meaning, *that which is vitally important, endowed with power, yet beyond immediate sense perception*. It is not present—yet powerfully present. It belongs to what is "other" to us.

This need not make spirit any more real than other figments of the imagination. Spirit can be either what traditional society took it to be, namely, a real, self-subsisting part of the universe in which we participate; or it can be what modern despiritualizing traditions take it to be, namely, a mistake of some kind, born out of wish and the limited power of human perception and cognition, and passively awaiting the correcting hand of science. In other words, spirit is a signifier, but whether what it signifies is worth talking about cannot be decided a priori.

We do not have to decide this now. All we need to affirm here is that it is worthwhile to look for such a signifier as spirit. This is because established science has never succeeded in telling us just what kinds of nonspiritual entities can stand in spirit's place, and because so much of importance has gone on under the name of spirit. If we conceive of a kind of imaginary volume consisting of all that human beings have held to be important about their existence throughout the time and the space of their stay on earth, then a very large part of that volume would be occupied by spirituality of one kind or another. Indeed, only in the very thin slice of time and space occupied by Western modernism and postmodernism would we find doubt about the priority of the spiritual and contraction of the life-space given to it.

Today people in the "advanced" industrial societies, separated from direct engagement with the production of life, spend about half their waking hours in one kind of alienated toil or another (for example, housewives in the age of the electronic home do more housework than their counterparts a century ago), and the remainder in personal relationships, tending to bodily needs, and what is loosely called leisure.[1] In other words, time is passed "nonspiritually," even according to the hazy understanding of the term we have for the moment. Yet in traditional society, and particularly in state-free society, virtually all activities were conducted with regard to spirit as a vital, intangible principle which suffused human existence and indeed the whole universe. Work (which interestingly takes up considerably less of "backward" peoples' time than of today's wage slaves) and personal life were spiritualized; and the proper destination of human existence was conceived as the full development of spiritual powers.[2] So striking is the difference between original society and our own in this respect that it may be said that state-free people would not think of spirituality as such. Nor would they think of religion as such, or of other notions such as "wilderness," which represent the impression made by an alienating civilization. That is, religion, spirit, and wilderness, or even external nature as a whole, are notions which occur to people after they have already lost some part of what these words signify. Those who are immersed in a thing do not have a word for that thing, because they do not need one. However, the age of despiritualization makes us separate spirituality from the rest of existence and search for it.

The term *spiritual* seems to apply then to some kind of basic, even original human condition. I would say it is in human nature to be spiritual, although this is admittedly a controversial idea.[3] However we look at the human species, the notion of spirit seems to be an essential one. Imagine if you will, that the science of some future society concluded that human beings really have no grounds at all for a spiritual life, and that the rulers of that society attempted to abolish the word *spirit*, and congeners such as *soul*, from the language. Imagine that they educated children, as Plato would have done with respect to poetry, to never use spiritual terms in their descriptions of the world. Imagine, in other words, a society which attempted to completely despiritualize itself instead of stopping halfway as our society does.

What would be the practical consequences of such a discourse? What could not be said? Could such people talk about what it is like to be human? I think not. Deprived of spiritual terms such creatures would be able to talk expertly about the external world as a collection of *things,* and they would be able to talk of themselves as things, too. But they could never converse about themselves as persons, real human beings. And indeed, such creatures would not really be human beings at all if the language of spirit were denied them. Nor would they have speech, so that the experiment as a whole is strictly fantastic, just as any idea of a human being without a spiritual dimension is unreal and fantastic, even in these bizarre and despiritualized times.

Varieties of Spirit

To assert the general significance of spirituality is one thing; to spell out the concrete forms taken by spirit under various circumstances is another. Since this is a work whose medium is words, we enter spirit through its traces upon language. Though spirit cannot be fully expressed in words, it can be partially expressed, and each expression forms a kind of tile in a gigantic mosaic whose final pattern gives some clue to the nature of the whole. We assume, therefore, that the varying meanings of spirit all provide clues to a larger pattern. Each use of the term *spirit* arises from some concrete situation in which people have expressed themselves spiritually, and employed the word *spirit* (or *soul*, etc.) for this purpose. It is only sensible, moreover, to make particular use of great teachers who have seen deeper and further into spirit.[4] I have thus used the various meanings of *spirit* and *soul* as archaeological sites, where I have dug up many pieces of the mosaic from a wide range of human situations. The approach is therefore both etymological and archaeological.[5] It is based on the assumption that no single meaning of the word *spirit* is logically prior to all the others, but that all are indicative of what spirit is about, as shards from a dig give clues to a lost civilization.

If the etymological approach makes it more difficult to think of spirit as a unified or homogeneous substance, so much the better. One often reads in some New Age text that humans are not simply mental and physical creatures, but that we also have a spirit, as though spirit were another compartment of being, a zone within which certain "spiritual" events happen. But this tripartite arrangement of body-mind-spirit is quite misleading, except as a rough metaphor. Spirit is not a substance or a place, but a kind of relationship which happens at certain points of human existence. We do not *have* a spirit; rather, we *are* spirit to the extent we achieve a certain kind of being. If body-mind is a unity, then spirit can be read as the coming-to-be of that unity. And this coming-to-be depends on the way we act and on our relationship to the world.

Taking our cue from the multiply registered dictionary entry, we find spirit refracted through language in five principal ways. These are not exclusive of each other, but overlap to provide a kind of five-dimensional plenum within which the various meanings of the term may nest. The dimensions all intersect and mutually determine each other, so that our distinction is actually quite artificial and no more than heuristic. In any case, it seems most useful to consider spirit from the standpoint of the following five significations:

- a vital force
- an occult or hidden being
- the authentic principle of a thing

- some relation to flesh, i.e., sexuality, or desire; the relation often being antagonistic
- a divine or higher way of being

We may take these in turn and meditate a bit about each one, expanding our sights as we go.

1.
Spirit as Vital Force

In the beginning God created the heaven and the earth. And the earth was without form, and void; and darkness was upon the face of the deep. And the Spirit of God moved upon the face of the waters.

Genesis 1 : 1–2 (KJ)

The immortal Self is the sun shining in the sky, he is the breeze blowing in space, he is the fire burning on the altar, he is the guest dwelling in the house; he is in all men, he is in the gods, he is in the ether, he is wherever there is truth; he is the fish that is born in the water, he is the plant that grows in the soil, he is the river that gushes from the mountain he, the changeless reality, the illimitable! . . . Man does not live by breath alone, but by him in whom is the power of breath.

Katha Upanishad

IT IS QUITE REMARKABLE that spirit, which we usually think of as primarily immaterial, and even as antagonistic to the world and flesh, should have as its original and primary meaning the direct apprehension of a vital and material force pervading the entire universe. In other words, spirit is power first of all. The famous passage in Genesis announces the spiritual attitude of the Old Testament, a document which expresses the views not only of the archaic world in which it was written, but of the tribal society which came before it. For the association of spirit with power is common, despite variations, to all traditional societies—that is, to societies before the despiritualizing effects of modernism set in, whether stateless societies or precapitalist statist societies. The Yoruba people of Nigeria, for example, have a religion which, in the words of Robert Farris Thompson, "presents a limitless horizon of vivid moral beings, generous yet intimidating. They are messengers and embodiments of *àshe*, spiritual command, the power-to-make-things-happen, God's own enabling light rendered accessible to men and women. The supreme deity, God Almighty, is called in Yoruba Olorun, master of the skies. Olorun is neither male nor female but a vital force. In other words, Olorun is the supreme quintessence of *àshe*."[1]

Note that we have already intruded into the domain of the next chapter, which is about "spirits" as occult and partial beings, bearing the power of the whole. To keep these two meanings clearer, let us agree to speak of *spirit-power* as "the sense of vital force associated with the spirit world," and *spirit-being* as "the division of the spirit world into individual entities called beings." These two categories go together, as do time and space in the physical world. In any case, the investiture of spirit-power in spirit-beings is a very widespread phenomenon. If we move a third of the way around the earth from West Africa, we find, in the words of Sword, a Dakota Indian, "Every object in the world has a spirit and that spirit is *wakan.* Thus the spirits of the tree or things of that kind, while not like the spirit of man, are also *wakan. Wakan* comes from the *wakan* beings. These *wakan* beings are greater than mankind in the same way that mankind is greater than animals. They are never born and they never die. They can do many things that mankind cannot do. Mankind can pray to the *wakan* beings for help."[2] Gerardus van der Leeuw, in his monumental study of the manifestations of religion, states that "*wakanda* [are] at one time a god of the type of an originator, at another an impersonal Power which acquires empirical verification whenever something extraordinary is manifested."[3] In other words, the term *wakan* expresses spirit-power and spirit-being in the same word.

For state-free people, the universal exists in and cannot be split from the concrete particular. This is not due to any defect in the capacity for abstraction, but to ways of thinking consistent with life lived in a relatively unalienated relation to its own production and reproduction. I am not speaking here of happy savages living close to nature, for state-free people, though they do live closer to nature than we, are complex and suffering creatures, capable of evil as well as good, as human beings have always been. The cardinal distinction between tribal and modern people lies rather in the fact that the former inhabit a society without a state apparatus or the peculiar distortion of human relations imposed by class division. The ways of the state and social class have been driven so deeply into our being that we accept them as natural, and can scarcely imagine what a difference they make in the fabric of human existence. The difference is manifested, among other places, in the spirituality of state-free people, with its emphasis on the notion of a vital power. A similar sense of power is projected, in more stratified societies, onto kings, popes, rock stars, or technology.

Although state-free people have religion, it is not institutionalized, since there is no state to regulate public life. Though there are certainly standards for correct ritual conduct, as well as certain individuals who carry out religious tasks, there is no superordinate social body to establish any church, nor any class of priests associated with that church and state, which sets itself off from the rest of society. Religious or spiritual activity emerges instead directly from the collective life of the community. The absence of the state and the class system removes the veil of alienation and abstraction from the experience of the self in relation to the universe. This prevents state-free people from developing rigidly monotheistic religions, or sharply opposed religious figures such as God versus the Devil. Instead, people develop a notion of a world-spirit which expresses itself through a rich and varied sense of vital power manifested in the smallest details of life. The best known instance of such a belief, and one which came to stand for all the rest, was discovered about a century ago another third of the way around the globe, as the *Mana* of the Melanesians. According to the British missionary, R. H. Codrington, Mana "is a power or influence, not physical, and in a way supernatural; but it shows itself in physical force, or in any other kind of power or excellence which a man possesses. This Mana is not fixed in anything, and can be conveyed in almost anything; but spirits . . . have it and can impart it. . . . All Melanesian religion consists, in fact, in getting this Mana for one's self, or getting it for one's benefit."[4]

Van der Leeuw observes that Codrington was mistaken in applying the term *supernatural* to the manifestations of Mana. In fact, Codrington, thinking along typically ethnocentric lines, failed to recognize that the state-free mind does not think in terms of a supernatural split-off otherworld, as we would, but sees the natural world as more fully alive than we do. In this perspective, Mana is the ubiquitous power in things, manifest wherever power and efficacy are present. Van der Leeuw comments that for the Maori, Mana can appear even in the latrine, "probably because excreta, like all parts of the body, function as receptacles of power."[5]

For about fifty years after Codrington's discovery, Mana, or some similar term connoting an inherent force, was considered by anthropologists to be the fountainhead and elementary unit of all religions. It was later realized that this could not be so, for the basic reason that religion is a specific kind of social formation of spirit, and can no more be derived from spirit than a building can be derived from the materials of which it is made. But even this metaphor is misleading if it conveys spirit as a kind of homogeneous substance like a brick that is everywhere available and transportable, instead of being produced in specific ways wherever it appears. This is why it takes so many forms.

But even if vital power is not the whole of spirit, it remains spirit's most elemental property, and is recognized as a sine qua non of the religious world. What the state-free person felt as Mana, or some cousin thereof, has passed into the religious and spiritual heritage of more complex societies, where it resurfaces in numerous ways as spirit-power.

Let us consider some of the phenomena of spirit-power as they have appeared in history, with no pretense of covering this ground comprehensively. It will be useful to consider spirit-power from two angles: the idea of the sacred or holy; and the various facets of inspiration. The former is a kind of a perception or intellectual construction of the world in the light of the experience of spirit-power; while the latter describes something of the state of being of the individual who experiences spirit-power. The notion of holiness and the state of inspiration commonly go together in life. We might say also that a person who is particularly inspired (or in-spirited) to experience sacredness or holiness is open to a *mystical* state of being.

Sacredness and the Mystical Consciousness

To speak of the sacred or the holy is to speak of spirit's power as immediately felt, as if it were bursting into consciousness. Awe and fascination are the psychological correlatives of this tremendous experience, which drives the human toward the divine. Until we realize how utterly compelling this sense of a force from the beyond can be, we will not grasp the core of religion, or some of its quirks, such as the fundamentalist faith in the literal truth of the Bible as the Word of God.

The fundamental importance of the sense of sacredness or holiness was evoked by Rudolph Otto in his influential work, *The Idea of the Holy*. For Otto, the holy was a special form of numinous experience: the "submergence into nothingness before an overpowering, absolute might of some kind."[6] This led to his description of the *mysterium tremendum* at the phenomenological core of the holy:

> The feeling of it may at times come sweeping like a gentle tide, pervading the mind with a tranquil mood of deepest worship. It may pass over into a more set and lasting attitude of the soul, continuing, as it were, thrillingly vibrant and resonant, until at last it dies away and the soul resumes its "profane," non-religious mood of everyday experience. It may burst in sudden eruption up from the depths of the soul with spasms and convulsions, or lead to the strangest excitements, to intoxicated frenzy, to transport, and to ecstasy. It has its wild and de-

monic forms and can sink to an almost grisly horror and shuddering.
It has its crude, barbaric antecedents and early manifestations, and
again it may be developed into something beautiful and pure and
glorious. It may become the hushed, trembling, and speechless humility of the creature in the presence of—whom or what? In the presence
of that which is a *mystery* inexpressible and above all creatures.

Otto emphasizes the irreducibility of the holy, the fact that it is
"wholly other."[7] The power of sacred spirit is the manifestation of
something radically outside the forces of nature, and of all ordinary
apprehensions of reality. "The facts of the numinous consciousness
point therefore—as likewise do also the 'pure concepts of the understanding' of Kant and the ideas and value-judgments of ethics or aes-
thetics—to a hidden substantive source, from which the religious ideas
and feelings are formed, which lies in the mind independently of sense-
experience; a 'pure reason' in the profoundest sense, which, because of
the 'surpassingness' of its content, must be distinguished from both the
pure theoretical and the pure practical reason of Kant, as something
yet higher or deeper than they."[8]

Otto's work, grounded in the phenomenology of Edmund Husserl,
brings us up against the problem of consciousness; for he discloses fissures and tears in consciousness, which arise, in his words, from a
"hidden substantive source." The presence of the holy implies a dis-
junction between consciousness and nature. Though common sense
might regard this as an illusion, it is rather an inherent property of the
world. For consciousness not only registers the world, but is part of
the world. If it breaks with nature at the moment of the holy, then it
must be that the way of the world is to have breaks incommensurable
with ordinary reason and logic. The sense of awe-ful power, the *mysterium tremendum* out of which is formed the idea of the holy, is therefore consciousness' representation of the rupture between itself and
nature.

The experience of holiness pursued inwardly to the actual alteration
of consciousness defines the sphere of mysticism. Any adequate discussion of the immense range of mystical phenomena here would certainly
take us too far off the track. However, certain common features deserve brief mention, to serve as launching points for later discussion.
First of all, the mystical experience involves an altered perception, not
merely a vague awareness. The world is seen differently. This seeing
may be with the inner or outer eye; that is, mystical perception may be
(in the terms developed by Stace)[9] introvertive, involving self-
perception of the mind; or extrovertive, involving perception of the

external world. Second, the experience is classically disruptive and sudden. In other words, a kind of quantum leap from one state to another is involved. Third, the experience defies ordinary logic. Things remain identical to themselves and thus different from each other; and at the same time are identical to each other, or seen to be unified as part of a larger entity. As Otto said in another context, "Black does not cease to be black, nor white white. But black is white and white is black. The opposites coincide without ceasing to be what they are in themselves." [10] We might recognize here the form of Hegelian logic known as dialectical, and consider some of its implications, to be pursued further later on. [11] The identity of things leads the mystic to a fundamental notion about the unity of the world. This insight has been repeated in countless guises throughout the history of mysticism. Here is a statement from Meister Eckhart of the fourteenth century, perhaps the most philosophically interesting of Western mystics (and the most related, albeit unconsciously, to Eastern mysticism). "All that a man has here externally in multiplicity is intrinsically One. Here all blades of grass, wood, and stone, all things are One. This is the deepest depth." [12] Furthermore, the mystical condition is never merely a perception (spirit-power has its objective as well as its subjective side), but is always connected with a bodily experience, which has physiological aspects. [13] These states are also usually accompanied by strong emotions—joy, rapture, even terror—and by trances and ecstasies. [14]

The mystical condition, then, is one that affects the whole person, and cannot be reduced to any psychological manifestation. If psychology plays a prominent role, it is because the mystic is concentrating every fiber on perceiving the source of spirit-power. But this perception is capable of transforming everything. As R. M. Bucke put it in a famous passage, it leads to a kind of cosmic consciousness.

It was in the early Spring at the beginning of his thirty-sixth year. He and two friends had spent the evening reading Wordsworth, Shelley, Keats, Browning, and especially Whitman. They parted at midnight, and had a long drive in a hansom. . . . His mind . . . was calm and peaceful. . . . All at once, without warning of any kind, he found himself wrapped around as it were by a flame-coloured cloud. For an instant he thought of fire, some sudden conflagration in the great city, the next he knew that the light was within himself. Directly afterwards came upon him a sense of exaltation, of immense joyousness accompanied or immediately followed by an intellectual illumination quite impossible to describe. Into his brain streamed one momentary lightening-flash of the Brahmic Splendor which has ever since lightened

his life; upon his heart fell one drop of Brahmic Bliss, leaving thence-
forward for always an aftertaste of heaven. Among other things he
did not come to believe, he saw and knew that the Cosmos is not dead
matter but a living *Presence* (italics added), that the soul of man is
immortal, that the universe is so built and ordered that without any
peradventure all things work together for the good of each and all,
that the foundation principle of the world . . . is love and that the
happiness of everyone is in the long run absolutely certain. . . . The
illumination continued not more than a few moments, but its effects
proved ineffaceable.[15]

This is certainly a classic example of Otto's *mysterium tremendum,*
in which a quantum of spirit-power bursts in upon the individual.
What distinguishes Bucke is first the intensity of the experience, and
second, his willingness to elaborate it into a systematic truth in which
an alternate order of things reveals the living and loving quality of the
universe. This reveals Bucke, a man of the nineteenth century, as a
spiritual person in the premodern mold, whose whole way of life prepared him to have the experience and to interpret it in the way he did.
Few today would be so willing to go out on such a conceptual limb,
much less have the feelings he had. Most of us would, I imagine, dismiss him as naive. Yet there remains something absolutely recognizable about Bucke's spiritual moment. And if there is a continuity between his experience of spirit-power and what remains accessible to
modern sensibility, it lies in the italicized term in the above passage:
Presence.

For spirit-power is experienced as a presence, as a making manifest
of that which comes from beyond the perimeter of consciousness.
Otto's phenomenology of presence kept a space for the God of traditional religion. The postreligious sensibility found this space closed,
and needed to derive new and nontheocentric terms to account for
presence. Freud's psychoanalysis represented one such pathway, in
which presence became the return of the repressed, the spiritual world
became the world of the unconscious, and spirit-power became the dynamics of the libido. Another, and less despiritualized, view came from
Martin Heidegger's philosophy.

Heidegger is credited with revolutionizing philosophy. But as with
many revolutions, the new was really a return to a lost past. Heidegger
gave philosophy a fresh start by returning to the question of being.
This emphasis placed ontology—the study of being—at the center of
his philosophy. Heidegger, whose background was strongly religious

(he had begun his career by studying to be a Jesuit), was able to transform the basic ontological concerns of religion into a nontheocentric philosophy. His thought returned to the pre-Socratics, moved on to existentialism and ended (after a disastrous embrace of Nazism which we shall consider further below) as a kind of Buddhism.[16] Faced with the irreducible question of what it means to be, Heidegger came to the conclusion that the being of beings, what makes something exist in the world, is precisely a thing's ability to present itself, to come forward, to emerge into a kind of "clearing," in our terms, to have for itself spirit-power, and to be known by a subject as spirit-power. We shall return to Heidegger, whose powerful influence extended to Herbert Marcuse,[17] precisely because of the ominous political implications of his spirituality. Here we want only to emphasize the common root of religious and nonreligious conceptions of spirit-power: the presence of spirit.

Spirit-power is the way we feel spirit come forward. This has been experienced in an infinite range of variations across the landscape of spirituality. However, there is a feature common to all of them which persists from the mystical tradition: a sense of discontinuity, or rupture. Spiritual experience is marked off from the rest of experience, and the sense of vital power is felt as spirit breaking through the boundaries. If we take this distinction and pursue it in the direction of action rather than perception, we arrive at the domain of inspiration.

On Being Inspired

When spirit-power fills a person so that it flows into practical activity, that person is *inspired,* which is to say, filled with spirit, or "inspirited." As in the phenomenology of spirit, inspiration is a state in which we become "other" than our normal self, filled with power, and capable of acting beyond our normal range. Religious people have spoken of this as the sense of the "living god." An especially important historical instance is that of Saul of Tarsus's experience on the road to Damascus. "Now as he journeyed he approached Damascus, and suddenly a light from heaven flashed about him. And he fell to the ground and heard a voice saying to him, 'Saul, Saul, why do you persecute me?' And he said, 'Who are you, Lord?' And he said, 'I am Jesus, whom you are persecuting; but rise and enter the city, and you will be told what you are to do.' The men who were traveling with him stood speechless, hearing the voice but seeing no one. Saul rose from the ground; and when his eyes were opened, he could see nothing; so they led him by the hand and brought him into Damascus. And for three days he was without sight, and neither ate nor drank" (Acts 9:3−9 [RSV]).

Here spirit-power is manifested as speech, the calling by the word. This is the *kerygma*, or the proclamation from the beyond, God speaking to the human.[18] Experiences of this kind would become translated, in the idiom of Christianity, into a visitation by the Holy Spirit. Note that the call (since it is in words, which humans use to describe things) pertains to a concrete relationship, that of persecution. As a result of the *kerygma* we see an evolution into another form of relationship, signified by Saul's conversion and change to Paul, and the founding of the Christian religion. The moment of inspiration, then, expresses a peculiar and highly important aspect of language: words stand for ("re-present") a thing, but also have an existence of their own. In inspiration, language also crosses a kind of boundary, and takes on a dual character.

Every spirit manifestation, then, needs to be described as both a force from the beyond and as having a particular rootedness in the present. This present has a past; it is history passing into immediacy, where it is met by spirit and transformed. Christianity, like any religion, is not some pure distillation of spirit; it is, rather, the spiritualization of certain definite social relations, the entering of those relations into a spiritual form. Among these relations, for Christianity, is one of "persecution." To be more exact, we could say that the Christian religion emerges within a structure of class and society for which the theme of persecution becomes a motif. These structures endure, in part because of the institutionalization of their spiritual expression. Enduring, they continually reproduce the spirituality.[19] In this way, the theme of persecution becomes a motif for the whole history of the Christian West, right up until the anticommunist witch-hunts of our recent past.

Some of the features of inspiration may be singled out.

Inspiration is essentially passive. It is as though a person has to yield, to become receptive, so that spirit-power can flow in. Friedrich Nietzsche, in describing the composition of *Thus Spake Zarathustra*, gave an excellent description of inspiration as it applies to the creative process: "The notion of revelation describes the condition quite simply; by which I mean that something profoundly convulsive and disturbing suddenly becomes visible and audible with indescribable definiteness and exactness. One hears—one does not seek; one takes—one does not ask who gives: a thought suddenly flashes up like lightning, inevitably without hesitation—I have never had any choice about it."[20]

To the external world such an individual may act with extraordinary verve and forcefulness; however, inwardly the experience is of something "other" than the self at work. The source of inspiration is variously thought of as either without or within the self. However, these alternatives are actually the same, since if inspiration comes from within the self, then it is "deep" within the self. In either instance, then, to be inspired means that spirit has come from beyond, from some place radically other than where ordinary consciousness dwells.

Inspiration is usually experienced as being filled with power. Subjectively this is felt as a kind of elation or "high." From this is derived another common word, *enthusiasm,* which means literally, "filled with god *(theus)*."

Inspiration is felt to be a discontinuous quantum leap, rather than a gradual transition from the normal. As with the experience of the Holy, spirit does not move continuously, but is more like a spark crossing a gap. This does not mean, however, that an inspired person is always being jolted around, though this happens often enough, as with Bucke. One can make a lot of small leaps—after all, quantum phenomena in physics are experienced on the macro level as smooth rays of light. And one can stay on a spiritual plane over an extended period of time.

Inspiration is a gift. The energy and power of inspiration, coupled with the passivity with which it is received, is typically experienced as a gift, not as something willed. In basketball, a player will describe his state of inspiration, in which he scores basket after basket irresistibly and without premeditation, as being "unconscious." Similarly, the Zen archer aspires toward the state of inner emptiness in which the arrow seemingly shoots itself.[21] The entire culture of Zen Buddhism, especially in Japan, is organized about making oneself ready for the spontaneous reception of inspired power. D. T. Suzuki has written about the art of swordsmanship, in which this principle is carried to the zenith:

> However well a man may be trained in the art, the swordsman can never be the master of his technical knowledge unless all his psychic hindrances are removed and he can keep the mind in the state of emptiness, even purged of whatever technique he has obtained. The entire body together with the four limbs will then be capable of displaying . . . all the art acquired by the training of several years. They will move as if automatically, with no conscious efforts on the part of the swordsman himself. . . . The mind, it may be said, does not know where it is. When this is realized, with all the training thrown to the wind, with a

mind perfectly unaware of its own workings, with the self vanishing nowhere anybody knows, the art of swordsmanship attains its perfection, and one who has it is called a *meijin* (genius).

This is no technical trick, but the manifestation of a cosmic spirit:

> When there is no obstruction of any kind, the swordsman's movements are like flashes of lightning or like the mirror reflecting images. There is not a hairbreadth interval between one movement and another. . . . This sword stands as symbol of the invisible spirit keeping the mind, body and limbs in full activity. But we can never locate it in any part of the body. It is like the spirit of a tree. If it had no spirit, there would be no splitting buds, no blooming flowers. Or it is like the spirit or energy (*ki, ch'i*) of heaven and earth. If there were no spirit, there would be no thunder, no lightning, no showers, no sweeping winds. But as to its whereabouts we can never tell. This spirit is no doubt the controlling agent of our existence, though altogether beyond the realm of corporeality. The Sword of Mystery must be made to occupy this invisible "seat" of spirit and control every movement in whatever external situation it may happen to find itself.[22]

We reserve judgment on how symbolic or metaphoric this spirit is, or on whether it is "altogether beyond the realm of corporeality." Still, the experience epitomizes the access of spirit-power.[23]

Inspiration is breath. Finally, and perhaps most remarkably, inspiration refers quite literally to a drawing in of air, that is, to the highly corporeal act of breathing. Most meditative practices within the Islamic, Buddhist, and Hindu traditions emphasize control of the breath as the *via regia* to inspired or enlightened states of being, and the notion is deeply enshrined in all the sacred texts of the world religions. Consider the following, from the ancient Hindu *Upanishads:* "Then Ushasta Cākrāyana asked him: 'Yājñavalkya,' said he, 'explain to me the Brahman that is immediately present and directly perceived, who is the self in all things?' 'This is your self. That is within all things.' 'Which is within all things, Yājñavalkya?' 'He who breathes in with your breathing in is the self of yours which is in all things. He who breathes out with your breathing out is the self of yours which is in all things. He who breathes about with your breathing about is the self of yours which is in all things. He who breathes up with your breathing up is the self of yours which is in all things. He is your self which is in all things.'"[24]

The Hindu texts talk of *prana* as variously "breath," "respiration," "life," "vitality," "wind," "energy," or "strength." There are five *pranas* within the body according to Hindu medical theory, and the breath is the path to *Atman,* "soul," or *Brahman,* "cosmic essence." R. C. Zaehner considers the Upanishad's preoccupation with breath to be paramount: "Breath, of course, is life: and the symbol is an obvious one, for where there is no breath, there is no life. Therefore, in the *Bṛhadāraṇyaka* Upanishad the 3306 gods are in the final analysis reduced to only one, and that is breath, and 'that they call Brahman.'"[25]

Similar preoccupations appear in ancient China, in Taoism, throughout the Buddhist traditions and in Islam, where the Sufi is enjoined to exhale while thinking of God. The Judeo-Christian tradition presents a special case, for here the relation of the breath to spirit undergoes a transformation. We have already quoted the Creation passage from Genesis, where the spirit of God moved upon the waters. Spirit here is the Hebrew word *ruach,* which can mean "breath," "life," "vitality," "words on the breath," or "animated emotion." The notion appears again in Genesis 2:7 (RSV), as "God formed man of dust from the ground, and breathed into his nostrils the breath of life; and man became a living being."

The term *ruach* occurs hundreds of times throughout the Old Testament. In the Greek of the New Testament, we find the word for spirit carried forward as *pneuma,* which means also "breath as life." A shift also occurred in the transformation to Christianity, revealed less in the terms for *spirit* than in those for *soul.*

The notion of *soul* runs parallel to that of *spirit,* and is as fundamental as *spirit* to our study. It reveals the same omnipresence in traditional society and the same marginalization under the despiritualized conditions of modernity. The chief distinction between *spirit* and *soul* for our purposes is that *soul* is the aspect taken by the person viewed spiritually. *Spirit* is the more general term, connoting a relation between the person and the universe; while *soul* is the more self-referential term, connoting the kind of person who undergoes that relation. In a sense, *soul* cuts even closer to home than *spirit,* because while spirits can be—and are—seen everywhere, *soul* refers to *who* we are, and, necessarily, to what we make of ourselves. We may define *soul,* therefore, as the spiritual form taken by the self. If *spirit* is a *relation* of the self to what is beyond itself, *soul is* the self insofar as it partakes of that relationship.[26]

To summarize, *spirit* in the Old Testament is indicated by *ruach,* and in the New Testament by *pneuma* (which today survives only in the sense of "filled with air," as in "pneumatic"). Correspondingly, the Old Testament Hebrew for *soul* is *nepes;* while the New Testament

Greek gives us the well-known *psyche,* from which all of "psy-" discourse arises, including psychoanalysis. According to John McKenzie, *nepes* occurs no fewer than 754 times in the Old Testament, with as might be expected, a multiplicity of meanings. In his *Dictionary of the Bible,* McKenzie states that "the concept signified by *nepes* can be signified by no single word in modern languages." However the integral sense of *nepes*—and therefore the whole meaning of *human being*— differs sharply from the Greek *psyche.* By the time of the New Testament, *psyche* had acquired its Neoplatonic meaning of a *disembodied* spirit. However, of all the meanings of *nepes,* the leading one is "life," and this is certainly meant in an embodied sense. At times *nepes* is meant as the seat of appetites; at times as the mental self. McKenzie concludes that *nepes* is the totality of a person as he or she concretely exists. "It is the self precisely as personal, as the conscious subject of passion and action, as distinct from other selves. . . . Consciousness is life as the manifestation of the *nepes.* . . . [Thus], *nepes* is the word which comes nearest to person in the psychological sense, i.e., a conscious subject,"[27] a subject seen spiritually, and a subject that is a unity of body and soul. The Old Testament recognizes no soul separate from a body, and no spirit separate from either body or soul. Spirit is rather the principle of energy, drawn through the breath, which infuses the soul. If spirit, soul, and body can be distinguished from one another, it is as dimensions of the totality, and not as separable parts.

Obviously this is very different from the New Testament meaning, for example, that given in Matthew 10:28 (RSV): "Do not fear those who kill the body, but cannot kill the soul." From this separation of body and soul emerged the dematerialized spirit-soul, which became a dominant theme in the history of the Christian West, and relates to the fourth major sense of the term *spirit* to be discussed below. It is fair to ask whether this well-known dematerialization of spirit, its splitting from flesh and matter, did not contain the seeds of the despiritualization now underway. For a spirituality severed from matter and flesh is also ultimately severed from life, which will find other ways of going on without it.

In any case, dematerialization is not the only way of conceiving spirit. In fact, it is something of an aberration in the history of spirit, and has never fully supplanted the primary material sense of spirit as vital power advanced in the Old Testament and all other spiritual traditions. It is, however, our aberration. Because of the dominance of dematerialized spirit in the Western tradition, the primary sense of spirit-power has become marginal. This has happened in two ways. Either the spirituality has been removed, or the invocation of spirit-power becomes the province of socially marginalized people.

The first kind of marginalization retains the infusion of energy characteristic of spirit-power but removes what is specifically spiritual, that is, the confrontation by the self of what is beyond itself. This sense, which we might call *nonspiritual spirit,* remains prevalent in common use as a way of invoking vital energy. We speak of being "high-spirited," or of making a "spirited defense," or of "animal spirits," as in the following lines from *Henry IV,* Part 1:

All furnisht, all in arms,
All plumed like estridges that wing the wind
Bated like eagles having lately bathed;
Glittering in golden coats, like images;
As full of spirit as the month of May,
And gorgeous as the sun at midsummer;
Wanton as youthful goats, wild as young bulls.
(act IV, scene i, lines 97–103)[28]

Nonspiritual spirit is a desirable state of being, whether as the ideal of a warrior or the expression of life's innate exuberance. In traditional society, nonspiritual spirit coexists with spiritual spirit as two accepted ways of being. In despiritualized society, on the other hand, nonspiritual spirit often represents the sole path open to spirit, a fact which may help account for the great value placed on youth in late capitalism.

The second kind of marginalization belongs to those who speak for a spiritually materialized conception of spirit—that is, a corporeal spirit that is not simply a metaphor or a symbol. In our tradition, to speak this way is to break with the dominant tradition and even be considered visionary or mad. A singular case is that of William Blake, who was called both:

Man has no Body distinct from his Soul, for that calld Body is a portion of Soul discernd by the five Senses. the chief inlets of Soul in this age . . .

The ancient tradition that the world will be consumed in fire at the end of six thousand years is true. as I have heard from Hell.

For the cherub with his flaming sword is hereby commanded to leave his guard at the tree of life, and when he does, the whole creation will be consumed, and appear infinite. and holy, whereas it now appears finite & corrupt.

This will come to pass by an improvement of sensual enjoyment.

But first the notion that man has a body distinct from his soul, is to
be expunged; this I shall do, by printing in the infernal method, by
corrosives, which in Hell are salutary and medicinal, melting apparent
surfaces away, and displaying the infinite which was hid.

If the doors of perception were cleansed every thing would appear
to man as it is: infinite.

For man has closed himself up, till he sees all things thro' narrow
chinks of his cavern.[29]

This is no doubt crazy, but it is the craziness which calls ordinary
reason into doubt. Blake differs from schizophrenics, those marginalized "others" who also have insights into the unity of flesh and spirit,
in that his madness is enunciated as true poetry. By this I mean poetry
where words and things come together and a new communicative
form is created. In Blake's instance, this effect is enhanced because
"printing in the infernal method" refers to his actual practice of en-
graving his own works—a technique (using "corrosives") so sophisticated that it has never been duplicated. Blake the seer shows that one
can be quite mad and yet technically astute—i.e., that there is no essential contradiction between spiritual insight and a science or technology which has conscious control over matter.

Some Politics of Spirit-Power

Spirit-power remains power, and power is the concrete way of
making a difference in the world. Despite some major disagreement
with Foucault, I am certainly in accord with his notion that power is
not some homogeneous substance like natural gas, to be used here and
there, but specifically produced according to the particular configuration of a given place and time.[30] Spirit-power is produced in the influx
of spirit at a given conjuncture, and is defined both by the here and
now (with its history) and the beyond (with its eternity). To use a
crude metaphor, consider spirit-power as if an "oxide" of one element
or another. Each oxide, whether of hydrogen (water), iron (rust) or
tarnish (silver), is produced by the reaction of oxygen; yet each is radically different, because of the other element with which it reacts.

The Zen swordsman or archer, for example, does not simply occupy the seat of pure spirit, or draw upon spirit as though from a foun-
tain. He is a concrete manifestation of spirit, expressing spirit in a
body that is itself shaped by its historical age. The moment the sword
flashes or the arrow flies may be relatively suspended from history, but
after the flash the swordsman or archer, the full, embodied man, continues living in a time and place that has one use or another for him

and his swordsmanship or archery. These are, after all, also means of violent combat arising from the defense of feudal privilege. They express fully the ideals of knightly behavior, and alo the social order of which knights—in the Japanese case, samurai—were the means of violent enforcement. In the modern age, when samurai no longer stalk the landscape, an individual (almost always male) who espouses this spiritual practice will be caught in a wind from the past. This defines political practice as, literally, reactionary, specifically in the sense of being tied to patriarchal authority. Take, for example, the case of kamikaze pilots dying for the emperor, or the neofascist Yukio Mishima, who chose similar ideals, finally realizing them in a public suicide.[31] A whole school of American politics, occupied by such figures as G. Gordon Liddy, Oliver North and some of the gentlemen who live by *Soldier of Fortune* magazine, are latter-day samurai in the same boat. I am not ruling out other political possibilities which might logically stem from the ideal of the Zen warrior. Empirically, however, this is one spirituality which moves rightward.

There are other notable contemporary instances of right-wing spirituality, a number of which have proven disastrous. We have already noted Martin Heidegger's ontology, which sought to restore "presence," and his influential notion of 'being' as a clearing within which existence unfolds. (We may also recall that in his later years Heidegger headed sharply in the direction of Zen Buddhism.)[32] Heidegger's philosophy was an effort to break through the dematerialized and static notion of 'being' which had burdened Western metaphysics throughout the Christian era. But it was no less an attempt to deal with the terrible crisis afflicting Germany—a crisis which came to a head in the wake of national humiliation following World War I, but whose roots lay deep in the soil of German and European history.[33] Heidegger's calamity proved to be his accommodation to National Socialism as both the vehicle of spirit and the resolution of the crisis. Hence for him spirit was a Nazified spirit. As a philosopher, Heidegger did not have to embrace Nazism[34] as a way out of the crisis—recall that his student Herbert Marcuse took a sharply opposed view of the same situation—but he had no choice about being thrown into the crisis, as a German coming to age in the midst of power, torment, and defeat (Heidegger was born in the same year, 1889, as Hitler). Having chosen an authoritarian, right-wing political ideal, he accordingly configured his notion of being. Spirit-power followed material power and flowed along the lines of fidelity to the führer and National Socialism.

We can observe some of this in the following passages from *An*

Introduction to Metaphysics, which was originally delivered as a series of lectures in 1935, after Heidegger had left the Nazi Party, but
while he still remained very much under its spell. Note how the notion
of being, which the philosopher was trying to pare to the bone, still
bears the impression of some very old-fashioned and malignant social
relations:

> Because being as logos is basic gathering, not mass and turmoil in
> which everything has as much or as little value as everything else, *rank
> and domination are implicit in being.* If being is to disclose itself, it
> must itself have and *maintain* a rank. That is why Heraclitus spoke of
> the many as dogs and monkeys. This attitude was an essential part of
> Greek being-there. *Nowadays a little too much fuss is made over the
> Greek polis.* If one is going to concern oneself with the polis, this as-
> pect should not be forgotten, or else the whole idea becomes insig-
> nificant and sentimental. *What has the higher rank is the stronger.*
> Therefore being, the logos as gathering and harmony, is not easily ac-
> cessible and not accessible to all in the same form; unlike the harmony
> that is mere compromise, destruction of tension, flattening, it is hid-
> den: "the harmony that does not (immediately and easily) show itself
> is mightier than that which is (at all times) manifest" (Fragment 54).
> Because being is logos, harmonia, alethia, physis, phainesthai, it
> does not show itself as one pleases. *The true is not for every man but
> only for the strong.*[35] (italics added)

It might be argued that these ideas, virtually dripping with fascism, are
exceptional in Heidegger's writings. However, one is also reminded of
the arm of Dr. Strangelove, at the end of Stanley Kubrick's film of that
name, compulsively reaching to salute the führer at a moment of great
pressure. As no less an authority than Heidegger himself said, "for the
most part, there lies at the basis of every philosophical conception a
personal position of the philosopher in question."[36]
The temptation to dismiss a philosophical position marked by so
repulsive a politics is understandable. However, it is not one we are
able to indulge. Reject Heidegger? Yes; that is an obligation for anyone who hates fascism. But he cannot be dismissed out of hand. After
all, Heidegger is to the twentieth century what Hegel was to the nineteenth: the philosopher who most compellingly articulated a spirituality no longer attached to religion; hence, the philosopher who most
fully met the challenge of despiritualization. And he failed in the worst
way imaginable—not because he was stupid, but in his very brilliance,
which wedded his notion of being to the most malignant political development in history. Heidegger's retreat to Zen Buddhism does not so

much remove him from suspicion as it casts suspicion on Zen Buddhism. Indeed, given the real implications of Heidegger's spiritual philosophy, despiritualization begins to look somewhat reassuring. For, whatever its limits, despiritualization at least seems to protect us from fascist regression.

Heidegger poses the starkest of challenges for anyone who is serious about restoring the notion of spirituality. This challenge is: can we develop a notion of being radical enough to encompass spiritual possibilities, yet one which leads in the direction of emancipation rather than fascism? Or is fascism the logical outgrowth of deep spirituality in the modern age? Being, after all, does not lie about like some indifferent natural resource. To a degree, it also is produced—and that degree is crucial. As we have seen, it does not suffice to merely invoke mystical power or inspiration to prove one's spiritual development. Only if a certain kind of being is spiritually presenced by inspiration can the results be deserving of our allegiance.

In the remaining chapters we shall see whether this is possible.

2.
Spirit as Occult Being

Prospero: These our actors, as I foretold you, were all spirits, and are melted into air, into thin air.

Shakespeare, *The Tempest,* act IV, scene i, lines 149–51

Now the Spirit of the LORD departed from Saul, and an evil spirit from the LORD tormented him. And Saul's servants said to him, "Behold now, an evil spirit from God is tormenting you. Let our lord now command your servants, who are before you, to seek out a man who is skilful in playing the lyre; and when the evil spirit from God is upon you, he will play it, and you will be well."

I Samuel 16:14–16 (RSV)

"ALL THROUGH the primitive and modern worlds," writes Mircea Eliade, "we find individuals who profess to maintain relations with 'spirits,' whether they are 'possessed' by them or control them. Several volumes would be needed for an adequate study of all the problems that arise with the mere idea of 'spirits' and of their possible relations with human beings; for a 'spirit' can equally well be the soul of a dead person, a 'nature spirit,' a mythical animal, and so on."[1] It is scarcely necessary to add that we cannot carry out here the adequate study that Eliade calls for. However, we need some understanding of what this sense of the term means, where "spirit" signifies a spectral kind of individual—a spirit-being.

Take, for instance, a definition of *spirit* by Wittgenstein: "When our language suggests a body and there is none: there, we should like to say, is a *spirit.*"[2] The customary sense of this usage of *spirit* refers to the nonmaterial, and also to the inner. Of all the dimensions of spirit, this one refers above all to the domain of the *self,* the mental representation of the person. In contrast to the sense of the previous chapter, *spirit* here can mean the self as well as the force of the universe.

There is a conventional usage of *spirit* which describes a whole person, analogously to the way we speak of "high spirits" as nonspiritual spirit-power. Thus we say of a bold, adventurous person, "She is a free spirit." In such usage, the proposition seems transparent, and the spirit-character of the self is a synonym for the whole individual. Here *spirit* is readily assimilated to the discourse of psychology. As psychology is the science of the mental processes and behavior of the person—and as it belongs historically to the epoch of despiritualization—we might regard this usage of *spirit* as a kind of anachronistic carryover from a former era into an age of positive knowledge about the self. I say "positive knowledge" because to have a science of psychology one has to have confidence that its object exists definitely, as a discrete entity in the world. Under the aegis of despiritualization, then, the self stands forth without any shadow of nonself.

Where such a shadow appears we approach the spiritual mode of spirit, and can begin talking of spirituality as such. Here, too, the self can be regarded as a kind of spirit, although now the relation of self to spirit is deep and problematic. We might say that a negative element exists along with the positive: what is not there coexists with what is there. When we talk now of spirit-being we mean to convey something of this negativity: an occult spirit, a spirit apparent neither in immediate self-awareness nor in the world of conventional sense experience. To address the self as spirit in this sense is to call upon the inwardness of human being.

On the Self

Self is one of those words, like *love,* which everyone uses, but which nobody can define. I would suggest that this is due to a fundamental problem in the relation of the self to language—which is to say, a fundamental problem in the very existence of the self.

Let us do the best we can and define *self* as "the cluster of mental representations whose center is referred to by the first person pronoun." The virtue of this notion is that it leaves open many possibilities. Thus the self can be compact, internally consistent, diffused, fragmented, and so forth. We might also think of the self as "decentered," that is, there is a conscious sense of self-identity—"this is who I am"—and an unconscious dispersion of this self-identity, so one may be said truly to not know who one is.

To recognize the presence of spirit-being is a way of decentering the self. It is to call the unity of the self into question, while relating the self to a larger entity outside its consciousness or self-awareness. A spiritual presence means that the self is something partial, gathered together more or less loosely, and not clearly bounded—fundamentally, not identical to itself. Thus there are alternate, multiple selves, or parts of selves within the same person or between people. The traditional way of speaking of such an alternate self-presence is as a "spirit" which comes back, haunts, possesses, and so forth. A spiritual presence can also mean that the whole self, or soul, can be like a spirit with respect to the bodily or socially integral part of a person. In such a conception, which forms the basis of shamanism as well as Hinduism, the soul can migrate as a spirit-being, leaving the shaman's body for a confrontation with the otherworld, or migrating across aeons and worlds.

The notion that we are souls internally composed of spirit-beings runs contrary to the common sense of the modern, technocratic age, in which people are forced to conform to the demands of a bureaucratic and rationalized society. The reality of spirit-being gets shunted aside in the modern state, for there is no way to manage the modern office or factory, not to mention the modern computerized tax rolls or the modern military machine, if the self is thought of as capable of migrating or splitting apart. Thus such notions are today automatically relegated to the sphere of insanity. However, they do happen to be the original view of the self, experienced by all the world's peoples until the modern age. And in the modern age, these original views have become relegated to the domain of "psychopathology," and replaced by a mechanical view of world and body, on one side, and a unified, homogeneous mind and self, on the other.

The notion of a fully individualized and rationalized self, that is, one devoid of the possibilities of spirit-being, did not appear in the West until the seventeenth century, born upon the Cartesian revolution in philosophy, which was less a revolution than a codification of the emergent self-experience of modernity. I do not mean to demonize Descartes in this process,[3] for he only put into words what was in the air; and if his thought came to epitomize the whole motion of modern scientific rationality, it was only the conceptual shaping of new forms of economic, political and social relations that were taking material shape in every quarter of Europe.[4] However, Descartes's thought provides a window on the emerging despiritualization in Western culture, especially as it affects notions of the self. A critique of despiritualization requires a critique of Descartes.

Descartes's overriding consideration is certainty and absolute knowledge—the kind of knowledge which can only be won through social control and mental totalitarianism. For Descartes, according to Copleston, "there is only one kind of knowledge, certain and evident knowledge. And ultimately, there is only one kind of science. . . . Hence there can only be one kind of scientific method."[5] Descartes believes that through his method, "there can be nothing so remote that we cannot reach to it, or recondite we cannot discover it."[6]

This philosophy searches for power over nature, and reduces nature to dead substance in order to win such power over it. In the Cartesian world, we "could render ourselves the masters and possessors of nature."[7] At the same time, his view refuses to recognize any indwelling of the spirit world, such as would cloud the consciousness of certitude. An attitude of splitting results, of which the celebrated division between the pure *cogito* and inert matter is the result. As Carolyn Merchant puts it: "All spirits were effectively removed from nature. External objects consisted only of quantities: extension, figure, magnitude, and motion. Occult quantities and properties existed only in the mind, not in the objects themselves. . . . Descartes reduced the imagination, source of universal knowledge in the holistic world-view, to an individual operation of individual souls. Chimeras, sirens, hippogryphs, and spirits existed only in the soul's imagination, as a result of the action of the will. Witches, monsters, nymphs, and satyrs became figments of the individual imagination."[8]

A particularly telling and—since it came from a woman—predictably ignored[9] critique of Cartesianism was launched by the seventeenth-century philosopher, Anne Conway: "For first, as touching the Cartesian Philosophy, this says that every body is a mere dead mass, not only void of all kind of life and sense, but utterly incapable thereof to all eternity; this grand error is also to be imputed to all those who affirm body and spirit to be contrary things, and inconvertible one into another, so as to deny a body of all life and sense."[10]

The justly famous critique by Alfred North Whitehead scarcely improves on Conway, although he adds the perspective of three centuries of the ruinous effects of Cartesian splitting. Whitehead sees the bivalent quality of Descartes's philosophy—its respect for the individual but also its annihilation of the interconnectedness of things. For Descartes,

[t]he emergent value of each entity is transformed into the independent substantial existence of each entity, which is a very different notion. . . . He implicitly transformed this emergent individual value, inherent in the very fact of his own reality, into a private world of passions, or modes, of individual substance.

Also the independence ascribed to bodily substance caried them away from the realm of values altogether. They degenerated into a mechanism entirely valueless, except as suggestive of an external ingenuity. The heavens had lost the glory of God. . . .

The doctrine of minds, as independent substances, leads directly not merely to private worlds of experience, but also to private worlds of morals. The moral intuitions can be held to apply only to the strictly private world of psychological experience. Accordingly, self-respect, and the making the most of your own individual opportunities, together constituted the efficient morality of the leaders among the industrialists of that period. The western world is now suffering from the limited moral outlook of the three previous generations.[11]

For all its philosophic depth, Whitehead's critique remains idealistic, as it implies that philosophic distortions led directly to the blight of modern society. The relations between ideas and institutions are much more reciprocal and dialectical than that. In the case of Descartes's thought, for instance, we can identify as an influence the emerging absolutist state, the political homologue of his search for absolute knowledge. As he says in the *Discourse on Method* of 1637, "there is seldom so much perfection in works composed of many separate parts, upon which different hands have been employed, as in those completed by a single master." And again, "if there are any imperfections in the constitutions of states . . . custom has without doubt materially smoothed their inconveniences . . . the defects are almost always more tolerable than the change necessary for their removal. . . ."[12] Or, with perfect lucidity, "God sets up mathematical laws in nature as a king sets up laws in his kingdom."[13]

We might dwell a moment on what the Cartesian notion of the self suppressed. All human societies save that of the modern West share a dominant view of the psyche as complex, dynamic, and composed of indwelling spirit-beings separated from objective reality by a kind of shell, or mental carapace. Modern technocratic society, by contrast, thinks of the carapace as the main body of the psyche. According to Marcel Mauss, all groups have ways of distinguishing between self and other, and all people develop a complex sense of corporeal and spiritual individuality.[14] An enormous range of "minds," that is, models of *psyche,* suitable to represent the great variety of social relations, can be encompassed within this framework. It is very striking, however, when one considers the whole range of human culture, to realize the essential formal unity underlying the diversity. There is a basic paradigm, expressed across virtually all cultures, and epitomized in the state-free person's view of the self. As Paul Radin put it in his *Primitive Man as Philosopher* (where the term *Ego* is used for "self"), "How does primitive man regard the Ego? It may be said at once that one thing he has never done: he has never fallen into the error of thinking of it as a unified whole or of regarding it as static. For him it has always been a dynamic entity, possessed of so many constituents that even the thinker has been unable to fuse them into one unit." [15]

The spirit-beings aggregate what is "infusible" into one collective unit. Virtually any description of state-free mental life will confirm Radin's generalization. Consider this from the same text: "Among the Maori a charm is recited over the corpse prior to burial in order to dispatch the soul to spirit land and to prevent it from remaining in the world to annoy and frighten the living. Practices of this nature are to be found among all peoples. What interests us, in this particular case, however, are the actual words of the charm. These run as follows: 'Farewell, O my child! Do not grieve; do not weep; do not love; do not yearn for your parent left by you in the world. Go ye for ever. Farewell for ever.'" [16] Here are all the elements of the original view: There are subsidiary beings—spirits—which inhabit and constitute the psyche. These spirits must be named, according to the oral logos, if their perpetuity is to be assured. They are taken in from external life and represent real figures in the world. And just as they can be folded into the self, so can they leave the self and be projected into the world. Finally, their relation to the self and to others is both socially and ontologically essential. The spirits are building blocks of a relationship to other persons and to the universe alike. They express the universal human condition of attachment to others, in both its loving and hating. The truth of who we are, in other words, requires recognition of the spirit-dimension; and the spirit-dimension requires recognition of the essential sociality of human beings—what Marx implied when he claimed in his *Sixth Thesis on Feuerbach* that the "self is an ensemble of social relations." [17] Thus a spirit-being is not simply some detachable particle of the self. It is the coming to consciousness of some part of the self's relationship to itself and to others. We need to be able to talk about this aspect of human being, so foreign to Cartesianism; to do so, let us use a term that combines both these relationships: the *Other.*

The Other

There are others—discrete other beings; and there is the Other—the mental trace of the fact that our life is with others and that our self is decentered. And there is possibly no term which stands more outside the net of language, hence no term harder to define. Consider the spirit-being. Is it one's self, or the Other? From the Maori ritual we would think the latter: the mourner addresses an absent other being, the dead child, on behalf of the parent. But the absent other cannot be a being radically separate from the self, like a ghost who lives "out there" in a haunted house, for the plain reason that spirit is not out there but inside, communicating subjectively to the mourner. Thus spirit-beings are indeed part of the self. And yet they are not part of the self, by the mere fact of being other. They are both a thing and not that thing—rather like the coinciding of opposites that do not cease to be themselves (e.g., the, "Black not ceasing to be black, nor white white, but black is white and white is black") we encountered in our discussion of mysticism.[18] That is, they are this way if one takes their existence seriously. Otherwise one can go the way of Cartesianism.

There is a way of looking at these things which at first seems complicated, but offers the promise of some clarity on the spiritual phenomena of human being. It consists of an attempt to regard the self—which is to say, all that we think of, in psychological terms, about ourselves—as a kind of precipitate issuing from a larger entity. Then we can begin to think of the Other as somehow belonging to the larger entity to which the self also belongs, as what is left over after we define all the aspects of the self that we can conceive of or articulate. Observe that thinking this way demotes the notion of self to a lower rank, so as to comprehend the phenomena of Otherness. But to a lower rank of what? Here I should say that we recognize the larger entity of which the self is a precipitate as *being,* the is-ness of the world, in which we share. In what follows I will use the simple gerund "being" to denote this elusive concept, rather than a circumlocution which might clutter up the text. I hope that the context will make clear when I refer to "being" as the ontological property of the "is-ness of the world," and when it refers to particular entities and/or agents who share that property.

In any case, I am suggesting that there *is* being, over and against particular beings; and that we have so much trouble talking about this being because as a human being we have a particular relationship to being which surpasses, or comes before, our capacity to think in words. I am also suggesting that the self is both necessary and essential for human being, yet not identical with being, even though despiritualized society would have people think it is. This means also that the discourse of psychology, which conforms to the contours of the self, is much less powerful in grasping our full reality than we ordinarily imagine. Thus the self is not only its positive self; there is also its Otherness in relation to being, and the things we call spiritual take place in the zone of Otherness that links the self to being. We are also implying that the way a person *is,* that is, the mode of being, or state of being, surpasses any psychological description. If we want to talk about what matters most fully and truly to us, we have to go beyond the language of psychology.

If this is puzzling it is because we are deeply attached to the delusory idea that the self is a separate and detachable entity from other selves, as if it were a body in the world, with an envelope of time and space separating it from other bodies. We view the self this way for a number of interlocking reasons: because the felt experience of the "I" peremptorily excludes all others; because we look at the physical body we inhabit and observe that it is substantially different and discrete from other bodies; and because we live in a civilization organized around the meeting of discrete individuals in the marketplace, the social ideal of which is the maximization and autonomy of the individual self. For all these reasons we conclude that the self is like a discrete body.

I would argue that this is all wrong. Indeed, it is even wrong for physical objects, for which the criteria of simple location are basically conventions shaped around the practical use to which such objects are put. Such a critique was one of the main ideas of the spiritual metaphysics of Alfred North Whitehead;[19] but it follows also from every advanced position in physics. And it is surely wrong for the self, or subject of experience. This is why we borrow the term *Other* from phenomenological theory. For the Other is that aspect of the self which is both part and not-part of the organization of the "I." The Other, we might say, is a spirit-being waiting to happen. If the lived world may be differentiated into the representations of self and of objects in the world, then the Other comprises that portion of the object world which penetrates into and overlaps with the world of the self. Here it becomes draped in the language of the self, as the traditional notion of spirits of ancestors or the forest, or Hamlet's ghost, Hitler's Jew, or Dante's Beatrice.

The condition for this, however, is that self and object are each beings sharing in a larger being. Aside from this common ground, Otherness need not have any kind of recognizable form or relation to the self. It can range from feeling or mood, a coloration of experience, to a sense of oppressive looming, or a hallucination. Spirit-being, on the other hand, implies an organized development of the Other into a definite individual (not necessarily human or recognizable), or even into an abstract category, as in Nazi anti-Semitism. The Other becomes a spirit-being, then, when its constituents become an object in itself, and then, subjected to desire, an object *for* the self.

Therefore the Other is part of the self, and the self is part of the

Other, and of all other selves. This does not mean that the ideal of self-autonomy is an illusion, or that we should seek some formless and mushy merging of spirit-beings. The self, after all, remains necessary to human existence. Certain religions, for example Buddhism, and certain philosophers, for example David Hume, have argued differently, but no one has ever demonstrated the absolute absence of self as a practical possibility or one which could be generalized as a rule for humankind. Barring this, the self, in some form, remains as essential as the brain to human beings. However, the self is never wholly itself, never what it takes itself to be, never identical to itself, and always prone to radical decentering. These qualities of the self comprised the rock upon which Freud built psychoanalysis. However, the spiritual traditions of the world discovered these insights centuries before Freud, whose principle merit was to reopen, within the perimeter of modern despiritualized thought, the notion of human being as *self-Other*, i.e., as a potential collection of spirit-beings.

Now if spirit-being is the formation of the Other into consciousness, the Other itself cannot be formless. If Otherness is an inherently difficult notion to grasp, the problem arises from the inherent opacity of human being to itself, not from the esoteric character of the Other. In truth, the Other is anything but esoteric; it is the mark made upon subjectivity by the real, historical conditions of living, in love and hate, with other beings, the very fabric of life. Otherness is not some uniform mush within the psyche, but the specific product of specific relationships. Since these all enter into spirituality, it will be useful to note some of the major configurations of Otherness.

The Otherness of the external world as a whole for human being is expressed in the notion of *nature*. Nature is not a simple universal so far as human beings are concerned; and the degree of Otherness experienced in nature at any given moment is a product of history. The more estranged, or split away from nature we are, the more does nature seem Other, and the more malignant is its Otherness. The notion of nature as a threatening wilderness occurs after "man" has reduced and conquered it.[20] On the other hand, there seems to be within people a deep and abiding drive to reestablish connection with nature, trammeled or not, or to become reconciled to it. Though there is no space for the notion within Cartesian thought, most people also tend to regard nature as a source of primary goodness and wisdom—the good Other, if not "mother."

For each person, childhood provides a matrix of Otherness, which becomes shaped by later experience. To a very considerable extent the essential problem of psychoanalysis has been to account for the nature of the Other arising from very early relations with parents. Let us imagine a person, say a grown woman in the presence of her mother, who feels annihilated by a passing remark made by this same mother, say, a criticism of the way her hair looks. Objectively, this is a trivial thing; the remark from any other quarter would not have had nearly the same effect. We are led thus to think that the self of this woman includes in some improperly integrated way (for reasons about which we need not speculate here) an Other comprised by her relationship to her mother and mediated in some way by hair. In the words of mainstream psychoanalysis, she has "internalized" or "incorporated" her mother as an "internal object" or a "self-object."[21] By the same reasoning her hair itself becomes part of this system fusing her to her mother. Input from her mother becomes then an alteration of her very self as it is composed of this Other. Realistic evaluation of her mother becomes impossible, because every judgment, however rational in terms of objective thought, is also a statement about her own inner 'being.' Similarly, anger toward her mother (such as could be automatically stirred up by the realization, at some level, of just how dependent she remains upon her) would never succeed in clearing the boundaries of the self. To be mildly irritated with her mother is to hate her mother, and to hate her mother is to hate herself, with resulting feelings of annihilation.

From the above example it may be intuitively obvious how all serious mental disturbances, whatever the cause, take the shape of various kinds of Otherness. In this sense, a variety of pathological moods, from anxiety, to depression, to depersonalization, etc., are indications of the presence of a malign Other; while delusions of persecution, or hallucinations of voices screaming at the sufferer, are each in their way instances of spirit-beings coming to life from the Other. In general, we might say that malignant mental disturbances are the product of a self-organization which is too weak and brittle to absorb or transcend its Otherness, and so cracks under its burden.

The language of spirit possession (see the epigraph relating to King Saul, perhaps the first mentally disturbed individual depicted in history[22]) is the oldest used to describe madness, and still remains remarkably vivid, even if psychology now talks of "bad inner objects" rather than of "evil spirits." For example, if in the story of the woman and her mother noted just above, the woman had gone on to develop a psychosis in which she was convinced that she was being eaten alive by her mother, then it would be possible to conclude that her Other had become a malignant spirit-being, i.e., an evil spirit. It would be possible but not desirable, however: for it is important to have some way of distinguishing between a madness in which the self cracks and a creative spiritual path (even if the two can be very closely connected in real life). To use spiritual language indiscriminately here would be a foolish discarding of what has been valuable in the tradition of psychology—just as the generalization of psychological jargon to all spiritual instances would be foolish.

But Otherness dominates normal life as well as the domain of madness. This is especially so in the sphere of love, or wherever desire exists.

> What is it men in women do require
> The lineaments of Gratified Desire
>
> What is it women do in men require
> The lineaments of Gratified Desire [23]

wrote Blake, knowing that the sexes are Other to each other, and that desire is desire for the Other, which is to say, never for the real. In his famous Master-Slave dialectic, Hegel elaborated the insight to claim that desire is for the desire of the Other. [24] Logically, this means that the Other is the same as the desire of the other in a relationship. Thus in the sphere of love, what we desire is in fact the desire of the other for ourselves. The universal desideratum is an abiding sense of being loved. But to do this requires that the Other—that is, a being radically different from the self—be accepted within the self. That is, to get what one wants in a love between full human beings, one must accept Otherness, the differences between people, and the finitude of the self. This is not an easy thing for people to do under any circumstances. It becomes excruciatingly difficult in a society that insists upon self-maximization. Hence the alternative is sought: a love in which the other person is treated as less than a full and reciprocal human being—in Hegelian terms, is made into the Slave in the Master-Slave dialectic. In this way, the other remains Other, yet is incorporated into the peripheral domain of an imperial self. The relationship now takes the typical form of sexual domination, especially that of male over female. As Carolyn Merchant has shown, the modern Cartesian attitude is organized around this theme. [25] But so is the situation of rape, and other manifestations of the deep, abiding fear and hatred men have for women. Hate and fear derive from an Otherness which is rooted in dependency, and which domination falsely tries to overcome. Indeed, domination only perpetuates Otherness and its hate and fear. Thus the more the male dominates, the more dependent he becomes and the more the relationship takes on qualities of the mother-infant bond, which only leads to greater fear and greater domination. This complex is anchored in and reproduces the political and economic inequalities of patriarchal society. The whole is embedded in the context of being mothered by the Other: the male-master remains dependent on the labor of his female-slave as an adult, just as he began life dependent upon a mother whose power was limitless to the infantile eye.[26] Meanwhile the female-slave grows to love her chains, because of the hidden power they afford, and because her own being has become absorbed in that of her man.

In general, the relation to the Other cannot be kept within bounds, and the various kinds of Otherness comingle and codetermine one another. This is the basis for Freud's view that humans are innately bisexual,[27] and for his theory of transference, as it accounts for the permeation of later relationships by earlier ones, thus reproducing the return of repressed spirit-being. Freud's aphorism that he had grown accustomed to seeing each sexual relationship as involving at least four people, was one of his truest insights.

But conscience is also a relation of Otherness. Conscience is a presence deriving from an internalized relationship with others, in which moral commands are laid down, so to speak, on the framework of identifications formed with law-giving authority. It is thus a dual Otherness: one part derives from social and intimate relations, the other part from the abstract necessity of the law. Perhaps as a result, conscience is endowed with tremendous spirit-power, indeed, power to make a person give up his or her life. This is why the moral commands are often referred to as "higher laws": they share all the peremptoriness and absolutism of the Old Testament deity.

It is not too fanciful to say that Freud, in a theory which caught the "spirit of his times," developed the Otherness of conscience into a spirit-being by installing it in the form of the superego. As with so many of Freud's notions, the superego has multiple dimensions. It is a descriptive concept, but also an explanatory one, which helps to draw together a range of mental relations.[28] But it also becomes a cultural form of its own, buttressed by Freud's authority as kind of seer for "modern man." In this sense, the superego becomes the way of thinking about, and more critically, being conscience: hence it is a spirit-being of its own. From a phenomenological standpoint, there is much common ground between Christianity's Holy Spirit and the superego.

Each is a peremptory voice of the Other calling the individual on-ward—the Holy Spirit from an age of intense spirituality, the superego in the age of despiritualization. We return to this theme below.

History is full of fissures, between people and within peoples. We have touched upon the split between men and women; but each major fissure—class, race, nationality—is represented subjectively as a rela-tion of Otherness. Thus the relations between workers and capitalists are never entirely given in the laws of political economy, but include an element or moment of Otherness. Marx's insight into the fetishism of commodities was his way of grasping the linkage between Otherness and political economy, by showing how the products of human labor become endowed with supernatural and quasi-religious power. It re-mains the key to understanding capitalist culture. From another angle, the malignancy of racism is as brutal an example of Otherness as can be found in history. To appreciate what Otherness means as a subjec-tive shadowing of historical relationships, consider the radical bond and simultaneous gap between black and white in United States so-ciety;[29] or those between Palestinian and Jew in Israel. Splits in the mind do not exist unless there are also splits in the world. The pres-ence of the Other is an element which structures economic and his-torical process. At the same time, relations of Otherness interpenetrate each other—for example, in the inevitable sexual twist given to rac-ism. These reflections return us to the generalization made in the previ-ous chapter, that the spirituality of state-free society differs from that of class-state society, insofar as a person of the former recognizes him- or herself in all things, while individuals of a statist society do not. The subjective reason for this is the degree of Otherness incorporated into the body politic over the course of history. Otherness, in sum, is a function of alienation. The Other is the stranger, the alien. The more alienated a society or person, the more horrific the Otherness. Within this scheme of things the state may itself become a kind of Other—a special, godlike creature. Hence the divine right of kings, and the ma-lignancies of Nazism, Stalinism, and Maoism.[30]

Otherness is not something that passively happens; it is produced. Because the Other tracks a realm which language cannot precisely des-ignate, it is subject to the fluid displacements and condensations of what Freud called the "primary process." In the terms of semiology we could say it becomes a "floating signifier"—a signifier which floats and is blown about by winds of Otherness. It is inevitable that Otherness should spill from one category to another, and be generated anew by various quirks of history. More to the point, such secondary Otherness is suitable for ideological manipulation by society's propaganda apparatus. We may add to this sketchy catalog, then, a few other varieties of a more synthetic nature, which have originated in the recent development of United States society.

One of the most consequential instances of synthetic Otherness is the ideology of anticommunism that has afflicted the United States for generations. I say "synthetic" because anticommunism can be shown to have been concocted and launched by elites who wish to legitimate themselves and destroy opposition to their power. In doing this they play on mass anxieties deeply rooted in the nation's history. These fears arise from pervasive doubts about identity summed up in the preoccupation with "Americanism" (as in the House Committee on Un-American Activities). As a result, the communist has come to signify an all-purpose Other for the American mind. The collapse of the Soviet system has removed one of the instigations for this national obsession—which can justly be called a state religion. However, since neither the root causes in the world capitalist economy nor the deep insecurities at the heart of our collective existence have been removed, the essential structures which have given rise to anticommunism remain in place. Within these structures, the signifier of the alien enemy can readily wander to other menaces such as the flag burner, the terrorist, the drug lord—and of course, the "narco-terrorist." It can also be seen how deeply connected anticommunism has been to racism, society's great reservoir of malignant Otherness.[31]

The most curious and deadly Other of recent historical times is that clustering around the representation of nuclear weaponry: the "bomb" (and nuclear power as well). What is unique about the bomb-as-Other is that it is the only object of Otherness whose real qualities match its fantastic properties. That is, nuclear weapons are in fact incomprehensible and wholly outside the range of normal experience. Indeed, of all the species of Otherness they stand the most remote from and hostile to being, to the extent of being capable of annihilating the being of this planet. If a person regards his or her mother as Other, that is due to the peculiar distortions posed by the infantile mind in a particular family setting; if blacks and whites regard each other as essential strangers, that is the result of history and not of an essential estrangement between races. The bomb, however, will always remain Other. The only way to eliminate its Otherness is to eliminate the bomb (or the nuclear power plant)—though even then, since the techniques for making the

bomb will persist, some trace of nuclear Otherness will remain so long
as civilization does. Indeed, the only absolute way to eliminate the
Otherness of the bomb is to use it—a truly nightmarish predicament.[32]

Splitting and Differentiation

Splitting refers to a kind of 'being' in which the Other is not recognized as having any common 'being' with the self. By the same kind of
reasoning we might say that a society or person which was not split
from nature, but rather *differentiated* (so that the Other was recognized as sharing 'being' with the self) would have less Otherness to
contend with, and, crucially, a more benign kind of Other. The notions
of splitting and differentiation pertain to a full state of 'being,' and are
to play a major role in our understanding of spirituality. And indeed
splitting is the basis for Western civilization's estrangement from nature and attitude of domination toward nature, exemplified in the philosophy of Descartes. Compare, if you will, the words of Black Elk, an
Ogalala Sioux holy man:

> So I know it is a good thing I am going to do; and because no good
> thing can be done by any man alone, I will first make an offering and
> send a voice to the Spirit of the World, that it may help me to be true.
> See, I fill this sacred pipe with the bark of the red willow; but before we
> smoke it, you must see how it is made and what it means. These four
> ribbons hanging here are the four quarters of the universe. The black
> one is of the west where the thunder beings live to send us rain; the
> white one for the north, whence comes the great white cleansing wind;
> the red one for the east, whence springs the light and where the morn-
> ing star lives to give men wisdom; the yellow for the south, whence
> comes the summer and the power to grow.
> But these four spirits are only one Spirit after all, and this eagle
> feather here is for that One, which is like a father, and it is also for the
> thoughts of men that should rise as high as eagles do. Is not the sky a
> father and the earth a mother, and are not all living things with feet or
> wings or roots their children? And this hide upon the mouthpiece here,
> which should be bison hide, is for the earth, from whence we came
> and at whose breast we suck as babies all our lives, along with all the
> animals and birds and trees and grasses. And because it means all this,
> and more than any man can understand, the pipe is holy. . . .
> Then I was standing on the highest mountain of them all, and
> round about beneath me was the whole hoop of the world. [Black Elk
> said the mountain he stood upon in his vision was Harney Peak in the
> Black Hills. "But anywhere is the center of the world," he added—
> showing that the deepest spirituality is compatible with a shrewd real-

ism.] And while I stood there I saw more than I can tell and I understood more than I saw; for I was seeing in a sacred manner the shapes of all things in the spirit, and the shapes of all things as they must live together like one being. And I saw that the sacred hoop of my people was one of many hoops that made one circle, wide as daylight and as starlight, and in the center grew one mighty flowering tree to shelter all the children of one mother and one father. And I saw that it was holy.[33]

This is the quintessence of a differentiated spirituality of nature. It unites the spirit-power of holiness with an Otherness in which every part of the universe is recognized in the self, and every part of the self exists in the universe as a whole. But even here some element of Otherness remains. Black Elk draws a vivid comparison between the natural universe and a happy, protective family. No one would claim, however, that the members of a family are totally fused with each other, except when children live in the mother's womb,[34] or when all members of the family are dead and returned to nature.

The identity between women and nature is an archaic symbolic foundation of society. First mediated through the mysteries of birth and mothering, the association became both reinforced and degraded in the emergence of modernity.[35] The degradation was manifested as a splitting in which women were to accept the dumbness and passivity projected into nature, hence to alienate their own specifically human powers, while men were to arrogate to themselves the functions of reason and self-autonomy. Acceptance of the degraded form of identity, and the alienated Otherness this imposes, has played a major role in the domination of women. At the same time, recognition of the strength inherent to nature-as-Other has provided a launching point for major feminist movements. These have reestablished a differentiated spirituality which develops a sense of the interconnectedness of things within the context of contemporary struggles for emancipation and saving the earth. It is no accident, then, that women have assumed leadership in the antimilitarist, antinuclear, and ecological movements.[36]

Among the views of nature expressed by spiritual political feminists, we have the following, written by Starhawk, a remarkable woman who combines psychology and political activism into the praxis of paganism, specifically as a witch. Writing of a woman, Joy, with whom she works, Starhawk says, "Casting the circle allows us to experience each direction as it is for us in the moment—to see where we are out of balance, what cluster of qualities needs work. So, for Joy, the East is warm and welcoming—a green garden and a sunlit forest.

The South is an ocean beach; it has been stormy in the past, but today it is calm. The West is a desert, bleak and uninviting. The North is another deep forest, green, cool and comforting. The directions do not correspond, necessarily, with the traditional associations of elements because they reflect her internal geography. Her West, her emotional life, does not feel like an ocean, with its deep tides and burgeoning life. It feels, at the moment, like a desert, blasted with heat, lonely, empty, with no oasis in sight."[37]

Note the striking convergence with Black Elk's differentiated view—and note too that the healing encounter with nature still preserves the Otherness of nature, for as Starhawk spells out, the "internal geography" and the external geography are not one. There is a powerful desire in us to establish this identity, but being the object of desire does not make a thing real. The distinction between humanity and nature remains so long as we are human; it can be differentiated infinitesimally, but it does not go away.

It is only within nature that beings are fully linked ecologically. By using speech and the word to signify that we cook our food, dress our bodies, and bury our dead, we also signify that, for us, some kind of irreducible and ultimately tragic gap exists between human being and purely natural being. Animals communicate, but at the level of the sign and not the word. Once the word appears, so does the tragic space between human existence and mere immediacy. I say "tragic" not to sound pessimistic, but to indicate the ineluctable tension between the desire for fusion and the reality of differentiation. The distinction is also wonderful, and is what makes life interesting and creative, for in that same space we transform the world. But wonderful or tragic, the distinction remains. This implies that Otherness does not simply pertain to other beings: it is, rather, inscribed in our own way of being; it is the way we have of being human. This means that consciousness and self-consciousness, indeed language itself, are manifestations of Otherness. The clearest evidence that even a differentiated human being such as Black Elk still regards nature as Other is spirit-being itself, and the whole state-free religious structure built upon it. On the other hand, we must not lump all this together into some grand and vague pronouncement about human being: it matters enormously whether the relation of Otherness is given in terms of differentiation or splitting. The whole question of domination is entailed in the distinction, for as we shall see, no domination occurs without splitting.

Otherness is associated with the entire range of passions, from extremes of love and bliss to terror, hatred, and persecution. And each

Other can become a spirit-being, invested with one degree or another of spirit-power and passion. The spirits of the lakes, the mountains, the sea, indeed, all of nature are Others made discrete, as is Freud's superego. So too are human figures of Otherness: relatives, ancestors, or anyone of significance. All these altered states of being—demonic possession, shamanism, trance, the speaking in tongues of Pentecostalism, spells, and so forth—resemble the pattern of Otherness studied under the various rubrics of psychopathology. Still, it would be the greatest foolishness to assume that whoever enters into an altered state of being is mentally ill, as if the shaman needed a psychiatrist to straighten him out, or that poor Saint Francis failed to realize how disturbed he was when he talked to the wolves and birds.[38]

Psychotechnology arrogantly thinks that it understands the ontological basis of what it calls mental diseases and ordinary people call madness. Psychiatric science has succeeded in classifying and tracing the trajectory of emotional disorders, and even in a number of instances, discerning their necessary neurophysiological accompaniments (necessary, because we are embodied, and whatever we think, feel, or do has a somatic dimension). All this can be useful; to repeat, I do not think we need go back to the language of spirit-possession to deal with emotional disturbance. But psychiatric science cannot say what it *is* to be "out of one's mind." One might as well say that love is really about the molecular changes in lovers as say that madness is adequately comprehended by study of the brain, or by psychological jargon. The fact is, madness has a spiritual component, and touches on the same ontological problems as spirituality. For both are a "going out of mind." This does not make madness, whatever its ontological nature, pretty or nice. Nor need spirituality be pretty or nice. Indeed, confrontation with spirit-being, even under the supposedly sublime conditions of religious mysticism, can be as harrowing as the darkest torments of madness, as conveyed in the words of Saint John of the Cross:

> This night, which, as we say, is contemplation, produces in spiritual persons two kinds of darkness or purgation, corresponding to the two parts of man's nature—namely, the sensual and the spiritual. And thus the one night or purgation will be sensual, wherein the soul will be purged according to sense, which is subdued to the spirit; and the other is a night or purgation which is spiritual, wherein the soul is purged and stripped according to the spirit, and subdued and made ready for the union of love with God. The night of sense is common and comes to many: these are the beginners, and of this night we shall

speak first. The night of the spirit is the portion of the very few, and these are they that are already practised and proficient, of whom we shall treat hereafter.

The first purgation or night is bitter and terrible to sense. . . . The second bears no comparison with it, for it is horrible and awful to the spirit.[39]

Let us say, then, that if spirituality is the passing beyond the self, madness is a kind of coming apart of the self in the process, because of the violent nature of spirit-being and its relation to the self. Thus not all spirituality need engage madness. On the other hand, madness can still remain spiritual, but it also can become real emotional illness. This happens if the state of being loses connection to the whole (i.e., becomes split), in which case it becomes asocial, uncreative, or frankly destructive.

On Shamanism

A number of these themes are played out in the processes of shamanism, a spiritual healing ritual common to much of the tribal world. Here is an example, from the Copper Eskimo.

The shaman of the evening was Horqarnaq, "Baleen," a young man with intelligent eyes and swift movements. There was no deceit in his face, and perhaps for that reason it was a long time before he fell into a trance. He explained before commencing that he had few helpers. There was his dead father's spirit and its helping spirit, a giant with claws so long that they could cut a man right through simply by scratching him; and then there was a figure that he had created himself of soft snow, shaped like a man—a spirit who came when he called. A fourth and mysterious helping spirit was Aupilalánguaq, a remarkable stone he had once found when hunting caribou; it had a lifelike resemblance to a head and neck, and when he shot a caribou near to it he gave it a head-band of the long hairs from the neck of the animal.

He was now about to summon these helpers, and all the women of the village stood around in a circle and encouraged him.

"You can and you do it so easily because you are so strong," they said flatteringly, and incessantly he repeated:

"It is a hard thing to speak the truth. It is difficult to make hidden forces appear."

But the women around him continued to excite him, and at last he slowly became seized with frenzy. Then the men joined in, the circle around him became more and more dense, and all shouted inciting things about his powers and his strength.

Baleen's eyes become wild. He distends them and seems to be looking out over some immeasurable distance; now and then he spins round on his heel, his breathing becomes agitated, and he no longer recognizes the people around him: *"Who are you?"* he cries.

"Your own people!" They answer.

"Are you all here?"

"Yes, except those who went east on a visit."

Again Baleen goes round the circle, looks into the eyes of all, gazes ever more wildly about him, and at last repeats like a tired man who has walked far and at last gives up:

"I cannot, I cannot."

At that moment there is a gurgling sound, and a helping spirit enters his body. A force has taken possession of him and he is no longer master of himself or his words. He dances, jumps, throws himself over the clusters of the audience and cries to his dead father, who has become an evil spirit. It is only a year since his father died, and his mother, the widow, still sorrowing over the loss of her provider, groans deeply, breathes heavily and tries to calm her wild son; but all the others cry in a confusion of voices, urging him to go on, and to let the spirit speak.[40]

A shaman is not merely possessed by spirit-beings; his or her own spirit can travel to engage them. As Saint John of the Cross emphasizes, this can be a hazardous voyage. The Eskimo shaman, Baleen, has to shed the skin of his normal self, and becomes Other-to-himself in order to achieve the desired condition of transport or ecstasy, which as *ek-stasis* means literally "standing outside oneself." Thus a person has to die to enter the spiritual world. The event is anything but tranquil or conventionally happy. For the true shaman (and there are many frauds), the issue remains long in doubt as to whether he or she will control the spirit-beings or remain possessed by them. What is involved in the confrontation with spirit-being is patently an exorcism, a driving out of noxious forces, whether called devils or evil spirits. Certain passages from the Gospels, for example, Mark 1:23–27, show very clearly that Jesus, too, had strong shamanistic qualities. The same could be said, with very different spiritual qualities, of Freud or any of the great psychoanalysts who followed him in trying to exorcise not "unclean spirits" but "bad introjects." Indeed, shamanism reminds us of the process of psychoanalytic treatment, and is based on the same insight, in Baleen's words, that "It is a hard thing to speak the truth. It is difficult to make hidden forces appear." The relations between Baleen and spirit-being are true relations—true because they are correct propositions about an edge of reality. They would not be true if one assumed that the spirits had corporeal being, like a common physical object—an assumption which shamanistic culture does not make.[41] But they are true if one wants to bring out the hidden forces of a situation. If the situation includes the complex of sentiments, feelings, and attachments—by no means all loving—between Baleen and his dead father, then the spirit is a true form for realizing that complex. That is, it makes real and objective what was latent. It does not make it real like a physical object, but real as a particle of activated consciousness changed into symbolic being and, crucially, shared among the community. The various spirits are not replications of separate beings, but transformations of Otherness—imaginative exfoliations of what had been compacted and obscure. Shamanistic possession is no more irrational or divorced from essential human reality than the theater.

Trance is a dramatization, then, and by this measure, a bringing to consciousness of what was merely Other. The Other is brought not to simple consciousness (as if there were such a thing), but to practical consciousness. We might even say it is a kind of "conscientization," in Paulo Freire's word,[42] a taking of responsibility, and a collective drawing together.

> "Who are you?" he cries.
> "Your own people!" They answer.
> "Are you all here?"
> "Yes, except those who went east on a visit."

Here spirit-being objectifies Otherness. By giving it a name, shamanism draws the group together. Spirit-being here enters into a kind of production, or labor, just as hunting food or building dwellings is productive labor; it is a conscious, active expression of human power, of object-making, of self-definition. Here we might qualify a bit: spirit-being is the creation of a new collective reality when it is not expressed in madness. And we can now amplify our definition of madness, as that configuration of Otherness and spirit-being which does not eventuate in new unity, which is not productive but annihilative. Yet even madness retains an active spiritual potential, for the mad person[43] is working to produce new being, too. That is, the tendrils of spirit-being grow even if they do not find their goal.[44] A spider keeps weaving a web even when there is nothing there to be caught, because it is "in" the spider to weave, just as it is in dogs to bark and roosters to crow. In the same sense, it is in human beings to produce spirit-being and to have that spirit-being seek realization. But although the mad person keeps weaving spirit-being, there is a failure in connection to others. He or she fails in the project, because of whatever makes him or her mad. However, this originating cause of madness is not located simply within the membrane of the individual mind or body, but in history as well.

Just as Freud revived the primary notion of mind as a dynamic ensemble of conflicting inner beings, so did he restore the practice of shamanistic exorcism as a form of treatment, giving it the name of psychoanalysis. But psychoanalysis came into its own under historical circumstances in which the splitting of inner and outer worlds had dampened hopes for spiritual realization. Under such conditions, not only spirit-beings but the entire subjective dimension of existence comes to seem Other. People begin to comfort themselves with psychotherapeutic change, and cultivate their mental garden, abandoning the very idea of transcendently going past the boundaries of the self. Spirit-beings now become "vibes," essentially remaining locked within the self.

Godhead and the Devil

Throughout most of human history, however, spirit-beings have found collective representation which has joined people into a community of belief. We know these forms as gods, and they focus spirit-power as well as spirit-being. When the god is a person, that person has to an extreme degree what is called *charisma*—the investiture in an individual of a sense of special power. The charismatic person stands out and is known by the capacity to draw others close, and to leave in their memory a lasting impression of spirit-power. The charismatic, in short, inspires. The charismatic has the capacity to funnel and transmit spirit-power, as if he or she were a lightning rod of the spirit.

Of course, not all charismatic individuals are godlike, though all godlike persons are charismatic. To become a god—i.e., to achieve godhead—a person has to find a way to link charisma with the defining function of logos, the word as the real. That is, the god must capture the dimensions of symbol and myth, in all their magical power. A person who achieves godhead synthesizes spirit-power, spirit-being, and logos. To do this a person must have a great spiritual ambition, or at least be the object of the spiritual ambitions of others. There is nothing in this that says such a person cannot be an utter fraud, or even a monster.

Gods are not necessary for religion, because there is no necessity for spirit to take the form of godhead. However in real history, the religious community has usually needed gods to define and express itself.

Hence gods are as different as religious communities. In this respect we might observe that the Christian Trinity is a dispersion and a representation of the three component parts of godhead. The Father (the breather of life into the universe) stands for spirit-power; the Son (the word made flesh) for logos; and the Holy Spirit (the indwelling experience of God) for spirit-being. They stand for these things in the context of a patristic, male-dominated class society. Even where religion has seemingly become atheistic, as in the case of Buddhism, the charismatic figure of Shakyamani Buddha (not to mention the hosts of bodhisattvas who followed him) is needed to infuse the logos with spirit-power and to define its spirit-being. In principle, Buddhism is an atheistic religion of pure detachment. But in practice it is full of gods—and politics.[45]

Where there are gods there also tend to be devils, or antigods, and also the absence or opacity of god. This latter condition is the primordial state of sin, a notion that began in Babylonia millennia before the Christians formalized it into "original sin," and which only fades with the despiritualization of society. Sin is a state in which the possibilities of being are denied because of a transgression. As Paul Ricoeur has written, "In the oldest Babylonian psalters the believer asks, 'How long, O Lord? What god have I sinned against? What sin have I committed?' Sin makes me incomprehensible to myself: God is hidden, the course of things no longer has meaning."[46]

The omnipresence of the notions of transgression and the devil must indicate a very fundamental tendency toward duality within human beings.[47] It seems as if every motion upward is matched by one downward: God requires the Devil; just as for Freud, Eros, the instinct of life, required Thanatos, the instinct of death.[48] But this tendency is not absolute; its precise character depends on how differentiated, as opposed to how split, the parts of the duality are. Differentiation and splitting in the realm of diabolism and sin are both compatible with genius. Blake was a genius of differentiation, who recognized the necessity of Hell but insisted that the voice of the Devil in Hell was full of wisdom, and that everything which lives is holy. Calvin was a genius of splitting, who damned us in the womb, and called matter itself evil. Hitler was another genius of splitting, whose diabolism extended to everything non-Aryan, and singled out Jews for special treatment.

Needless to say, Hitler did not invent the diabolization of the Jewish people. The recurrent thirst for a persecutory, diabolic object arises from deep within the bowels of Christian civilization. In this grim and recurring spectacle the Jew has taken first rank. Blamed for the murder of Christ, the breakup of the medieval commune, and the rise of heartless capitalism, the Jews have been made to pay again and again—from the expulsions of the Middle Ages to the Holocaust. As a result of this monstrous misery, the Jew was turned into an all-purpose Other to pay for the accumulated guilt of Christianity. Their maginality and exclusion gave the Jewish people a painfully won insight into the potential for emancipation—before the building of the state of Israel turned the tables by putting Jews in the role of oppressors.

It is worth pointing out that an intellectual enterprise is necessary to establish just what constitutes god, the devil, and sin. Myth making is an essential part of notions of both evil and good; and in more advanced societies, the myth is hardened through the activities of experts wielding logos. In fact, the construction of a devil can be an even more prodigious work of logos than the making of a god. In these instances, the scientific mentality enters the fray. Perhaps the most stunning episode was Sprenger and Krämer's astounding *Malleus Maleficarum,* or "hammer of evil," a treatise written in 1486[49] in order to "diagnose" the form of diabolism known as witchcraft. In the persecution of witches, the Otherness of the female had to be elaborated into a compelling moral rationale for eliminating the threat of woman healers and paganism. It was necessary therefore to rigorously prove that the women accused of witchcraft were in league with the Devil; and in order to do this a detailed and complex set of objective mechanisms had to be devised. Thus witches were accused of causing the male organ to disappear, of consorting with Satan, and so forth, all with the utmost attention to correct reason. Logos provided a juridical and quasi-medical precedent for what eventually became the system of mental diseases.[50]

Whether differentiated or split, human being seems to need the polarity provided by god and devil. We are left to wonder, however, about the origin of this tendency to dualism. Is it a peculiarity of the intelligence, or a structure within human being itself? And if a structure, is it a true or full expression of spirit? Can this question even be answered? It seems we have to expand our notion of spirit.

3.
Authentic Spirit

*But as regards the inner life of the soul, it has another form.
This inner life can the external not attain. Hath the soul's fire
not God's light, neither can the soul's will enter into God's light;
it must remain in the darkness of the external Nature.*

*[External] Reason knows no more of the soul's origin than a
cow does of a new stable door. She looks at it, and it seems to
her to be strange; so also to external Reason the inner world
seems to be something strange.*

Jakob Boehme, *Six Theosophic Points*

IF WE WERE TO LIMIT the domain of spirit to the revelation of
power from beyond, or the visitation by spirit-being, a great deal of
what the term signifies would remain unexpressed. For example, consider the phrase, "the spirit of the agreement was not honored." Here
spirit connotes both "hidden power" (i.e., the "real force" of the
agreement) and "hidden being" (i.e., there is another meaning to the
agreement beyond what may be apparent). However, these connota-
tions certainly do not get at the heart of the statement. Or, at the risk
of being precious, the "spirit" of the statement. For in the phrase "the
spirit of," *spirit* means "the authentic meaning of something." This
authentic or real meaning includes the sense of force, but not of blind
force. It also includes the sense of things not immediately present, as a
spirit-being is not present. But this sense adds a whole dimension. It
asserts that the force inherent in the agreement can be expressed only
if the truth of the agreement is respected; and it means that what is not
immediately apparent is of superior value, that it is the "real thing," as
opposed to mere appearance. To speak of "the spirit of a thing," then,
is to condense truth and value into a unity.

Taken no further, this meaning would express another nonspiritual
sense of spirit, in the same way that the expression "animal spirits"
expresses a nonspiritual sense of spirit-power, and "a noble spirit" ex-

presses a nonspiritual sense of spirit-being. But what distinguishes this third sense of spirit is its demand to go further, its insistence on radicalizing the meaning of any spiritual phenomenon, its commitment to make meaning an active force and not a mere matter of definition. In contrast to spirit-power and spirit-being, we are now in the domain of *spirit-meaning,* where *meaning* signifies not an intellectual problem but the conduct of life. In sum, spirit is a way of being.

What distinguishes the more radical spiritual meaning is the quality of the negative. Since spirituality consists in a going beyond the self, true spirituality means to truly go beyond the self; thus the true spirit is the radical spirit. As the self is a kind of precipitate of being, a radical spirit goes beyond the given state of being into a radical being which negates ordinary being. And as our state of being constitutes all that exists to our understanding, radical spirit goes beyond what exists to the understanding. That is to say, the truly spiritual includes risking the abyss, what cannot be named. We call this domain, *nonbeing.* Nonbeing does not connote an absence of being, or an annihilation, as would occur after nuclear holocaust. It means rather that aspect of being which is beyond our ken; it remains being but, one might say, "empty being"—being which cannot be grasped by what Boehme calls "external reason."

The spiritual, in going beyond the self, is most authentically a reaching from being to nonbeing, one that preserves yet transforms being. Thus the hidden spiritual meaning of things is not a secret code, the disclosure of which would supplant or even erase the manifest meaning of the decoded proposition. Indeed, there is no secret code to spiritual being. To spiritually engage the negative does not abolish the manifest meaning of things. Neither, however, does it rest with that meaning, nor accept it. To live with the "spirit" of negation means to accept rather a certain indeterminacy to being, while remaining faithful to reason and truthfulness. It means to seek a truth which resides in the negation of what is. This sense of the spiritual is represented in the legend of the quest for the grail: a striving for that which is of surpassing value yet cannot be grasped or named.

The combination of meaning and power belongs to the dimension of logos, which as we have seen can fall into domination. But we must risk ourselves in the belief that there is also a truthful logos which acts as a spiritual force. Not to do so means acquiescence in nihilism; while to do so means an opening of immeasurable potential. This was the path of Gandhi, as revealed in a remark made by a disciple:

Einstein has given us his well-known equation setting forth the relationship between mass and energy which states that when even an infinitesimal particle of matter attains the velocity of light . . . it acquires a mass which is infinite. The corresponding law governing the release of spiritual energy is to be found in the formula enunciated by Gandhiji, viz., that even an infintesimal of an individual, when he has realized the ideal of Ahimsa [i.e., not injuring others] in its fullness so that in thought, word, and deed, he—in short his whole being—becomes a function of Ahimsa as it were, he becomes filled with its power, the power of love, soul force, truth force, or the godhead within us, to which there is no limit and before which all opposition and hatred must cease: "With Satya combined with Ahimsa you can bring the whole world to your feet."[1]

For Gandhi, *satyagraha,* the name given to his praxis of nonviolence, was "truth-force," or "soul-force," or in our terms, a kind of practical power released when spirit-being and truthfulness are aligned with each other. To put it another way, spirit-power is released spiritually in concert with an authentic, true way of being. This way of being has at least two prerequisites—first, some kind of correct conduct in the world; and second, an encounter with nonbeing.[2]

It is at this point that the modernist rupture with spirituality comes into view. For what we have been referring to as the despiritualization of modern culture may be more specifically defined as resistance to the encounter with nonbeing. Despiritualization adopts the strategy of unmasking hidden meaning. This is necessary, but not enough, because it does not touch upon nonbeing. In fact, despiritualization cannot tolerate nonbeing, the affirmation of that which is radically not present, as part of what is present. And this brings us to Freud, who found hidden meanings, and had an ambiguous relationship to nonbeing.

The Spirit of Freud

Psychoanalysis sways uneasily between the spiritual and the despiritualizing traditions, and meets the requirements of neither. On the one hand, it has been perennially accused by "hard" positivist science of dealing in imponderable, unmeasurable, and ultimately mystical spiritual domains such as the unconscious.[3] On the other hand, psychoanalysis has understood itself to be the bearer of the demystifying "spirit" of the Enlightenment in reference to problems which had been regarded as of the soul.[4] I recall the smug remarks made by one of my teachers of psychoanalysis, claiming that with Freud, the once mysterious soul had come out into the light at last, to be resolved by the gaze of the analyst. To the modern analytic psychotechnician, what the ancients and state-free peoples regarded in their ignorant spiritual way could now be spelled out as a set of hidden meanings. Spirit-beings were only mom and dad; and spirit-power was no more than . . . why, it was only libido, which as we all knew, was simply our sexuality, grounded in neural wiring and chemical messengers, and waiting to be made healthy.

Jung challenged Freud on just this point, and has been savaged ever since by the Freudian psychoanalytic establishment as mystical and irrational. A separate study would be necessary to deal adequately with the many issues raised by Jung, who was the most explicitly spiritual of psychoanalysts, and whose system has continued to draw the most interest from those students of psychoanalysis with spiritual inclinations. I cannot do justice to the subject here, and will set it aside except for some brief comments in a footnote.[5] Whatever one's general views on Jung, however, I think he was on the mark in his claim that Freud, and mental science in general, had falsely reduced questions of the spirit.

This is not to deny that Freud was greatly concerned, indeed preoccupied, with spiritual questions.[6] However, he deliberately aimed to debunk any independent basis for the spiritual world, and to reduce all its manifestations to the play of nonspiritual forces. When he held, in *Future of an Illusion*, that religion was essentially the search for the protection of the father, Freud was trying to destroy a notion of godhead which he considered a fetter on human development. Similarly, in *Civilization and Its Discontents*, Freud said that the "oceanic feeling" of oneness with the universe was essentially a recall of the state of oneness with the mother's breast experienced by the infant after having been fed. Since the oceanic feeling may be taken as the elementary state of mystical being, and is more or less the correlate of Rudolph Otto's *mysterium tremendum*, Freud was trying to demolish the phenomenological ground of spirituality just as he had attacked religion's intellectual pretensions.

But all he succeeded in doing was in establishing how firmly he stood in the camp of despiritualization. For the only truly radical conclusion drawn by Freud was that these hidden meanings of religious and mystical spirituality were the *only* meanings, or at least the only essential ones. That is, for Freud, spirituality was nothing more than another kind of infantility to be outgrown, so that the "soft" voice of scientific reason could take charge. Or as he put it in his noblest stoic prose, "Our God, Logos, will fulfill whichever of these wishes nature outside us allows, but he will do it very gradually, only in the unforeseeable future, and for a new generation of men. He promises no compensation for us, who suffer grievously from life."[7]

And so the atheist Freud did have a god: logos without spirit. Hence the spiritual could be reduced to a hidden meaning of infantile life, and left at that. But this principle is only asserted, and nowhere proven. Nor can it be proven. Who could deny that infantility persists within spirituality as it does elsewhere? Anyone can see that in the rich complexity of religion, God the Father is also the father, or that the state of helplessness which arises when we contemplate our weakness in the face of the universe or society evokes in the mind a yearning for the protection afforded by parents. Similarly, it stands to reason that the satiation of an infant at the breast should be one of the first occasions for spiritual experience in an individual's life. But none of this exhausts the real meaning of spirituality—indeed, it fits into that meaning and is implied by it, since for there to be transcendence there has to be something to transcend.

Freud's dismissal of an authentic spiritual dimension is of a part with his dismissal of all experience that does not privilege the being of males. As Catherine Keller has written, "To find intimations of interconnection so mysterious, so misfitting, may indeed be 'men's' problem and prerogative. Such a feeling contradicts Freud's psychology . . . because it has been omitted from the ideals of the androcentric civilization to which his analysis is limited."[8] It is no accident that, in the field of psychoanalysis, it has taken women—of whom Melanie Klein and Margaret Mahler are the outstanding examples—to grasp the significance of the primary phase of life represented in the oceanic feeling.[9] Similarly, it has taken women within theology—one thinks of figures such as Dorothée Sölle, Rosemary Radford Ruether and Elisabeth Schüssler Fiorenza—to establish that one can authentically relate to a deity who is not God the Father.[10]

Freud's path of reduction seems essential to a masculinist view of reality that dreads immersion in any formlessness which might suggest the maternal body. But to make this critique is only half the task. One also must establish the ontological authenticity of the sense of connectedness conveyed in the oceanic feeling. David Michael Levin has made an admirable attempt to describe the necessity of the oceanic feeling: "This 'archaic' feeling, which once, in Freud's own words, 'embraced the universe', this guardian awareness of our interconnect-edness with all other beings and our grounding in the wholeness of being, and which Freud himself, under pressure, did finally recognize, is of the most decisive importance for our present critical task. It is this 'feeling', this awareness, which preserves, through all the vicissitudes of ego-logical history, a sense of the ground, the 'unifying unity' of subject and object. Its retrieval and redemption are therefore *necessary* for the deconstruction of structures of experience reified under the influence of our prevailing metaphysics. The 'archaic' feeling does not have to remain forever archaic; it remains archaic only as long as it is split off, excluded, in some way denied." [11]

Sociology and psychology confirm for us Freud's insights into the persistence of infantile being in religion and mysticism. Our ontology must tell us, in addition, what Freud would not, that there is more than infantile being behind the surface of religion and mysticism. Or, equivalently, we might say that there is more to infantile being than Freud thought—that infantile being also has the potential for spirituality.

Paradoxically, Freud himself is more spiritual than he admits; indeed, he is profoundly ambivalent on the subject. Freud is a kind of intermediate figure between traditional spiritual thought and a more fully despiritualized, technocratic mind-science, and there are many encounters with nonbeing in his psychoanalytic writings. Still, we should take Freud at his word, that his work had as one of its prime goals the despiritualization of the world.

How is this matter to be decided? Are we left with a leap of faith, the *credo quia absurdum,* as the only means of deciding the validity of spiritual experience beyond the place assigned to it by Freud? I think not. For while there can be no positive proof of the independent exis-tence of the spirit realm, and therefore no "spiritual science" as such, we are still able to say whether the dimension of spirituality makes hu-man existence as a whole more coherent. We are still able to think about whether human beings are more intelligible, more fully them-selves, when considered spiritually or through the lens of despiri-tualization; and whether history becomes more intelligible, whether the ceaseless struggle of classes, the fitful march of progress, the as-tounding and horrific abyss over which history teeters, all become clearer. Remember, a spiritual perspective on human existence does not deny any of the findings of science, from psychoanalysis to neu-rophysiology to the sociology of religion. It simply says that these findings, the "nonspiritual spirit of things spiritual," if you will, are a backdrop to the encounter with nonbeing which is the "spirit of spirituality" itself.

The Quest for Being and Nonbeing

In one of the more amusingly snide passages in *Civilization and Its Discontents*, Freud pointed out that "the question of the purpose of human life has been raised countless times; it has never yet received a satisfactory answer and perhaps does not admit of one. Some of those who have asked it have added that if it should turn out that life has *no* purpose, it would lose all value for them. But this threat alters nothing."[12] This is very clever indeed. Freud is shrewdly calling attention to the way our attitude toward fate can be transferred from the child's attempt to threaten and cajole the parent who is supposed to be the source of all knowledge and power. Once again the infantile nature of a seemingly mature behavior has been traced. Beyond this, Freud is implying that life is its own purpose: it simply *is,* and sweeps consciousness along with itself, indifferent to the questions we vainly put to it. Such questions as the purpose of life are thus essentially childish ways of denying our helplessness before the universe and introducing some sense of mastery into an essentially chaotic situation. The great Master of Suspicion (to use the phrase of Paul Ricoeur)[13] has again deflated a bit of narcissism.

Has the corrosive edge of Freud's logos finally destroyed all spiritual possibilities, all utopian hope? For the statement, "life has no meaning, it simply *is,*" is in fact a statement about the meaning of life, yet one which seems to demolish spiritual ambitions by denying any interrogation of being.

To say that life simply *is* means that its purpose cannot be interrogated as if it were a question about the price of milk. But we are left with a fact which is to be explained, namely, just why the question keeps arising. Must we accept Freud's fully despiritualized view? Is the interrogation of being, as Freud seems to suggest, merely a product of outraged narcissism and feelings of helplessness? Is there another, spiritual, way of interrogating existence, which includes the nonspiritual spirit of narcissism yet transcends it—and does the spiritual way of looking at these things surpass the way of despiritualization chosen by Freud? To demonstrate that *a* means *b* does not prove that it does not also mean what it says, *a,* or even something entirely different, *c.* This is particularly consistent with Freudian discourse, which stresses the multidetermination of all meanings. But we are not content with simply multiplying meanings, either. The real issue is whether the spiritual belongs on a different plane than the psychological—that is, whether the spiritual transcends the psychological. If so, then the infantile meanings are entirely consistent with spiritual meanings, and psychoanalysis does not require its framework of despiritualization. The spiritual question, then, is not about the content of the self, but about the existence of a "nonself" to which the self relates—a "beyondness" to being which does not invalidate psychological propositions yet sets their limit. And the insistence of the question about the ends of life calls attention to this.

Why does the question of the purpose of existence arise so regularly? It seems to come as naturally to human beings to interrogate the ground of their existence as it does to make love or to speak. It may be true, as Freud says, that this has something to do with feeling helpless—but what is that something? It is not helplessness itself which leads to questioning existence, but human helplessness. After all, we are no more helpless than a duck, yet there is no suggestion from any quarter that a duck bothers about the end of existence. I have seen ducks panic in the face of a perceived threat to their existence, but they do not respond by wondering but by huddling together and quacking. Certainly one reason for the difference lies in the tremendously enhanced scope of the human central nervous system, with its billions upon billions of neurons hooked together into one prodigious sensing and questioning device. Ducks simply do not have the capacity to form representations of the universe and to ask questions of them, as we do. But the presence of a capacity does not imply that the capacity will be utilized. It depends rather on how the capacity is organized. Capitalism, for example, has the capacity to provide full employment and abundance vastly in excess of that now realized, but because it is organized for the profit of the few against the many, it systematically wastes its own potential. Similarly, all human beings have the spiritual capacity of a Buddha or Saint Francis, yet all save a tiny few squander these powers beyond measure.

Notwithstanding, the spiritual urge is so powerful that even in its state of desuetude it still makes itself heard. And why? Not because we are helpless, or so smart—but because we are positioned in such a way that the question of life's purpose is bound to arise. That is, the question inheres in the structure of human being and its kind of consciousness.

Freud derived the activities of spirit from what we *wanted*. But this overlooks who we *are*. And who we are includes the way in which we are conscious. Consciousness is not simply like a screen, passively registering the qualities of things, but active. And its activity goes beyond the merely cognitive sorting out of the world. Consciousness itself has the character of spirit. I mean here human consciousness, because there is also a consciousness of ducks, and, one should think, of every being, proper to the nature of that being. The insight that human consciousness already has, at least potentially, the character of spirit is Hegel's, whose entire philosophy is spent developing the insight. If Freud stepped outside this position, it is not because he disproved Hegel. There is no evidence I know of that he ever bothered to think seriously about Hegel, who was only a woolly-headed philosopher so far as the tough-minded man of science was concerned. Instead, Freud decided a priori to adopt a despiritualizing attitude. One key way in which this assumption affected his system was in the conception of consciousness and Freud's reluctance to take it seriously as anything more than a membrane, like the inner surface of a cathode ray tube, specially designed to register impulses from the outer world and the interior of the mind.

A Discourse on Consciousness

Viewed psychologically or physiologically, consciousness is an opaque mystery. Freud concluded the same when he abandoned his 1895 "Project for a Scientific Psychology," in which he tried to explain the phenomena of consciousness on a strictly natural and scientific basis, that is, as a property of the organism—that aspect of our being which has duration, extension, and mass. But although Freud abandoned its natural-science conclusions, he remained a prisoner of the style of thinking of the "Project," which resurfaces, for example, in his usage of the term "mental apparatus" to describe the psyche.[14]

However, consciousness cannot be produced by neural tissue, as though it were a secretion. It is better to say that consciousness may be gathered by the brain. One cannot, after all, learn anything about electromagnetic radiation by turning on one's radio. One uses certain properties of the radiation as bearers of information; and the radio functions only as a sophisticated gatherer of the radiation. The nature of the radiation remains a fundamental phenomenon of the world.

When we see, we use electromagnetic radiation of the visual range as the radio uses radiation of its proper wave length. Yet seeing is not consciousness, nor is it even a form of consciousness. Seeing is rather the impression of visual electromagnetic inputs on consciousness. Nor is consciousness bound to other physical forms of energy. Hearing,

smelling, tasting, and feeling are not consciousness. Rather, the senses
are the impressions made upon consciousness by the organism's transformation of various kinds of physical inputs—electromagnetic radiation, propagated mechanical waves, chemical transmitters (which are
ultimately other permutations of electromagnetic radiation), and gravity. It would seem that the organism, through its senses, has devised
means of drawing the physical world into itself. But consciousness is
there irrespective of whether the eye sees or the ear hears; or else blind
and deaf people would have no consciousness. In a sensory depriva-
tion tank, deprived of all perceptible difference between the self and
the external world, an individual does not lose consciousness, but
takes on a consciousness of a relatively unmediated inwardness. Where
does it come from?

The most elementary observation seems to confirm the fact upon
which Descartes built his philosophy—that consciousness arises from
within the self or, depending on how one looks at it, the head. Now
there is no doubt that if you knock a man on the head hard enough he
will lose consciousness. The fact that consciousness seems to come
from within the brain leads people to believe that it is a property of
neural tissue. But this tells us no more about consciousness than the
disappearance of an image after smashing the television set tells us
about electromagnetism. Psychology makes the self the locus of consciousness, while physiology makes the brain the locus of consciousness; yet each seems off the mark. Not only does the traditional mind-
body bifurcation fail to get at the problem of consciousness; it can be
seen that each half of the split is inadequate. It is with some relief that
we realize we need not choose between mind or body: we need only
recognize that each is a kind of fiction, and look for a more adequate
representation of reality.

In brief, we should be able to do better than to speak of mind versus
body in the discourse of consciousness. This is not to deny that consciousness is an inherent property of living creatures, and certainly
more highly developed living creatures, so that some distinction has to
be made as to just what aspect of us has consciousness. But if consciousness is inherent, why must this belong to the organism as such,
that is, to the *material* dimension of our full being? There is also the
ontological dimension. We are *beings* as well as organisms; and if our
being cannot escape materiality, neither can our organism escape the
spiritual dimension of being. Thus we have the property of "is-ness"
which no purely physical or chemical calculus can understand. Just
because modern analytic philosophy has thrown up its hands in the

face of the question of being with which all previous philosophy had been preoccupied does not make the question invalid—especially as it can be shown that the reasons for an abandonment of being are ideological.

Should we not accept the reality of this being, not as something outside of our organism but as something linked to it, in being-organism? If so, then being is part of the natural world, and has the natural world's properties. We do not replace the ancient western metaphysical dualism of body versus mind with another when we write of being-organism. We say rather that the universe differentiates itself at the point of our existence so that, in a way we do not yet understand, there is a "beingness" to us as well as an organismic nature. The "as well as" conjoins being to organism: it differentiates one dimension from the other without splitting them apart. The problem here is no less and no greater than to wonder why time as a dimension exists in the plenum of "space-time." The time dimension is distinct from the space dimension to our eyes, yet joined in space-time. Similarly, being and the organism are distinct, yet joined in us. The organism is the presence of space-time, of matter and the laws of physical extension and duration. And being is something else, whose presence is given in consciousness. Thus instead of the *splitting* into mind versus body, we can think in terms of the *differentiation* into being and organism, the point of differentiation manifested as consciousness. If this differentiation is denied, the situation takes on the appearance of a mind-body split.

It might be said that consciousness is an aspect of being rather than of organism. But since consciousness is a function of a differentiation, it also belongs to the organism. It is better to say that consciousness is the way being presents itself to the organism. Consciousness is not simply a property of being; it is the hyphen, so to speak, in being-organism, the link between the being of the universe and the organic substantiality of the universe as perceived through the work of the organs of sense and the nervous system.

Let us pursue this with a speculation, perhaps wild, but useful in any case. Imagine that consciousness functions in relation to being the way gravity functions in relation to matter. If gravity is the attractive force between separated centers of matter, and the universal force which holds matter together as a single space-time continuum, may not consciousness be the homologue at the level of being—the response of universal being to the presence of individual beings? In this view, consciousness is the registration upon each being of other beings and of its own state of being.

This leads to an important consideration: consciousness is that aspect of being which expresses the separateness of beings, and at the same moment undoes that separateness. That is, a being conscious of other beings has them presented to itself. The presentation by consciousness recaptures what has been detached. It connects beings across a distance. Where there is no separation, there is no consciousness, so that beings are identical to each other—or, what is the same thing, fully absorbed in a larger being. Where, however, beings are distinguished from one another, consciousness is an aspect of this. Consciousness is that which, within a being, announces and undoes the lack of other beings. In the case of human beings—and we would claim that this is virtually definitive for human being—a peculiarly intense conflict over separation and attachment creates unique conditions for consciousness. For human being, consciousness cannot simply be a screen, that is, an inert membrane intercepting stimuli.[15] It is an active process indicating the general predicament of our species: discontinuity with the rest of being. Human being cannot be reduced to being as such, but has its species-specific characteristics. Though our organism is part of nature, our form of being breaks with nature, and our consciousness is the living manifestation of this break.

The constitution of human consciousness in which the break with nature is fought out is language. It is not enough, in our opinion, to consider language functionally, as that marvelous tool by means of which culture is established and "man masters nature." We do not deny that these things happen through the institution of language. We insist only that the institution of language is not simply a neural or a pragmatic event (though it is these), but an ontological event as well. Consciousness itself, in Freud's profound view of the matter, is the acquisition of "word-presentations" to replace the "thing-presentations" of the unconscious world.[16] The word, in this view, is the coming-to-be of human being out of Universal Being. This acquisition is the true Promethean act, and it accounts for the power of logos, for good or ill. With the word, the universe is now more than presented; it is represented to us in a way that permits its infinite reworking. Yet at the same time language institutionalizes the separateness of being by placing the word before direct apprehension of the thing. If the presentation of being in consciousness is an effort to undo separateness, the representation of being by the word reproduces separateness. It masters the world at the cost of losing it further. This is the tragedy of abstraction which poetry, prayer, and spiritual speech seek to overcome. In any case, all language is of estrangement and never transparent to being. Speakers may not lie, but speech does. This fact has brought the philosophy of language to the forefront of contemporary thought. An epoch which despairs of its spirituality and retreats from questions of being replaces these with the scrutiny of language and representation.

But consciousness is self-consciousness as well as the representation of other beings through language. This means it is of itself as well as of the other. The peculiarly human property of a self-reflective subjectivity either differentiates or splits the field of consciousness into the knowing subject and the object known. The division becomes the distinguishing mark of personhood, reflected in that portion of consciousness which encompasses the knowing subject and is called "self." Yet this division makes the self fundamentally problematic. Because of the basic differentiation or splitting within consciousness, the self never fully knows itself.

On the other hand, the self knows more than itself, though we tend not to recognize this. The whole sphere of knowing which goes under various rubrics such as "intuition," "intersubjectivity," or "empathy," is at heart consciousness at a more direct being-to-being level, with only secondary (though still necessary) contributions from the organism. It is characteristic of all such forms of knowing for them to take place without the immediate intervention of language. The word, rather, follows upon and codifies intuitive and empathic knowing— and this is just as we would expect from our ontological view of language. "The heart has its reasons of which the reason knows nothing," wrote Pascal in describing this sphere.[17]

We have already observed that the self is a kind of precipitate of being. Thus a quantum of being is left behind, so to speak, as the self forms. This residual being is incorporated into the field of consciousness without being attached to self-representation. It is rather that which the self left behind but still desires. This primordial Otherness is deployed within the remainder of the field of consciousness. The remainder of the field (the object known) is not homogeneous, but is itself differentiated or split into those objects which are there in themselves, and are merely utilized by the self as object—this pen, this dish, this table, and all other things which are invested with residual being. The former kind of objects are beings, but in themselves; while the latter are beings as any discrete entity is a being, yet with an additional investment of desire. This latter category comprises the dimension of

Otherness. The practical distinction between the two classes of objects is given in the notion of *value*. Any old pen is an object; the pen I value has residual being—and has some quality of Otherness.

Even though I own a pen I do not fully appropriate it. The *lack* of those beings which embody Otherness is experienced as *loss*. This experience is a representation of the primary loss of being and signifies that human being is intolerant of the separation from which its consciousness arises. With the sense of loss arises a valence to recover the loss: *desire*. We shall explore this more fully in Chapter Four.

The range of the consciousness of other beings extends from intuition and empathy, as forms of knowing not dependent on language, all the way to what has been called "extrasensory perception" (ESP). Here we have consciousness of other beings occurring essentially without the mediation of organism. I do not pretend to know how this takes place, though I think it does take place—and think, therefore, that an expanded theory of consciousness must make room for extra-organismic transmission of presentations of the world. Those who pooh-pooh ESP in the name of hard-boiled scientific skepticism are in my opinion guilty of obscurantism. Though the vast majority of reported ESP occurrences may be superstitions, often quite ridiculous, it takes only one genuine instance to force a reconceptualization of the relations between consciousness and the physical world.[18] We see then why it is important to be able to detach the existence of consciousness from any particular medium or organismic effect, and to make it a property of the "separatedness" of beings, as gravity is a property of the "separatedness" of masses. One can assume either that authenticated ESP events are raw coincidences, or that there exists a mode of transmission of consciousness which does not require the media of ordinary matter and the organs of sense perception dependent on them. I would adopt the latter assumption. It must be only an assumption; there can be no hard proof of these things, nor any way of convincing the confirmed skeptic.[19]

It might be noted that valid instances of ESP often involve mothers. Now I do not wish to inflate the value of mothering by raising it to the level of a supernatural instinct. The prevalent apparitions of maternal figures which enter into world religions can, after all, be explained on psychological grounds. But there is something special about mothering, as though the production and birth of another being sets going an intense nexus of attachment and separation. We might imagine that this "primes" maternal consciousness, and creates the possibility for reactivation at later moments of separation. I would speculate, too, that such activated consciousness would be able to immediately perceive the loss of or hazard to those other beings to whom one is "attached." "Attachment" here is not a metaphor, but an aspect of the actual condition of beings, which is ordinarily masked by the separation necessary for the sustenance of individual organismic existence. This is, again, speculation, but I am not persuaded that any alternate explanation does better.

The ideas stated above may cast some light on certain issues and phenomena. They might help explain consciousness during sleep, when the neural apparatus which connects certain aspects of the organism to a being is switched off. The organism persists, but its being for a period moves toward the being of the whole universe. In the dream state word-presentations become thing-presentations once again, and language moves toward being, hence the peculiar psychology of dreaming. This explanation would leave room for more recent neurophysiological—i.e., organismic—insights into sleep and dreaming without invalidating Freud's basic discoveries.

In addition, group relations become more comprehensible. Standard psychological discourse has never been able to account for the power of the group in human existence. Freud's classic account[20] remains the most important effort to do so, though limited by ideological prejudice against the rationality of collective action. Freud could not shake the idea that the basic group was constructed along the lines of the mob, or at best, the army. He would not recognize, so far as I know, group activity in which people would actually grow and become more intelligent in the process—for example, the exhilarating, then horrifying events in Beijing in May and June of 1989, where observers reported that the entire city was occupied spontaneously by its people, who differentiated themselves to perform complex functions before they were wiped out by the authoritarian state.[21]

We need a perspective which does justice to the primacy of group experience in its creative as well as deformative possibilities; and which also explains the tension between individual and group. For the group is ontic before it is psychological; it is the larger being from which individual being emanates and to which it returns. A dialectic arises between the individuated self and the group being to which it belongs. The group, be it family, clan, tribe, class, nation, or church, becomes the intermediary representation of being to the self, a way station between the isolated particle of consciousness and the universe. It becomes being in human form, combining the familiar (hence the elementary primacy of family relations in all group relations) with the awesomeness of Universal Being. Thus groups are the scenes within which spirit-power is manifested, and the locus for the politics of spirituality when the spiritually moved group becomes the religious community or church. And charismatic leadership becomes the ability enjoyed by certain individuals to draw back into themselves the spirit-power belonging to the group.

The complexity of this dialectic must be appreciated. It has as its elements

- human being separated from Universal Being;
- the group as reconstitution of being toward Universal Being;
- the charismatic leader as appropriator of reconstituted being; and finally,
- group-with-leader as setting within which being is remediated back to individuals in the socialization process. This final stage is what we know as self-formation.

Marx states that the self is the "ensemble of social relations."[22] This summarizes well the last stage above, but neglects the vital preceding ones. Freud's view does the same, with attention to the infantile and deeply subjective aspects of the process ignored by Marx. In both Freud and Marx, however, the group psychological process is picked up, as it were, after it has departed from being. Thus both end up explaining group activity reductively. Freud recognizes that individual psychology and group psychology are different manifestations of the same thing, but he sees both within a framework where bourgeois standards of rationality reign. Thus for Freud there is no rationality to collective action as such, nor do individuals seek anything, ultimately, but egoistic gain, however masked by the grand scale of group ideals. These ideals, then, are only illusions, and individual being must be seen as checked in any motion through a collective project toward a larger being. Marx, of course, sees the foundations of rationality in collective endeavor; therefore, the group is open to a fuller being. However, the sources of this being in the individual are closed by Marx's insensitivity to depth psychology and the roots of subjectivity in nature. This, too, is grounded in an unwillingness to go beyond the frame of egoic rationality and consciousness.

We need to regard consciousness, too, as absorbed in the group, and group consciousness as a kind of intermediary being. This substitutes for and may or may not obliterate the consciousness of the individual, according to how "group-being" is gathered with respect to other beings. Here the question of class consciousness enters as a function of how alienated a group is from being and of how authentic its practice is. We will return to this theme later.

This notion of consciousness also permits us to make sense of the fact, noted earlier, that creative and mystical experience seems to occur discontinuously, in leaps: sudden flashes of insight, the agony of creation, developmental jumps of young children, being seized by the muse, and so forth. It allows us to see this discontinuity as the product of two existing modes of consciousness, the one holding the other back, the other now bursting through and altering the conditions by which the other functions.

Thus if we cease thinking about consciousness as a passive sensor, and regard it instead as dynamically and actively engaged in self-constitution, we will see that consciousness spontaneously generates questions about the ends of existence. To the extent that consciousness is spirit, it is structured so as to interrogate being. We can frame the questioning of being stupidly or well, can do so in the pattern of a sulky and frightened child or a spiritual warrior, can repress questions of existence, scientize them like Freud, make jokes of them like Woody Allen, or use these questions to evolve a coherent spiritual practice. These are all real choices. They are both socially conditioned and ultimate matters of existential freedom. But we can begin with the hypothesis that human being is structured to bring them to the fore: questions concerning the ends of life emerge from the womb of the spirit as ova are brought forth out of the ovary on an uncertain journey of fertilization.

With his splendid ambivalence, Freud made it possible to see this—even if the psychoanalytic tradition has largely chosen not to follow its own spiritual implications. In any case, psychoanalysis discloses consciousness itself arising, not independently of the world, but in the course of separation from the world. That is, consciousness grows out of the praxis of the developing person—his or her self-transformative activity—and not from some group of cells in the nervous system. The praxis of the developing person is organized around the dilemma of being with and being separate from another. If we could learn to see consciousness as a transformation occurring within praxis instead of as a cathode ray screen or a photographic emulsion, we would be on much firmer conceptual ground. In any case, a human being does not become conscious as a self-contained monad, but as a creature who begins existence inside another, and only constitutes its being, its consciousness, and its spirituality in relation to others. Freud showed that the world against which consciousness forms is the human world; that is, the world of human others encountered by the infant. From these others, with whom we are first fused and from whom we separate, arises the Other. The "ego is a precipitate of abandoned object cathexes," wrote Freud; or again, the "shadow of the object falls on the ego."[23] Human being is consequently always poised between the affirmation of individuality and the lost fusion with the Other. Because of this painful yet creative paradox, we are not simply conscious, but self-conscious. Our consciousness is then of separateness, as is our language. For us, being is discontinuous—and yet this discontinuity is experienced as loss, and life is spent in trying to overcome it. It comes naturally to us, then, to sense nonbeing along with being, and to try to rejoin the two, that is, to be spiritually. For nonbeing is the space between the discontinuities, the space beyond the Other. It is in this context that human beings are led to wonder about the finitude of their existence against the universe's infinity, to ponder the ineluctable mysteries of birth and death, and the origin and passage of the soul from the world.

The occasion at which this first takes place is the attachment and separation of the human infant.[24] That the parents are the earliest primary objects is crucial for the understanding of human existence. But there is a tremendous difference between making the parents the *cause* of human consciousness, on the one hand, and on the other, recognizing that parents are essentially an *occasion:* that which fills the role of "world" at a vital stage of human development. The former position confines human being in what may be called a "psychological" mode determined principally by intrafamiliar relations; the latter position recognizes those relations as one occasion of a larger and continuous whole, which is the inevitable and natural unfolding of human power and consciousness. In this unfolding, parents occupy a strategic role at a strategic time; they are not however the alpha and omega of human existence, but rather the occasions for transmitting reality—including of course social reality—to the developing person. This latter point of view is the spiritual one; the former, the despiritualized one of a society which clings to familial relations as the only conceivable authenticity. But the spiritual position may also be called ontological, as against psychological. That is, it is a position which begins from and returns to the being of human being; while the psychological position begins and returns to the self, or subjectivity, of human being. The self-subject studied by psychology is a creature traced by immediate relations with those parts of the world considered within limits of conventional reality. Psychological science is essentially a readout of the given

consciousness of things, which, to nobody's surprise, is immediately
defined by the family and personal relations. That is why so much psychology ends up as a laughable elaboration of the obvious. Psychoanalysis is the only branch of psychological science to scratch beneath
the surface of things, but all too often it too stops at the level of hidden
relations within the family, that is, with the nonspiritual spirit of the
self. Feminist scholarship has succeeded in unmasking the ideological
distortions of masculinist bias in Freud and the whole psychoanalytic
tradition.[25] The same challenge exists with respect to the mystique of
the family.[26]

Freud's cynicism about the meaning of life is self-contradictory, because no one wrestled more profoundly with the problem than he.
This was reflected in Freud's willingness to go all the way into a
frankly speculative metatheory which confronted nonbeing. The results, particularly in *Beyond the Pleasure Principle*,[27] have continued
to embarrass the technocrats who plug away in his name. *Beyond the
Pleasure Principle* is a permanent scandal to the psychoanalytic establishment, not because it postulates instinctual aggression as a root of
human nature (in itself a comfortable bourgeois illusion), but because
it claims that the very "instincts" which are supposed to be the hard,
scientific part of psychoanalysis are grounded in the frankly spiritual
categories of Eros and Thanatos, the life and death instincts. These are
tendencies within the universe. They are not just beyond the pleasure
principle, but beyond psychology and biology, and by extension, beyond the grip of logos altogether. Eros and Thanatos can only be regarded as notions at the level of being—and though Freud would not
use the term, this was the source of the scandal of *Beyond the Pleasure
Principle*. Both Eros and Thanatos are reactions against the separateness of being. Eros is the attraction of beings for each other, that is,
the denial of separateness through activity; while Thanatos is the denial of separateness through a merging with the source of being.[28] In
addition, Freud proposed to derive the instincts, and hence biology
and psychology themselves, from being. If there could ever be any
doubt as to the basically spiritual bent of Freud's metatheory, it should
be dispelled by the association of Thanatos with, of all things, the nirvana principle. This was the return of Freud's own repressed spirituality in the acceptance of nonbeing, hence an acceptance of being. To
Freud's credit, he refused to back away from the line of reasoning set
forth in *Beyond the Pleasure Principle*, as outrageous as he knew it to
be, and even though he also refused to integrate its ontological perspective into the body of his thought. Freud's greatness had something

to do with his ability to freely move within what lesser minds would regard as impossible contradiction. There can be no question that this was a spiritual strength in him.

The interrogation of being cannot be evaded; it is the one question before all others. Of course there is no answer to this question, because the notion of an answer is of something that can be grasped by human cognition. An answer belongs by definition within the perimeter of the knowable, while the question of existence is essentially posed of something about which all we know is that it is not knowable, and that it is outside ourselves; indeed, it is defined by the negative of the self; nonbeing. To expect the universe or God to answer the question posed by spirit deserves the sarcasm of Woody Allen or Mel Brooks, for it is no better, really, than scanning the astrology columns in the daily papers. To complain about the universe, or threaten it, as in Freud's wry example, quoted above, is to reveal a spiritual motion trapped within the limitations of psychology. Need we add that this is very common, especially when a whole society is structured to cretinize the spiritual capacities of human beings?

It is the questioning and not any particular answer which opens the door to spirituality. Spiritual questioning is neither empty nor idle, but shapes action in the world, or praxis. Spirituality is not some mooning about for pie in the sky or reassurances from big daddy God, but a way of being and acting in the world with decisive effects on real life. If we recognize that human beings are configured spiritually, that spirituality is an interrogation of being from the standpoint of nonbeing, and that there is no discrete answer to the interrogation and therefore no prescribed spirituality, we are saying that spirituality is a continual process of discovery and struggle, enacted in this world, which is to say, in history. It is a process, moreover, of no particular valence or virtue: necessary for the good, but no less prone to generate evil.

States of Being: Ego and Soul

There are many variations in consciousness with many different relations to being. A kind of duality seems to hover over the ensemble. We have called attention to the pernicious effects of splitting apart the terms of these dualities, and have introduced the notion of differentiation as an alternative to splitting. But this seems to have succeeded in introducing yet another kind of duality: that between differentiation and splitting.

We have written also of the self as a precipitate of being, which can either be differentiated or split from being according to its spirituality.

We have already used the traditional term *soul* to refer to the spiritual form of the self. Now we need to employ another term for the non-spiritual form of the self. For this purpose we will make use of a much-worked word that nevertheless best conveys the kind of reality we are trying to describe—*Ego* (capitalized here to indicate its special use). The notions of Ego and soul provide a pair of concepts serviceable for the discussion of spiritual life.

Ego and soul are forms of the self, but since the self is a relation to being, on a larger scale Ego and soul are states of being: positions of the whole being-organism acting in history with a certain kind of consciousness. Although psychoanalysis has employed the term *ego* as a way of describing an objective structure of mind, the word will do equally well as a way of calling attention to the state of being of the isolated self. For in fact that is all psychoanalysis wants to see.[29]

Two qualifications are worth noting here. First, to say that Ego is a form of the self on the opposite end of a spectrum from the "soul" form of the self does not mean that some of us are (bad) Egoic people and others are (good) soulful people, the way some have blue eyes and others brown eyes. In other words, Ego and soul are not meant to distinguish types of whole persons (although it would be impossible to avoid some informal usage of this kind). Rather are they states or ways of being which commingle in the concrete individual, and in the concrete historical situation. Each of us, in other words, has Egoic aspects to our being, and soul aspects to our being, which are in a conflict played out through our historical agency. One side or the other may prevail or come to the fore at a crucial juncture, and so define that juncture. This is after all the spiritual flux of history. But we are never all one mode or the other; and each mode, so to speak, is the shadow-side of the other. Another way of saying this is that we wish, here as elsewhere in this study, to advance a differentiated way of doing things rather than a split way: we want to learn to see ourselves as differentiated into Ego and soul modes, and have the two recognize one another. In this way the soul itself develops and overcomes Ego, as it never could if we held, with spiritual pride, that we were all one way or the other.

Second, it is also important not to limit the predominance of the Ego form of the self to the world of capitalism, for Ego is a possibility open under all conceivable social conditions. But it is just as important to recognize that capitalism is the one social system specifically organized around the Egoic mode of being. An analogy may be drawn here with wage labor, as a kind of production relation spread throughout history, yet only systematically developed by capitalism. In any case, capitalism is that kind of social order which functions, at the level of the self, so that Ego overcomes soul.

The way of Ego is splitting and nonrecognition; and the various psychological properties of Ego—for example, an emphasis upon domination and control, the use of intellectualization and rationalization as defenses, a sharp distinction drawn between itself and the world, and the well-known drive toward self-aggrandizement—are all derivatives of this splitting mode. The fact that people think of "ego" as a kind of prideful—i.e., "egotistical"—self is noteworthy here, because the kind of self-formation we have in mind is subjectively as well as objectively aggrandized. At the same time Egoic being is prone to an endless proliferation of splits. Freud called attention in his last years to "splitting of the ego" as a mode of psychological defense.[30] I think we should extend this insight: splitting as a way of being is essential to the Egoic self. I imagine this is because Egoic being lacks a spiritual center, hence is capable of going off every which way, the ways losing cognizance of each other. Because it denies itself recognition of the internal relatedness of the Other, Ego is capable of adopting wildly disparate and even contradictory patterns of praxis. At the same time its masterful arrogance enables it to blithely ignore its own fragmented being, and even to coexist with soulfulness in certain instances. It is this tendency which allows men to be kindly fathers at home and planners of nuclear war or child pornographers at the office—and never experience a twinge of self-doubt. The fact that psychoanalysis makes such a fuss over Ego in its ego psychology tells us, too, that Ego is an ideologically precious piece of mental territory. In a despiritualized world, where people are not supposed to have souls, and spirit-beings are psychopathological, Egoic being is a last refuge. Indeed, we could call its naturalization under psychoanalysis the fetish form of the self. As a fetish is a part made to stand for the whole,[31] so does Ego tend to become all—repressing the formless id, setting up its boundaries with reality and between people and controlling the gates of reason. Ego stands over mere nature, keeps genders rigidly separated, and flees oceanic being as madness. Hence it attempts to control the nature of consciousness.

Although ESP or states of mystical awareness are powers vouchsafed to only a few, there are endless variations in the ordinary life of consciousness which approach them, according to one's state of being. We tend to think of these states as abnormal, and they are, but only by the standards of Ego—which is that state of the self which sets rigid standards and worries about them. Once we get over regarding Ego as the summum bonum of human existence and recognize it instead as a very partial way of being, it is possible to take a more balanced view of the abnormal; or rather, of normalcy. For it now appears that if a fuller being is not recognized, this is due to a terror of nonbeing rather than to the sanity of the normal.

In any case, there is a consciousness peculiar to Ego, which is sharply bounded and excludes whatever the senses cannot immediately verify. There is also a consciousness proper to soul, which is not bound by any envelope, is less sharply bounded, and employs to varying degrees the direct apprehension of other being. The emergence of the Other and of spirit-being, as we have noted, is an indication of this.[32]

As Ego and soul coexist in varying proportions in each individual, we would argue that soul-consciousness and Ego-consciousness are everywhere present together. If it does not seem this way, it is because a main function of Ego-consciousness is to suppress soul-consciousness. The soul-consciousness which is felt so strongly in instances of telepathy is also present in numerous other settings. Two factors determine the "varieties of consciousness" of which William James and other students (esp. van der Leeuw) of mysticism and religious phenomena write. The first is the relative degree of soul-consciousness admitted by Ego, and the second is the specific contents "written" upon soul-consciousness, which are determined by history, religious tradition, culture, individual psychology, etc.

Another way of talking about this is through Freud's image of the oceanic experience. This is dismissed, we may recall, by the great pathfinder of modern psychology as the derivative of an infantile memory in which the immature ego was without a boundary from the world. On this basis Freud argues that religious and mystical phenomena are remnants of immature experience, that they are sought as consoling escapes from the real world, and that they are therefore without any rational basis. The same critique could also apply to any transportive feeling, such as orgasm, being in love, and strong political passion. If it is true, however, that instances of the oceanic experience are not simply the return of lost gratification, but actual instances of soul breaking through chinks in Ego, this whole class of phenomena is put on a different basis. In a word, they have a rational core: oceanic experiences are not illusions but visions, grounded in the immediate perception of the existing unity of all beings.

If this line of reasoning is true, beings are united at the level of being, while they are divided at the level of self. Soul-consciousness may be difficult to achieve, disorganizing to the sense of reality, seemingly outside of reason and deeply troublesome—but it is no illusion. Rather, it is the perception of linkage to being, as real in its way as the isolation of Ego-consciousness. It would be wrong to assert one side of this at the expense of the other. Both are true—and contradictory. We see separateness more readily, for the simple reason that consciousness itself is of separateness. We ordinarily do not become conscious, then, of the actual existing unity of beings, their participation in Universal Being.

The same is true at the level of organism as of being: there is a real connectedness masked by the illusory Egoic separation. I do not dispute that creatures have a degree of separateness, and that the existence of beings manifest this, for a property of being is in fact its own self-perpetuation in relation to others. I do dispute, however, the absoluteness of this separateness, and claim that this notion is the result of Ego's fear of connection. Indeed, biological science cannot even define an organism as something radically discrete from all other organisms. The entirety of ecological consciousness depends upon this fact. Ordinary experience seems to confirm the radical discreteness of organisms, but the notion is easily broken down. Think about it: where does your body truly end and that of another begin? How many other organismic beings are part of our own? How much is our own flesh in constant exchange with the rest of nature? The inability to see anything but individual organisms is only another instance of the splitting inherent to Egoic attitude. In fact, the discreteness of organism is the true illusion, foisted by Egoic terror upon mute being.

Junctures of Being

Consciousness is critical to the understanding of being, but cannot be separated from the whole of being. Consciousness flows through being, which is to say, from the way life is lived.[33] Human being is a project, and never determined in advance. The self does not crystallize out of being all at once to become the seat of psychological relations. Rather the relation of the self to being continuously evolves throughout life, with critical moments defined at great existential junctures. Coming into the world and differentiating from parents are two such existential occasions for spiritual development because they represent critical junctures in the development of being—points when being has to redefine itself, and shed preexisting forms. We have no choice in going through these junctures—except to choose whether to go through the juncture or to stop being altogether.

Birth and differentiation are junctures of being peculiar to the immature self, and the ones most fussed over by psychology. But they certainly do not exhaust the category of significant life junctures, for human being is so constituted as to require continual redefinition. There are, in other words, junctures appropriate to the mature self, which comprise an equally necessary set of choices.

I have no intention of cataloging an inventory of the "phases of life," a task already done in tedious detail by psychology. For our purposes these may be summarized as two elementary and enduring problems: how to live, and how to die. Although the two problems cannot ultimately be separated, we are obliged to make a distinction for purposes of exposition. But in expounding a notion of the conduct of life, we will also have to introduce a fuller reflection on history. Once born, we are thrown into the historical world, and the way we configure our being—in dying as well as in living—is shaped accordingly. Our consciousness does not grow in relation to some abstract tendency in the universe, but according to the precise way self and Other are made.

> Hitherto individual mind as such has been under review, and this is an abstraction from social mind or spiritual existence. . . .
>
> Spirit is thus the self-supporting absolutely real ultimate being (*Wesen*). All the previous modes of consciousness are abstractions from it; they are constituted by the fact that spirit analyses itself, distinguishes its moments, and halts at each individual mode in turn . . . Spirit . . . is that type of consciousness which has Reason. . . . Finally, when this reason, which spirit "*has*," is seen by spirit to be reason which actually *is,* to be reason which is actual in spirit, and is its world, then spirit has come to its truth; it *is* spirit, the essential nature of ethical life actually existent.   Hegel, *Phenomenology of Spirit*

The notion that consciousness unfolded as spirit[34] was first developed by Hegel, the greatest expositor of the life of spirit outside the religious tradition. Hegel also asserted a kind of rationality to the unfolding of spirit. In brief, he assumed a conformity between consciousness and spirit on the one hand, and reason or logos on the other. That is, being emerges through an orderly succession of stages, the order reflecting an objective and absolute world-spirit whose effects are present in every sphere, from the consciousness of self to political structures such as the German state. This kind of harmony manifested the hopeful attitude of the rising bourgeoisie, which felt it had within its power the unification of the globe. For this class, then, the problem of how to live and die could be answered: in conformity with the objective unfolding of absolute spirit. Events were to bring this illusion crashing down.[35]

It became clear to the followers of Hegel that the association between the real and the rational was murky for those fated to live on the historical earth, and had to be created rather than found ready-made.[36] One's being had to be chosen; it could not be objectively read in the motions of spirit. Nor, therefore, could spirit be regarded as an absolute, standing above history and human being. The post-Hegelian tradition became as a result mainly existential in temper, and the philosophy of Kierkegaard, Nietzsche, Heidegger, and Sartre was preoccupied with the choice of being and the confrontation with nonbeing, variously conceptualized. In this sense, all existential thought is intrinsically spiritual. Unable to accept Hegel's absolute spirit, the existentialist is led by spiritual need to create an authentic spirituality.

Existentialism is now in eclipse, victim to a triumphant despiritualization. But the involution of existentialism was not the result of a purely philosophical defeat. It has been part, rather, of the narrowing of historical possibilities. Kierkegaard and Nietzsche, to mention the two major existential thinkers closest in time to Hegel, lived in stifling autocracies marked by bourgeois prejudices, which they endlessly savaged in their writings. Both were also antidemocratic, anticlerical and (especially Nietzsche) hostile to socialism. Yet they lived in the fading, but still powerful, light of religious salvation, and in the rising light of social revolution. The possibility of transcendence was in the air. A thinker could reject the prevalent forms taken by transcendent ambitions, yet still feel obliged to hold a vision of life marked by real hope for self-transformation. Kierkegaard's radical Christianity of "fear and trembling," and Nietzsche's invocation of the "eternal return," were particular existential responses, devastating to conventional logic and values, yet asserting a more valid possibility of spiritual renewal.[37]

Where real choices are seen as narrow and meaningless, so will the sense of existential possibility contract. With the further decline of religion and the atrophy of revolutionary aspirations, the choice of the conduct of life and death has, in the advanced industrial nations, become confined to a shrinking zone defined by dominant political and economic interests. Within this zone, which is called "democracy" because people can vote into power the faction of the ruling class they dislike the least, choices in conduct are made to seem infinite, with as many entries, at least, as in *The Guinness Book of World Records,* or articles in *National Geographic*. But these are sideshows in a carnival owned by the few and administered to the many. After all, one can divide even a very small piece of ground into a million parcels. What counts is the person or class ultimately in control, and the chance of asserting self-determination against him, her, or it. It is a very good thing for people to struggle for control over local government, as in trying to alter the zoning commission or the school board. But if these issues are pursued in the context of resignation over the direction of society as a whole, they tend to become truly parochial and spiritually vacuous.

Thus the existential contracture of modern society is in the deepest sense a political process, which is to say, it is dependent on human struggle and not on some law of nature. And the outcome of the struggle has so far been a victory for those who would have us believe that the world cannot be organized other than by the terms of the capitalist state. And as the sense of real choice has shrunk, so have philosophical horizons.[38] This is consistent with our reflections about the group as an intermediate station of larger being, where society as a whole becomes the fullest stage to which this direction of being can extend. As our relation to being determines consciousness, and as philosophy represents the largest reflection into consciousness, a contraction of social possibility implies a contraction of philosophy. This point of view is also consistent with Marx's view of ideology as the ruling ideas of the ruling class—and it tells us why Marx broke both with the philosophy and the politics of the Young Hegelians.

Post-Hegelian philosophy may have despaired, but it never accepted the hegemony of bourgeois society. In fact, it battled that hegemony fiercely. Kierkegaard continued to think in the terms of Christian eschatology and of faith, although on a radically new, and highly critical, basis of dread; Nietzsche looked toward the *Übermensch* and the confrontation with nonbeing entailed in the eternal return; Heidegger reconceptualized authentic being and associated it with the spiritual renewal of the German people in fascism; while Sartre pursued being and nothingness, and later, the critique of dialectical reason, in the framework of the politics of the revolutionary left.[39] All of them, therefore, even those who were seemingly apolitical (Kierkegaard and Nietzsche despised ordinary politics, and Heidegger turned away from ordinary politics and towards a kind of Buddhism after the fall of Nazism), looked toward a kind of world radically Other than the present. All, that is, were in one way or another utopian. None of them felt obliged to accept a world order whose outer perimeter was defined by bourgeois democracy. From the right or left, all the existential thinkers—and the great existential novelists, too, such as Dostoevsky—drew spiritual strength from raging against bourgeois society and its relentless despiritualization. This perspective gave a certain high seriousness to existential spirituality. The choices made by being really mattered, in the real world. Today, when the world order defined by Coca-Cola ("It's the real thing") and General Electric ("We bring good things to life") has become internalized as necessary by philosophers and the academy in general, the choices offered by contemporary thought become mainly internal. Indeed, they are pushed back to earlier phases of personal existence, even infancy, when there is not so very much to choose, after all. Hence the great fashion of psycho-technocracy, or the furor for deconstruction and textual analysis which sweeps through the academy. All are, in one way or another, philosophies of resignation.

The Meaning of Meaningfulness

I think we would all agree that every life has meaning, but that some are more meaningful than others. But few would agree on the meaning of this "meaningfulness." Obviously it is not a quantitative term, as though the meaningful life were simply full of more meaning. Nor is meaningfulness a product of social station, or any objective fact. The most externally degraded individual is able to infuse life with meaning; while the lord of the realm may live meaninglessly. Meaningfulness has rather to do with how a person encounters reality. To live meaningfully, then, is a way of creating meaning and giving it to life. It has to do with the active and passive senses of the verb *to live*. A meaningful life is life we live; a meaningless life is life which is lived for us. It might be imagined therefore that the more meaningful life is the one over which we have the most control. There is some truth to this, but a narrow and ambiguous one. For it begs the questions: with what state of being do we control or not control life; and what, in any case, does it mean to control something? It would be better to say that a meaningful life is one we have *appropriated*. It is interesting that *appropriate* should have descended to the level of an adjective denoting socially correct behavior, while its now-faded usage as a verb signifies the active, full taking in of life, the making life part of the self.

An important ambiguity remains: should appropriation be regarded in terms of the expansion of the self, as though taking life in and making it one's own were a kind of acquisition; or, on the other hand, is appropriation a kind of opening up of the self to life? The first alternative focuses on the self and aggrandizes it; hence it builds the boundaries of the self. The second alternative, however, focuses on a kind of dissolution of the self's boundaries.

Capitalism affords the prime example of the first alternative in action; indeed, capitalism builds itself upon it. For capitalism tells us that the meaningful life is the life that maximizes the self. Whatever is "me" has more, does more, achieves more; such is the good life, whether measured in terms of compact disks, muscles, orgasms, publicity, or cash. This is the philosophy of individualism. It is no mere idea, but an essential configuration of human relations to grease the wheels of economic accumulation. Thus the meaningful life is held to be the life in which one profits and succeeds the most. The principle of self-maximization is the personal ideology of capitalist society: it makes the society seem worthwhile, and provides an endless supply of eager beavers to hustle their way to the top.

This is the way of Egoism, which aggrandizes Ego at the expense of soul. The problem with capitalist Egoism is that it also aggrandizes the Ego at the expense of other persons. Individual success in the marketplace is always at the expense of others; the meaning of self-maximization is the minimization of others. The capitalist firm, the individual worker, the manager, the woman seeking the richest man, the star seeking the highest ratings, the nation-state seeking total control over markets—all are bound to the same wheel, which spins with each triumph or loss, each exchange in the market.

There is a shadow: each success of the self is another's failure. And whether or not one succeeds, in this scheme of things all others are reduced to antagonists. This means that each other person becomes radically Other, and is not recognized as a fellow being of the self. Thus the way of the Ego seems natural, because it meshes with social relations so basic that the words to question them are excluded from ordinary thought, and indeed seem mad.

The control over life achieved by this way of being is strictly illusory. Thus I read [40] that Apple Computer Company—a firm for which I have some feeling, as they made the machine upon which I wrote this work—is in deep trouble and woe. Having grown from nothing to sales of a billion dollars a year in five years, and from one billion to five billion in another five years, Apple is now stagnating. Its product line is not keeping pace with the competition; its marketing effort has flagged; and sales have dropped to "only" a 6 percent increase in the last six months.

Great anguish has seized the firm, and three of the top six positions are now empty as the chairman, John Sculley, seeks to regain the initiative, or as they say, the cutting edge. Layoffs are to follow. What misery! That such power and success can bring so much anxiety in its wake. And what is the source of this angst? It is the honored capitalist principle of grow or die, and the vicious climate of competition in which it exists. If living a meaningful life is having some inner control over one's existence, then this path, despite all its Egoic power and control, is meaningless.

This effect spreads to the inner world of the person because of the breakdown in communal life and the rise of the privatized family in capitalist society.[41] In this arrangement, family means more, and public existence less. The former conduces to neurosis, the latter to estrangement; and the entire situation makes the dominant relationship to Otherness one of splitting. A bitter paradox, specific for capitalist society, results. The moment of the self's triumph, and the summum bonum of the system as a whole, is also the moment of its alienation: that occasion when the self stands apart and radically separated, surrounded by a world dimly populated by Otherness. Thus alienation describes the spiritual as well as the economic life of capital. In this world of estrangement, the development of Otherness into spirit-being is inhibited. Spirit-beings are not experienced as such. Indeed, Ego sees itself only as self, the other only as Other. The mediation between self and Other provided by spirit-being is denied. We might say, then, that spirit and soul have also been inhibited. Soulless conditions are the result.

No one is actually told not to have a soul. By soulless conditions is simply meant that those ways of being which are conducive to soul are not rewarded with worldly success. The main institutions of society train people to be efficient techno-bureaucratic workers, jolly consumers, and aspiring winners in the game of life. In this scheme of things, soulfullness is strictly a residual category, and does not help one get ahead, indeed, can well make for failure.

To break out of the shell of Ego, then, requires a radical rupture with the logic of the system as a whole. At the same time, the system needs oppositions and breaks to function—so long as they are kept under control and do not threaten the mainsprings of power. Our religions are excellent candidates for this controlled negativity. As Marx said, religion is the "spirit of spiritless conditions."[42] Religion may also be the "opium of the people," that is, a kind of narcotic easing of the pain which might otherwise lead to transformative action. The established religions offer Otherness a kind of safe-conduct pass, on the condition that it return to its cage when the service is over. But even so, religion provides that spark of light which can illuminate the Other and undo, however momentarily, the loneliness of existence.

Our line of reasoning leads to the second sense of appropriation as the criterion of a genuinely meaningful life: appropriation as the opening of the self to life, so that the self and life flow together. But *life* here must mean the whole world of being, which presents itself as Otherness. Therefore the fully meaningful, appropriated life is one whose meanings consist of openings to the Other; from another angle, a life led according to differentiation rather than splitting. For it is in the mutual recognition of difference that the richest meanings arise. And since meanings are mental representations of practical relations with others, the meaningful life (a life, that is, consistent with the needs of the soul), is a life led with others, so as to overcome Otherness. It is important to add that such a life is not antithetical to the development of the self. It only rejects and opposes the self as an isolated particle over and against others—the form of the self that we call Ego. To overcome Otherness is to accept Otherness, not to repress or abolish Otherness—to accept it, perhaps as spirit-being, make it part of the self, and then transform the self. But this kind of self-transformation is the spiritualization of the self, the recognition of self in Other, the transformation of self into soul. And it is also a practical matter, with political implications.

Considering this, we might reflect a bit on the following quotation from Karl Marx which appeared in his column of 15 March 1859 for the *New York Daily Tribune* (and may have been written by Engels, who did many of the *New York Daily Tribune* pieces, obviously with Marx's full approval). "At the same time I take advantage of the occasion to express my admiration for those British factory inspectors who, in the face of all-powerful class interests, have assumed the task of protecting the oppressed masses. In these days when Mammon is worshipped one can hardly find any parallel for their moral courage, their unflagging energy and their spiritual superiority." This passage was drawn from Jose Miranda's *Marx Against the Marxists*,[43] a work which culls through Marx's writing to demonstrate that the founder of modern communism—a doctrine widely denounced for its hostility to religion and spirit—was in fact a spiritually motivated man (though certainly not a religious one).[44] In the symphony of historical materialism, the above passage is no more than a slender grace note. Yet it is consistent with the moral and spiritual logic of Marx's entire project.

Four interconnected ideas may be drawn from this vignette: that the factory inspectors had to overcome "all-powerful class interests" to do what they did; that what excites Marx's admiration is caring for the oppressed masses; that Mammon is worshipped in a capitalist society; and that moral courage and spiritual superiority is demonstrated by this behavior.

This can be restated in terms of our discourse. In class society certain people are systematically oppressed. That is, their oppression follows from forces which, though ultimately human, have sedimented and appear as facts of nature, beyond individual human volition and comprehension. These people—the "oppressed masses"—can be workers and, with certain distinctions that do not concern us for now, also anyone who is systematically excluded, like women, blacks, homosexuals, all the "wretched of the earth." They comprise the historical Other; and their Otherness is the dialectical counterpoise to the worship of mammon—naked, elemental, materialistic greed, fetishized into an idol. The systematic nature of the forces in class society is inscribed in consciousness and ideology ("class interests"). Ordinary, normal consciousness is calibrated so as to exclude this reality: hence what passes for received truth is actually false consciousness. The falseness of consciousness accounts for the inability to sift critically through the various kinds of meanings given to different ways of life. It takes, therefore, a special leap, or opening to Otherness, to see beyond the naturalization of oppression sedimented in the system, and to achieve genuine meaningfulness. Such a leap requires what Marx calls moral courage, and it is proof of spiritual realization. The spiritually realized person, the person of soul, breaks across the class barrier. He or she not only becomes open to the Other but actually appropriates the Otherness of the oppressed. That is, the spiritually realized person makes this Otherness his or her own, through an act of protection. This act also constitutes a risk to the normal, Egoic self—hence the element of courage. The result is a mutual empowerment of the person who had been Other and of the person who has made the leap. Such is the best way of describing what a meaningful life might be, for it is a way of being that most fully encounters Otherness as it appears in society.

In practice the logic of this process might stop at the level of charity—of giving the oppressed a handout, or a home, or even better working conditions. But a person who pauses at the level of charity in protecting the oppressed masses is doing so at the behest of Mammon and violating the motion of spirit, for it is ultimately the systematic, class-based nature of the whole which generates oppression and Otherness. Therefore to fully overcome oppression and Otherness, one cannot settle for charitable handouts to individuals; one can never rest until the bases for Otherness have been overcome. The only real way of protection is to foster conditions for the development of the oppressed to the point where they no longer need protection. This might be done for an individual through a job training program; but if that program reinforces the class system, it would be self-contradictory. Hence spirit cannot rest but must drive onward; and the only word which does justice to this motion of spirit is the anathematic one of *revolution*. Or to put it in less heated—and corrupted—terms, radical social transformation. This is what was missing in Hegel's account of the rational ascension of spirit. Although he is commonly misunderstood as a philosopher of a kind of woolly Idealism, Hegel grasped quite well that spirit must be revealed in work and real transformation of the world. His shortcoming was that he failed to recognize the class-based system which rigidly occluded the ascension of spirit and its union with reason.[45]

On the other hand, so systematic is class society, so buttressed with institutions and ideologies, and so deeply sunk, through the family and culture, into the self, that the revolutionary spirit cannot itself avoid the charges of quixotism or madness. Hegel may have been shortsighted and chauvinistic, but was not his idealism more realistic than Marx's materialism? For Hegel postulated that the fulfillment of spirit lay in the perfecting of the existing political system, rather than an inevitably disruptive and, by all odds, futile revolutionizing.[46] The charge of quixotism is a grave one, and has all the weight of pragmatic reason behind it. But since reasonableness is only the shallow reflection of a reality which is distorted by class interest, we are not obliged to confuse what seems reasonable with what is rational. In fact, on closer inspection, the reasonable position looks much less persuasive. And this is because the existing political system can no longer support anybody's illusion of progress. All we can expect now from "business as usual" is economic contraction accompanied by an increasingly rapid degradation of the environment and the horrendous impoverishment of great portions of humankind.[47] I say this not to be apocalyptic but to point out the intolerably obvious: that despite the tremendous short-term success of capitalism and its ideology, none of the current social orders points elsewhere than disaster; and that in consequence, the social agenda is open as never before. I will not dwell now on the specifics or merits of any socialist alternative. That is not the issue. What is at stake is recognizing the bankruptcy of the established order;

and for this recognition I would submit that a spiritual rupture is essential.

No ideal worth its name can be made real. Nonetheless, it matters just what those ideals are and in what spirit they are pursued. The first question concerning a radical spiritual practice is not whether one adheres to this line or that, but whether or not one accepts the given state of affairs or rejects it. The hallmark of spirit is a basic rejection of the given and a principled commitment to radical change; not a correct political line. Indeed, if the line is necessary, it is as a way of organizing a basic rejection and giving it substance. Thus one can profoundly reject the given without going mad or turning to a politics of desperation and violence, even when it is perfectly clear that one has no more than the vague outlines of a blueprint for a better alternative. In fact, it is a good thing to bear in mind the inherent limits of any totalized vision of a society, for such would inevitably work to destroy the rich texture of spirit by imposing a stifling uniformity. Differentiation in the spiritual sphere means pluralism in the political sphere—a true diversity, not the administered consumerism we call democracy.

One can accept limited practical goals within the framework of a radical spirituality. One can even be shrewdly practical in the pursuit of limited goals, when those are the only realizable ones, while radically rejecting the social order. To cite one of those clichés which happen to be true, the journey is more important than the goal—yet a journey requires a goal lest it become rudderless drifting.

The reason for this lies less in the pragmatics of politics than in the unsurpassable nature of spirit. To take a deeply spiritual attitude toward politics means the recognition of nonbeing behind the Other. It means that spirituality is a dialectic which negates the real yet pulls the real toward itself, so that the synthesis is neither here nor there, but just beyond. Spirit risks the abyss, and reaches for what cannot be named; and because of this the authentically spiritual person is quite content with the notion that nothing real can suffice, and does not lose interest in material reality because of that, because he or she knows that the direction of spirit is contained in the real, even if the end cannot be prefigured. Therefore a fully realized spiritual politics does not delude itself with slogans in place of reality, and works prefiguratively within reality, rejecting the existing order, while studying it closely and moving with it even as radical transformation is sought.

Utopia has been made a dirty word by the ideological blitzkrieg that promotes capitalist democracy as the only possible society. Usually this is done by associating utopia with a dream of social perfection and absolute unification. Such a form of society would be inherently repressive and violent, since anything that fell short of the definition of perfection promulgated by the party in power could be split off into the category of the subhuman, and eliminated. Accordingly, no educated Western person can avoid being told insistently of the crimes committed in the name of utopian revolution. The French Terror, Stalin's atrocities, and Cambodia under the Khmer Rouge—all these nightmares serve to remind us of the criminality possible when society is organized under a utopian tyranny.[48]

Yet utopian politics are precisely what we have been describing here as the authentically spiritual path through the tangle of history. There is no contradiction, however, if we recognize that the spiritual path to utopia requires a social transformation yet exceeds any possible social realization. This insight is indeed the precondition of genuine tolerance, as it spares us the illusion that any real social alternative we may offer is more than a grain of sand to the spiritualized universe. Thus the notion of a perfect society (which was one of the delusions of Stalinism), along with the repressiveness attached to the dream of a realizable perfection, are both foreign to spirit. However, spirit continues to demand that the given be measured—and transformed—against the horizon of *utopia*—a "noplace" to go with nonbeing. Let us put it more broadly yet: if the climate of despiritualization characterizes the modern era, the utopian vision represents the dialectical persistence of spirit this epoch; represents, that is, the transcendent hope rather than the repetitive recycling of modernity. Maynard Solomon has suggested the scope of this impulse:

> During the millenia of religious channeling of Utopian desires into ritual, Utopia moved underground, into the folk-traditions of the common people, into a synthesis of social and pagan-religious strivings. Utopia and the negative-theology of paganism merged; the outlaw and the Utopian hero became synonymous: Sherwood Forest is both the image of a tree-worship in paganism and an archetypal image of Utopia—the shaded Eden of the British poor. The folk-tale and the fairy tale . . . keep alive man's attempt to lighten the burden of a supposed mythic (class) destiny. (Walter Benjamin: "the fairy tale tells us of the earliest arrangements that mankind made to shake off the nightmare which the myth had placed on its chest.")
>
> The church had harnessed Utopia to religious eschatology. With the bourgeois revolution, however, the entire force of dispossessed eschatology is released and reconverted into Utopia. . . . Utopia explodes into philosophy and the social sciences—creating the foundations of

Communist theory. Utopia surfaces in the ballad and folk-tale revival, and from the creative arts—where it had been kept alive within Don Quixote's Cave of Montesinos, in Kepler's Somnium, in Dante's Earthly Paradise, on Crusoe's island—and becomes the transcendent swan-song of an enlightened but doomed feudal aristocracy. Utopia explodes into view once again in *The Magic Flute* and the *Caprichos,* in the *Grosse Fuge,* in Daumier's *Emigrés,* in the pre-Raphaelitism of Morris' Brotherhood, in Goncharov's *Oblomov* (who says "No" to a progress which excludes beauty and love), in Dostoevsky's *Myshkin,* in Melville's *Typee* and *Omoo,* in Cooper's primeval forest, on Mann's *Magic Mountain.*[49]

Note that Marx's communist theory is but one instance of the explosion of "dispossessed eschatology" (that is, the doctrine of ultimate things) which occurs with the breakup of traditional patterns of faith. It is important to recall this at a time when Marx, ever the bugbear of capitalist ideology, is being flushed down the drain with the remains of Bolshevism. It is also important to bear in mind that of the whole range of utopian impulses, Marx's had special value because it was wedded to an appreciation of the real forces which move the world. As Ernst Bloch, the greatest of modern utopian thinkers, has observed in his monumental *Principle of Hope,* "The very power and truth of Marxism consists in the fact that it has driven the cloud of our dreams further but has not extinguished the pillar of fire in those dreams, rather strengthened it with concreteness."[50]

Marx has been considered the most antispiritual of thinkers. Hopefully, the discussion so far has cast doubt on that judgment, though it should not lead us to think that Marx was an angel in personal life, or without serious spiritual limits in his thought, which have been reflected in socialist practice.[51] It will take a much more extended discussion to pick a way through the various relations between Marxism and spirituality. But whatever the complications, the spiritual core of Marx remains, for two linked reasons. First, Marx saw, better than anyone before or since, that this real society which shaped every human endeavor, including spirituality, cleaves primarily about the issue of class. He saw, too, that everything was set up so that this reality would be mystified and kept from those who needed to grasp it most—the workers and the oppressed. Hence these people would lose touch with the nature of class oppression and with the possibilities of class consciousness. And second, Marx opened up such possibilities for the workers and the oppressed, more than anyone before or since.

Why is this spiritual? Recall our discussion of consciousness and group consciousness, in which we saw that the group is a kind of way station toward a fuller being, but that the nature of this being depends on the concrete way group activity is carried out. Now consider what happens, say, to a collection of unorganized workers at a factory who come together to form a union.[52] Prior to this event, the workers tend to be a mass of disconnected particles of consciousness, their being determined by an alien force.[53] Various Egoic temptations—opportunism, alcohol, drugs, consumerist fantasies, or the consolations dispensed by the culture industry—flourish in this atmosphere. Visualize the males of the American working class sitting home Sundays, each in their little box, isolated from one another and from women, each plugged into another box from which emanates the fortunes of "their" football team. Instead of an appropriation of real life, we have the administration of militaristic fantasies of grandeur and male bonding. The spectacle tells us everything about the decline of a genuine collective practice and its substitution by the synthetic Otherness put out by the industries of culture.

Now imagine the formation of the union: a collective practice which appropriates some of the worker's powers of production. The union, as its name implies, joins. It does not simply connect people, but creates a group being through which individual being can connect with Universal Being. We do not need the technical language of ontology to convey this, for there is a word within the tradition of workers' movements which does it better: *solidarity*. To call the sense of full life evoked by solidarity a manifestation of "group psychology" is an utter mystification, because it avoids the question of what makes this group different from others—the unmistakable power which comes from historical agency. Nor can any objective economic factor explain the power of solidarity. Once workers break free of the Egoic indoctrination of the system, and undertake collective practice, they experience a change in the whole of their lives—i.e., in their being. Workers engaged in collective struggle tend to overcome racial[54] and gender Otherness, develop democratization in their union activity, and deepen their insights into society as a whole. We cannot say more than "tend to," of course, considering all the countervailing forces massed against solidarity and its appropriation of full being. In fact, these events are all too rare in recent United States history, though the recent sustained—and "inspiring"—struggle by miners in West Virginia against the Pittston Coal Company may indicate a change in the wind.[55]

All collective struggle of oppressed groups is spiritually authentic practice, though workers' struggles are of special significance, given the importance of production. Marx saw the furthest into this principle, even if he did not describe his vision in spiritual terms. As Bloch writes, "First, this acute and sensitive man was aware of his own humanity; secondly, others with the same human countenance were being treated like dogs. No mercy could be spared for those who treated them this way; on the contrary, to tolerate the oppressors would really be inhuman in regard to the oppressed and humiliated. . . . the humanitarianism of Marx was not general and abstract but personally addressed and directed to those who alone needed it. Like Münzer,[56] Marx took up the whip with which Jesus had driven the money changers from the temple. Therefore, his humanitarianism, precisely because it is concrete depending on the direction in which it faces, simultaneously manifests a pervasive indignation, while calling men to action and seeking, finding and proclaiming their objective redemption."[57]

This side of Marx links his project with a familiar line from the New Testament: "Blessed are the poor in spirit, for theirs is the kingdom of heaven" (Matthew 5:3 [RSV]). The quotation has a twofold meaning, as a statement about the spiritual nature of poverty and the inherently poor nature of spirit. Another, equally famous passage from Matthew drives home the point even more fully, identifying the wretched of the earth with Jesus himself: "'for I was hungry and you gave me food, I was thirsty and you gave me drink, I was a stranger and you welcomed me, I was naked and you clothed me, I was sick and you visited me, I was in prison and you came to me.' Then the righteous will answer him, 'Lord, when did we see thee hungry and feed thee, or thirsty and give thee drink? And when did we see thee a stranger and welcome thee, or naked and clothe thee? And when did we see thee sick or in prison and visit thee?' And the King will answer them, 'Truly I say to you, as you did it to one of the least of these my brethren, you did it to me'" (Matthew 25:35–40 [RSV]). The spiritual implications of this will become clearer if we bear in mind that poverty is more than a statement about one's level of material possession. It is that, to be sure, and no value supersedes the right to decent living conditions; but poverty is about social relations in addition to possessions. To speak of poverty in the way the Bible does—and, later, as Marx does—is to see possessions not as things but as materialized relations between historical agents. Thus the poor are also the oppressed, at the victim-end of domination. As such, the poor are also the repositories of nonbeing. It is this which connects material poverty to the dialectics of spirit.

The location of nonbeing in the oppressed follows from the elementary character of domination. For the person who dominates another does not merely extract the labor of that other without compensation, nor force sexual obedience, nor beat, nor humiliate. Yes, at least one such material relation is present whenever domination exists, for domination does not grow out of thin air. But domination is always more than such a power relation. Power, however much it may grow out of the barrel of a gun or with the connivance of the state, is ontologically a condition of *being-over*. That is, the dominator exerts power by extracting being from the dominated. We should not think of this difficult relationship as if being were a substance, like ore from the earth. Rather, extracting being means to establishing—violently, if necessary—a kind of force field, a polarity of being between dominator and dominated. The orientation of that field is experienced and manifested as power over the other. We might say that just as theft is the expropriation of property, so is domination the expropriation of being. The capitalist gets more than the exploitation of labor power and surplus value from the worker; he also degrades the worker's being and puffs up his own being, whence the unmistakable narcissism of class superiority. The white racist does not simply exist in a materially exploitative relation to the black; he makes himself into more of a human being, and the black into less, indeed, into something of an animal. And the sexually exploitative male does more than control the labor and body of the woman: he makes himself into the bearer of logos, of history itself, while the woman is made into dumb nature. In each relation of domination, then, there is the creation of being and nonbeing, and a polarization, in which being accrues to the pole of the dominator and nonbeing to that of the dominated. This is, however, another side of the making of Otherness—for the Other is that figure from which being has been negated. Hence the far edge of the Other is the edge of nonbeing; and spirit, which seeks nonbeing, seeks Otherness as the vehicle of nonbeing, and therefore seeks the poor. And because of its confrontation with nonbeing, a life given over to the struggle for justice is more than just a "spirited" life, that is, a life full of animal spirit and enthusiasm. It is that, but also a genuinely spiritual life. This is the spiritual basis for the special option for the poor which forms the core of liberation theology—and it is also the basis of the convergence between liberation theology and Marxism, for no one has ever done more than Karl Marx to devise a special option for the poor.[58]

Dying

The question of how to live confronts only one half of what is spiritually meaningful. We need also to attend to the second part, which is how to die. For in death we immediately face nonbeing, not shrouded behind Otherness, but presented directly, at the terminus of our own separate being.

The confrontation with nonbeing through awareness of death is what shocks many into spiritual reflection. For to face the reality of nonbeing smashes the illusions fostered by everyday life. Freud thought of God the Father as an illusion, but there is no greater illusion than to deny the contingency and finitude of our being. Once the denial is overcome, we feel the radical contradiction between the ordinary certitude of consciousness which takes its evidence of the everyday as real; and the realization, sometimes sudden and blinding, sometimes slow and insidious, that this everyday reality can be no more than a flimsy screen shielding our eyes from an unfathomable abyss. Often it is a brush with death that excites this realization. However, death is not simply something that happens later on, but is an everpresent shadow. There is a death in life, the presence of nonbeing that comes into the foreground when death itself arrives.

In any case we proceed day by day, proud of the gardens we cultivate, warming ourselves in the sun, enjoying food, love, and the charms of children, grateful for existence. Yet we forget, or cannot conceive, that this brief span of being we call our own has no conceivable meaning in the larger scheme of things; that there is no parity between our existence and the universe; that we inhabit a body and an earth which are specks of matter scaled to the universe as a neutrino is to earth; and that the processes of this universe show no cognizance of our existence, gardens, children, lovers, art, or ideas.

The larger scheme of things is somehow bound up with that infinitely mysterious yet overpowering entity called nature, and the question of dying encompasses the question of spirit's relation to nature. In death a person rejoins nature once and for all; yet in life, too, there are a host of lesser joinings. Every walk in the woods is to some degree a joining with nature, and to some degree, therefore, an oceanic experience. Normal sleep is also a kind of oceanic return to nature insofar as it is an abandonment of the self. All those manifestations of spirit which involve some dissolution of self are at the same time a joining of nature and a kind of dying. That is why the relation to nature is so crucial, and why it sums up and relates all aspects of spirit to itself. At the same time, no one relates directly or immediately to nature, which is in any case a construction of the mind before it is anything "out there." This does not mean, of course, that the spiritual relations a person establishes with other people and those with nature are parallel and equivalent. It asserts only that spiritual pathways are complex and unresolved, so that every person relates to nature according to the dialectics of the self. In this respect, we might expect discontinuities at the lower levels of being which we all inhabit. Thus a man can be an utter fascist politically, yet feel a deep rapport with birds and trees—remember Hitler's fondness for dogs. Heidegger lived in the mountains, had a wonderful appreciation of wilderness, and a caring attitude toward nature, but this did not improve his politics as far as I am aware. Another person, however, can be saintly in his dedication to the poor and be terrified of grass. Evidently Marx had little or no feeling for nature, while Lenin is said to have suppressed ruthlessly such feelings as he had because the revolution had to crowd everything else out. Attitudes of this kind have been prevalent in Marxism-Leninism and have cost it—and the world—dearly, as a look at the blighted landscapes of the Soviet bloc will attest.

We can expect that at the further reaches of spiritual development a person will show convergence in his or her relations with all beings, human and nonhuman. Saint Francis is the exemplar here—though perhaps that supremely blessed man paid for this in the harshness of his attitude toward himself. Nor should such convergence between the human and nonhuman be misinterpreted as equivalence, as do certain "deep ecologists" who would just as soon save a tree as a starving child.[59] For any such convergence is at the level of spirit, not of external behavior. And spirit consists of a relation to the concrete Other which is based on that Other's specific character, rather than some indiscriminate loss of boundary which destroys the individuality of the Other.

There is a dying to a spiritual walk in the woods, as one's being moves toward joining the universe; and there is dying in orgasm and in sleep, in which the self transiently steps aside. These are, as has been proverbially said, kinds of little deaths, deaths succeeded by awakening. But there is also the big death, the dying of self which comes with the return of bodily flesh to nature. Here there is an equilibrium at the level of substance, as one's flesh returns to nature.

No one wants to die, for to be "one" is to be set off against others, and being resists abolishing itself. But being that is human also experiences its separateness as a burden and longs to reestablish connection to its ground, and to undo its discontinuity. Death is ambivalently conceived, therefore, as the ultimately horrific termination of being, and also a rejoining of individual being with universal being. Commonly this ambivalence is uneasily resolved by populating the nonbeing of death with spirit-beings drawn from the Otherness of life. The universal human trait of burying the dead is another expression of this ambivalence. The dead are sacred, and a human being cannot tolerate the desecration and insult of simply abandoning a corpse to nature. This is more than a maintaining of respect and care for the individual who is gone. It is also a maintaining of self in the Other, and a denial of the power of death to terminate being altogether. Thus a dead human being is rejoined to universal being with appropriate ceremony, to announce to nature that human being means to extend itself into nature even beyond the grave. People may want nonbeing, but only as a completed being, that is, still attached to being. Emptiness, the unbearable thought that our existence is for nought against the aimless scurrying of the universe, is unendurable and unthinkable. So the corpse that was once flesh is encoded with the symbols of humankind as it passes into nature.

Because everyone must die, and because human being is always constructed about the dialectic of separateness and attachment, a special reaction to death is a universal tendency in all societies. An archaeologist has no surer sign of the presence of human remains than evidence of a burial ritual. This universal is not uniform, but undergoes the most remarkable variation across the scope of human conditions. We need not review this, which has been done exhaustively elsewhere,[60] except to comment briefly on several aspects of present interest.

First, the different modes of the self will regard death very differently. To Ego, death is an absolute loss and horror. Deprived of spirit-being as a conduit for Otherness, Ego can see in death nothing but nothingness, for there is no recognition between nonbeing and being. So absolute is Ego's terror of death that the whole subject tends to be repressed in those societies dominated by Egoic being. This taboo extends backward from the grave to include anything which smacks of death, or reminds Ego that its time may be approaching. Old age also is therefore repressed in Egoic societies, and since of all societies we are the most Egoic, United States society goes to amazing lengths in order to deny death and age. Consider only the rage for plastic surgery among the better heeled.[61]

As was his wont (and in the teeth of his own theory of Thanatos), Freud tried to despiritualize the psychology of death. He built his reasoning on the fact that death itself can be no object of knowledge. By pointing out that the actuality of death could not be known, Freud concluded that such deep ideas as were formed on the subject were variations of infantile fantasy—of separating from parents, killing or being killed, sleeping, etc. Thus death was replaced with what was death-like, or led to death, and Freud concluded that the unconscious mind had no registration of personal death.[62] Here as so often, however, the question has to be asked, *which* unconscious mind; or rather, the unconscious belonging to which state of being? The problem is that psychoanalysis reads the mind of its time and place. Its psychology is of that state of being known as Egoic, and moves within the assumptions made by Ego about reality, namely, that spirit-being and nonbeing have no substantial role in human existence, but are only derivative. Thus psychoanalysis cannot move outside the trap of Ego, and cannot see that the repression of death in Egoic societies is a function of Ego's terror of nonbeing, which is experienced not as a fusion with nature but as pent-up Otherness.

Soul remains deeply unhappy about death as the end of its being, yet is able to accept death to the extent that it has been able to accept and overcome Otherness. Soul knows that it cannot die as a separate particle of being because it has never really lived as such. That is, compared to Ego, soul makes less of the self, more of the Other. To draw the conclusion of the great Oriental religions, soul accepts its own illusory nature. Although elaborated to the greatest extreme in Hinduism and Buddhism, this attitude is not confined to any specific religious context. It is common rather to all instances of the unfolding of spirit, the dubious as well as the valuable. Each spirituality, from transpersonal psychotherapy to holy warfare, is experienced as a kind of ablation of Ego (for there is Ego in everyone), and a motion toward the Other, with or without the mediation of spirit-being. For soul, then, living is also a kind of dying. There is a saying that one cannot accept death unless one has lived, nor life unless one is ready to die, and it seems to me that this is no platitude, precisely because it is intolerable to Ego.

We may add, then, to our repertoire of definitions of spirituality that it would include a willingness to die. One would have to also ask how and for what to understand the value of spirituality in any given instance. But the overall point is clear enough: the meaningful life, the authentic spirit that knows how to live, is a life that has accepted Otherness and made itself ready to die. Of course this does not mean that such a being wants to die. Quite to the contrary, a full soul finds life all the sweeter and more intense. If spirituality were not for life, it would not be worth very much, after all. But it is for a life in respect to which death has been taken into account, understood, and accepted, within the limits of human being to do so. Indeed, the awareness of the presence of death, the vision of its shadow, does nothing so much as throw life itself into perspective. In traditional Japanese culture this insight was elaborated in the samurai tradition which made one's actual way of dying a validation of the entirety of life. The ideal of this culture was the search for sincerity, that is, a purity of motive which could only be manifested when all the corrosive compromises of life were put aside and real death was encountered. The logical extensions of this were the kamikaze pilots of the closing months of World War II who rapturously flew their planes into the U.S. fleet.[63] The type reappears in many non-Japanese contexts as well, including instances of fascism as well as communism, Christian martyrdom, and so on. This underscores again the need to submit all spiritual practices to critique, but the extremes may at least illuminate a generally valid point: that one fully pursues spirituality as a kind of warrior. Not necessarily a violent warrior, but one who anneals the self in the fire of struggle until able to live according to the needs of the soul.

Human Spirit

> *The Spirit of the Lord GOD is upon me, because the LORD has anointed me to bring good tidings to the poor; he has sent me to bind up the brokenhearted, to proclaim liberty to the captives, and the opening of the prison to those who are bound.*
>
> Isaiah 61:1 (RSV)

And so we are led to the ultimate sense of spirit as "truth of." The question of human spirit is closely related to the hoary one of human nature. In fact, we might say that human spirit is a sublimation of human nature, as the latter term is popularly used. Where human nature is said to be base, opportunistic, greedy, and exploitative, human spirit is given to rise, to resist oppression; in short, it is the drive to be free. "You can't kill the spirit," goes the expression, to indicate the immortal, transcendent character of human spirit. Whether or not this notion is objectively true, it seems that human beings cannot live without invoking it.

To me, there is something profoundly wrong with the opposition of human spirit to nature, human or otherwise. If human spirit exists, then it exists in nature, as a natural, essential element of human being, not as something split off from human being or from the body. If human spirit exists, then human nature is not as one-sided as the popular conception makes it out to be. And this is to be expected, because the popular view of human nature, even the view of conservative ideologues such as Freud, is essentially ruling class ideology displaced onto cracker-barrel philosophy. In the reigning views of human nature[64] we see all the cowardice and defeatism which the established powers could demand of their subjects, suitably dressed up as stoic resignation.

But the fact remains that if human spirit exists in nature, then it is not one whose emergence can be "naturally" expected. To speak of human spirit means a commitment to a philosophy of becoming, in which the self can become Other to itself, and from that position either remain alienated or transcend itself. The notion of human spirit does not have, therefore, a simply objective truth: it is rather something which has to be proven in each instance; something, too, which can be suppressed or turn into its opposite. To speak of human spirit is to speak of a practical wish to be free—I say "practical" to indicate a wish that is to be put on the line in struggle, as a spiritual warrior. In this sense, we cannot say that the wish to be free is transhistorical, because there are too many instances in which it has become inhibited, or turned into its opposite—as in the love of the slave for the chain. But I cannot imagine any reading of human existence which can deny the fact that the wish to be free is always immanent in human affairs.

What, concretely, is this wish to be free, or human spirit? It may be considered as follows: that a person in some situation of domination, in which his or her being has been expropriated by another, resists, saying in effect "I am a person, not a thing." This statement can be rephrased thus: "I am a subject, not merely an object; and I am not a Cartesian subject, whose subjectivity is pure inwardness, but rather an expressive subject, a transformative subject; I am a subject, therefore, who needs to project my being into the world, and transform the world as an expression of my being; and finally, I will appropriate my being rather than have it expropriated." And since we do not want to split human nature from human spirit, but rather differentiate the two, we would add that it is in human nature to have such a drive to expression, that human beings cannot be constituted or grasped without such a drive—although it is also a possibility open to human nature to fall away from such a drive, or to reverse it, to make the person into a thing. In any case, human spirit is characterized by the tendency of spirit to define itself expressively, and in conflict. We could say that human spirit reflects the struggle of soul to express itself in history.

Human spirit can be no abstract universal, however, since what is expressed through consciousness is spirit-being, and spirit-being is determined by the concrete, historically determined Otherness through which a person has passed. It is in the expression, deployment, and interaction of spirit-being that the attainment as well as the falling away from human spirit is decided.

The language of human spirit belongs to that dialectical tradition which has been more or less thoroughly rejected by the prevailing centers of intellectual power. Dialectics—the notion that truth and being alike emerge from conflict, that nonbeing gives birth to being, that the negative determines the positive and coexists with it—all this is marginalized or made anathematic to the power structure, yet it is the logic of spirit.[65] We will not make an idol of the dialectic, and worship it as the key to the universe. We should try to use it, rather, to gain a glimpse of the fleeting negative, a notion beyond any arithmetical determination. Dialectic cannot, therefore, be a key, or a master plan, or any kind of logocentrism (even if words must, perforce, be used—as here—in describing the dialectic). The dialectic is, rather, an opening of being, and a clearing of false, encrusted Egoic being; therefore it is critical before it is prescriptive, and a letting go before a seizing. The motion of despiritualization consists of wiping thought free of dialectical influence, of determination by the negative. Psychology, taken all in all, is the effort to stake out the subjective, inward world as a preserve without the troublesome demands of human spirit. Correspondingly, although there have been a few attempts in this direction, a fully dialectical psychology has never emerged.[66]

An elaborate technical discourse, however, is not required to express the needs of human spirit. Human spirit, it is safe to say, will survive whatever experts do to it, short of nuclear or ecological extermination. Indeed, the notion has significance only because it has been continually rediscovered over the span of history. Small children discover human spirit as they struggle for a self adequate to their own individuated being; and grown persons rediscover it within the ebb and flow of domination. The tribes of Yahweh discovered it in the twelfth century before Christ, and the Jews kept losing and rediscover-

ing it thereafter.[67] Slaves and serfs discovered it according to the unfolding of the conditions of their domination. Luther discovered it, and
Thomas Münzer, and countless religious radicals since; as did Blake,
Tom Paine and the antireligious *philosophes* of the eighteenth century,
and Marx and Engels of the century to follow. The abolitionists discovered it, and the suffragettes, along with Rosa Luxemburg, Emma
Goldman, Gandhi, Cesar Augusto Sandino, Martin Luther King, Malcolm X, Frantz Fanon, Aimé Cesaire, Ho Chi Minh, and Fidel Castro.
And women and men in occupied territories all over the world discover and rediscover it every day. Even Saul of Tarsus discovered the
basic motion of human spirit, and despite his terrible repressiveness,
no one has ever put it better or more dialectically than he: "But God
hath chosen the foolish things of the world to confound the wise; and
God hath chosen the weak things of the world to confound the things
which are mighty; And base things of the world, and things which are
despised hath God chosen, yea, and things which are not, to bring to
nought things that are" (1 Corinthians 1:27–28 [KJ]).

4.
Spirit and Desire

However innumerable beings are, I vow to save them;
However inexhaustible the passions are, I vow to extinguish them;
However immeasurable the Dharmas are, I vow to master them;
However incomparable the Buddha-truth is, I vow to attain it.

The Four Great Vows of Buddhism
Daisetz T. Suzuki, *Manual of Zen Buddhism*

THE RELATIONS between spirit and desire are so diverse as to strain
the bounds of a single chapter. For the sake of clarity, then, the discussion will be divided into three parts. The first, "Sacred Sex," considers
the traditional opposition between sexual and religious practice and
introduces the notion of desire. Next, in "Pride and Violence," we
move to politics, to consider what happens when desire invests the self,
how this eventuates in violence, and the overcoming of selfish desire in
the practice of nonviolence. "The Spiritual Body" returns to ontology
and picks up the track of desire as the manifestation of spirit in nature.
This is revealed as the *flesh,* and, in the discourse of being, as a kind of
plasma out of which Freud's notion of the unconscious is derived. This
chapter rounds out our discussion of the spiritual aspects of psychoanalysis, and prepares for a confrontation with Ultimate Being.

SACRED SEX

Usually when people speak of the relations between spirituality and
desire they mean erotic desire. This is understandable, since desire is
most clamorous when expressed sexually. Still, a great deal of desire is
manifestly nonsexual, while a great deal of sexuality can be carried out
without very much desire. This latter is what is often referred to as
"animal sexuality," perhaps an unwarranted slur on the animal king-

dom, though a way of calling attention to the fact that "desire" seems to be a way of describing a peculiarly human aspect of sexuality, just as "spirit" calls attention to the peculiarly human aspect of existence as a whole. In any case, desire cannot be divorced from sexuality, just as spirit cannot be divorced from religion. Moreover, sexual desire often seems to be at some kind of odds with religious spirituality.

Indeed, the opposition between religion and sexuality, and the assumption therefore that the sentiments underlying these dimensions of being have no more in common than oil and water, has been more or less axiomatic in many quarters. Thus William James in his famous study, *Varieties of Religious Experience,* writes, "The plain truth is that to interpret religion one must in the end look at the immediate content of the religious consciousness. The moment one does this, one sees how wholly disconnected it is in the main from the content of the sexual consciousness. Everything about the two things differs, object, moods, faculties concerned, and acts impelled to. Any *general* assimilation is simply impossible: what we find most often is complete hostility and contrast."[1]

This is what happens when dialectical thinking has been driven out of one's brain—and, it might be added, when one remains the victim of ethnocentrism, since the traditions which do not split the erotic from the religious realms are those which have not been organized by white civilization. Despite what William James claimed, however, erotic experience forms one of the original and enduring bases for religion.[2] At the beginning of society, sexual being and religious being were not split from one another, because both were united at the level of spirit. Consider "The Vulva Song of Inana" from ancient Sumer, perhaps the oldest civilization:

I am lady I
who in this house
of holy lapis
praying
in my sanctuary say
my holy prayer
I who am lady
who am queen of heaven
let the chanter
chant of it
the singer sing of it
& let my bridegroom

my Dumuzi my wild bull
delight me
let their words fall
from their mouths
o singers
singing for their youth
their song that rises up
in Nippur gift to give
the son of god
I who am lady sing to
praising him
the chanter chants it
I who am Inana
give my vulva song to him
o star my vulva of the dipper
vulva slender boat of heaven
new moon crescent beauty vulva
unploughed desert vulva
fallow field for wild geese
where my mound longs
for his flooding
hill my vulva lying open
& the girl asks:
who will plough it?
vulva wet with flooding
of myself the queen
who brings this ox to stand here
"lady he will plow for you
"our king Dumuzi he will plow for you"
o plough my vulva o my heart
my holy thighs are soaked with it
o holy mother.[3]

We know Inana more commonly as Ishtar and later, Astarte; while Dumuzi is also Tammuz. Jerome Rothenberg comments that in "the fragment presented here, the direct celebration of female sexuality conjures a descent from the stone venuses and incised vulvas . . . of an earlier time;" while Mircea Eliade adds that Inana-Ishtar-Astarte "will enjoy an 'actuality' in both cult and mythology never approached by any other goddess of the Near East."[4]

The evidence from state-free society is equally striking. Consider the following chant, from the aboriginal culture of Australia's Arnhem Land:

> Go, put out the *rangga,* making it big: open your legs, for you look
>   nice!
> Yes, take Miralaidj, my Sister. Yes, the mouth of the mat is closed.
> Yes, go rest there quietly, for the vagina is sacred, and the *rangga* are
>   hidden there, like younger siblings, covered up so no one may see.
> Thus, climb up, put it into the mouth of the mat!
> What is this, blocking my penis? I rest above here, chest on her
>   breasts!
> Do not push hard! The sound of her cry echoes.
> Covered up, so no one may see, like a younger sibling . . .
> Do not move what is within, for it is sacred!
> For it rests there within, like the transverse fibre of the mat.
> Blood running, sacredly running!
> Yes, they, the *rangga* clansfolk, are coming out like *djuda* roots, like
>   spray . . .
> Go, digging within, causing the blood to flow, sacred blood from the
>   red vagina, that no one may see!
> Very sacred stands the *rangga* penis![5]

Here sexuality is drawn into a creation myth. *Rangga* is a sacred emblem identified with the phallus. However, the *rangga* clansfolk are also distinct spirit-beings, ancestors of the Arnhem Landers. As spirit-being, the *rangga* represents Otherness drawn from the life history of the individual, and also the body-as-phallus. There is no contradiction, because Otherness is accepted. In oral cultures the tyranny of logos is absent, and different ontological dimensions can be rationally thought of together. The conjuncture between body-as-phallus and the spirit-being of ancestors indicates the differentiated life of soul, while the sensuous commingling of being makes the chant erotic. Such eroticism is not linked with a terror of nonbeing, rather the reverse: a profusion of beings ensues through the mingling of being. The *rangga* folk from the past become the progeny that carry life forward. Being proliferates in this creation myth where there is no shadow of possessiveness or institutionalization, and where, in consequence, male and female can freely interflow. Thus the imagery is phallic but not phallocentric. This does not mean that the relations between the sexes in Arnhem Land are free of domination, but it deprives domination of its systematic and life-negating character, and so preserves an openness between sexuality and spirituality.

The body expressed here is a spiritual body—which we may also call flesh, using a common word in the sense developed by Maurice Merleau-Ponty.[6] As used here, *flesh* will connote the organism as both the subject and the object of perception. Flesh is a spiritual body, because it is an organism, composed of the matter of life, yet alive with spirit-power and spirit-being. We will return to the notion below.

Sexuality in archaic societies is a more or less universal accompaniment of the sacred. Usually this is understood as a peculiarity of native agriculture, in which sexuality is said to be the magical propitiation of nature to encourage the yield of crops. According to this line of reasoning, the generativity of sex and the generativity of nature are aligned with each other. Thus the vulva of the Sumerian goddess awaits its flooding and the land awaits the water from the Tigris or Euphrates rivers. With the emergence of technological civilization, so the argument goes, "man" learns to trust in "his" scientific powers, abandon magical thinking, and leave the sacredness of sex to rude savages.

But this is the crude materialism that recognizes only the mode of being known to its own despiritualized age, which it essentializes and projects backward. What gets ignored is the inclusivity of the state-free worldview. To be sure, the state-free person wishes to propitiate "mother-nature" by sexual ritual. The mistake is to think that the event can be reduced to a hierarchical set of logical operators. For tribal culture (and extending far into peasant culture of traditional society), there is no contradiction between productive life and other spheres of existence. Sex is sacred because it is the occasion for the encounter with being as embedded in the body. And yet it is also matter-of-fact, because the encounter is one of differentiation.

In a fragmented society composed of numberless Egos, sex is made into something sui generis, with a special place all its own; or rather, a series of places. Logos marks sexuality (the very word is a recent creation) the way a dog will mark a hydrant, delimiting the erotic into discrete categories: stimulation of special subcutaneous or olfactory pleasure centers linked to subcortical neural networks, hormones circulating, fantasies popping away, and lots of fun away from the dreary work world, along with the reproduction of the species. This splitting avoids the ontological unity of sex, which is re-creation before it is recreation. In the commingling of genitals, and more basically, in the overpowering urge to merge with the entire flesh of the other in the sex act, the origin of being is sought again. And not only individual being, but also phylogenetic being is sought in sex, as Freud's disciple, Sandor Ferenczi, recognized in one of his many inspired insights. Ferenczi speculated in his *Thalassa* that the sexuality as well as the reproductive physiology of more complex organisms reverses the process by which life emerged from the seas. Hence the most mature sexual level was also the most primitive, and the most ontologically close to the origins of being.[7] We can see, then, how sexuality and desire, and religion and spirit, tend to occupy the same domain, albeit entering from different sides. The question is one of differentiation: to what degree are sexuality, desire, religion, and spirit permitted mutual recognition?

Though religious ecstasy cannot be reduced to sexual ecstasy, it does appear that erotic and religious experience each draw from the same well. They share a common substratum in a transformation of being. These common features are not everything, but they are quite a lot, and deserving of much more reflection than is usually given. Religious and erotic life are each immanently spiritual pathways. The paths move on common ground, cross, then go their own ways. State-free peoples live close enough to the crossing to allow a flux between religious and erotic elements to freely occur. We tend to forget that the crossing exists.

Sexuality cannot be encompassed in any purely objectivist-calculus because it involves states of being which have classically been the occasion for spiritual experience. That is, erotic life is both ecstatic (*ekstasis* means "standing outside the self") and enthusiastic ("filled with god"—a term deriving principally from Dionysian rites).[8] It sweeps the self outside its boundaries and fills the self with a kind of spirit-power. Rudolph Otto's sense of the numinous and van der Leeuw's sense of power have already been cited as classical descriptions of the phenomenological basis of religion. However if we turn again to Otto's famous description of the *mysterium tremendum* we would be hard-pressed to deny that it also tells us something of the phenomenology of sexual passion:

> The feeling of it may at times come sweeping like a gentle tide, pervading the mind with a tranquil mood of deepest worship. It may pass over into a more set and lasting attitude of the soul, continuing, as it were, thrillingly vibrant and resonant, until at last it dies away and the soul resumes its "profane" . . . mood of everyday experience. It may burst in sudden eruption up from the depths of the soul with spasms and convulsions, or lead to the strangest excitements, to intoxicated frenzy, to transport, and to ecstasy. It has its wild and demonic form and can sink to an almost grisly horror and shuddering. It has its crude, barbaric antecedents and early manifestations, and again it may be developed into something beautiful and pure and glorious. It may become the hushed, trembling and speechless humility of the creature

in the presence of—whom or what? In the presence of that which is a *mystery* inexpressible and above all creatures.[9]

Otto is at pains to deny anything beyond a crude analogy between sexuality and religiosity in the *tremendum,* and gives the holy its own laws altogether. And there are, to say the least, major differences between Otto's notion of the numinous and what transpires during sexual passion—distinctions in object, ideation, and the deployment of bodily sensation. But everybody knows this. What usually slips through our grasp is the common substratum of rapture, transport, ecstasy: being swept away by a force experienced as beyond the self, and far more peremptory than anything in everyday life. It appears that religion and sexuality both ride this flow, and follow it into different channels. But this metaphor should not be followed too literally, because religion and eroticism also switch between channels. One might think of another metaphor, of a variable barrier between two flows, which determines the switching. In the religious sexuality (equivalently, the sexualized religion) of state-free society, the barrier is permeable and switching occurs readily—indeed, it would be possible to say that in certain instances there is no barrier at all, so that the two channels become one. And in the religions of more complex and stratified societies the barrier becomes more or less rigidly institutionalized.

There are a number of ways to define the boundary between the religious and the erotic channel. It could be regarded as a more or less permeable membrane, in which there is no fundamental felt difference between the two, no more than the difference between playing Bach's *Musical Offering* on a keyboard or in a small chamber ensemble. Spiritual expression in these cases can be immediately transcribed to the flesh. Arnhem Land erotic spirituality is of this free-flowing type, without formal religious institutionalization, or logos of spirit, or a unified, imposing, and overbearing theological conception of God.

At the opposite pole, the boundary could be seen as a more or less closed barrier, which goes with formal religious institutionalization and literate cultures. If the barrier is relatively less closed, we have the presence of ecstatic and/or orgiastic elements in the religion, such as temple prostitution, or as in Tantrism, a tightly controlled prescription of sexual ritual. If the barrier is more closed, we have efforts of one degree or another to impose repression. If we turn to the tangled history of the Christian religion, we may find a range of variations on this theme.

The dominant attitude of the Christian faith has been overt antisexuality, that is, frank repression. This is heir to a similar struggle within

Judaism,[10] although it should be noted that the Hebraic attitude toward sex as evinced in the Old Testament was considerably more open than the Christian, certainly throughout the early period.[11] The Ten Commandments contain only one sexual injunction, that against adultery. Beginning about 500 B.C., however, a theme of mounting sexual guilt appears, along with a broad assault on female sexuality, and the condemnation of homosexuality. The rebellious Eve became the symbol of the wild female principle, henceforth to be tamed by phallic logos. This interpretation was carried forward into Christianity with a vengeance, with the emergence of the Virgin Mary as the ideal of female subservience to logos and its mission of sexual repression. Thus the virgin birth of Jesus raised the barrier against eroticism to new heights. By the High Middle Ages, worship of the Virgin Mary began to rival the worship of Jesus at the center of the faith. A special reverence for the Blessed Virgin characterizes the harshly antierotic Pope John Paul II.

> But I say, walk by the Spirit, and do not gratify the desires of the flesh. For the desires of the flesh are against the Spirit, and the desires of the Spirit are against the flesh; for these are opposed to each other, to prevent you from doing what you would. But if you are led by the Spirit you are not under the law. Now the works of the flesh are plain: immorality, impurity, licentiousness, idolatry, sorcery, enmity, strife, jealousy, anger, selfishness, dissension, party spirit, envy, drunkenness, carousing, and the like. I warn you, as I warned you before, that those who do such things shall not inherit the kingdom of God. But the fruit of the Spirit is love, joy, peace, patience, kindness, no law. And those who belong to Christ Jesus have crucified the flesh with its passions and desires.   *Galatians* 5:16−24 (RSV)

The essential attitude of Christianity was summed up by Paul, the founder of the religion. For Paul, spirit and flesh are not only different, but opposed, so that spirit becomes frankly repressive. Indeed, church dogma teaches a positive hatred of the body, whose impulses are made to bear the weight of all the sins of the world.[12]

However, the split-off erotic spirituality could also reappear on the margins of the ecumene, as a revived paganism. We have already mentioned the notorious, and ferociously repressed, example of witchcraft. The attack on witchcraft reveals clearly that for Christianity, the Devil has been the split-off Otherness of the erotic body. Needless to say, the entire project was also part of the patriarchal oppression of women and the advance of male-dominated Christianity over the more open spirituality of paganism. The bull of Pope Innocent VIII, *Summa desiderantes,* which launched the major persecution of witches in 1484, expresses fairly well the attitudes involved:

> Desiring with the most heartfelt anxiety, even as Our Apostleship requires, that the Catholic Faith should especially in this Our day increase and flourish everywhere, and that all heretical depravity should be driven far from the frontiers and bournes of the Faithful, We very gladly proclaim . . . those particular means and methods whereby Our pious desire may obtain its wished effect. . . .
>
> It has lately come to Our ears . . . that in some parts of Northern Germany . . . many persons of both sexes . . . have abandoned themselves to devils, incubi and succubi, and by their incantations, spells and conjurations . . . have slain infants yet in their mother's womb, as also the offspring of cattle, have blasted the produce of the earth, the grapes of vine, the fruit of trees, nay, men and women, beasts of burden, herd beasts, as well as animals of all kinds. . . . These wretches further afflict and torment men and women, beasts of burthen . . . with terrible and piteous pains and sore diseases . . . they hinder men from performing the sexual act and women from conceiving, whence husbands cannot know their wives, nor wives receive their husbands.
>
> Wherefore We . . . decree and enjoin that the aforesaid Inquisitors be empowered to proceed to the just correction, imprisonment, and punishment of any persons, without let or hindrance.[13]

The dominant mode of repression is functioning poorly, and is threatened by its negation. In witchcraft, Eve returns and supplants Mary. The Slaves will rise against the Master, and the things which are not will overcome the things which are. From this alarum came the systematic persecution of witches, masterminded by Sprenger and Krämer's *Malleus Maleficarum.* A typical persecution, it stemmed more from the fears of the master than the behavior of the slaves. And these fears were sexual fears.

The great majority of the victims were women, old and young, and their principle crime was that they were sexual, embodied creatures. In Sprenger and Krämer's words, "All witchcraft comes from carnal lust, which in women is insatiable."[14] When a sexual economy is based on domination, its contradictions become projected onto the female sex. Many of the women tortured and burned had nothing to do with witchcraft at all, but were victims of some other vendetta. Notwithstanding, there really were pagan cults of witchery, distinguished from established Christianity by a greater role afforded to women, and a sacramental view of sex. Consistent with ecstatic religion, worship was not split from eroticism, indeed, could eventuate in orgy.[15] It should be added that the adherents of this cult were, like the early

Christians themselves, often willing to die for their beliefs. There is rarely, if ever, a persecution without the thing persecuted having some deep and abiding attraction.

The persecution of witches was part of the slow and tormented transformation of Christianity from a religion radically open to spirit-being to one of logos and modernity. We should recall that the original religion of Jesus was, if not erotic, certainly ecstatic, which is continuous with the erotic, and therefore potentially subversive to the rationalized building of religious institutions. Paul's admonition to the Corinthians against speaking in tongues is a recognition of this hazard.[16] Paul's problem was of course complicated by the fact that he had himself been converted ecstatically, through a sudden infusion of spirit-being on the road to Damascus. In any case, the earlier ambivalence, even differentiation, of the Christian religion with respect to erotic matters hardened decisively into a mold of patriarchal repression as soon as the religion was embraced by the Roman imperial state.[17] Thus the characteristically antisexual—and anti-female—attitudes of Christianity are basically functions of the degree of power and domination incorporated within the religious body.

Another vicissitude is for the split-off eroticism to appear within the religious field as a more or less negated impulse. Through much of church history sexual gratification, while officially repudiated, was indulged in by the hierarchy with scarcely a wink. This is, however, a manifestation of the splitting of Ego, and not the expression of soul—a well-known kind of splitting in which Ego simply divides itself and goes several ways at once. Sexuality here is an ignored contradiction, unmediated by spirit-being and carried on with patriarchal degradation of the object. And it is commonplace: witness its appearance in novels such as Sinclair Lewis's *Elmer Gantry* and Somerset Maugham's *Rain*. The scandal in 1988 concerning the charismatic televangelist Jimmy Swaggart provides another example of this kind of split-off and degraded sexual expression. Perhaps it counts to his credit that unlike a Renaissance pope, Swaggart remained tormented by sexuality, which in his case consisted mostly of clandestine visits to a prostitute, whose pudenda he would view while masturbating. Notwithstanding, Swaggart preached against what he practiced, and accompanied his sexual life with a hellfire diabolism worthy of Sprenger and Krämer.[18]

Although Christianity has been the antierotic religion par excellence, the exclusion of sexuality has been a good deal less successful than the defenders of the purity of the faith care to admit. We should not need Freud to remind us that the practice of a violent asceticism often brings about what it tries to suppress. And it goes without saying that the sexuality which results is full of misery. The list of sexual torments that afflicted the faithful and which they strove to suppress or transcend is a very long one, and includes the self-flagellation and rapt asceticism of the early (and many later) monks. Florid antisexuality demands inclusion in the category of the sexual. That is, if a sect practices ritual castration as a proof of its adherents' religious devotion, we are obliged to call this a manifestation of sexuality (not very healthy sexuality, no doubt, but sexual nevertheless). For it can only be an erotic eruption, hated as it may be, which gives rise to the effort to extirpate sexuality. Here is the testimony of Saint Jerome as the presence of sexuality in antisexuality: "How often when I was living in the desert which affords to hermits a savage dwelling place, parched by a burning sun, did I fancy myself amid the pleasures of Rome. I sought solitude because I was filled with bitterness. . . . I, who from the fear of hell had consigned myself to that prison where scorpions and wild beasts were my companions, fancied myself among bevies of young girls. My face was pale and my frame chilled from fasting, yet my mind was burning with the craving of desire, and the fires of lust flared up from my flesh that was as that of a corpse. I do not blush to avow my abject misery."[19] Or as Gibbon said of the efforts by the early Christian fathers to dictate the terms of sexual relations, "The enumeration of the very whimsical laws, which they most circumstantially imposed on the marriage bed, would force a smile from the young, and a blush from the fair."[20]

However, eroticism can appear directly within ascetic religious experience, then be transcended. This compares to the repression attempted by the Christian hierarchy as differentiation to splitting. Where patristic orthodoxy tries to stamp out the directly erotic, erotic desire has also been at times recognized, accepted, then passed beyond. This pathway is a minor one within Christianity; and notably it belongs to the mystical tradition, in which holy consciousness is cultivated. The most famous example is that of Saint Teresa of Avila. Here is a sample of her testimony:

> I saw close to me an angel in bodily form . . . the angel was not large but small; he was very beautiful, and his face was so aflame that he seemed to be one of those very sublime angels that appear to be all afire . . . I saw in his hands a large golden dart and at the end of the iron tip there appeared to be a little fire. It seemed to me that the angel plunged the dart several times into my heart and that it reached deep within me. When he drew it out, I thought he was carrying off with

him the deepest part of me; and he left me all on fire with great love of God. The pain was so great it made me moan, and the sweetness this great pain caused me was so superabundant that there was no desire capable of taking it away; nor is the soul content with less than God. The pain is not bodily but spiritual, although the body doesn't fail to share in some of it, and even a great deal. The loving exchange that takes place between the soul and God is so sweet that I beg Him in His goodness to give a taste of this love to anyone who thinks I am lying.[21]

William James seems not to have noticed, or been able to assimilate, this reflection in his *Varieties*. The psychoanalyst Princess Marie Bonaparte, friend and protector of Freud,[22] sagely concluded that Teresa had had an orgasm. Meanwhile, the cynical have often made much of Saint Teresa's effusion, regarding it in the same light as Gibbon did the repressiveness of the church fathers. But this attitude is seriously mistaken, because Teresa's relation to the orgastic pleasure which she finds on her mystical path is essentially nonrepressive. She was, as the poet Crashaw called her, the "undaunted daughter of desires," and much closer to the differentiated soul-eroticism of the Sumerian priestess or the Arnhem Land aborigines than to the tormented Egoic sexuality of Jimmy Swaggart or the grim antisexuality of Pope John Paul II. One would have to wonder about the adequacy of using the word "Christian" to describe such widely disparate forms of experience. Unlike Swaggart or the pope, who hate the flesh, Teresa recognizes that the body has a share ("and even a great deal") in her spiritual voyage, and she does not reject this so much as pass through it. She differentiates between erotic and nonerotic phases of a spiritual path, and does not try to split the one from the other—as would the vast majority of opinion from both the religious and psychological schools.[23] In other words, spirit need not reject flesh, though it remains different from flesh; rather it passes onward.

I do not want to make this picture hygienic. Remember that Teresa experiences her rapture as akin to violent rape. It entails a great pain and the feeling that her entrails are being drawn out of her. It is not "the joy of sex" which she confronts and transcends but the terror of annihilation which lies on the path toward nonbeing. Lack of repression does not imply lack of suffering, but openness to the suffering one has. What is drawn out of the unrepressed soul is the terror of being. Georges Bataille put this well in his great and truly spiritual work, *Erotism:*

For the Christian apparently, sacred things are necessarily pure and impurity is profane. But for the pagan sacred things could also be unspeakably foul. And if one takes a closer look one must admit that Satan in Christianity is not so far off from the divine, and even sin could not be regarded as completely foreign to sacredness. Sin was originally a religious taboo, and the religious taboo of paganism is in fact sacred. The fear and trembling that modern man cannot rid himself of when faced with things sacred to him are always bound up with the horror inspired by a forbidden object. I think in the present instance that it would be a distortion to conclude thus: "The conjugal symbolism of our mystics does not have any sexual significance. Rather sexual union already has a transcendental significance." Transcendental? That means denying its horror, the horror connected with earthly reality.[24]

Courage to face up to one's demons is necessary for every spiritual practice, from mysticism to psychoanalysis. This should not be taken to dispute the joy of sex; it only claims that the deepest joys can also head toward an abyss.

The Meaning of Desire and Its Differentiation from Spirituality

Just as it is necessary to detach the notion of spirituality from religion, so is it necessary to distinguish the notion of desire from sexuality. The relations are both parallel and complex: sexuality is to desire as religion is to spirituality. But sexuality and desire are also manifestations of spirit, and spirituality is a form taken by desire. How, then, are we to distinguish desire from spirituality if the former is not always sexual and the latter not always religious?

The notion of desire refers to the "wishfulness" of human being, the fact that as a species we seem to want more than we need. But desire is more than a wish. It also reflects the fact that at a very basic level we cannot name what it is that we want, and that we are not sure of who we are in relation to our wanting. Desire signifies that human being is suffused with a kind of longing, and that this longing, without name or certain goal, seems to determine a good deal of what we do. Desire is a property of consciousness; to be more exact, of the lack which consciousness expresses. Because Freud was never very interested in consciousness except as a screen on which "qualities" were projected, he did not bother to talk of desire as such. Instead of the deeper reflection into consciousness which would have revealed desire, Freud chose to explain our longing as the product of biological instinct.

However its source is construed, desire is the very stuff of which psychoanalytic thinking is made. Freud's project is predicated on taking desire seriously and psychoanalysis is at heart a logos which

puts desire at the center of human existence.[25] The method of free association, and the peculiar relationship between analyst and analysand,
produce a decomposition of normal speech into which might be called
desiring speech; and bring to the foreground of consciousness those
inchoate longings in which the subject is no longer fully constituted
and the object no longer fully nameable. The great fascination of psychoanalytic work derives from the fact that under its terms ordinary
language, thought, and consciousness can no longer be sustained as
truthful renditions of being. The attempt to identify speech with propositional truth about reality becomes a kind of self-deception; the
speech which sustains itself under the conditions of psychoanalysis is
desiring speech, speech suffused with and polarized by desire—and desiring speech knows neither itself nor its object.

To say that desire is primarily erotic does not mean that it is only
erotic. It does mean, however, that the erotic is not what it is commonly taken to be. Freud was perennially accused of a kind of pansex-
uality—of reducing all human motivations to erotic ones. He re-
sponded defensively time and again by detaching the notion of desire
from sexuality, saying that yes, all human motivations (all serious
ones, at any rate) were sexual, but that no, sexuality for him was not
what people ordinarily took it to be. Rather sexuality was subsumed
ontologically into the Platonic notion of Eros:[26] the great universal
binding force through which beings connected themselves to each
other and the universe. The key discovery of psychoanalysis was that
Eros makes itself known through bodily desire; and it was at this point
that Eros entered human existence; hence the sexual form taken by the
deeper structures of the mind.

Since these deeper structures are composed of Otherness and revealed in spirit-being, we can begin to spell out the relation between
desire and the spirit. *Desire* is the direction and magnitude of the binding force between the self and the Other. It appears in consciousness as
a pull or polarization between beings which have been separated. Thus
desire is the kind of wanting which arises when the entity wanted is
Other to the self; that is, perceived as belonging to an original, yet separated unity. From this standpoint certain features of desire, namely,
its essential inability to name its object and the doubt it casts on the
identity of the subject, come into focus as properties of Otherness. For
as we desire we activate Otherness, which cannot be named, and is
part of the self as well. Therefore in the quest for the Other we seek it
somewhere, giving names and transforming things as we go, including
the "thing" of our own self. It follows, further, that there is no distinct

end to this road, for each desire containing the Other will not rest with any act of transformation, but must continually press onward. Nor is there any limit within the frame of what the human mind can conceive as to the object of desire. We can desire, literally, anything: the love of others, another's body, self-perfection, beauty, youth, commodities, wisdom, fame, power, virtue, justice, logos, reunion with nature, the future or the past, eternity. . . . Hence the numberlessness of desires, and the Buddhist insight that it is desiring itself which is the condition of suffering, or its cause.

If spirit is about soul, then desire is about the *heart,* linked to soul in popular discourse, and indeed a path toward soul, albeit an unreliable one. As language intuits, *heart* is the force which sets the body in motion as flesh, its pulsation, its desire, obscure and hidden: Pascal's heart with reasons which reason knows not. But reason can learn this much of the heart—that its ways are essential but also unrealizable and even treacherous.

We do not need psychological experts to tell us this. Emily Brontë—isolated on the Yorkshire moors and with little to navigate by except direct observation of the human heart—told more of the anguish and torment of desire than Hegel, with his hierarchical discourse of Master and Slave. Hegel showed that the encounter between human beings was not a mere greeting, but a struggle to the death for recognition. A person does not simply desire the other. Rather one desires the desire of the other. One wants the other to desire oneself; such is the primary desire before the exfoliation into numberless desires. Hegel's conception illuminates the history of class, race, gender, and nation. But Hegel's focus on the rational ascension of spirit blinded him to the realization that desire does not go in logical progression up to death and stop there, but insists on going beyond, into madness and nonbeing. Brontë's Catherine and Heathcliff love with a love that is stronger than death, yet is also a dying. This desiring love has located each within the other; and they are unable to prevent themselves from crashing, like moths intoxicated by the light, headlong into mutual annihilation. "I *am* Heathcliff," realizes Catherine. "He's always, always in my mind: not as a pleasure, any more than I am always a pleasure to myself, but as my own being." The insight forces her to leave the succubus—and ultimately to die. To this Heathcliff reacts: "Be with me always—take any form—drive me mad! only do not leave me in this abyss, where I cannot find you! Oh God! It is unutterable! I *cannot* live without my life! I *cannot* live without my soul!" As he says—or "howls"—this, Heathcliff smashes his head against a tree "like a savage beast getting goaded to death with knives and spears."[27] A romantic fancy, no doubt, this association of love with death. But it is also an accurate rendering of the ontological horizon of desire for another person.

Desire does not stop at being a master or a slave; it is not content with recognition by the Other. It wishes also to annul being itself, to achieve nonbeing: nirvana. This is its threat to Ego (and to ego psychology), and the true meaning of Freud's *Beyond the Pleasure Principle*, a work not about the "bio-logical" instinct of aggression, but the "onto-logical" dialectics of desire. I say desire, not the person, or the self, or any particular instinct. The self stands opposed to the tendency of desire to annihilate being. But it cannot oppose absolutely, because the self, in its narcissism, is also an object of desire. Thus when desire expresses the ineluctable wish to overcome the duality of human being, the wish is one inherent to being itself. At bottom desire expresses human being's intolerance of separateness. In this sense desire, the locus of the non-rational, manifests the law of the universe—that all beings are connected—and that human being has strayed from the law and is willing to annihilate itself to set matters straight. It is as if there is a law of the conservation of being; and desire represents the action of this law when being pushes itself beyond the limit.

Desire refers to the ontological state of wanting. It seeks an object, and according to whether the object is seen as good or bad, defines the attitude taken toward the object as loving or hating. Thus love and hate are organized deployments of desire toward the world, in which the attitude toward an object crystallizes out of desire's matrix. Love and hate each assume some breaching of the unbearable loneliness of the self by the Other. They differ essentially in the attitude taken by self toward Other according to the program of desire—and as folk wisdom can tell from the beginning of the world, and throughout all forms of society, desire is configured so that its loving and hating can coexist and flow back and forth into each other.

The fact that love and hate begin in infancy and are carried forward for the rest of life reflects our deepest and most authentic attachment to the universe. Babies will not survive unless they are loved. And they will not flourish unless they are loved unconditionally, simply for their own being. To love a baby means to love a being who is not yet formed and is relatively speaking, being as such; which means that the baby is an object of desire, onto whom the parent projects his or her own aspirations. As the parent, one loves the baby as an object that cannot be named, and—for the mother especially, though others can identify with this—as an Other who, having been part of one's flesh, is as close to union with the self as life provides. In the animate dialogue with the parent the infant experiences the central Other as a desire for itself. This is the elementary basis of knowing, and therefore the root of knowledge is desire and not logos. To survive and come into one's own being means that the first thing known is the desire of the Other for oneself. This is what we learn of the Other if life succeeds and thrives; and so we automatically associate the survival of our being with the desire of the Other, and seek to bring this desire into our own being. But this means that we experience the power of our own being as the desire of the Other. I do not mean this as some metaphorical approximation, but the actual structure of human ontology: who we are is the Other desiring us—which means that we can never be simply identical to ourselves. Iago spoke for the human species when he stated, "I am not what I am."

The difficult paradox in all this, which human beings have never been able to escape, is that this Other whose desire is oneself, is also a separate being—and to be sure, one for whom the self is also the desire of another. Desire seeks to annihilate the separate being of the other even as it abolishes the separateness of the self. Harsh experience tells us that this cannot be done. We necessarily depend on real, separate others, with wills and desires of their own. A mature person realizes this, and even comes, though not without painful struggle, to value the individuality and desires of others.[28] But for this to happen a remodeling must occur, which takes two broad forms.

First, one internalizes the other, differentiating—or in less fortunate instances, splitting—the self into the I proper and Otherness. By means of this ruse, one preserves the facticity of separate being yet maintains inner relations of desire. What Freud called superego refers to the internal preservation of the sense of self as desire of the Other, now given the contents of the moral law. Within the Christian tradition, the Holy Spirit is experienced as the same kind of phenomenon. As we shall study below, the central Christian notion of love—*agape*—is precisely the experiencing of the other's desire to its full realization—for *agape* is the unmotivated, unmediated and unbounded flow of love from God to the human being, unconditioned by any deed or reciprocity.[29]

If the first step is a transformation of the subject, the second maneuver affects the object. We are uniquely capable of displacing and otherwise transforming the object of desire. Because desire cannot be sated with any one object, it seeks another object, and ultimately all objects, and relates them to one another and to the self according to its loving or hating.

Spirituality, however, is also a transformation of the object of desire. All of the world's spiritual traditions emphasize this, claiming, in effect, that for spirituality to happen, we must abandon Egoic desiring, with its ties to the world and flesh. This however still leaves open the question of the intrinsic relation between desire and spirituality. That is, is desire simply an instrument of spirit, is spirit antithetical to desire, or is spirit somehow a transformation of desire?

The main features of spirit reviewed so far—the experience of spirit-power and emergence of spirit-being—obviously do not conflict with desire. Indeed, their presence can be as well explained by the workings of desire as by any spiritual force, as the appeal of Freud's psychoanalysis testifies. Similarly, the authenticity of spirit does not rule out desire. As we have seen, deeply authentic spiritual experience such as Saint Teresa's can engage a truly erotic desire in a nonantagonistic way, while a spirituality which is hostile to desire sinks into a slough of contradiction. It seems as if spirit has to transcend desire if it is to be realized. However, to transcend does not mean to abolish but to raise to another plane. To simply speak of transcendence without spelling out just what that other plane may be is to speak emptily. In sum, the difference between spirit and desire is just that difference between planes. But planes of what?

It might be helpful to turn to another instance of the dialectic between spirit and desire. As we have seen, a simple opposition between sexuality and spirituality cannot account for the complex reality of spiritual life. Nor, however, can a simple identity between desire and sexuality. Another dimension is needed, the exploration of which will direct our attention toward different regions of existence. We need to look at the fate of desire when turned, not toward sexual objects, but toward the self.

PRIDE AND VIOLENCE

The Spiritual Agony of Angelo Roncalli

The *Journal* of Angelo Roncalli, later Pope John XXIII, is a highly spiritual document which casts doubt on the thesis that a holy man has to push back sexual passion all the time, lest he slip off the tracks.[30] It is not that Roncalli's *Journal* lacks reference to Christian asceticism, or to his own arduous struggles with flesh. Quite to the contrary, it is a highly typical example of Christian hostility to flesh ("of our own nature we are but filth, so far as our bodies are concerned," p. 71) and abounds with self-mortifying exhortation and rituals:

(1) Above all evils beware of bad or unworthy companions, [this was written during Roncalli's early adolescence] those whose speech contains impure suggestions, filthy or cynical words, or dialect expressions. Avoid those who cultivate the company of the other sex and talk about love making; those who hang around in inns, or are intemperate, particularly in drinking. . . . (2) Never converse familiarly or play or jest or in any other manner show too much confidence with women . . . never confide in them the slightest thing which might in any way be dangerous or suspect. (3) Never play at forbidden games or even at games which are permitted, such as those with cards or dice . . . never linger to look on at these games. (p. 70)

And so forth. This is worthy of Saint Paul. As Roncalli matures, the anticorporeal fervor of these missives wanes, though there are still occasional references to "distractions," suggesting a loss of sexual continence. It is plain, however, that sexuality is considered an antagonist to spirituality from the beginning to the end of his life. It is also clear that some kind of sustained negation is taking place, the outward manifestation of which is a constant stream of self-admonition, chastisement, and exhortation. Psychoanalysis would have no problem in recognizing this as a kind of "transformation of an instinct." To take it a step further, psychoanalysis would invoke a harsh superego enabling a continuing "countercathectic discharge of energy" to ward off the forbidden sexuality and turn it into spirituality.

But this reasoning is too crude. It assumes that Roncalli is in the grip of a biological force which he has to continually turn back. This is not so. There is an organic impetus behind sexuality, of course, which wanes with age, so that, as might be expected, the directly sexual character of Roncalli's spiritual travail diminishes. But the travail as a whole does not diminish. It simply shifts its ground from the relatively more sexual to the relatively less sexual side of things. As it does so, the real issue of a spiritual ascension is revealed.

The essential problem is *sinfulness,* which is not a matter of concupiscence, the temptations and "distractions" of the flesh, but of losing one's way, of having God turn opaque. Sinfulness therefore depends not on sexuality as such, but on the "spirit" of sexuality, that is to say, how sexuality is appropriated. For Angelo Roncalli, as for any true Christian, the spiritual path was the overcoming of sin. Insofar as he considered eroticism sinful, it too had to be overcome. But what is "sin?" Here we may refer to the words of Pope John XXIII, as quoted in the preface to his spiritual journal. When asked for permission to publish his personal journal, he agreed, then added, " '[These notes] are a more intimate part of me than anything else I have written; my soul is in these pages.' He paused to read over again the first pages of 1895–9, and with his mild eyes suffused with tears he went on: 'I was a good boy, innocent, somewhat timid. I wanted to love God at all costs and my one idea was to become a priest, in the service of simple souls who needed patient and attentive care. Meanwhile I had to fight an enemy within me, *self-love* (italics added), and in the end I was able to get the better of it. But I was mortified to find it constantly returning. . . .'" (p. xxi).

The master sin, as ever, is pride or self-love, and this constitutes the point of differentiation between desire and spirit. For this is a feature of desire we have not yet sufficiently appreciated. This is that desire is inherently for the self. It seeks objects, but selfishly. Desire does not know the self; indeed, desire inevitably mistakes the self, because it seeks the Other as the self. But this is immaterial from the standpoint of desire. One who gives oneself over to desire is to that degree self-centered, even if at the behest of a false self at the center.

The proposition becomes more radical yet if looked at from the end of the self rather than that of desire. We are, after all, accustomed to looking askance at desire. However, if desire is fundamentally for the self, then the self is that which desire is for. And since desire is unable to find a true representation of reality, then the self as desire is equivalently false. Thus we cannot know ourselves as long as we are captives of desire. This is the bedrock on which Freud built psychoanalysis, but it raises the more general question of *false consciousness*—that is, a consciousness which might be objectively or factually correct but remains spiritually false because it denies the truth of being. Freud did not have full insight into false consciousness, as shown by the glaring inability of psychoanalysis to comprehend that major determinant of being known as social class.[31] It would seem that the extent of a critique of false consciousness depends on how far its insight reaches into the protean nature of desire. Marxism fell into illusion when it exclusively (if only implicitly, since the notion is scarcely developed at all in Marxism) rooted desire in the dynamics of class struggle, just as psychoanalysis did when it refused to look beyond the family and the infantile body as desire's source in the world. In both instances, a fuller appreciation of being would have forestalled this tendency.

In any case, false consciousness never held anybody back, as the whole world of huckstering, jingoism, and greed testifies. "Vanity of vanities! All is vanity. . . ." The line from *Ecclesiastes* (1 : 2) expresses perfectly the realm defined by desire. One feels a bit foolish to reinvent the wheel, but there is no mistaking the perennial realization that the stem of evil is self-aggrandizement at the expense of the other. All of the traditional sins, for example, lust, greed, envy, gluttony, and so forth, are variations on the self-centeredness of desire, and the debasement of one object or another in the headlong rush to live according to the dictates of the desiring self. Those who have taken a dislike to the abuses of the human condition have always expressed that abuse as one variation or another of the self-centeredness wrought by desire. Buddha, Lao-Tzu, Chuang-Tzu, Jesus, Saint Francis, Marx, Freud, Simone Weil, Martin Luther King, and, to be sure, Pope John XXIII. Thus Roncalli's attack on erotic sexuality, like any valid critique of sexuality, attacks the propensity of sexual desire to aggrandize the self and annihilate the object. The spiritual critique of desire does not rule out the possibility of a nonaggrandizing eroticism, nor, as we have seen, the possibility of interweaving eroticism with religious experience. In any event, the sin associated with sexuality is not sexual pleasure but the narcissistic aggrandizement it may bring in its wake. Hence the body can never be a valid object of spiritual opprobrium, in spite of Saint Paul.

By the same token, I do not want to write a hagiography of Pope John. All saints were sinners once, and the sinfulness is not made to disappear simply by its moral condemnation. Some great Christians, such as Paul and Augustine, achieved spiritual transcendence after a life spent in dissipation and persecution. But their greatness was not achieved, in my opinion, by their violent antisexuality, but rather in spite of it. At best, we might say that this antisexuality allowed some psychological stabilization to take place, which then permitted spiritual development. However, the sexual attitudes did not share in that spiritual ascension, but remained behind as a permanent curse upon Christianity. And today, when modern civilization has, for all its miseries, at least attained a certain respect for the body, such an attitude is simply indefensible.

So it was for Roncalli, whose sexual torments are no more spiritual in themselves than another's indulgences. The greatness of a person does not depend on the absence of warps and scars in his or her being, but in the manner by which those limits are transcended. If the young Angelo Roncalli had a dread of sexuality, it must have been because some concrete, historically determined hatred had become sedimented into his sexual being. To the self, nature—in this case, the sexual drive—is always *second nature*—that is, nature that has been structurally affected by internalized history. Growing up in patriarchally dominated society as young Roncalli did makes internalization of a destructive sexuality quite likely; and this sexuality becomes an evil and split-off Otherness. By blocking this Roncalli created some space for spiritual development. He then took splendid advantage of his opportunity, and became spiritually great, but not through antisexuality. For every Roncalli who ascended spiritually from the place of his sexual repression, countless priests and nuns have remained stuck, leading miserable, stunted, and essentially spiritless lives, for all their piety. And the Catholic church is rapidly decaying as a force in the industrialized societies because of a sexual repression which has lost touch with history.

To repeat, this is culturally and historically specific. Arnhem Landers contend with much evil, too, but deal with it through a flexible and socially articulated soul which allows spiritual expression to incorporate erotic spirit-being. For a European white man at the turn of the twentieth century the situation was drastically different, and we can no more expect a young Roncalli to have developed an aboriginal spirituality than we can expect a dog to be indifferent to smells. In its seeming automatism, second nature mimics first nature. It differs in that second nature—the nature defined by internalized desire—remains after all capable of transcendence; and this is what Roncalli set out to do, using the materials at hand, i.e., Roman Catholicism. We make history, but not as we please, said Marx: each of us inherits a conjuncture of second nature with a concretely unfolding historical dialectic. Within this manifold we are free to transcend ourselves or not, free that is, to undergo one kind of spiritual path or another. For Roncalli, an authentic spiritual path was wide enough for an antierotic spiritualization, and no wider.

His spiritual development gave Angelo Roncalli an openness to the Other with which he was able to transform the Catholic religion itself. The term *catholic* implies an open adaptability which has characterized the religion of the same name in some features—such as its ability to incorporate the faiths of conquered peoples—but has been radically denied in others—the above-mentioned antisexuality, for example. Equally fundamental was the Vatican's implacable hostility to socialism and movements of popular empowerment; indeed, despite the origins of Christianity as an emancipatory movement, no more conservative institution existed in the first half of the twentieth century than the Roman Catholic church. As the first pope in modern times from a poor background, however, John XXIII brought with him an in-

grained sensitivity to the outsider. He recognized the growing importance of the nations breaking free from imperialism and set about
mending the Vatican's fences with the communist movement. This was
elaborated theologically in his great encyclical, *Pacem in Terris,* which
approached a synthesis of the original Christian dream of emancipation with Marxism's secular vision of emancipation. John XXIII did
not have to be a "Marxist" (whatever that is) to do so; he needed only
to respond to the same configuration of spirit that Marx revealed in his
life's work: the critique of domination and the "option for the poor."
We should add that Marx did not invent this position, either, but inherited it from the radical Reformation, which in turn inherited it
from Jesus, and so on backwards into the abysm of time. To be more
accurate, Marx shepherded the critique of domination and the option
for the poor, holding it in escrow, so to speak, until the church could
evolve to the point of uncovering its own roots.[32] Angelo Roncalli—
among many others—became, in his spirituality, the bearer of this uncovering. Thus Pope John XXIII introduced, in a highly original and
transformative way (which emphasized detente, a condemnation of
militarism, and the assertion of the rights of self-determination for
emerging nations) a critique of imperialism within and not external to,
the faith. This made his spirituality the bellwether of Vatican II and a
catalyst for the theology of liberation.

Can we say now with more precision just what spirituality means in
relation to desire? Is it not, in light of the above, a mutation of desire
away from its self-centeredness? At the same time, it is a new, qualita-
tively different species of desire. And since the self is a precipitate from
a larger being, while desire points to the ground from which separation ensued, we may now define *spirituality* as the desire for being.
There is, then, a spiritual desire which expresses, like all desire, the
longing for connectedness, the inability to name its object, the self-
dissolution at the core of desiring. But this is a new form of desire because its attraction is not toward the self but toward being, from which
the self arose. And it is a nonpsychological desire, although it leaves its
traces upon psychology. Nonspiritual desire wishes to pull the Other
into the self: its motion is taking or possessing. Spiritual desire wishes
to dissolve the self toward the Other, because it sees in the Other an
opening toward being: its motion is giving, even giving over. Spiritual
desire recognizes the source of all Otherness in the dark corners of
being itself; and it is willing to forgo the island of self-certainty we
have hewn out of history, to voyage toward that obscurity. The pull

toward being and the associated ablation of the self introduces the terror of nonbeing into the spiritual quest—but also the possibility of
transcendence.

We foreshorten the fullness of being in order to put things into
words. Thus when we speak of "spiritual desire," we abstract something from the concrete unity within which the process is taking place.
In reality, spiritual desire in itself does nothing: it is a desiring person
who is spiritual or not. And because the self emerges in desire and can
never escape desire short of death, a person is spiritual with others in a
social collective shaped by desire, and with an embodied and already
desiring self. This is a way of saying that in reality, all spiritual desire
coexists with desire proper. Spirituality, even at its most sublime (for
we have been talking of a kind of sublimation here), is never pure and
cannot be pure; it must always be admixed with ordinary self-
motivated desire. This repeats, in essence, what was said about religion—that no religion can be fully spiritual, that all are to some degree
bound by concrete historical relations of domination, such as those
which have been manifested in Christian antisexuality. But it is not an
idle repetition. Unless we bear constantly in mind that all concrete
spirituality includes self-desire and second nature along with desire for
being, we are unable to offer any critique of the diverse spiritual practices of humanity. These spiritualities range from the top of the moral
scale to the bottom, from the sublime to the ridiculous, from philosophical greatness to mere crankiness, from the most heroic and creative selflessness to the most rigid, nihilistic, and barbaric ruthlessness.
And this depends upon the concrete relations of spiritual and nonspiritual desire, along with all the historical and psychological relations mediating these relations.

These reflections may cast some additional light on the despiritualization endemic to the modern era. Under the late capitalist ecumene,
desire is administered in the interests of economic accumulation and
political stabilization. At the same time, as the family cracks and mass
culture and the psychotechnocratic professions rise, the self is continually subject to invasion. Infused with heteronomous desire, the self
becomes a battleground, the last shred of being accessible to the
person. As a result, the modern person typically has too much invested
in the self to let it go in a spiritual quest. Selfhood is to be defended
and not undone in the quest for being. In the defense of the self, a frantic search for stimulation results, goaded by the economy of consumerism and the expression of desire caught within the self and split off
from being. Fetishization of the erotic arises, and such spiritual needs

as remain become expressed as a series of compromises in which self-integrity, self-maximization, and spiritual release are uneasily synthesized. New Age spirituality emerges, along with a host of political movements, as countercurrents expressing the persistence of desire for being. But the dominant tendency remains one of selfish and ever increasing desire.

A Few More Thoughts about Sin

In a despiritualized time the last taboo is the one on guilt: "thou shalt not feel guilty." This should not be at all surprising, because despiritualization involves the defense of the self, and the essence of sinfulness is Egoic being—being entirely for the self and at the expense of the other. The feeling of guilt, therefore, spiritually conceived and transformed into *conscientization*,[33] would undermine the entire system. The taboo is felt less at the psychological level, for individuals remain by and large capable of feeling guilty, as in the cultural substitution of the ethos of "health" for that of responsibility. Health ethics are a recycling of traditional morality under conditions of late capitalism, where the good is transformed into the healthy, and the bad into the sick, thus absorbing guilt feelings into a clinical mode of reasoning. The shift corresponds to the rise of massive industries of health. It also stems from the glorification of machinery in despiritualized culture, associated with a double reduction—of persons to their bodies and of the body to a machine. On a wider scale, health ethics are better for business than the old ethos of renunciation and hellfire, because they impel us toward commodity consumption rather than acts of expiation. And they are much less disruptive to the order of things than would be an ethos of responsibility, that is, one grounded in a sense of the possibility that one's action could make a difference in the world. Thus the ethos of health blunts the sense of personal responsibility, distorts it into one neurotic framework or another, and generally prevents the drawing of connections between the individual and the whole.

Spirituality, by contrast, requires a sense of sin—neither to preach about, nor as a life-denying attack on the flesh, but as a way to root spirit in real moral existence. Or to use the term just employed in the spirit of its originator, Paulo Freire: to *conscientize*. Between the consumerist hedonism of late capitalism, and the repressiveness of traditional religion, lies another path, grounded in an acceptance of responsibility and one's situation in history. Moving away from Egoism, this path recognizes the frailness of the self in a violent world defined by

domination. It is less concerned with guilt than with conscientiously ad-
dressing reality, and chooses responsibility over an illusory purification.

Such a moral spirit is "critical" in a threefold sense of that word:
recognizing, differentiating, then going through. This notion of sin
does not imply an attack on sensual pleasure. Pleasure, after all, is the
sign of desire finding an object, which is the very stuff of life. However,
a critical notion of sin should recognize the limits inherent in pure sensuality. For sensual desire is not capable of sustaining a coherent and
lifelong project. The life of the libertine is inherently self-defeating, because desire needs an object, yet disregards the reality of that object,
and, if left to itself, would annihilate that object. While pleasure is essential for the fully lived life, no one can consistently live for pleasure,
that is, direct one's being in an exclusively sensual direction. Pleasure
is an essential sign that desire is achieving gratification. It is therefore
necessary for any realization of being. Yet pleasure has to be subsumed
within a larger scheme; it cannot direct that scheme. The supreme example in history of an existence dominated by pleasure is the Marquis
de Sade, brilliant and doomed, a monster of egomania.[34] By refusing to
treat the Other as more than an object of desire, Sade locks himself
into the Master position in Hegel's famous dialectic. To be locked in,
however, means to be no real master at all, but an abject slave of desire, and an eventual prisoner in society's system of confinement.

If sinfulness is not inherently a matter of sensual pleasure, nor is it
essentially linked to hatred or rage, as an exaggerated Christian piety
would have it. Hatred is a sign of the badness of the object of desire: its
inability to gratify the self. However many things in this world are
bad, and it is necessary to hate them. Indeed, it is necessary to hate in
order to exist, since every infant must go through the pain and rage of
separation in order to become a person. To accept the existence of hatred, however, does not deny the existence of evil. But if evil is not
simply a matter of rage, then what is its source?

Psychology has tried to subsume the propensity of humans to
behave hatefully and destructively under the technical rubric of "aggression." I say, technical, because the notion of aggression as it is
prevalently used removes any intrinsic spiritual element from destructiveness by regarding it as an animal instinct. The primary spear car-
rier for this endeavor has been, of course, Freud, with his well-known
dim view of the human condition. He succinctly expressed this in *Civilization and Its Discontents:* "Men are not gentle creatures who want
to be loved and who at the most can defend themselves if they are attacked; they are, on the contrary, creatures among whose instinctual

endowments is to be reckoned a powerful share of aggressiveness. . . . As a rule this cruel aggressiveness waits for some provocation or puts itself at the service of some other purpose, whose goal might also have been reached by milder measures. In circumstances that are favorable to it, when the mental counter-forces which ordinarily inhibit it are out of action, it also manifests itself spontaneously and reveals man as a savage beast to whom consideration towards his own kind is something alien."[35]

This is pretty strong stuff, and it plays nicely into the self-hatred of a society which has lost its hope for transcendence. Variations on Freud's approach are widespread and can be read frequently in the popular press. There is only one problem with his reasoning (which has been echoed down through the years in psychoanalysis):[36] the central concept, that "aggressiveness" is an "instinctual endowment," is false. This is because aggression is no instinct in itself, but the *apparatus* through which a complex of desire works itself out. One might as well blame the engine of the car for the fact that the driver crashed it. What Freud called aggression and tried to subsume into an instinctual formation is as diverse, therefore, as the possibilities of desire. We know from experience that there is no singular reckoning of the phenomena which fall under the rubric of aggression. Freud's attempt to boil all this down to an instinct for destruction lurking like a coiled snake at the core of human nature must rank as one of the low points of his intellectual career—as if he needed a counterweight to the sublime flight of the death instinct. The culprit here is the biological assumption that beneath the surface of human being lies a natural essence—the aggressive instinct—which is its real determinant. Biological notions are a useful way of calling attention to the Otherness of human being, to its rooting in nature, and to the limits of psychology. When they are taken literally instead of metaphorically, however, the dialectic is abolished and the results are repressive. History, as the specific locus of human becoming, collapses into nature and disappears, and people become reduced to that which they cannot overcome. This is purely a bourgeois prejudice into which Freud fell when he mistook the "bio-logical" scaffolding, on which he had climbed to such heights, for a substantive reality.

There is ample "aggression" in nature and in humans alike. However its only sensible definition is "the active capacity to achieve an end." Aggression uses the musculature, is associated with considerable pleasure (for example, in sports, or in the animal joy of exercising one's body, or in lovemaking), and can get pretty rough at times. But it has nothing intrinsically to do with sinfulness or destructiveness. Children having a pillow fight are showing plenty of "aggression;" while Adolf Eichmann, who calmly sent millions of Jews and others to death camps, showed virtually none.

The evil in this world is rather a matter of one degree of violence or another. Hence *sin* may be defined substantively as "the propensity to commit violence." Violence often entails aggression, but is definitely not identical to aggression. Violence means what the word suggests, namely, a violation, that is, the disruption of the integrity of another being. A bird is violated when killed by a cat, a woman is violated when she is raped, a child is violated when it is not loved, Palestinians are violated when their homeland is expropriated by the state of Israel, ghetto dwellers are violated by heartless ugliness and terroristic police, workers are violated when their power to labor is alienated by capitalist production, and the forests are violated by acid rain. Some of this requires aggression, but only as an instrumental means. All of it, however, is some specific, violent fate suffered by a concrete being. Thus the notion of violence requires an ontological conception—that there are beings in the world with specific needs and integrities: i.e., rights. If we did not think that a woman has a right to determine what happens to her body, the concept of rape would be meaningless; if we did not think that children need unconditional love to thrive, we could have no sense of a violated child; if we did not think of a forest as requiring rainfall of a certain pH, the notion of acid rain would be meaningless; if we did not think that people need land and organs of political expression, we would have no conception of the violent expropriation of Palestinians; if we did not think that persons need to express their being through unalienated work we would have no critique of capitalism, and so forth.

What these reflections tell us is that an adequate notion of sin, or violence, cannot occur so long as psychotechnocracy preempts spirit and walls off human relations within the boundary of the self or its "bio-logical" substratum of instinct. But to say that spirituality is a superior conception of human existence does not mean that spirit is necessarily "nice." In fact there is violence inherent in being, an ontological necessity which gives rise to the notion of "original," i.e., necessary sin. Ontological violence is as necessary as Freud's instinctual aggression, but it moves on different terrain. It is not the necessity of a biological automatism but of a predicament. And where there is a predicament there can be a direction out. There is an irreducible violence to being, but to speak of violence is also to speak of a capability for transcendence.

Watch a birth, in which one being breaks loose from another, and the violent quality of being will become clear. Even the baby bird, hatching from the egg, must break the shell. We may generalize: the expression of any being requires the negation of another being. The egg is broken so that the chick may hatch—or, proverbially, that the omelette may be made. Similarly, the ground must be overturned if crops are to be planted, and weeds must be uprooted if the vegetation which nourishes human beings is to flourish.[37] Hegel's dialectic of Master and Slave, and the flux of desire, applies when this negation is carried out by human beings with self-consciousness, but the principle holds for all living beings.

Our existence begins with the fertilized zygote, and enters the world with birth; but each transformation of the life cycle is also a negation of prior being, and at least potentially violent. The more radical the new being, the more violent will its emergence appear—and the more widespread the effects on related beings. As children are born and develop, they change, and so does everyone else related to them. No child can exist as a real being on its own unless the desire of parents for a clone is violated, often with great upheaval, especially in adolescence. But the storms of adolescence, as painful as they may be, are also the occasion for new life. The same applies to revolutions, and also to religion. The born-again Christian must destroy his or her old self. Jesus, the Prince of Peace, also brought not "peace, but a sword" (Matthew 10:34 [RSV]). This does not make Jesus a militarist, but it tells us he was anything but passive. Or consider the following passage from Luke: "John answered them all, 'I baptize you with water; but he who is mightier than I is coming, the thong of whose sandals I am not worthy to untie; he will baptize you with the Holy Spirit and with fire. His winnowing fork is in his hand, to clear his threshing floor, and to gather the wheat into the granary, but the chaff he will burn with unquenchable fire'" (Luke 3:16–17 [RSV]).

As desire turns toward being, new states of being emerge, mediated by spirit-being and expressing spirit-power, often in outbursts of radical upheaval. The vast history of ecstatic possession is evoked here: shamanistic trances, rites of Haitian vodun, raptures of the bacchante, whirling dervishes—whole continents of human transformation, now fading from view.[38] Behavior of this kind, of course, is "aggressive." But it bears only the most tenuous relation to Freud's notion of aggression as intraspecies malevolence waiting to be unsprung. Nor can ecstatic religion be called inherently violent, even if violent excesses may occur in its course.[39]

The salvific moment in ecstatic religion is a wrenching, often terrifying state of being, wresting the self out of ordinary existence with all the force and terror of birth. In the Christian tradition it has manifested itself as glossolalia, or speaking in tongues. This has become a core of modern Pentecostalism, which emphasizes its Biblical roots:[40] "And suddenly there came a sound from heaven as of a rushing mighty wind, and it filled all the house where they were sitting. And there appeared unto them cloven tongues like as of fire, and it sat upon each of them. And they were all filled with the Holy Ghost, and began to speak with other tongues, as the Spirit gave them utterance" (Acts 2:2–4 [KJ]).

Spiritual Pride

To return to the matter of sin, it is obvious that the overt violence of an event does not make it sinful. Sin is rather an expression of the inner state of being accompanying a violent act. To repeat, sin is not violence in itself, but violence done with the *propensity to commit violence*. To sin is to have violence "in one's heart," that is, to have a *desire* for violence. Adolf Eichmann, who showed so little aggression, nonetheless had a desire to serve his führer, and sinned through that path. By contrast, the baby who bites the mother's breast does so with no desire and therefore sins no more than a chick breaking through its egg—except, of course in the twisted mind of a John Calvin, who held that even babies in the womb were liable to sin. It is not the deed in itself, but the deed taken together with its "spirit," which constitutes sin.

Many things have been called sinful, but the deadliest has traditionally been a subtle state of affairs known as "spiritual pride." Spiritual pride is an insidious phenomenon which extends well beyond the bounds of religion and mysticism. It does not necessarily entail any manifest violence. Indeed, the spiritually proud person may have courage, tenacity, and love, and may stand for the highest ideals . . . including, of course, the ideal of spiritual self-effacement. This person may as a result experience bonds of brotherhood and solidarity with all beings, may work for all the good causes, even give away all his or her possessions, may deny in all external ways any sense of domination, i.e., being-over—and yet feel in his or her heart superior precisely because these goals have been attained. But of course this means they have not been attained.

Spiritual pride is an aggrandizement of the self, a pride in being spiritual, though the true motion of spirituality is to overcome the self. Thus the spiritually proud individual negates transcendency by experiencing him- or her*self* as transcendent. The self, in reaching for being, finds only itself once more. It puts on a mask of soul, but remains Ego within. Self-deception is intrinsic to spiritual pride, then, and violence is latent within it, because spiritual pride thwarts the development of being, and thereby violates being. And when violence becomes manifest, spiritual pride enters the dialectics of sin with peculiar deadliness. The reason this form of sin is so deadly is its terrible and self-perpetuating loneliness, for the spiritually proud person can neither enjoy the pleasures of Egoism, nor find the integrity of soul. Such a person hates the world with all the venom of an unlived life, and seeks revenge without even knowing it.

The violence occurring in the course of spiritual pride is cold and correct. Blood-lust and the scenarios of revenge are missing. Desire seems absent. Such violence is usually not committed directly against the other, but through intermediaries. Meanwhile the spiritually proud killer continues to feel virtuous. Thus the witches who were to be put to the stake in Pope Innocent's bull (see p. 118) are, like all "enemies of the state," sacrificed calmly for the greater glory of God. The story has been endlessly repeated, and plays an increasing role in the history of modern society. Indeed, because spiritual pride has so radically lost its connection to being, and seems so stripped of messy desire, it is peculiarly well adapted to the needs of technological society. It is epitomized in the modern bloodless ritual of capital punishment, carried out under medical supervision and piously intoned as the impersonal will of justice.[41] Whenever a victim is ground under the heel of the state, or sacrificed for the abstract necessity of the economy, spiritual pride is regularly displayed by the master. The most extreme instance was that of Nazism and the Holocaust. Consider the words of SS Commander Heinrich Himmler to his officers in Poland in 1943:

> It is absolutely wrong to project our own harmless soul with its deep feelings, our kindheartedness, our idealism, upon alien peoples. . . . One principle must be absolute for the SS man: we must be honest, decent, loyal and comradely to members of our own blood and to no one else. What happens to the Russians, what happens to the Czechs, is a matter of utter indifference to me. Such good blood of our own kind as there may be among the nations we shall acquire for ourselves,

if necessary by taking away the children and bringing them up among us. Whether the other peoples live in comfort or perish of hunger interests me only in so far as we need them as slaves for our own culture; apart from that it does not interest me. Whether or not 10,000 Russian women collapse from exhaustion while digging a tank ditch interests me only in so far as the ditch is completed for Germany. We shall never be rough or heartless where it is not necessary; that is clear. We Germans, who are the only people in the world who have a decent attitude to animals, will also adopt a decent attitude to these human animals, but it is a crime against our own blood to worry about them and to bring them ideals.

I shall speak to you here with all frankness of a very serious subject. We shall now discuss it absolutely openly among ourselves, nevertheless we shall never speak of it in public. I mean the evacuation of the Jews, the extermination of the Jewish people. It is one of those things which it is easy to say, "The Jewish people is to be exterminated," says every party member. "That's clear, it's part of our programme, elimination of the Jews, extermination, right, we'll do it." And then they all come along, the eighty million good Germans, and each one has his decent Jew. Of course the others are swine, but this one is a first-class Jew. Of those who talk like this, not one has watched, not one has stood up to it. Most of you know what it means to see a hundred corpses lying together, five hundred, or a thousand. To have gone through this and yet—apart from a few exceptions, examples of human weakness—to have remained decent, this has made us hard. This is a glorious page in our history that has never been written and shall never be written.[42]

This may well be the furthest extent of Egoic Otherness in human history; yet I hope the reader will see it as an endpoint on a continuum rather than an isolated freak occurrence.

There is no fathoming the depth of spiritual pride, or its subtlety, as it blends with the "normal" narcissistic investment of Ego. It is difficult to make this point clearly enough, perhaps impossible—at least in words. For there is nothing more blind than a self-consciousness which takes its being as apodictic—i.e., as radically certain—and says, "I am—and therefore I know!" Any critical challenge to this certitude is accepted, perhaps pondered over, but not believed, because it has already been assimilated into narcissism. Here is where Freud's introduction of the notion of narcissism[43] becomes so radically important—and so neglected, because the notion of narcissism, indeed the word *narcissism* slides harmlessly off and is already outside of what narcissism is meant to signify. And it must stay outside.

What narcissism is meant to signify is desire for the self. This is radically distinct from the self-regard that stems from achievement, or from looking good in the eyes of others—that is, from the standpoint of desire for the Other's desire. Ordinarily we limit our thinking about narcissism to the level of self-esteem. Pop psychology loves to talk about self-esteem and spews forth an endless series of works anxiously hoping to make us feel better about ourselves. But this summum bonum of modern life is only the proverbial tip of the iceberg as far as narcissism goes. One may call self-esteem "secondary narcissism" if one likes, so long as the idea is not severed from the deeper narcissism, the "primary narcissism," the narcissism of grandiosity and apodictic certitude. This more elemental narcissism appears in psychosis, where it invests an entire being and comprises the scaffolding of delusional thinking. But it also appears in ordinary life, where it is kept in bounds by being wrapped inside a socially correct sense of self.

To feel good about ourselves is a gratification of desire in which we internalize the desire of the Other and thus become Other to ourself. Hence the felt experience of self-esteem is dialogic: "You are a good-looking boy today." Gratification of this pathway of desire is experienced as the pleasures of self-esteem; and its frustration as the torments of self-hatred. These, however, are secondary; they reflect an already constituted self formed as the object of desire. A more radical narcissism arises when the self is both the object and the subject of desire. At this point we do not experience what has happened to desire; we feel, rather, the immediate pressure of desire forcing its way into self-consciousness. The subject-object unity of self cancels out desire experienced through external objects. What results is an experience seemingly closer to the navel of being and yet profoundly antispiritual: desire in itself.

We think of desire as a kind of longing, but this is so only when desire is turned toward another person in a situation of lack. This no longer applies when desire is contained in the self, where the illusion of no-lack can be sustained as long as reality is warded off. Then the immediately felt edge of desire is experienced not as longing but as prideful certitude—for the object is already possessed as Other. Though it is often masked by rational and seemingly objective language, in fact this state of being is based on establishing the self as being-over the other, in order to contain the other and deny separateness. When we say, "I know this," not as a testable statement about reality but as an expression of desire, we are claiming "I am all, I have no lack." Logos is an institutionalization of this position—the assertion of the identity of knowing and what is known—not to know as truth but as an expression of narcissistic power. This kind of thinking is at the core of every delusion—but also at the core of much ideology. It is implied in the truism that people's minds cannot be changed on matters of politics and religion.

Desire wants fusion with the ground of its being and the undoing of the distinction between humanity and nature. The prideful Ego accomplishes a pseudoresolution of this problem by making itself the ground of being. Ego becomes both object of the self and the self-as-object. But desire is also for the desire of the Other. In narcissism, Ego becomes this Other whose desire one desires. The self loves Ego as an ideal form of being, then identifies with Ego and becomes in fact like Ego, Egoic and prideful. Desire is therefore kept within the bounds of the self, and separation and differentiation are denied. The price of this denial is an exclusion of real others as integral beings; and yielding of opinion becomes annihilation. Since annihilation here means reunion with an Other which has been hated, expelled, and reduced below the level of being, the experience is catastrophic. Indeed, doubt is equivalent to nonbeing and is equated with death. This may help us understand the vehemence of certain points of view and the difficulty many people have in changing their "mind." For it is not opinion, but one's being which is at stake. Reinforced as a defense against the terror of nonbeing, Ego goes on its way—especially if it can find other Egos to go along with it. The oppression of its own solitude is relieved by collective acceptance of certitude and collective rejection of the bad Other. Then the real others who are excluded become the lesser races.

Though we have been speaking in a highly abstract shorthand, we are referring to very widespread phenomena, the political results of which have quite often been disastrous. Spiritual pride is certainly not the worst sin when it accompanies genuinely virtuous acts. Then it is a reminder of the tragic limits of human being, and perhaps ironic as well. It is another story when the false consciousness of spiritual pride is associated with material power, which is then spiritually justified and so reinforced.

Let us consider in this light the Israeli occupation of the West Bank and Gaza, and the *Intifada,* or uprising of the inhabitants of those areas. Here is what the Israeli prime minister, Yitzhak Shamir, had to say about these events at the beginning of the Intifada, as reported in the *Los Angeles Times* of 26 December 1987: "To Shamir, the Palestinian youths throwing rocks in the face of Israeli assault rifles are just another in the long history of trials that the Jewish people have faced. 'Our people . . . fought for 3,000 years for its land, for its freedom, for the right to preserve its culture and heritage, and it is certainly continuing to fight,' he said during a Hanukkah candle-lighting ceremony at his office on Monday. 'There is no end to this war, and it is a war in which we must triumph, in each and every generation.'" This is spiritual pride with a vengeance, accompanied, as so often in human history, by religious symbolism of the "God is on our side" variety. Here spiritual pride is in the context of an equation between the Jewish people and the Zionist project realized in the state of Israel. This state of being is very definitely one of being-over and violence. Hence the "we" and the "they" are sharply etched and opposed. Splitting is essentially complete in the being of Shamir; there is no recognition of self in Other, or Other in self. The world is divided into a "we"—a brilliant people which has fought for the highest ideals and suffered for those ideals for nearly the whole span of human history; and the "they"—vermin, subhuman filth, "terrorists," not humans, but things and even nothings. This degree of splitting ensures perpetual violence; thus in Shamir's universe, the being of the Jewish people is a permanent and irrevocable state of war. The state of being mirrors and expresses the permanently mobilized Zionist state apparatus. Warfare provides the occasion for this being to assert itself; without a permanent state of war, one suspects, Shamir would feel empty. In any event, this state of being, like the state apparatus it serves, must have its enemy-Other.[44]

One of the striking things about Shamir's statement is the falseness of the history it proclaims (and institutionalizes). The Jewish people have in fact had an extraordinary and brilliant history going back more than three thousand years. Moreover, it is a history of nearly continuous struggle, just as Shamir claims. The very identity of Jewishness seems to have been framed as opposition and adversity, from the tribes of Yahweh to today's confrontations in Gaza. Although it had profound effects on Jewish national character, the long diaspora, with its ghettoization and victimization culminating in the Holocaust, does not mean that the Jews are not capable of being a warrior people. They have been just that for considerable stretches of time in the past; and the present militarism of the state of Israel is certainly not a historical anomaly.

What is wrong with Shamir's view of history is the denial of history itself—in denial's dual sense of creating falsehood and as a sign of spiritual pride. Denial of history is inherent to ontological splitting. Where related peoples—here the Jews and Palestinians—are forbidden any moment of recognition, they are also deprived of negativity: the coming into being of the "things which are not." To deny the negative is to posit Nietzschean "eternal return of the same;" here, the "war in which we must triumph, in each and every generation." Heidegger does this, and Freud as well, for the notion is essential to any ontology or politics which defends the Master position in the dialectic of history. That is of course just what Shamir does.

But the history this denial expounds is also untrue, as any denial of the dialectic must be. Spiritual pride demands eternal victory for the "we." However, the Jews have not always triumphed, and not always been the Master. More important, their greatness as a people derived from struggle against Masters, not from being Master. Indeed until the present moment (and it is but a moment) of history, the Master role has been anything but characteristic of Jewish being. The Jews became great 3200 years ago by fighting against Canaan and Egypt when they could be best characterized as an irregular band of guerrillas with an egalitarian social base; and they became great again when they fought heroically and tragically against Rome, in the epoch of Jesus, and when their social condition bore a striking resemblance to that of the Palestinians whom Zionism now oppresses.[45] The remarkable irony is that Shamir himself was treated by the British in the 1940s exactly as he now treats the Palestinians, as a "terrorist" deserving of expulsion.

A fuller discussion of the conjuncture of Israel and Palestine would have to consider as well the unspeakable horrors of the Holocaust, as a calamity the Jewish people vowed would never again happen to them. The Holocaust is perhaps the ultimate in violence received by one people at the hands of another, the ultimate in reduction from the level of being to that of a thing, as the discourse of Himmler, quoted above, makes chillingly clear.[46] Undoubtedly the Holocaust sharpened Zionist resolve through an identification with the aggressor. But it did not create such resolve, the institutional bases of which were laid down before World War II, and extend deep into history. Unhappily, Zionism is and has always been integral to the motion of Western imperialism toward the south; that is ultimately why the fortunes of Israel, South Africa and the United States have been so deeply linked. The Holocaust played a role, but in speeding up the wheel of domination, not in starting it.

The recycling of victim and oppressor can be read as an instance of the "compulsion to repeat" which Freud saw at the heart of instinctual life.[47] Or we could see in it Nietzsche's "eternal return of the same," in this case, a recycling of domination.[48] But though it is certainly true that history reveals a tendency to recycle itself, the return can never be the same. Human "instincts" are not biological instincts like the urge which leads spiders to weave the same web over and over, or spawning salmon to return to the river in which they were born. Our instinctual drives incorporate second nature—nature which already contains history and which operates therefore according to desire and not the scurrying of molecules.

Because the Master in the dialectic of domination arrogates being to himself and assigns nonbeing to the Slave, domination is the one human condition in which spiritual and nonspiritual desire converge. That is, in the struggle of the oppressed to be free there is no inherent contradiction between the two modes of desire. The spiritual desire for being runs along the same course as the desire of the self to be free. The combined power of this desire is the spiritual force in history, which continually interacts with material elements. It is not immediately connected to any religious impulse, although it has often enough been engaged religiously, just as the erotic has been engaged religiously. Rather the desire to be free appears utopianly, as the dream of a society beyond domination, a dream employed by Marx but which he by no means originated. For it was Marx's Jewish ancestors who first conceived this wish as the destiny of a people. This is the real source of the greatness of the Jewish people—a greatness forfeited, needless to say, in proportion to the degree Jews play the role of dominator.

Zionism, the modern imperial form of Judaism, mystifies the desire to be free into an ideology of domination. It says, just as bourgeois economic ideology has said, that freedom is of the one against the many, in this instance, of the Chosen People against an undifferentiated mob of subhuman Arabs. Indeed, no matter how much the defenders of Israeli "democracy" deny the allegation, Zionism engenders racism at the most fundamental level. Ontologically, racism is the license of Ego—the isolated particle of being, which can sustain itself only by nonrecognition of the Other, a position which implies the reduction of the other person to a subhuman thing. A violent suppression is the inevitable means of enforcing this reduction. This is a tragedy for the Jewish people even as it is a calamity for Palestinians. It proves once more that humans are at most bearers of their own greatness; they cannot become identical to their own ideal. In this phase of the dialectic, then, the desire to be free has been turned over to the rejected Other. Zionism has succeeded in transferring Jewishness to the Palestinians.[49]

The Violence of the Master and the Oppressed

"All things come into being by conflict of opposites, and the sum of things flows like a stream."[50] "*Panta rhe,*" said Heraclitus: everything flows. Ceaselessly, back and forth through historical struggle, human being arises, projects its desire, and transforms reality. There is no necessary end to this, no "law of conservation of being," except as desire gropes for it. Thus there can be no master plan, for such a plan is nothing but the projection of Egoic being into the cosmos. A master plan is a plan of the Master. Being does not need a plan; it flows on its own, without any help from the Master. The logos of the Master cannot know this, but he responds violently to it. Ego, defined by splitting, is necessarily cut off from the flow of being. Egoic being is consequently not fully alive; it stands *over* life, not *in* the living stream. Though the Master flourishes, he does not really live. And since he is a living being with desire, he is in a state of unfulfilled desire, and hence, hatred. The hatred of the Master tends to be, moreover, absolute and boundless, because the unfulfilled desire of the Master ultimately arises out of his very dominion. It is intrinsic to the splitting which makes him Master in the first place. This hatred born of unlived life can be overcome only if the Master ceases to be a Master.

In speaking of a Master, I mean no particular individual of the dominant group, but those who choose to represent that group, i.e., the ruling class, in the activity of domination. And since everybody is to some degree divided internally in this regard (just as we all have Ego aspects and soul aspects), so do I mean to designate by the term "Master" the tendencies within individual beings which reproduce the domination of the ruling class. Certain people are more or less completely identified with this tendency; while others, who may objectively belong to the wealthy and powerful sector, can make some degree of spiritual and material break with it. In any event, it is at the level of the collective that significant historical change occurs. And from this standpoint we can say that those classes which dominate can heal themselves only if they voluntarily lay down their wealth and power. This has never happened, to my knowledge, in the whole history of the world[51]—which must mean that there are some very powerful ontological reasons behind it.

It seems to me that the tendency toward ruthless violence is inherent to any ruling class, or, since the state is an instrument of a ruling class, to any state apparatus (more concretely, to anyone who represents this, such as the military or police). Obviously the violence of the Master is expressed in a myriad of ways and is subject to all kinds of modifications and controls, which are not within our scope now to describe. But it applies in its essential characteristics whether the class is aristocratic or bourgeois, and whether the state is monarchical-absolutist or bourgeois-democratic, as well as to socialist states to the extent they have failed to overcome class differences (which is to say, to actually existing socialist states, all of whom have done poorly on this score).

The extreme violence of the Master is fueled not simply by pride, but also by the nonrecognition of the Other intrinsic to the Master's split state of being. To the Master class, the underclass is less than human. And when social unrest rears its disturbing head, the subjugated class is readily put on the block, with scarcely a qualm or moral inhibition (except as a tactic, to appease world opinion). The name given by bourgeois society to underclasses in a state of unrest—or anybody who represents this possibility—is "communist."[52] This is the daemon, the "spectre haunting Europe," to use the remarkably insightful phrase of the *Communist Manifesto*. The "communist" is the diabolic spirit-being of capitalism, projected on whomever stands in the way of the continued plunder by the ruling class. Once this association is made, all lingering moral considerations are cleared away and the violence of the Master can be unleashed.

For the Master, the blockage of desire, and life itself, forces desire back onto the paths outlined by Freud, epitomized in the compulsion to repeat. The only direction desire can take under such circumstances is toward the instincts organized around the death instinct and epitomized by sadism. In sadism nonbeing is not accepted, but rather displaced entirely onto the victim, who is forcibly made into a passive piece of meat, a thing. It is scarcely a play on words to proceed from death instinct to death squads, or the equally inhuman cold ruthlessness of their patrons in the CIA and related organizations of death. Rather than yield, the Master resorts instead to the logic of annihilation—though given his spiritual pride, he arranges for surrogates to do the actual dirty work.

An unyielding Master often provokes revolutionary violence by the oppressed. With the defeat of the Sandinistas in Nicaragua, a cycle of these revolutions seems to have run its course, broken by the overwhelming and implacable power of imperialism. Yet the reality which gave birth to them is still present, and their lessons are still before us.

It is a verifiable fact that the oppressed are in general less violent than the oppressor. Indeed, the major carnage of most revolutions occurs in one of two contexts: either the counterrevolution and civil war unleashed by enraged Master classes—as was the case in Nicaragua; or in instances such as Cambodia under the Khmer Rouge when a fanatical clique takes power in a chaotic situation and immediately reproduces the worst features of a ruling apparatus.[53] But these are, in any case, abstractions and averages: the "in general" as opposed to the existential given. Violence is still violence; revolution generates war; and war is an unacceptable option, especially for the poor who always bear its burden disproportionately.[54]

What is to be done in the face of this? We cannot deny to an oppressed people the same force of life that we recognize in our children, or in the *kerygma* of the word, unless we deny life itself. The pharisees who preach against revolutionary struggle in the current state of the world deny this life. Yet to affirm it runs the gauntlet of violence and war. This is not the place to discuss the politics of radical democratic struggle necessary to effect real emancipation. Yet we should not pass on without commenting on the chances of enduring the gauntlet. Specifically, can there be a spiritual mutation of violence, if not a transcendence of it? If spiritual desire can move with selfish desire in the wish to be free, it can also do so in the matter of violence, converting it into militancy for democratic struggle. Here the distinction follows that already drawn between differentiation and splitting—between the giving and opening of soul and the taking and closing of Ego. We have already written of the splitting epitomized in the spiritual pride of the Master, his radical schism into I and Other, and the violence which ensues. What of the militant differentiation of violence—of nonviolence?

Nonviolence

A great deal has been said by many voices over the years concerning nonviolence. We can only deal here in the broadest terms with this complex subject, which concentrates the question of spirituality in the arena of political action.[55] For nonviolent practice is the spiritualization of violence, the overcoming of violent desire. Nonviolence is not an absence of violence, for that is inconceivable. And it is certainly not passivity or inertia, which would violate life itself. To be a nonviolent activist, rather, is to make oneself a kind of spiritual warrior. To block the entrance to a nuclear submarine base is neither passive nor free of violence (for one is violating the rights of workers to enter their workplace); similar considerations obtain wherever nonviolence is practiced.

It is important to take this to another plane, where the particular violence of an act is seen in full context. Here we can say that nonviolence is, rather than the mere absence of violence, the negation of sinfulness. In other words, nonviolence is a propensity to transcend, rather than commit violence. Thus nonviolence is primarily a matter of spirit in its third sense, of authenticity, and it involves a spiritual, as against an Egoic, desire.

How does a nonviolent act actually take place? It would seem that two major criteria must be met. First, the act must be a conscious intervention in some situation of violence, the purpose of which is to create a crisis within that situation, to raise the level of consciousness and conflict about it, and to cause a realignment of forces towards the reduction of violence. Thus the intervention is directed against the cause of the violence, and its authentic spirit is to overcome violence. Usually this entails an act of refusal, but can also be the dramatic commission of a lesser violence to sharpen conflict about a greater violence, e.g., smashing a nuclear nose cone. It goes without saying that at this level of action one behaves in a minimally violent way, with Gandhi's *ahimsa* (doing no harm), always in mind.

The second dimension is subjective. It is to take into the self a degree of the violence, and accept it. In a word, the nonviolent person accepts suffering. He or she does not do so as a masochist, which would be the Egoic reversal of sadism. Masochism and sadism are mirror images of each other; and both manifest a kind of spiritual pride. But nonviolent suffering is accepted for the sake of soul, for a way of being that allows nonbeing, and recognition of the Other. Suffering brings this about because it undoes the Egoic self. In masochism, Ego suffers in order to hold onto the object (and covertly to torment the object, hence true masochists are sadists at heart); whereas in nonviolent suffering the self releases the object and moves toward soulfulness.

The consumerist culture rejects the ethos of suffering as forcibly as it rejects the notion of sin, and for the same reason: it is not the "healthy" thing to do. But no spiritual path can avoid some degree of consciously accepted suffering; and nonviolence defines itself by accepting suffering in the course of political transformation. Such a suffering is not an end in itself (which would be masochism); nor is it strictly speaking a means. Suffering is rather something one finds already there, as the sediment of domination encrusting the living being. It has to be picked up and shouldered before it can be thrown aside. By suffering and acting according to *ahimsa*, the nonviolent person is breaking the cycle of revenge by means of which violence reproduces itself. And at the same time he or she is establishing a bond with the oppressed, at the level of nonbeing.

The nonbeing and suffering accepted in nonviolence had been the province of the underclasses, the oppressed, the poor, and the wretched of the earth. That is why nonviolence is uninterested in peace as an abstraction, but always focuses on peace with justice. The bumper stickers with the slogan "Visualize Peace" or some such New Age jargon, are repeating an empty phrase;[56] for peace as such is nothing but the hypothetical world without violence, that is, nothing. Everybody, after all, wants peace. Hitler, Ariel Sharon, Pol Pot, Deng Xiaoping: they all want peace; but on their own terms, the peace of the Masters. Unless the overcoming of violence includes also the coming into being of the "things which are not," it cannot be nonviolent and cannot move toward spirit. I think this is what Jesus intended when he offered not peace but a sword.

Nonviolence is more than a recognition of violence. By accepting suffering—which may mean standing in a vigil, or picket line, or fasting, or going to jail, anything up to and including martyrdom—the nonviolent warrior also accepts responsibility and attempts restitution. Nonviolence is, therefore, a kind of conscientization, to recur to the expression of Paulo Freire. But the acceptance of suffering and responsibility, the restitution, and the general opening toward soul embodied in nonviolence, are also aspects of sacralization. That is, a nonviolent motion is also a motion toward the sacred. The sense of the sacred derives from a recognition of the violence inherent in being. In earlier times, this entailed a recognition and restitution made to those parts of nature transformed and negated for the sake of human being. The hunter who killed the prey made this animal sacred; the horticulturalist who pulled crops from the earth made the earth and its harvest sacred. From this developed the tradition of sacrifice, which has been at the core of religion from the beginnings of time, and is now at the core of nonviolence. More than guilt or dependence has been involved, and certainly more than Freud's "just-so" story of the totem as the restitution made for killing the primal father.[57] These emotions are, typically, the projection backwards of certain reigning obsessions of bourgeois society. The actuality of the sacred, on the other hand, is the recognition of the spiritual need to reclaim Otherness. This entails an objectively responsible attitude toward nature as the whole ground of Otherness—something which has been obliterated in despiritualized society, with nightmarish consequences.

The notion of sacrifice has, according to van der Leeuw,[58] the greatest range of meaning in the entire religious tradition (an honor it shares, significantly enough, with "soul"). We may take this to mean that the concept is most pregnant with historical implication. In any case, the notion of sacrifice takes on a new dimension in the Hebrew tradition. As Mircea Eliade pointed out (building on the insight of Kierkegaard),[59] when God demands of Abraham that he sacrifice his only son, Isaac, religion confronts for the first time the dimension of faith. Abraham's sacrifice is an act to be committed without any rationale (such as paying nature back for one's violence, or coercing the heavens to rain upon one's crops), but rather entirely prospectively and on God's word alone. Indeed, the deepest sacrifice is demanded of soul and is not soul's own volition; it runs against the grain, does not come "naturally." It is, so to speak, an "intervention:" not yet a political intervention, but an instance where suffering (imagine the suffering of Abraham!) is to serve an end in the world which cannot be foreseen. It is a suffering, then, which creates, and then enters, historical time.

The supremely violent act asked of Abraham has, then, a hidden nonviolent content, which is to grow through history. It reaches a pinnacle in Jesus, the apostle of nonviolence and Prince of Peace (with justice) who is sacrificed for the redemption of the human species.[60] It continues today, dispersed into the myriad of nonviolent practices, all of which are ventures in faith. But there is a paradox here which needs to be elucidated. If a hunter sacrifices an animal, it is a reflection of immediate responsibility for killing animals. But if a nonviolent protestor takes onto him- or herself a token of the suffering for the bombing of Hiroshima or the violation of Nicaragua, he or she is acting on behalf of the real perpetrators of violence. These gentlemen, we may be reasonably sure, are enjoying a good meal while others fast in the name of a conscience the Masters refuse to assume.

But this is precisely why somebody must adopt the sacrifice—to show that everybody is in the same boat. Everybody, that is, at the level of soul. Ego remains inherently divided, while soul connects. Needless to say, in any concrete instance soul may be only a potential space for being. One need not think, say, of Henry Kissinger or Margaret Thatcher as having very much soul. But even Kissinger and Thatcher have the possibility of soul; and nonviolence has to act as the proxy of soul which cannot yet be for the Master. This should require, it may be added, releasing the Kissingers and Thatchers of this world from the bondage of their Masterdom, since this is the source of the sinfulness which keeps them from realizing their spiritual power.

To extend the argument, we might say that the spiritual heart of nonviolence is the dissolution of Egoic boundaries in the moment of political struggle. Once this is begun, it is impossible to say where it will end, except in the utopian and evidently unattainable goal of a

classless society beyond domination. Essentially this means that the
goal of nonviolence is a world where no person is worth more than
any other at the level of Ego. This *u-topia,* in the original meaning of
the word, is "nowhere." It can only be said to be a path toward the
beyond. Yet on the way to that goal, nonviolence can stop off at a great
number of political places in the here and now, where we live. Properly
understood, this has two immediate implications. First, one never
fights for "my country, right or wrong," or a Chosen People, or a Master Race, or any other Egoic distinction; thus an American life is not
worth more than that of an Iranian or Guatemalan peasant. Second,
one always fights—nonviolently above all, but fights nonetheless—for
those who have had nonbeing thrust upon them, and who contain,
therefore, the germ of the spiritual ascension of human being.

If these principles are conscientiously adhered to, wars will disappear, and true human history will begin.

THE SPIRITUAL BODY

Having pursued something of the track of desire through society,
we need to retrace our path to the point where desire intersects with
nature and arises from nature. For no social arrangement can contain
desire. Even after true human history begins desire will persist, because desire is the intrinsic manifestation of the unfulfilled nature of
human being. To expect otherwise is to wish suffering out of the
world—a wish which is nothing but a trick of desire and its intolerance of incompleteness and separateness. Desire, as we know, can
take for its object whatever entity can be formed by the mind. Desire
can even desire itself; and commonly does—turning into one addiction or another—when spiritual development grinds to a halt. In any
case, desire cannot be avoided. To suppress desire is the same, at heart,
as fetishizing it: in either case one becomes obsessed. We have already
seen how ambiguous are the relations between spirit-as-religion and
desire-as-sexuality. The same complexity holds throughout the range
of spirit and desire. Its root lies in that peculiar and strategic part of the
world called the body.

The body is the one part of the universe claimed at the same time by
the self and nature. A basic way of referring to this doubly registered
part of the universe is *flesh*. Flesh is matter which is also the presence
of subjectivity. It is matter as subject-object: the subject that feels, the
object that is felt and at the same time the place of the feeling.[61] Flesh is
more than the "physio-logically" describable organism, though it is
that as well. Flesh is that body as it enters and constitutes the subject.

The physiological body is the substratum of being. But flesh is the material place where being transpires. Erotic desire, the desire which looms so noisily in life, is desire whose object is flesh—desire focused on the bodily site of being, desire which seeks being insofar as being is embodied. The erotic vision sees the universe itself as flesh.

Typically in statist societies, spirituality has been opposed to the body, just as it has been opposed to the erotic expression of the body. In traditional Christian dogma the body-as-flesh is despised as a place of corruption. The hostility is centered about sexuality, as we have seen, but is more general than that. Indeed, its wider target is the body as that which sickens, ages, and dies—the body as a source of a suffering which comes to all irrespective of their place in society and history. Along another dimension, this body, of corrupt nature, is also identified with the female who both repels and fascinates the church fathers.[62] It is this aggregate carnality which is apparently negated in the Christian doctrine of the resurrection of the flesh: "So it is with the resurrection of the dead. What is sown is perishable. What is raised is imperishable. It is sown in dishonor, it is raised in glory. It is sown in weakness, it is raised in power. It is sown a physical body, it is raised a spiritual body. If there is a physical body, there is also a spiritual body" (1 Cor. 15:42–44 [RSV]). In the King James version, the "physical" body is referred to as the "natural" body. On the basis of these and countless other behaviors the conclusion has been drawn that Christianity is fundamentally hostile to flesh. Now this is certainly so as an empirical statement about the attitudes of the fathers of the church, up to and surely including the current pontiff.[63] Historically, Christianity has regarded the body as no more than a prison of the soul. But this is not the same as saying that the above famous words of Paul—or indeed the whole Christian tradition—admits of no other interpretation of the relations between flesh and spirit. As Karl Rahner, the great Catholic theologian—and scarcely a fire-breathing radical—has pointed out in his *Dictionary of Theology*, "The body is the substantial 'expression' of the soul in which the soul first achieves its concrete reality; the soul cannot fulfill itself without making use of matter; the greater its self-fulfillment, that is to say, the more man [sic] becomes spirit, the more the soul (man) becomes the body. This means that the body is the medium of all communication and that conversely the soul fulfills itself in proportion as man lives with bodily men in a bodily world." And again, "It was an error ill beseeming Christians to banish grace to the realm of the 'soul alone,' for in that Body, possessed by grace and become the expression of grace, is the one entire man

and the whole of humanity, blessed bodily in the bodily presence of
Christk."[64] The lines resonate with Blake's *Marriage of Heaven and
Hell,* quoted above: "Man has no Body distinct from his Soul for that
calld Body is a portion of Soul discernd by the five Senses. the chief
inlets of Soul in this age".

Thus flesh may be differentiated from soul, as in the Blakean-
Rahnerean (which is also, it may be added, a Thomistic) view; or flesh
may be split from soul, as in the views of the patristic church and Pope
John Paul II. The "spiritual" body and the "physical" or "natural"
body need not, therefore, be radically opposed dimensions of being.
Rather the "spiritual body" can be seen as a body-with-spirit, a body
that *is* spiritual. Now to speak of a body-with-spirit is not the same as
tacking on a spiritual dimenison as though it were another organ or
faculty of flesh, or as ego psychology attaches the ego to the "mental
apparatus." This mode of discourse is rooted in traditional Protestantism and often continues in New Age circles, where we hear talk of a
tripartite division of human being into "body, mind, and spirit." This
recalls Lewis Carroll's *Hunting of the Snark;* it bids us pick up dissect-
ing kit and magnifying glass to go looking for the location of spirit,
and a scale to weigh it in once the beastie has been found. To tri-
chotomize being into body, mind, and spirit is not much different or
better than to dichotomize it into mind and body. The tripartite division is just that—a division, or splitting, rather the way pop psychology views Freud's famous differentiation of mind into ego, id, and
superego. Freud himself was careful to point out that the notions he
coined could not be mapped as contiguous regions of space-time, except in the roughest and most heuristic way.

To speak of a body-with-spirit as differentiated means that being
and the organism are two sides of the same entity, so that flesh is inherently spiritual and open to the Other, and only ceases being spiritual through repression. Entities which are differentiated are distinct,
yet constituted through mutual recognition—a dynamic interrelation
which leads to change and the expression of new historical being. We
see this in the sphere of gender. In the timeless war between the sexes
men and women tend to split apart, each refusing to recognize the
Other in him- or herself. This position is the one specific to patriarchy,
and it freezes the genders into "natural" yet false molds. Individuals
who live out lives of such splitting cannot evolve erotically or in terms
of gender identity. When, however, life leads a man or woman to begin
recognizing the Other in him- or herself, a greatly enriched set of possibilities opens up, which can lead both to conflict and growth. In this

respect, a sexual transformation becomes a spiritual one as well, as a portion of Ego becomes soul.

That most spiritual of psychoanalysts, Wilhelm Reich, held that orgasm is the concrete realization of the spiritual body, the flesh transformed.[65] The essential moment of orgastic experience is Ego dissolution, and the flowing of self into Other. Or we might say that it is the joining of beings through flesh, flesh combining with flesh in their overflowing. Orgasm is the acme of sexual life, yet is not confined to objectively sexual practice. It is, rather, a state of flesh mediated by the imagination—witness the orgastic experience of Saint Teresa of Avila. Indeed the sense of orgastic flooding cannnot be divorced from spirit-power, and appears, transformed, throughout the range of ecstatic spiritualities.

The rapid gratification of desire (signified organismically by convulsive discharge and subjectively by the sense of merging with the other) accounts for the pleasure of orgasm. This cannot be correlated, however, with the mechanical event of tension buildup and release. Psychoanalysis traditionally held that pleasure was the release of physiological tension—indeed this is the basis of Freud's pleasure principle. However this does not account for the fact that the *buildup* of tension during the sex act is also highly pleasurable. It makes much more sense to think of pleasure as a vicissitude of desire than as an organismic tension. It would seem that the gratification of desire—along with its organismic accompaniment—is directly transformed into pleasure. Similarly, the blockage of desire will be experienced as sharp displeasure—again associated with painful stimulation.

Whatever these theoretical niceties, the fact remains that for many, orgasm is the concrete bridge to a kind of heaven, the single most intense reminder in life that Ego can be broken through and the self rejoined to the world. Despite Reich's hopes for using this bridge as a way of building a heaven on earth, however, orgasm remains only a harbinger of spiritual fulfillment. The reason lies partly in the inherently transient character of orgastic experience—and more substantially in the fact that orgasm is linked to the program of desire, which cannot in itself mediate a spiritual pathway because it annihilates its object. When flesh merges with flesh in orgasm, the being of the other is dissolved into one's own. There is nothing in the program of orgastic release which would inherently sustain the full being of the other. Orgasm is therefore essentially prespiritual. It is certainly not antispiritual, as Saint Teresa showed. Yet it must be passed through, because of its transience, dissolution of practical capacity, and bondage to desire. This does not mean that a person cannot have a rich sexual life and a full spirituality; it only asserts that full spirituality occupies a different place from the erotic, so that the conjunction "and" may have to link sex and spirituality (not, by contrast, "or").

Orgasm is an extreme state of being in which Ego approaches dissolution and opens onto the spiritual dimension. But it should not be assumed, therefore, that this possibility, in a less dramatic form, is absent from the ordinary life of flesh. We would hold, then, that flesh is inherently a "spiritual body," and that we only see the distinctions, and think at all about a spiritual dimension which gives form to the energy of the body, because of our estrangement.[66] The situation is analogous to the use of the term "wilderness," which is needed as a word only by those who have become estranged from nature.

In normal Egoic being, spirit and flesh are split so far apart that they seem wholly distinct realms, while in fully differentiated soul-being they are so close together that separate words are scarcely needed for them. But if flesh is inherently spiritual, then spirit is also inherently flesh—and desire is a material force as well as a longing.

Consider people in the midst of radical social transformation. There is no more impressive phenomenon in the human world than the discovery by a hitherto oppressed and, literally, stupefied people of fantastic reserves of energy and brilliance once they have embarked on a revolutionary course. The whole mystique of *morale* is involved here— that peculiar force which lifts and inspires according to the authenticity of a spiritual practice. The differences in morale between oppressor and oppressed can, as history has witnessed again and again, cancel out the most extraordinary material differences. But this means that morale makes a material difference. Despiritualized science falsely limits the understanding of such phenomena to the infusion of adrenaline and corticosteroids—i.e., to its physiological substratum. However, no one has yet been inspired by an injection of any hormone, and only a fully inspired person—or group—can mobilize spiritual power.

And why do we feel such an infusion of power, along with a sense of wholeness and integrity when we experience "nature?" I offer inverted commas here, because the only nature we know is that already affected by human activity. However, there are great relative distinctions in the experience of nature, arrayed once again along the axis of splitting and differentiation. To the degree we achieve differentiation, opposed to splitting, with nature, then we let nature into our being. This must be more than merely subjective, else untold millions of people who have found strength in encountering the mountains or the sea have been victims of illusion since the beginning of human society. And it is more than merely objective as well—that is, the whole range of power which comes into play when spirit and body are differentiated and no longer split cannot be merely a matter of molecules scurrying about. In other words, something real takes place to the extent that a person places his or her spiritual body more immediately in contact with the natural universe—and this real something can be limited to neither a bodily nor a mental process.

We must therefore postulate the presence of spirit in nature. This squares with our speculations about consciousness, in which we considered it an inherent property of the "beingness" of nature. It is hardly necessary to add that the precise relation is not to be fathomed so easily, if ever or at all. Yet many things have been known to be necessary before they were fully comprehended, from the curvature of space-time to viruses. So it will have to be, for now, with the grounding of spirit in nature. If spirit exists, and nature exists, then spirit is part of nature—and nature part of spirit. Our desiring flesh as the scene of spiritual events is fully part of nature: it is nature's infolding in our being. In the human form, nature achieved a mode of organization which permitted the concentration of spirit, and its self-realization in consciousness and history. Human being, then, is a dialectical conjuncture, whose inner tension is expressed in desire. Desire is no instinct, then, but the roiling of indwelling nature striving toward spirit. It follows that to liberate spirit, one must listen to desire, not as an end but as an indication of where liberation lies—a direction, it may be added, which encompasses the feeding, clothing, and housing of flesh, and provides flesh with clean water and air, medical care, and security against the blows dealt by nature in old age. Thus there is no spiritual liberation without material liberation. And we should extend this, as Buddhism reminds us, to a society which frees all sentient beings.

In sum, there is no inherent antagonism between spirit and flesh; when such antagonism occurs it must be regarded as a spiritual perversion and an aspect of historical domination. Desire in itself is not the culprit in this perversion, but a familiar kind of desire is. As to what that may be, consider the following from Meister Eckhart, one of the great spiritual geniuses of our civilization.

It is written: "You have become rich in all virtues" (1 Cor. 1:5). Truly that can never happen until first one has become poor in all things. Whoever wants to receive everything must also renounce everything. That is a fair bargain and an equal return, as I said a while ago. Therefore, because God wants to give us himself and all things as our own free possessions, so he wants to deprive us, utterly and completely, of all possessiveness. Yes, truly, God in no way wants us to possess even as much as I could hold in my eye. For none of the gifts he ever gave us, neither gifts of nature nor gifts of grace, did he give for any other reason than that he wishes us to have nothing that is our own; and he never gave anything as their own to his mother or to any man or to any creature in any way at all. And so that he may teach us and make us aware of this, he often takes away from us both earthly and spiritual possessions, for it should not be for us but for him alone to possess them as honors. But we ought to have everything as if it were loaned to us and not given, without any possessiveness, whether it be our bodies or our souls, our minds, powers, worldly goods or honors, friends, kinsmen, houses, lands, all things.[67]

The actual and ancient antagonist to spirit is not the part of nature known as flesh, but rather those parts of nature that are falsely claimed by desire and made part of Ego. I refer, in the spirit of Eckhart, to the common word, "possessions." It is possessions which constitute the true denial of spirit. But a possession has to be seen in a different context from the common usage of the phrase "private property." Otherwise we would be unable to differentiate between harmless pride in one's books or curios, and harmful pride which materializes in expropriated wealth. Possession in this sense is what Ego claims through a relation of domination—specifically, exploitation of the fruits of another's labor, along with the seizing of another's being, the denial to another of being, or of the expressive powers inherent to being. That is, possessions are the concretization of being-over. To possess exploitative wealth (or to be more exact, the means of production) certainly comes under the heading of being-over, but so does a possessive attitude toward flesh. It is this latter juncture which is the point of a spiritual critique of eroticism. For whether the body possessed is another's or one's own, to try to possess it is a denial of the self-subsisting being of that body, and a frustration of the desire for being.

The spiritual critique of eroticism is a critique of the fetishization of the erotic, of making sexuality an end in itself, in sum, of pornography and phallocentrism. It is a critique of a form of desire for being-over flesh, in Nietzschean and Sadean terms, a will to power over flesh, whether one's own or that of another. By the same reasoning such a critique does not demand asceticism. If a spiritually inclined person is, like Angelo Roncalli, so configured by historical and personal accident as to require an ascetic denial of flesh to fulfill his or her particular pathway, so be it. Given the dependence of spirit on the historical position of the self, however, there can be no universal prescription of this sort, and no need, therefore, for asexuality as a condition for spiritual development. Some great spiritual figures, Leo Tolstoy and Martin Luther King, Jr., for example, lived highly sexual lives. It is a bit foolish to say that if King had been as ascetic as the pope, he would have been even greater spiritually than he was. On the other hand, the sexuality of Tolstoy and King was compulsive and exploitative of women. Their sexual behavior was thoroughly unworthy of their spiritual ambitions—and they knew it and were tormented by the fact. Perhaps as a result of their torment some portion of desire became detached from flesh and moved in the direction of being. The pattern would be similar to that of Angelo Roncalli, who remained ascetic. But there is no necessary sequence here, given the plasticity of desire; and in any case, it is at the level of desire, and not of any particular sexual practice, that a spiritual struggle is waged.

The Plasma of Being

We have been led to the notion that spirit is part of nature, and would follow the track of this idea further. To do so we need return to the puzzling matter of consciousness and reflect some more on the interrelations between consciousness, nature, and being.

As Hegel says, consciousness and spirit are way stations on a path of being. But consciousness is also a mark of the separateness of beings, and self-consciousness is a reflection of radical separateness, which is to say that the individual is a freak of the universe. In the universe as a whole, there is no real separation between things; there are only, so far as the most advanced science can tell us, plasmatic quantum fields; one single, endlessly perturbed, endlessly becoming body.

The degree to which an illusion of individuality is sustained is correlative with the degree of consciousness possessed by a being. A being identical with all other beings (which is to say, no being at all), would have no consciousness of anything. Consciousness, therefore, has two aspects: it is the sensory registration of entities with varying qualities; and it is the manifestation of separateness itself, of the difference between a being and the universe.

It does no good to say that we are at one with nature, except to express an illusion which is comforting to desire, for we are not one with nature until we are dead and our substance rejoins the eternal flux of matter. Before that, we are human beings, whose distinctness from nature is expressed in the notion of production. We produce not simply to live, but to express our being. And by producing, we throw being forward in a process of active, conscious transformation of nature. Production for economic purposes is only a fraction of the whole of production for human being. Thus we have to eat to live, a quality we share with caterpillars and every other animal. But while the caterpillar directly takes a leaf into its body, transforms it further inside its organism, and rests with that; we cook our leaves, spice them up, decorate them, and mix them with other elements of the world *before* ingestion. We make salad—with a set of social relations which bring the entirety of history into the most mundane acts as well as the most spiritual.[68] The world is transformed anterior to incorporation into the body of human being; and because of this, cooking, and other practical, productive activity, become the constituents of new consciousness. From this angle, self-consciousness is not merely a mental property, but more essentially the result of a projection of human being into a world transformed by praxis.

And we also produce language. We assume that nature has granted us an inborn neural apparatus capable of generating language. But it is only when we *use* this, that is, when language is produced and expressed through the body as speech, that human being arises. And as we enter the realm of speech we both produce our consciousness and break with nature.[69]

By using language, the self sets itself off from nature. But the self does not only use language as an instrument; the self is constituted through language. Language is not outside the self; it is the way of being of the self. The self which the "I" signifies, and the signifier "I," grow and dwell together in human being. This however does not make them the same thing, for if the word-representation, or signifier, and the signified were the same, then human being would be perfectly transparent and present no problem to itself—which is a manifest absurdity, for whatever else is true about human being, it is clearly a profound problem to itself. The fact is, we are part of nature—and we are irrevocably outside nature. There is no way of evading the dialectical character of human reality forced upon us by this contradiction—or the spiritual path set into motion by the dialectic.

To leave the womb and begin life as a self-constituted human is to face separateness. Along with its instrumental purposes, speech is the effort to reclaim this distance by substituting words for lost things. For speech is fundamentally addressed to another, and connects the separated self to that other. Speech, like consciousness, fills the space between being and the world. One might say that speech is an inscription of consciousness, and the expression of that inscription for purposes of social being. The word names the Other; forms the Other as an object; presents and re-presents the object to being; and thus occupies the space between being and its Other. In this sense speech reconstitutes being. But the word also develops the powers and the separateness of a being. In this way speech can become a means of domination over the Other through logos, and a source of further estrangement from the ground of being.

Now if consciousness and language are produced, we may ask, from what? From the unconscious, it would seem, for the unconscious is the primary reality of the psyche.[70] But what is the unconscious? Of what does true psychic reality consist? The answer given by psychoanalysis has run along the following lines: the unconscious is a system of meanings without awareness. It contains thoughts under the influence of the instinctual drives and ordered according to the primary process. The thoughts are remnants of infantile experience, which have been driven back by repression. These thoughts press peremptorily toward discharge, but they are held back by a "countercathectic" wall of mental energy. Thus the unconscious can never be known; only its derivatives are knowable, as they become inhibited by the secondary process and enter the system of the "preconscious," those mental contents which are potentially conscious and can be verbalized. In sum, the unconscious is said to consist of dynamically charged ideas denied access to awareness.

It can readily be seen that this is a very difficult theoretical position to hold; and a brief reflection will convince us that another understanding of the unconscious is necessary if the entire notion is not to fall apart. The difficulties arise at two levels.

First, it is both unprovable and inherently contrary to psychoanalytic thinking to assume that the unconscious "contains" anything as recognizable as a discrete idea. Let us qualify this. No doubt there are "strata" of the unconscious which consist of repressed memories: the whole theory of dream interpretation, the understanding of slips of the tongue, neurotic symptoms, and much else depends on it. But to say that this layer of the unconscious is the whole entity is simply a kind of anthropomorphizing—a projection of what is familiar, namely, verbalizable thoughts, into what is radically different and strange. Indeed, by saying that the unconscious "contains" something, or that it consists of certain contents, is to objectivize it, to make the unconscious resemble an object in the external world. It is not that we cannot employ words to say something useful and descriptive about the unconscious. It is only that we have to recognize the limits of these words, and employ them in a much more subtle and differentiated way than is conveyed in phrases such as "a system of meanings outside awareness." If there are hidden meanings in the unconscious, they cannot be considered identical with the whole.

Second, the genesis of the unconscious is inexplicable according to these terms. If the unconscious consists of repressed ideas alone, then how did it get started? What was the first repressed idea? No doubt, a very archaic experience of infancy, perhaps of the intrauterine phase. Fine. But how can this be called an idea, when we are certain that the inner processes of this epoch are radically different from anything we experience, and prelinguistic to boot? Obviously, the unconscious, that most powerful and necessary construction of psychoanalytic thought, cannot be restricted to any set of verbalizable ideas, or fantasies. These must be present; they cannot, however, be the core of the unconscious, but rather something which stands between this core and preconscious thinking.

Freud recognized this. In the most important study of this bedrock of his theory, "The Unconscious," he asserted that the unconscious consists of "thing-presentations" (*Sachvorstellungen*), while what becomes conscious consists of thing-presentations plus "word-presentations" which have become linked to them.[71] This is clearly a much more satisfactory way of describing what is going on; the very opacity of the notion of thing-presentation serves to remind us that we are not dealing with ordinary verbalizable or objectifiable reality. For whatever a thing-presentation may be, it is not linguistic. It must be, rather, the dialectical precursor of the word—the "that which is not" becoming "that which is."

However, Freud never told us more about what "thing-presentations" may be; nor did he ever link the idea in a major way to the rest of his theory;[72] nor, finally, was anything substantial ever made of the notion by the Freudian tradition. Jacques Lacan surpassed the orthodox establishment in attempting to comprehend the unconscious. However he built his system out of the proposition that the unconscious is "structured like a language," thereby setting aside the non-linguistic implications of the thing-presentation. We are thus in the strange position of having a putatively scientific profession doing virtually nothing to investigate its most basic concept. An analogy would be for physics to pay no attention to the puzzle of subatomic structure, except to somehow continue thinking that the atom was a bunch of very small billiard balls circling another knot of balls.

The deficiency arises from staying on the familiar but isolated ground of psychology instead of confronting radically different onto-logical territory. Freud in his philosophically naive way was boldly venturing into such terrain with the notion of the thing-presentation. He was treading across ground declared closed by Kant, who held that we could not arrive at knowledge of "things-in-themselves," the noumenal world. At one level, Freud is confirming Kant, by claiming that propositional knowledge, which depends ultimately on speech acts and consciousness, is closed to the unconscious, and vice versa. However, he is also boldly challenging Kant, since Freud claims—and psychoanalysis would be empty without the claim—that the uncon-scious interacts with and plays a major role in determining conscious-ness and knowledge. The thing-presentation cannot be a "thing-in-itself" if the unconscious acts as a kind of force field influencing lan-guage and thought. This effect is seen in the upper layers (to resort reluctantly but necessarily to physical metaphors) of repressed fantasy and memory—the layers appropriable by psychoanalytic praxis, and which are considered by those who wish to rationalize Freud's discov-eries to be the full extent of the unconscious world. But as the saying goes, in for a penny, in for a pound: if we see repressed memory and fantasy—the "hidden meanings"—as intermediate formations, then there must be something they stand between: the phenomenal world on one side, the noumenal, thing-in-itself world of the unconscious on the other. Once we admit that this unconscious can deform language into the fantastic shapes disclosed by psychoanalysis, then we have ad-mitted into our chambers some idea of how the unconscious is, and what, if you will excuse the expression, it does. That is, the uncon-scious is such that this deformation comes about in language; it has the property of pulling language into itself and twisting it about, de-composing the word along the lines of the thing. Thus in contrast to Lacan, we would not say that the unconscious is structured like a lan-guage; but rather that it is that which comes before language, out of which language declares itself logos, and under the spell of which lan-guage becomes destructured, if not destroyed.

The beauty of Freud's notion of the id (*das es*, "it") now comes into view. For *it* is perhaps the best-suited word in the Indo-European lan-guages to suggest such a view of reality. *It* is the pronoun standing for the thing: any entity, without value, standing before being. *It* stands

for any-thing; and yet no-thing except that which is indicated, and always some-thing which surpasses the indicated. And yet this no-thing
which surpasses any verbal representation is also a living part of us, if
not yet as presence, then as prepresence.

It would seem now that to talk about "the unconscious" is not to
speak of any discrete entity in the world, but rather that out of which
language comes; and more, that out of which individuated being
comes. The unconscious is our indwelling presence of the such-ness,
the that-ness, the it-ness of reality. It is thus not right to shape our halt-
ing words in such a way that the unconscious comes out looking like
an object, or a system, with functioning, interrelatable elements. In
fact, it would seem that only mystical experience, with its primary, unmediated, nonverbal contact with such-ness, is adequate to encounter
the reality signified by the term "the unconscious." For now, still
working within the confines, but also within the wealth of connections, of a critical form of logos, we are reduced to saying that the unconscious seems more like a zone of becoming, a kind of place out of
which being emerges bearing language with itself. I do not want to see
the unconscious as someplace on a map of the mind, but rather that
out of which the map appears. To say the same somewhat differently,
the unconscious, in its fullness, is more than nonconscious, it is non-
psychological as well; or, from the standpoint of becoming, it is prepsychological. We think of it in psychological terms because our consciousness is shaped, by history, to think in this way. Therefore the
Egoic self projects its own kind of being into other realms. Driven by a
fear of aloneness, we want to recognize ourselves wherever we go, and
so project "psy-nature" in a kind of internal animism, not allowing
ourselves to realize that our being extends beyond language and representation, beyond behavior and mental processes. Thus a fine dialectical point: Freud's "true psychic reality" is not "psycho-logical" at
all. Nor, however, is Marx's "true reality" primarily social. Recall that
Marx said, in his *Sixth Thesis on Feuerbach,* that the "self is the ensemble of social relations." The proposition is both true and necessary.
But it is not sufficient, and it limits our view of human reality. This is
because the self is not sufficient, or primary. The self is that ensemble
of social relations which precipitates out of a primordium which
comes before social causation—a core which, crucially, remains active
throughout life. Before the self, there is being; and before being is
the unconscious primordium. Society intersects with the individual
through a set of cultural representations. It is a naming, a designation, an affixing from without. Without this naming, the stuff of a

person would never take form. But the unconscious, in its core, is prerepresentational.

To call attention to the radical nature of the unconscious, the fact that it is prepsychological, presocial, and preontological as well, I should like to call the unconscious the "plasma of being." By the unconscious, then, we mean the stuff out of which being comes. From the Greek root, *plessein*, we have "to mold" or "to spread out," (hence, plaster or plastic). Plasma itself refers to the sustaining medium in which cells are suspended; or in physics, to an ionized gas composed of the primary particles of matter. Hopefully this usage will call attention to certain characteristics of the unconscious, without burdening with too much literalism an entity which must always remain beyond the power of words to describe.

We need not grouse about the ineffability of the plasma of being, but should rather celebrate it. For it is the source, in nature, of the wish to be free. Even though we are, by "nature," social beings, there is something in each person which surpasses any kind of familial or social representation. No matter what the family or society tries to make of a person, no matter what molds a person is forced into, there is a core to human being which comes from elsewhere, and to which one must be true if one is to authentically fulfill one's nature. Psychoanalysis discloses the social roots of our psyche, by showing how family, society, and individual mutually inscribe one another. But psychoanalysis also discloses a zone beneath the root, in which this mutual inscription trails off into the void. Though we are never asocial, we are each at some point presocial; by which I mean that we come from a place before society, even if we are always directed toward society. Neither of these dimensions can exist without the other; together they define the dialectic which is the precondition of tragedy and freedom.[73]

The plasma is an alternative conceptualization to Freud's "instinctual drive" as a zone beyond civilization. It preserves the alterity of the unconscious, but deprives this of its conservative and conformist implications. Although psychoanalysis discloses a moral dimension of human being, it should give no comfort to the morality of the existing system—precisely because it shows how this system cannot reach all the way into being. Rather, the notion of a plasma of being opens onto the ground of a "higher," or at least an Other, law to challenge the law of the state.

Freud's unconscious viewed as a plasma of being and Heidegger's clearing of being share this: they are both figurative locations where being becomes and gathers itself. Moreover, Freud and Heidegger are both strongly critical of the extension of Cartesianism into psychology (a critique made with a great deal less self-consciousness by Freud than by Heidegger). Each, in other words, rejects the dualism between psyche and soma, and the categories of the unconscious and the clearing of being are essential for this. Nonetheless, there is a sharp difference between the two thinkers, even if the distinction is nowhere critically elaborated within their work. For Freud, the unconscious remains radically cut off from being; it has no presence at all, even though it exercises a determining influence. We might say that Freud remains a kind of Calvinist here: God is utterly beyond the human. Heidegger, on the other hand, is a kind of Lutheran, even a Catholic;[74] God is a voice which can be heard if one opens oneself to it. By the same token, Heidegger lacks a firm conception of negativity; the dialectic slides off the surface of his clearing. The idea that being can be self-deceptive, that the psyche can be built from a set of coherent lies, is foreign to him.[75] He was not, in the words of Paul Ricoeur, a "master of suspicion." Freud, along with Marx and Nietzsche, was.

In poststructuralist thought, the limits of language have been recognized, yet nothing has been seen beyond these limits, and indeed any presence beyond the text is denied. In a justifiable reaction to the violence associated with the metaphysical tradition, the notion of a transcendental signified—a reality beyond signification—has been refused. Thought thus turns even further in upon itself, and since it knows itself to be inadequate yet cannot let go of logos, it continually tears itself to shreds like a mythical beast. One major result has been the fixation upon the text. A powerful yet profoundly aimless technique of "deconstruction" emerges, spearheaded by Derrida, and perfectly tooled for the academy of postmodern society, in which it takes on the function of a varsity sport.[76]

I would argue that the retreat to the text is a classical and unwarranted retreat from the world, a new scholasticism. It is a denial of the reality of production (for logos is also the mode of academic production) and of the spiritual, desiring ontology which production expresses. No doubt this results from the defeat of emancipatory social movements, but it also perpetuates that defeat. It seems to me that the notion of the plasma of being, as an entity to account for the incapacity of language to find its center in being, is a way of refusing defeat without lapsing into the tyranny of logos. But in any case, I do not see how we can comprehend human existence without recognizing the reality of the plasma, even if it cannot be named and dissolves all naming. It is the precondition for our being: with no plasma of being, there would be no being at all, nor any possibility of emancipation. The notion offers a real ground for the constitution of a transcendent signified adequate for emancipation—one outside the bounds of logos yet within reason. What is transcendent occupies ontic terrain which is radically Other: it is that which is not. The way now lies before us for a view of deconstruction which is neither nihilistic nor academically trivial: one open to the text as the produced shard of being, yet open to the world as well.

The Relation of Desire to Being

We will be disappointed if we think too much has been gained by these verbal maneuvers. All we have accomplished has been to redirect attention and gain a better vantage point. If this can keep us from trivializing the problem of spirit, so much the better. But we should not be under the illusion that more than a proper orientation can be achieved.

A suggestive link to this orientation, however, may repay further examination. And this is the association of plasma with fluid, which reminds us that we all began in a fluid environment and refocuses us on nature. Before there was a discrete "I" which could form the notion of self and other persons, there was a proto-"I." And before this, there was a creature floating about in its mother's womb, in the plasma of amniotic fluid. At some point, this creature was not a being but part of another being, without boundaries, but wholly absorbed into another being. This leads us to ponder not when a human being begins, but *how,* and with what consequences. We are able therefore to expand the inquiry from an abstract conception of a plasma of being, an ontoplasm, if you will, to a more articulated conception of *ontogeny,* as the growth and development of being out of its plasma.

Meister Eckhart wrote, "If a man will work an inward work, he must pour all his powers into himself as into a corner of his soul, and must hide himself from all images and forms, and then he can work. Then he must come into a forgetting and into a not-knowing. He must be in a stillness and silence, where the Word may be heard. One cannot draw near to this word better than by stillness and silence: then it is heard and understood in utter ignorance. When one knows nothing, it is opened and revealed. Then we shall become aware of the Divine Ignorance, and our ignorance will be ennobled and adorned with supernatural knowledge. And when we simply keep ourselves receptive, we are more perfect than when at work." [77] The mystical traditions of the world religions may be said to have uncovered the "thingness" of the world. Freud's discovery—and it is the main source of the philosophical interest which has adhered to psychoanalysis—was to demonstrate this thingness in relation to desire, that is, as unnameable longing. We have observed that Freud differs from Heidegger in denying "presencing" to the unconscious. Where Heidegger speaks of the clearing of being, Freud's unconscious is mute, if powerful. It "speaks," however, in desire. Originally, for each individual, there was no difference between things; neither inner subjective world, nor outer objective world. The difference is created through praxis, and desire is the preverbal voice of praxis as it breaks loose from, then reapproaches the plasma of being. If we conceive of the unconscious plasma along the analogy of physics, as a kind of fluid of ionic particles—of words-as-things, prior to speech—then desire represents the coming together of those ionized words. It is praxis before speech, the foreground of speech.

The unconscious is not a static formation. It constitutes the emergence of world-being into individual being, and retains its core as long as the individual draws breath. However it is continually elaborated and enriched through praxis. Thus there are developmental levels within the unconscious plasma of being (which is where the layer of discrete, verbalizable fantasy may enter). These do not replace, but combine with each other, the later transforming and being transformed by the earlier. They may be crudely schematized as follows:

1. *No-thing:* world-being as such, the suchness of nature, prior to any differentiation of being. For the human we may regard this as that phase of being from the inception of the zygote to the emergence of nervous tissue sufficient to gather and concentrate experience. This epoch must be regarded as devoid of any practical capacity—and devoid of desire as well. Such experience as is acquired occurs wholly passively. Being is simply participated in, by virtue of belonging to nature (though even here, what the mother does affects the fetus).

2. *Thing + No-thing:* the registration of experience prior to any signifying capacity. We may hypothesize this mode as belonging to the later stages of fetal life, through parturition and the immediate postnatal period (perhaps up to three months of age). The being of the individual is already separable from maternal being, though not viably so. Therefore, practically speaking, being remains entirely attached. However, we may infer the existence of consciousness, which implies some differentiation within being into "inner" and "outer"; i.e., being which pertains to itself and being which belongs to the Other. This development emerges without any evidence of differentiation within

consciousness. That is, there is consciousness but no self-consciousness. We would regard this stage as the archaeology of praxis—a proto-praxis carried out before the presence of any conscious guidance or self-reflective capacity. And it is part of the archaeology of desire as well, when desire cannot discriminate between subject and object. In psychoanalytic parlance, we would call this the stage of "primary narcissism," and it is the stage recovered in the oceanic experience.

3. *Word-thing* + *Thing* + *No-thing:* In infancy the child enters the world of cultural codes, as its own capacity for speech matures. In this stage, being is suffused with language, both from the coding imposed by others and the child's own exploratory babbling. This language is not, however, experienced as speech, i.e., as the distinctive expression of human being. Words are therefore experienced as another kind of thing. The child enters the human, signified world bearing all the marks of nature. At this point we would postulate a recognizably human form of consciousness and a gradually developing self-consciousness. It is quite obvious that humans at this prelanguage stage are capable of a kind of discriminating desire in which objects are constituted as distinct and separate beings; here, too, the infant is capable of praxis—conscious and purposive transforming activity. Observation of any healthy six-month-old infant will settle this question. Indeed, a practical capacity must be regarded as necessary for the acquisition of language. Thus praxis has to come before speech, both ontologically and ontogenetically, though the form of speech known as *poesis* reaches to this level where words are things.

4. *Word* + *Word-thing* + *Thing* + *No-thing:* Finally and gradually, beginning generally in the second year of life, the child develops speech, and speech becomes the dominant mode of praxis, until the capacity for logos is attained. This would, broadly speaking, be signified by the emergence of a developed mental structure with an articulated self-consciousness, and a corresponding level of desire. Education, science and law, politics, economics, and "theo-logical" religion—all the appurtenances of civilization enter the range of human possibilities. However, at no time is the archaic substratum of the unconscious, as No-thing and Thing, surpassed. Such would be quite inconceivable for us as living beings.

5. *Spirit:* the gathering and transcendence of the above, once a developed being experiences the contradictions of desire and realizes its futility. In terms of the above, spirit represents the direction of self-consciousness, guided by the desire for being, toward the growth of soul. We shall return to this theme in our final chapter.

A developmental sequence is postulated here within ontogeny: first, being as such, emergent from world-being; then, praxis and rudimentary consciousness; and finally, speech as differentiated human being. Speech, though a quintessential human property, is therefore a third-order phenomenon of being.

Within this framework, desire is called upon to settle two unbearable contradictions, which are at bottom, however, one: that we are part of nature, yet other than nature; and that our being is separate, yet the universe from which it comes is a unified whole. Desire is the abolition of these contradictions, while spirit is their transcendence. Desire affirms that speech, our otherness from nature, is in fact part of nature; and it affirms that we exist both independently and attached, that we are ourselves and yet are one with the being from which we have separated. Being here means both our own prior states of being, and other individual beings from whom we have come. Desire is aligned then to the past, which it tries to recapture in the present for the sake of the future. Desire is temporalizing, and, as Hegel and then Marx recognize, places us as the historical animal. And yet desire is the condition of each of us before we enter the historical arena. In this respect, desire is at bottom, in all instances, for the mother. And yet it is also for the plasmatic precursor that was ours before any differentiation was conceivable. By overcoming desire through a spiritual praxis, we return in life to that precursor. In this sense, the spiritual body is indeed the resurrected body, because it has once again glimpsed its source.

5.
Divine Spirit

In the beginning was the Word, and the Word was with God, and the Word was God. He was in the beginning with God; all things were made through him, and without him was not anything made that was made. In him was life, and the life was the light of men, the light shines in the darkness, and the darkness has not overcome it.

John 1:1–5 (RSV)

The Search for Ultimate Being, or, On God-Building

When I was a boy we were taught through a saccharine text in Hebrew School that although there were a great many religions, there could only be one god. Indeed, the multifarious nature of the human religious impulse proved that "man" was everywhere reaching for the same thing, even if men could not agree on just what this was—and (though this was not a point dwelt upon in the text) had on many occasions over the centuries slaughtered one another as a way of settling their disagreement.

The text also assumed that the transhistorical striving humans show toward godhead meant that the object of that search was a one god. That is, since looking for god is a common feature of humankind, there must be a common and singular god who was looked for, a god, moreover, who was a discrete being somewhere up above us. In fact, this one god began to look remarkably like Yahweh, God of the Hebrews. Now Yahweh has been one of the most influential gods of human history, for the simple reason that He represents the first sustained notion of monotheism. In this respect Yahweh was a giant leap forward, and the remarkable history of the Jewish people is unthinkable without Him, as is, indeed, Christianity and even Islam. But the god Yahweh had other features as well which have remained attached to the notion of monotheism. For a singular god always teeters on the edge of being a particularistic god. And in the case of Yahweh, the god-builders of the Hebrews went over that edge with the claim that He made the Jews His Chosen People. This claim, however, creates severe difficulties.

It is certain that all the mysteries surrounding the notion of God will never be cleared up, but some of them are accessible to proof. This is not because they are about God, but because they are about propositions made by human beings about God, and propositions have to pass the test of logic: niggling things such as *a* not being the same as *not-a,* and so forth. In this respect, if a group of human beings says that there is one god and that "He" is their own God, that is, more the God of the Jews than of the non-Jews, then they are not speaking truly about God. For the proposition must imply one of two things: either that all human beings have an equal right and access to God, in which case other groups will have their Gods, so that Yahweh is not monotheistic, but only one god among many—or, on the other hand, that there is something essentially wrong with non-Jews to have been denied God's favor. The first point contradicts the monotheistic basis of Judeo-Christianity. And the second contradicts the emphasis Judaism places on moral development; indeed it is unworthy of the moral greatness of the Jewish people. Surely a deity such as Yahweh who is made to stand for the moral development of humankind would not choose one people over another—and certainly not a people guilty of such exceptionalism. The same contradiction haunts the religion of Judaism as besets the state of Israel, which claims the universal spiritual principles of democracy yet restricts them to one people. Hence the proposition that Yahweh is the one god is manifestly untrue.[1]

I think the same could be said for the singular God advanced by any particular religion, whether couched in the moral eschatology characteristic of ancient Israel or not. This does not mean that there is no God, or Ultimate Being; it only means that such a Being, whatever its existence, will be supremely difficult to talk about. Once, indeed, we let slip a personal pronoun: "He," or in less frequent usage, "She"—the game is already up. To speak of God as He is to repeat the particularization of the Old Testament, making males into the Chosen People. Indeed, the very idea that God made "Man" in His own image, or Woman in Hers, is not much relieved by claiming that God made Man and Woman in Its image. Aside from the recurrent logical difficulties posed here (is God therefore hermaphroditic? If not, and God is an It, can an It have any sexual distinction? Considering that God has no sexual distinction, should humans abandon sexual dimorphism?)

there is the nagging question posed by making the Chosen People . . . people. What gives us the right to claim our species as the model taken by God? If we consider spiritual pride a sin, then is this not sinfulness, too? It does not degrade the wonders of human being to recognize that we are only one evolutionary line of the universe—one, moreover, whose terrible pride and egocentrism may terminate the whole experiment. But if we destroy ourselves and our civilization, will not the universe keep on going? Will the galaxies even blink at the spectacle?

A critique of god-talk[2] is not a verbal game, but an exposure of the gaming inherent in language, and language's radical incapacity to name any conceivable Ultimate Being.[3] It is a reminder of the prison house which is language, whose words draw down, delimit, and necessarily narrow the possibilities of being.

To Ludwig Feuerbach must go the credit for first developing the insight that what we call "God" is a projection into the heavens of our unfulfilled being on earth.[4] Marx and Freud (the latter seemingly unawares) both followed in the path of Feuerbach, which has become the standard modern interpretation of God-building. The God of state-free agriculturalists is the Spirit who lives in and through the life-giving elements; the God of the Tribes of Yahweh dispensed justice according to their struggle for self-determination; the God of the subjugated is a delivering and redeeming Messiah; the God of expanding Islam is a warrior, and so forth.

Feuerbach's line of reasoning has often been used to disprove the existence of God entirely. But all Feuerbach does is to unmask the essential human contribution to the idea of Ultimate Being. A Feuerbachian critique tells us that the predicates to the proposition "God is _____" are inextricably deformed by the partial and contingent position of the person who makes the statement. Thus Feuerbach merely offers a critique of the necessary anthropomorphism which enters into any kind of God-building.

God cannot be any particular Other, because one person's Other is not another's. An agriculturalist living in a small classless and communal society will not be interested in salvation by God-as-Messiah; and a ghettoized and victimized people living in the midst of a complex urban civilization will have no interest in a universal nature-spirit. Some have tried to solve this problem by calling Ultimate Being the "Absolute Other," that is, the Other which encompasses all forms of Otherness. However, the notion of an Absolute Other leads nowhere, because insofar as Ultimate Being remains Other, it also remains part of us. Thus we are unable to give any positive properties of God that are not also properties of ourselves, and since we are finite and historically contingent while God is by definition infinite and not dependent upon any other being, God cannot be described. The predicate in the sentence "God is ____" must be left blank.

Ultimate Being is, finally, "un-predicate-able." No description can quite grasp its existence, simply because all descriptions come from humans who must remain to a degree separated from Ultimate Being. Perhaps the most extreme and consistent statement of this principle comes from Christian thought of the sixth century:

> Again, as we climb higher we say this. It is not soul or mind, nor does it possess imagination, conviction, speech or understanding. Nor is it speech, per se, understanding per se. It cannot be spoken of and it cannot be grasped by understanding. It is not number or order, greatness or smallness, equality or inequality, similarity or dissimilarity. It is not immovable, moving or at rest. It has no power, it is not power, nor is it light. It does not live nor is it life. It is not a substance, nor is it eternity or time. It cannot be grasped by the understanding since it is neither knowledge nor truth. It is not kingship. It is not wisdom. It is neither one nor oneness, divinity nor goodness. Nor is it a spirit, in the sense in which we understand that term. It is not sonship or fatherhood and it is nothing known to us or to any other being. It falls neither within the predicate of nonbeing nor of being. Existing beings do not know it as it actually is and it does not know them as they are. There is no speaking of it, nor name nor knowledge of it. Darkness and light, error and truth—it is none of these. It is beyond assertion and denial. We make assertions and denials of what is next to it, but never of it, for it is both beyond every assertion, being the perfect and unique cause of all things, and by virtue of its preeminently simple and absolute nature, free of every limitation, beyond every limitation; it is also beyond every denial.[5]

Pseudo-Dionysius, the author of this remarkable passage (the "pseudo" derives from the fact that his life is shrouded in obscurity), is known as a "negative" theologian, and we can see why. For according to his conception, only total negation, the complete emptying-out of language, can express the characteristics of godhead.

The fact that the predicate of the sentence "God is ____" may be unspecifiable does not erase its verb. Indeed, there is no conceivable Feuerbachian, Marxist, Freudian critique, nor any other critique of the existence of God which can positively eliminate the being, or "is-ness" of God. This curious situation does not apply only to God's being. We use the verb "to be" all the time and cannot say, really, what it means.

This realization spurred the philosophy of Martin Heidegger. However great a philosopher Heidegger may have been, it is fair to say that his treatment of being failed to erase the ineluctable darkness at the center of the notion.[6] And yet we still speak of being or is-ness, though our words cannot penetrate to the heart of being. In this respect, we assert there is being without being able to assert what being may be; and what we can do for being in general, we can do for Ultimate Being, the being of all beings.

The existence of God can neither be proven nor disproven, because proof and disproof are exercises in logos, the human attempt to master reality through language, and God surpasses logos. Nevertheless, though the existence of God cannot be settled one way or another, propositional statements about God can be evaluated—as by denying the validity of the claim that Yahweh was the one god and also the God for the Jews. On a more general plane, we are able to say that any notion of God which asserts a providence in individual lives is not a true notion of God—for the simple reason that such a creature looks rather too much like the father in the sky about whom Sigmund Freud wrote in *Future of an Illusion*. The notion of a directly provident God who rewards good and punishes evil also runs up against the problem of theodicy,[7] that is, the relation of God to the evil of the world. For it has been well objected that a God who would intervene directly, say, as an answer to prayer, is a very busy as well as omnipotent God, in which instance one may ask further, why would He, She, or It allow misfortune and evil to come into the world in the first place?

Indeed, the whole idea of monotheism is dubious. The notion of one god is thought of as a high point in human development, the final breaking by "man" of his primitive chains, and his emergence into the light of universalizing reason. But this idea, as a predicate of God and a projection of "man," has always been stained with domination—that is, incomplete being. The God of Pharaoh Akheneton, after all, was a projection of empire and the state; and the God of Moses was suffused with jealousy and the need to eliminate all rivals. To posit God as a being, that is, a singular entity, means that "He" (for the masculine pronominal address is forced upon us by this maneuver) must stand over others—and Otherness. In this sense, the Hebraic claim that they were the Chosen People of Yahweh is quite consistent with monotheism itself. "Theo-logy" is inevitably brought into this struggle as its intellectual arm, and a further instrument of exclusion and domination. Monotheism, in short, never escapes Ego and its splitting. In this respect, monotheism is not so much of an advance over polytheism after all. Or we might say that all theisms are equally suspect so long as they posit individualized gods.

We could pursue this discourse for some length, covering ground that has been worked over endlessly down through the ages as one person or another has wrestled with the mystery of Ultimate Being. However, we choose to break it off instead. For there is an offshoot to the enquiry that may be particularly intriguing to follow.

It is curious that while it is impossible to prove or disprove the "isness" of Ultimate Being, and while all predicates about God are to a degree false because they only describe humans and not God, we still find ourselves asserting with a sense of validity that predicate *a* is closer to the way God is than predicate *b*.[8] In other words, though all statements about the nature of God are more or less untrue, it seems possible to say which are more untrue and which are less untrue. This must mean, however, that there is some notion of Ultimate Being which is valid, even if this notion surpasses the understanding and can never be precisely detailed, nor, of course, have anthropomorphic qualities. To offer a critique is to limit logos but not to deny it. After all, if we were to flatly deny logos, there would be no point in saying anything. This would be a violation of human nature, for we are fated to speak, even without words. Simeon Stylites, the mute who sat upon a pillar for many years, went very far in denying logos, but certainly kept on saying quite a bit, in his way.

Ultimate Being as Asymptote

Let us recur to a sentence in the recently quoted passage of Pseudo-Dionysius describing negative theology: "We make assertions and denials of what is next to it, but never of it, for it is . . . beyond every assertion." Here, even in the most radical assertion ever made of the indescribability of Ultimate Being, some quality remains, namely, that of a "next to it." It seems then that though Ultimate Being possesses nothing in itself, yet it has some kind of "locatability." But how can there be something which surpasses any descriptive statement such as location, yet provides the possibility of contiguity, which implies location?

A notion from mathematics may help here. Since Pythagoras, who introduced the notion of the music of the spheres to Greece in the sixth century before Christ, the purely formal relations of mathematics have been recognized as expressing a kind of homology with the spirit.[9] We cannot say exactly why this is so, except to suggest that by expressing a harmony with the eternal and universal, mathematics transcends the contingent and narrow boundaries of the self. In any case, it seems that the kind of god-building we have been undertaking can be expressed in an elementary mathematical gesture, namely the inverse function, $y = 1/x$. If we plot the graph of this function with values of x from zero to infinity, we observe that y varies inversely from infinity to zero:

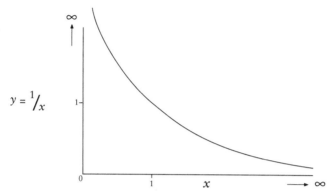

Note the infinitesimal character of this relationship, for y never reaches zero for any real x, but only if x is infinity. That is, for any countable number x, no matter how small, there is a y which is correspondingly large, and vice versa. Yet the end of the graph, being infinite, can never be drawn. The line of the graph reaches as close to the axis as one wants, yet never reaches the axis. Such is the asymptote. It allows us to think about infinity, although it does not represent infinity, which is not directly representable.

In the same way, it seems to me, the spiritual mind can accept some such modeling to predicate the un-predicate-able, Ultimate Being. This means that God can be talked about and approached, without ever being reached in thought or practice. The direction in which Ultimate Being exists can be determined, even if the endpoint of that direction— the unity of the graph with its axis—can never be attained by any act of consciousness or praxis. However, a direction is what praxis needs, a sense that a given path is the way to go, and not another. We can say then that spirituality can be directed toward Ultimate Being; and that the way we determine spiritual adequacy is fidelity to the path by which spirit approaches God asymptotically.

If this is so, then a considerable amount has been achieved, even if the ambitions of particular religions to attain a full logos are disabled. Nietzsche's famous aphorism, "God is dead!" no longer has the sting with which it demolished the metaphysical pretensions of the nineteenth century, for we can see that God was never alive in the first place, except as an idea. Nor need we say, as postmodern philosophy and criticism has said, that there are no transcendental signifieds, no truth behind the surface of a text. There is no Truth as the Word of a dominant authority, but there is truth revealed in the motion—now haphazard and seemingly unconscious, now patient, now "inspired" with flashes of power and insight—toward Ultimate Being.

The "death of God" is not the denial of Ultimate Being, but only of that conception of God which directly extends human propensities and characteristics into the heavens. In other words, Nietzsche killed off the theistic God who was worshipped as a separate and special being. And to this I would say, good riddance!—because such a God has been an essential feature of the splitting and spiritual pride which have dogged history. As bitter a blow as it must be to narcissism, we are better off entirely without an Ultimate Being[10] who is dedicated to the advancement of any one of us, either as individuals or nations. It may gall one to no longer have a God who is there to bless one's own side in war, or justify whatever form of domination happens to be in fashion. But we should celebrate the demystification and hasten the demise of this crude, brutal, and superannuated idol. Its influence still unhappily abounds—in the late Ayatollah Khomeini's brand of Islam, in Shamir's Zionism, and in the crusading Protestantism of American ideology. I think we could even recognize It in the fascist meditations on Being of Martin Heidegger. Such a God is not the omega point of history. He is Moloch, the Old Testament deity who demanded bloody sacrifice of the young. If there is a "challenge to the modern age," to advert to one of those embarassingly lofty barbarisms which dog the discourse of spirituality, it is to recapture a notion of divinity no longer tied to the projections of monotheism, yet adequate to the present condition of spirit. But this notion is already present in the direction of the asymptote.

The Living God

> *Jesus answered him, "Truly, truly, I say to you, unless one is born anew, he cannot see the kingdom of God." Nicodemus said to him, "How can a man be born when he is old? Can he enter a second time into his mother's womb and be born?" Jesus answered, "Truly, truly, I say to you, unless one is born of water and the Spirit, he cannot enter the kingdom of God. That which is born of the flesh is flesh, and that which is born of the Spirit is spirit. Do not marvel that I said to you, 'you must be born anew.' The wind blows where it wills, and you hear the sound*

of it, but you do not know whence it comes or whither it goes; so it is with every one who is born of the Spirit."

John 3:3–8 (RSV)

Ultimate Being defined abstractly as the asymptote of a graph is no consolation. Unless it can be shown that the "God-without-predicates" is a living God, a God mobilized in human existence, then there is not much good in the notion of Ultimate Being. A purely abstract God might as well be dead—for the representations of it in the mind are devoid of all spiritual power. And an utterly remote God, like the God of Kafka's hopelessly aspiring creatures, is as good as dead also. One might as well go with the purely "psycho-logical" incentives of the age of despiritualization as invoke so pale a shadow. The theistic gods all had one unworthy quality or another, but they were also capable of drawing forth and integrating spiritual energies. They provided, in their limited way, a real anchoring point for morality; and when they were gone, Dostoevsky and others were correctly able to intuit that a moral order had gone with them, leaving the way open for nihilism. It is not at all clear that Ultimate Being without predicate can restore the balance and harmony of historically earlier spiritual epochs. But it can only begin to do so if it is a living God and not a dim lodestar.

The asymptotic character of Ultimate Being tells us only that God cannot be predicated. It is an abstraction from the nature of this being, which in itself is anything but abstract. If we move away from the mathematization of God and toward living experience, we find that what the formula $y = 1/x$ stands for is a relationship already given in this text and which can be rephrased here as follows: spirit (y) is the dialectical overcoming of the self ($1/x$) and its opening toward being through the Other. Here all our previous reflections, on spirit-power, spirit-being, spiritual authenticity and spiritual desire, are focused and drawn together toward a single point—a point nowhere given in any logos or perception, but indicated by the "toward which" inherent in spirituality. We may call this point God, though we have no need to say that "it" should care for us even if our imperfect spiritual being is such that we are led to project ourselves forward into its nonbeing, and clothe it in various kinds of raiment depending upon the historical location of the self and its prevailing illusions. But we can say that it is no illusion to call this nonpredicatable God a living God, because those spiritual moments in which the self is overcome and the soul is expressed are manifestly the most intense points of life.

We may employ this God-point as though it were a North towards which a compass points, or the star chosen by sailors for navigation. But we do not do so directly, since this Ultimate Being is rather more like a black hole than a perceptible star, and we cannot see it at all. But we do sense its presence according to the spirituality which guides us toward it. That is, we know that we are heading in the right direction when we become more spiritually alive, when spiritual practice evokes within us the greatest degree of spiritual resonance—that is to say, when spirituality expands in practice. In this sense, the notion of Ultimate Being invoked here is that of a living God. We know that we are reaching beyond ourself most fully when we live most fully the life within ourself and with others, and directly, sensuously experience its coming-to-be. There may be no question of attaining the omega point, or even of knowing what is to be attained. But there is every opportunity to live spiritually, to engage consciously in the dialectic of spirit-becoming.

A more valid idea of God, then, is one corresponding to a fuller spirituality. But what does this mean in practice? Spirituality is too diverse, too contingent upon history, and too poised over nonbeing, for there to be any kind of formulaic answer as to what constitutes its fullness. But though there may be no formula, there are traditions, paths worn by practice in the rocks of history, in which the notion of Ultimate Being has become channelized. We may consider some of the better-known of these traditions.

The God of Nonattachment and the God of Love

> *For God so loved the world that he gave his only Son, that whoever believes in him should not perish but have eternal life. For God sent the Son into the world, not to condemn the world, but that the world might be saved through him.*
>
> John 3:16–17 (RSV)

> *So therefore let us pray to God that we may be free of "God," and that we may apprehend and rejoice in that everlasting truth in which the highest angel and the fly and the soul are equal— there where I was established, where I wanted what I was and was what I wanted. So I say, if a man is to become poor in his will, he must want and desire as little as he wanted and desired when he did not exist. And in this way a man is poor who wants nothing.*
>
> Meister Eckhart, *Sermon 52*

> *The men of old, their knowledge had arrived at something: at what had it arrived? There were some who thought there had not yet begun to be things—the utmost, the exhaustive, there is no more to add. The next thought there were things but that there had not yet begun to be borders. The next thought there were borders to them but there had not yet begun to be 'That's it, that's not.' The lighting up of 'That's it, that's not' is the reason why the Way is flawed. The reason why the Way is flawed is the reason why love becomes complete. Is anything really complete or flawed? Or is nothing really complete or flawed?*
>
> Chuang-Tzu, *The Seven Inner Chapters*

Here are three classical passages of spiritual thought. Each mobilizes spirit-power, spirit-being, and spiritual desire in an authentic synthesis. Observe, however, that they seem to go off in different directions, if not to openly contradict one another.

The Gospel of John expresses *agape*, the core of the Christian tradition, namely, that God sends an unconditional love to redeem those who believe in Jesus. However, the Taoist sage and the Christian mystic each offer visions of spirituality that seemingly deny the main features of the Gospel. Chuang-Tzu would not give love such a singular place; he sees love rather as a derivative of an already-fallen age. Eckhart meanwhile denies the primacy of God, seeing it as an idea deriving from the separated ego and needing to be overcome. It is safe to say that had Chuang-Tzu the opportunity to reflect upon Judeo-Christian God-building, he would have come to a similar conclusion about God. In fact, he might have disagreed with Eckhart as well, for being excessively attached to the desire for transcendence. Perhaps the key sentences in the Taoist text are the last two, playfully mocking the notions of being "complete" or "flawed"—and with them, the whole mania for progress, the whole insistence upon a *telos,* or eschatology, or positing of final things, which obsesses the historical Western world, Christian, Marxist, and capitalist alike. In this gentle and humorous reminder of the folly of all God-building and progress can be seen the whole of the Oriental philosophy of nonattachment, including Zen Buddhism, which has caught the tormented imagination of the West in these days of the declining pull of traditional ideologies and the rise of the New Age spiritual movements. Indeed, the ideologies which have guided Western history all seem to be in an advanced and irreparable state of decay. Christianity is profoundly splintered and out of touch with modernity; socialism has collapsed as an economic alternative and has been betrayed by too many of its exponents; while capitalism, the standing survivor, is spiritually cancerous and ecocidal. Thus countless numbers of people in countless ways have wearied and grown disillusioned with the axial notions that have driven the West for two millennia. To this profoundly disenchanted yet spiritually hungry sensibility the Oriental sages appear as godsends—even if they deny that there is a god to send anything.[11]

I think there is a common "spirit" to the great Eastern traditions of Taoism and the various schools of Buddhism[12] (with important contributions from Hinduism, Jainism, etc.),[13] despite the many distinctions between these systems of belief. Chuang-Tzu, in his spirit of nonattachment, is a major representative of this.[14] Yet we may still wonder whether this great and gentle demystifier was himself entirely free from the wheel of logos—or whether Taoism, indeed any philosophy of egolessness, still remains bound to logos. For if the Taoist sages do not actually engage in God-building, they are not without their godhead, namely, the Tao ("the Way") itself. Now the Tao is certainly no discrete being, and does not stand over any other in domination.[15] In this sense it seems to me an advance beyond monotheism. But though the Tao indicates emptiness, it is not an empty construct, as the spirit of Pseudo-Dionysius demanded for propositions concerning Ultimate Being. I think this is a good thing, as Pseudo-Dionysius's extreme strictures as to the conception of Ultimate Being leave us nowhere to go. In this respect, the Tao is such a way of going; indeed, it is most commonly translated as "the Way." Yet a "way" which is posited as better than other ways constitutes a demand, however gentle and nonviolent. After all, the sage is *telling us* to be spontaneous. His self-mockery differentiates logos, but does not release him from logos. Nor does the notion of a path convey all of what the Tao signifies. For the Tao is both a possible kind of conduct and a primordial reality of the world.

Moreover, it is a human reality. I think we can give the passage from Chuang-Tzu an interpretation which connects it to the development of persons. The "ancients" in his text can be read not only as the "persons of long ago," but also as the "long ago of persons." The Tao here becomes a statement about the plasma of being, the ground of the unconscious, referring to an "age" when we each were at one with the substance of another, had no individual being, and therefore had the knowledge which "thought there had not yet begun to be things," much less "borders," between things; that is to say, words and judgments of discriminating value.

The *Tao Teh Ching,* the other great text of Taoism, offers many glimpses of the Tao as a kind of plasma of being emergent from a nameless absolute, or Ultimate Being:

> The Tao is like an empty bowl,
> Which in being used can never be filled up.
> Fathomless, it seems to be the origin of all things.
> It blunts all sharp edges,
> It unties all tangles,
> It harmonizes all lights,
> It unites the world into one whole.
> Hidden in the deeps,
> Yet it seems to exist for ever.
> I do not know whose child it is;
> It seems to be the common ancestor of all, the father of things.[16]

The Tao may be read as a narrative of the growth of the self, its relation to desire, and the longing for nonbeing which lies at the ends of desire. But Chuang-Tzu does more than remind us of this—he valorizes it. One does not read Chuang-Tzu, Lao-Tzu, or any of the great Zen thinkers who drew from them as a way of getting an objective account of the growth of the "mind" from its primordial Egolessness to its Egoic state. That is the province of psychology monographs. Nor do we read the Taoist narrative of the growth of the self to bring the mind back to the Ego-established reality of toil and domination.

A Taoist text is to be read, rather, to direct spirituality to its Way, playfully and spontaneously, because of the practical conviction that life is better lived by the Tao. That was the intention of the sage himself. For Chuang-Tzu, the master of nonattachment, is paradoxically attached to at least one thing: the Tao, that is, attached to nonattachment. Chuang-Tzu knows this—which is why he and the other Taoist and Zen sages are so full of wry humor and self-mockery. But knowing it does not get them off the wheel, on which they are placed by the simple fact of being human beings who have to contend with desire and the limits of language as long as they draw breath.

We have used three kinds of terms, whose signifieds share the common properties of being beyond description and spiritually associated: the plasma of being, the Tao, and Ultimate Being. Are they not different kinds of words—precipitates of logos in different circumstances, yet circling about one thing? The plasma of being, which we infer from the psychoanalytic reflection into subjectivity, can never be a direct object for the senses or conscious thought, any more than a black hole, which is deduced from astrophysical reflection, can be an object for the senses. Nor does the notion of the plasma seem to contain any sense of a path, or "way of being;" thus it lacks the third sense of spirit, that of authentic being. The Tao, on the other hand, is an orientation deduced spiritually from the nature of human existence. Hence it combines a prescriptive statement—this is the way one should be—with a substantive statement—this is the way things are. The Tao is also a statement about Ultimate Being as well as the plasma of being, for it claims the asymptote in its bottomlessness. Putting the above together we arrive at the notion that Ultimate Being should include that entity, or property of the universe, necessary for the plasma of being to be in us. It is what comes before the self, and from which language and the self arise. And the plasma of being itself is the world-being within us. It is also "nature" within us, if nature be read free of the bondage imposed upon it by logos. Thus right conduct—Tao—inheres in maintaining contact with the plasma.

Still, this may seem like cold porridge, given the impenetrability of the plasma of being and the un-predicate-able nature of Ultimate Being. After all, "nature" in this respect is only the "suchness" of reality, radically removed from the petty narcissism of the self. And indeed the vision of the Tao offers no guaranteed reward, nor any particular spiritual path. It claims, rather, that spirituality has to be made anew, and can never be taken as found, nor can its fruits ever be exactly predicted. But this is anything but cold or lifeless, for it places God within us as the presence of the universe manifesting itself, if we can but learn to listen. And more, the Tao places spirit and matter on the same plane of being, for there is no differentiation between subject and object on the level of plasma of being.

There is a beauty to the Tao, a kind of perennial tug which has lifted spirit from the ancient days of the Chinese sages to those of Thomas Merton, who felt Chuang-Tzu to be "my own kind of person." [17] With the collapse of traditional Western notions of spirituality, the sayings of Lao-Tzu, Chuang-Tzu, and the great Buddhist masters seem very close to the eternal wisdom.

The essence of this Eastern spirituality is receptivity to being, sought through a discipline which releases Ego into a state of receptive awareness and silence. We may roughly sum this up as meditative practice. This is passive in one sense only, namely, in its rejection of the Egoic attitude of being-over. However it would be as wrong to characterize meditative practice as psychologically passive as it would be to regard nonviolent politics as passive. For the soul which results is, for all its calmness, characterized by a clarity and activity not given to grasping, striving Ego. This silence begins to put the quietus to illusory logos; and as desire and logos are conquered the plasma of being can be heard.[18] Desire attaches the self to objects in the world, and desire generates time as an element of experience. Subjectively, time is compounded from memory and anticipation, both functions of desire. The spirituality of nonattachment tends to annul desire by getting beneath desire, and cuts the strands by which desire holds the self to objects. To the extent this is done—and there seems to be no limit short of death up to which a virtuoso of nonattachment can go—objectlessness and Egolessness are achieved together, and with them, an overcoming of temporality itself. A state of fusion is achieved, which, although never complete, pushes differentiation of the self toward its limit. This oneness with world-being is given many names, which would be distracting to enunciate at present. But among them we should include oneness with the plasma of being. And insofar as the plasma of being constitutes our bridge to Ultimate Being, it would seem that this form of spirituality has authentic value: it is, at this level, a "full spirituality."

However there is more to spirituality than this; and things are not so simple at the practical level. The plasma of being is not in itself a bridge to Ultimate Being, but only as it is materially expressed in the relations of history. The plasma of being belongs to our existence from the time anterior to individuated being, and we only approach it as individuated beings of a particular culture and epoch. To be precise, spiritualities are dialectical negations of the self as it moves toward being; and in this relationship the omega point, whether we construe it as plasma of being or the Tao, never stands completely outside the self, but is always mediated by the fact that the self remains "an ensemble of social relations." The various elements of spirituality are not to be regarded as mere raw fuel lying about to be chucked into the furnaces of spirit. Spirituality always inheres in the concrete transformation of a real self in a real world. In practice, therefore, the ideal of the Tao cannot be used to simply bypass the self; and Taoist spirituality must always contain features of that self and its darker "second nature."

Thus different ages of the world provide different forms of spirit. We should not forget that the great religions of nonattachment are all flowers of feudal society, and reflect, sometimes nostalgically, its organic character. There is much to be reclaimed in the communality of feudal society, but much which we do not accept either, because spirit itself, as it has evolved over time, introduced new modes of being elaborated around an ideal of freedom which does not pertain to the feudal worldview. As the following passage from the *Tao Teh Ching* reminds us, the actual application of the Tao included sustaining a social practice which spirit has long since overcome:

> From of old there are not lacking things that have attained Oneness.
> The sky attained Oneness and became clear;
> The earth attained Oneness and became calm;
> The spirits attained Oneness and became charged with mystical
>   powers;
> The fountains attained Oneness and became full;
> The ten thousand creatures attained Oneness and became
>   reproductive;
> Barons and princes attained Oneness and became sovereign rulers of
>   the world.
> All of them are what they are by virtue of Oneness.[19]

The "spirit" of the *Tao Teh Ching* is certainly nonauthoritarian, but its humility and gentleness germinated within a rigidly hierarchical system; indeed, Chuang-Tzu was a minor official in an immense imperial bureaucracy. Obviously, this needn't contaminate a modern-day practitioner of Taoist spirituality, but it is not irrelevant, either. To practice the Way one must live a certain way, and not just release the mind. Within the frame of feudal society, the Way, with its spontaneity, emerges as a precise dialectical counterpoint to the established order. Indeed, it had an immediately emancipatory content, and was used as such by the Taoists against the formalistic Confucians. Within late capitalist consumer society, on the other hand, with its youth cults and commodity fetishism, notions such as the Tao are eminently colonizable by dominant interests. How many T-shirts and pop psychology books have "Tao" written upon them? Indeed, there is even a Tao of investment, and, I am sure, a "Tao-Jones average" somewhere. This might be amusing, but one may doubt whether the *Tao Teh Ching* was composed to facilitate the accumulation of capital.

Paths of withdrawal from the world to pursue some imagined spontaneity or inwardness—up to and including immersion in a monastery for Eastern religion[20]—are similarly ambiguous. Fundamentally this is because the spiritualities of nonattachment are caught in a particular historical present when withdrawal from the world is tantamount to abandoning the earth to destruction and injustice. The global society of today cannot be treated as if it were the feudal society of Chuang-Tzu. Thus Taoist or Zen spirituality today has a radically new valence from its original nature, when it was a productive element of society.[21] This does not make it valueless—it only means that the Tao has to be mediated with the historical moment.

The Tao, then, is not eternal wisdom, because no wisdom is eternal. It is as it says, no less but also no more than a way of being, a way of noninterference and spontaneity. Therefore the Tao cannot choose a path for the expression of being. According to the path, the Tao can turn into a narrow bourgeois indulgence or expand into a sublime and transformative praxis. To repeat, this is not to downplay the notion of the Tao, which comes as close as anything ever devised by the human spirit to express an orientation toward Ultimate Being. It is only to insist that the Tao must be found anew, and in the world.

Another path in the direction of Ultimate Being traverses the spiritual horizon: the God of Love, epitomized in the famous Johannine passage, "For God so loved the world that he gave his only Son, that whoever believes in him should not perish but have eternal life." Chuang-Tzu was, I think, right when he wrote that the Way becomes flawed as love becomes complete. For love is the fate of a separated being who wanders according to desire. Love is for that reason never far removed from hate, and the great religion of love, Christianity, has been the religion through which the most concentrated hate and persecution have been inflicted upon the world.

We have said that love is the attitude taken toward the object which gratifies desire. In this sense, love is dependent on the vicissitudes of desire and may be called psychological. But there is also a non-psychological notion, a kind of love which stands above desire as a force which moves the universe, the universal attraction of all beings for each other, as in the closing lines of the *Divine Comedy:* "To the high fantasy here power failed; but already my desire and will were rolled—even as a wheel that moveth equally—by the Love that moves the sun and other stars." [22] Here Dante subordinates desire to love as a cosmic force which draws the purified soul to God like a spiritual gravity. God to the Christian has evolved beyond the form of Yahweh to become that which generates the love which draws all being to itself. This notion arose from feudal relations as surely as the harmonies of the Tao—but it expresses a different spiritual motif, in which being has passed beyond the plasma of being, to the level of word and thing. The being subject to Christian love is in the world, and must define itself in relation to the world to find its source. Its trajectory is still toward Ultimate Being, but as if from a different range on the spiritual asymptote. In the spirituality of love, the function of desire cannot be abolished, because desire is already polarized by love's cosmic field. The Christian thus finds nonattachment at the outer edges of his or her faith, defined by a contemplative mysticism which is a tradition within, but not the center of, the religion.

Therefore, rather than extinguish desire, as does Taoism, Christianity directly engages desire, seeking, through acts of spiritual purification, to transmute it into love. This places Christianity in the way of second nature, with its internalized domination. The effort to build a religion of love leaves the Christian faith peculiarly prone to hateful perversion, but also peculiarly fitted to the actualities of history, in a way that the great Eastern faiths tend to bypass. Christianity therefore has been, of all religions, the most actively historical, its only close competitor being Islam. The Buddha could indicate a path of infinite acceptance and compassion; while Jesus brought "not peace but a sword." This is not to be interpreted as the sword of militarism, of "Onward Christian Soldiers." That belongs to Christianity's tenure as a state religion. The sword of Christ is what cuts through, what does not accept, and transforms in order to transcend. The sword of Christ is desire turned to love, which in the practice of Christianity became differentiated into two forms, that of Eros and that of *agape*.[23] Eros was Christianity's inheritance from the Greeks, and remains, for example, the dominant form of love in the Dantean universe. Agape, on the other hand, represents Christianity's unique contribution.

Originating outside of Christianity, Eros does not remain confined to Christianity, but reappears in settings as anti-Christian as Freud's metaphysics. In essence Eros has the twofold property of reciprocity and value. It is the love which brings one being to another according to the qualities of the beloved. Thus erotic attraction is mediated by sexual traits, and expects sexual love in return. Hegel modeled his notion of desire after Eros, where Eros is love according to the attraction of the object: thus desire is for the desire of the other. This fixation upon the object allows Eros to be drawn on by capitalism, taken away from spiritual paths, and fetishized according to the laws of accumulation. Thus Eros, being grounded in self-centered desire, is pervertible. In genuine religious and spiritual experience, Eros remains the love for God, or nature, expressed as a desire that the object, God or nature, will be a good object, i.e., answering one's prayers, providing favorable weather, etc.

Agape, by contrast, is unreciprocable love. It upsets the orderly procession of Hegel's Spirit, and has no place in Freud except as a neurotic distortion of narcissism.[24] It is not pervertible, although it can be very readily made to vanish. Agape is the experience of a love coming bountifully from God, without any conditions attached. To merit this love one has only to be a believer, and open one's heart to Jesus. The genius of the Christian faith has been to devise liturgical means, for example, the Communion in which the believer incorporates the body of Christ, which permit the experience of agape to happen. But whatever these means, the phenomenology is the same: an overpowering feeling of being loved. In agape, spirit-power and spirit-being are as fully realized as in any moment of mystical illumination. It is, we might say, Otto's idea of the holy, experienced as desire coming from the beyond. R. M. Bucke's cosmic consciousness, noted in Chapter One, is a good example. So strong is this emotion that believers will gladly give their lives for it, and it stands at the emotional center of all that Christianity has meant.

Such an experience is highly abnormal, indeed a rupture with the patterns of ordinary desiring being. In agape, one feels the joy of being loved without the ache of an Egocentric desire. The believer desires, but from the center of an emptied self, spirit or soul from which Ego has been abnegated. The self has become nothing, the Other, everything. The emptiness of nonbeing is like a vacuum in the soul, into which the love from God floods.

This remarkable occurrence is made possible for the Christian by the belief in Jesus as the redeemer—the Lamb of God in whose blood sin is washed away. Psychoanalysis has an explanation for this at the level of the self. It ascribes the phenomenon to an overcoming of the superego through an identification of the self with the Son of God, and the diversion thereby of the guilt which had prevented feeling worthy of love. The agency of Christ thus allows the soul-building work of conscience to go forward without Egoic destructiveness. The hatred which afflicts Ego is put aside; and as it is hatred which produces splitting, Ego is allowed, so to speak, to wither away. What was superego in the ego psychology of Freud is now, because of agape, the power of the Holy Spirit. Thus the Christian (I speak now of the individual who has either avoided falling into, or successfully extricated the self from, the abyss—may we call it Hell?—of second nature) achieves soul and the opening toward being. Now one's own love can be felt—not coming from the self but from the Other. And since the Other is the shadow side of the self, we might say that in agape a person expresses love without having to know it. The very "beyondness" of the deity[25] ensures that the origins of love in the self are kept obscure. By this means, the painful vulnerability that comes from loving is no longer a problem, because the object has been established, by an act of radical belief, as wholly good and trustworthy. And the belief is reinforced by its blissful inner consequences—the overcoming of separateness.

So much is "psycho-logically" true. And yet the psychodynamics of agape cannot account for the wonder of the phenomenon itself. Christianity, like any religion, has adapted a set of symbolic practices which makes possible the generation, expression, and expansion of spirit. But the astounding influx of spirit-power and spirit-being which characterizes the moment of agape remains as a fact of existence. One does not have to accept the literal reality of the myth which brings this variety of the holy into being (though it is virtually incontrovertible that there was a historical Jesus). But it seems to me that one's vision of the universe is tremendously foreshortened if the experience itself is not seen as integral to reality.

Now just as we decided that Ultimate Being had to be such that the plasma of being could exist, so must Ultimate Being be configured so that agape can take place. These ends of spiritual reality are not split and separate, but differentiated. Love is that condition when, through the union with another being, subject and object are rejoined within the individual. In this coming together, being experiences its plasmatic core—and receives spirit-power as a result. Through union with the beloved, the separateness of being is reconciled with its origin. All love involves a flowing between self and Other; but in the love of God, precisely because its object has been displaced from any particular other to Ultimate Being, the source of the Other is also recognized as the plasma of being: God within, the living God.

Since the plasma of being belongs to nature, the force of love has a material reality. Love is in nature—not manifestly, but immanently— and it is the evolution of spirit itself which can bring love into historical being. Christian spirituality brilliantly succeeds in concentrating this and extracting love from nature. Hence its great power, not built on illusion so much as the transforming of existence under unfolding historical conditions. Notably, we see this in the emergence of nonviolence, first manifested in Jesus and the early Christians, then inhibited when Christianity became a state religion, until it reappeared in Quakerism.[26]

Christianity employs desire, because desire is what organisms of our degree of ontological complexity have at our disposal to reach toward being. Yet desire is pervertible through its misshaping by domination into the forms of second nature. And the religion of love has been stained with domination, beginning with Paul and reaching full force when Rome adopted Christ as the God of empire. Then Christianity became perverted: the religion of nonviolence became the bearer of bloody crusades, violent persecution and hatred of the body; and Christian love turned into submission—the love of the slave for its chains.

Centuries of complicity in state power and repressiveness have so misshapen Christian institutions as to make the continued presence of love seem miraculous. And yet the religion which burnt witches and expelled Jews also produced Saints Teresa and John of the Cross; the religion whose flaming sword helped lay waste continents for imperialism gave us Quaker nonviolence, Simone Weil, and Dorothy Day; and the religion which produces the repressive John Paul II and scoundrels like Jim Bakker also has produced a John XXIII and the hosts of saintlike figures, mostly anonymous, who have labored and sacrificed on behalf of the poor in that great transformation known as liberation theology. While Jimmy Swaggart hopped about the globe blessing apartheid and every dictator he could find, while Pat Robertson gave benediction to the terrorist contras in Nicaragua, and while the born-again mass-murdering President of Guatemala, General Efrain Rios Montt, practiced genocide in the name of Jesus on the Indians of that tormented land,[27] other Christians struggled in the authentic spirit of Jesus, to bring "good tidings to the poor." Many have died, but many more continue, throughout Latin America and wherever Christianity and class struggle come together.[28]

The struggle over liberation theology is perhaps the most crucial matter now at issue in world religion. Predictably, the doctrine is under heavy attack from an entrenched church hierarchy, abetted by the centers of wealth and power. Liberation theology's success in recapturing the soul of the church is at this writing quite doubtful, given the campaign of the present pope and the overall retreat of revolution. To the extent that liberation theology diminishes, so will Christianity's last chance to authentically capture the soul of modernity. It will not be the death knell for organized religion, to be sure, but it will render religion irrelevant for the spiritual development of humanity.

But however it turns out for liberation theology, the struggle for the spiritual realization of our species will continue. This is not something which goes along one line only, nor in any kind of linear progress, but across multiple fronts, as humans struggle to pick themselves up from history and second nature and rejoin Ultimate Being. In this sense, spirituality is as much cultural diffusion and interpenetration as it is a political struggle. Nor has nonviolence ever been limited to its Christian manifestation.

In the course of this process, different spiritual lines will intersect and interact, as have liberation theology and Marxism; or ecology and New Age spirituality; or feminism and nonviolence. There is no formula which can encompass the concrete particulars of these encounters. But there is, I think, a general asymptotic motion of the spirit, fidelity to which can guide spiritual paths. It was given as well by Meister Eckhart as any, in the quotation offered above, which stands as a kind of dialectical synthesis between the nonattachment of the Taoist and the agape of traditional Christianity. I reproduce it here: "So therefore let us pray to God that we may be free of 'God,' and that we may apprehend and rejoice in that everlasting truth in which the highest angel and the fly and the soul are equal—there where I was established, where I wanted what I was and was what I wanted. So I say, if a man is to become poor in his will, he must want and desire as little as he wanted and desired when he did not exist. And in this way a man is poor who wants nothing."

Eckhart's spirituality, being Christian, should be spoken of as "detachment" rather than "nonattachment." The distinction is between a taking away, and a not having in the first place, and its basis is twofold: first, it proceeds from and negates a desiring which is more sharply inscribed in Christian than Taoist texts (due, one might speculate, to the higher degree of sexual repressiveness in Christianity); and second, it remains more otherworldly than the Zen tradition, which always delights in immediate reality. In any case, Eckhart's detachment bids us overcome not just desire as such, but even the desire for God.

This may be read as a call for utter withdrawal from the world. However, for reasons offered already, I find such a course of spiritual action utterly self-contradictory and ultimately antispiritual. Because spirit is in material nature, and we are in history, spiritual action is historical, nature-transforming action. But what kind of action? I see Eckhart as setting out the asymptotic point, the azimuth toward which spirituality must aspire. And because it sees through logos, the namer of God, Eckhart sees through any particular dogma or church, or political line or party, as the exclusive arbiter of spirit (which is essentially why he was anathematized).[29] Yet he does say this, that there is an "everlasting truth in which the highest angel and the fly and the soul are equal." There must be some such point insofar as spirit ascends toward Ultimate Being. It follows then that those spiritualities are truer which act so as to move closer toward this goal, groping as they go through the maze of historical inertia and false consciousness; using what they can and discarding what moves the search backward. I do not know of any foreseeable world in which angels, flies, and souls would be equal. But I feel reasonably certain that a world in which human beings are equal and live in loving respect for nature—in other words, a world beyond domination—is along the asymptotic curve toward Ultimate Being. And I feel therefore that Eckhart's call for detachment—like that of Buddha, Lao-Tzu, and Christ—is most of all a call for radical transcendence of domination. I do not mean a passive contemplation, for that would be empty navel-watching which would only reproduce the system of domination. True detachment is not withdrawal, but active differentiation, in which a demand is placed upon society to bring it into line with the spiritual needs of the earth. It involves contemplation, but actively, as critique, a moving back and forth from within to without, knowledge which flows from doing and leads to more doing. This is an act of love as well as of detachment. It asks the most radical giving of self, the most naked impoverishment, the utmost commitment to those in whom nonbeing has been located, those "who are not." And it brings new being into existence, through a rupture with what was. To cite another spiritual authority, "At the risk of seeming ridiculous, let me say that the true revolutionary is guided by a great feeling of love. It is impossible to think of a genuine revolutionary lacking this quality. Perhaps it is one of the great dramas of the leader that he must combine a passionate spirit with a cold intelligence and make painful decisions without contracting a muscle. Our vanguard revolutionaries must idealize this love of the people, the most sacred cause, and make it one and indivisible."[30]

Well, nor do I wish to seem ridiculous by mentioning in the same breath a veritable communist with the sublimest of Christian mystics, especially in these days, when all sensible people are supposed to trample even the memory of revolution. But it seems to me also that these lines of Che Guevara indicate with painful honesty what is, in our present unfolding of world-spirit, the path of genuine detachment toward the equality of the highest angel and the fly and the soul. For the spirit of agape is incomplete unless it tells what is to be done with the bounty of God's love. The full soul must, so to speak, metabolize love lest it return to narcissism and Ego. Love should not be spilled in some New Age indulgence, returning to the bosom of an annihilating society and restoring Ego in the flight from Ego. Its spiritual place is rather with the suffering sentient beings to whom the Buddha first called our attention—except that the intelligence should also differentiate between suffering from human and natural causes, and pay special attention to the former, for this is the furnace of spirit. Thus the agape one receives from the divine spirit and source of all being needs to be utilized: practically transformed through outward turning and a non-Egoic identification of soul with Christ, which seeks those others who have become Other. In so doing soul embarks upon the riskiest of its adventures, one despised and feared by the whole world of power, and with only the most dubious of outcomes. In short, the perfect opening for spirit.

6.
Paths of Soul

On Being Spiritual

And now we see—through its refractions into power, Otherness, authenticity, desire, and Ultimate Being—what spirit is: No-thing in itself; rather, the relatedness, the coming together of separated elements of being—of nature through the organic body; of language through the self, or psychological body; of history through the social body. Thus biology is true; psychology and psychoanalysis are true; economics and sociology are true. But they are more true, more conscious, more directed toward Ultimate Being, when they come together spiritually.[1]

But what does this mean for the practice of life? Or from another angle, what is the life of the mode of the self taken by spirit: "soul"? There can be no formula for soul—because there is no absolute, universal spirit, nor an absolute, universal self. Yet the term *soul* persists in everyday speech, and for reason. If spirit is a journey, conditioned by its starting point and without a prescribed end—then soul is the traveler and spirituality is the way of travel. If two people were to travel toward Los Angeles, for example, one from New York, and the other from Mexico City, and if it were impossible to reach Los Angeles, then their journeys would be greatly different from each other, in fact, might traverse no points in common. So it is with spirituality, which involves the motion of the self toward being, where selves differ at least as much as cities. And for spirituality, there is no map to the destination, nor knowledge of how long the road may be. To paraphrase Marx, we make spirituality; not as we choose, but rather according to the history into which we have been thrown. And we make history as we make spirituality. Still, there are broad types of spiritual development, as there are routes to Los Angeles from New York, and different routes from Mexico City.

Spirituality is *the practice of spirit*—the conscious, goal-directed activity which brings spirit and soul into being. I say conscious and goal-directed because these qualities are what makes raw activity into practice, or praxis. All activity has some degree of spiritual potential. Some acts open up the self and are inherently spiritual, or at least prespiritual: one thinks here of climbing a mountain, making love, or listening to music.[2] Others tend to keep the self closed and are inherently unspiritual: reading the newspaper, working in an office or on an assembly line. Others are ambiguous, for example, riding in a car or sitting on the toilet. (Lest we ignore this humble activity, recall that Luther achieved some of his spiritual breakthroughs while defecating.)[3] But everything human is open to spirituality. Religions sacralize the tasks of everyday life, as in the traditional Jewish conduct of the Sabbath meal; and revolutionary movements also prescribe everyday tasks of the party in the spiritual movement of the revolution.

Spirituality responds to spirit, but also produces spirit. Wherever a state of being open to spirit occurs, spiritual desire can seize it and, through spiritual practice, create spirit as a new form of relationship. Spirit so produced will then become the basis for the next occasion of spirituality, and so on. This is a way to account for the extraordinary array of spiritualities, and their vastly different values.

Just as natural selection leads to the evolution of species, so does "spiritual selection" mediate spiritual evolution. But spiritual evolution is also history. Spiritualities that succeed bind together a historical project and ensure its survival. A successful spirituality must ensure material development, group cohesion, and cultural continuity, and provide a practical basis for individual spiritual experience. Each viable religion does this; but so do the spiritualities or potential spiritualities of the modern age—revolutionary political movements, schools of psychotherapy, and New Age spiritualities, to mention a few—which have abandoned the traditional religious emphasis on a divine spirit, liturgy, prayer, and otherworldly rewards. The survival of secular spiritualities, like that of traditional religions, depends upon their ability to adapt to and transform reality so that continuing spiritual development can take place.

At the level of the individual, these grand abstractions come down to the simple and existential truth of choosing one's life. This is not the same as choosing a new pair of shoes, for in order to find a new life, the old one will have to be given up. Desire will become detached from its previous objects and find new ones, including being itself. In the process, all the violence hidden by Ego may be summoned up, like all the demons of traditional lore. In short, a spiritual transformation is an existential crisis, and must involve a rejection of the given world.[4] The rejections themselves come in a thousand shapes and forms, depending upon what the self has to leave behind. In the differentiated worldview of state-free peoples, self and Other freely intermingle. Hence the fluid interchanges of shamanistic spirituality, which are less a rejection of the external world than of moving back and forth between the external and internal worlds. For us, for whom the "world is too much with us," to be spiritual requires a sharper sense of rejection.

Spirit has to be made; and the making is spirituality. Like any craft, spirituality is done a certain way; certain skills, such as meditation and prayer, are essential to many spiritual pathways, and have to be done well if the pathway is to be traversed. This is not, however, primarily a matter of technique. The bookstores are full of "how-to" works of spirit, many of which defy parody. Spiritual praxis requires technique, but surpasses technique in the same way that an artist is more than a technician.[5]

Praxes are situated in a historical place, and synthesized from a number of elementary factors. In the practice of spirituality, we might think of these factors as follows: what parts of the world are suitable for rejection; the social matrix of the spirituality, i.e., institutions, leaders, fellow-seekers; the kinds of cultural narratives available to make spirituality intelligible, i.e., to provide spirit with a logos: the makeup of the self, especially its balance of Egoic and soul forms; and the character of Otherness.

The spirituality which results cannot be identified with any of its elements, any more than a work of art can be reduced to the medium with which the artist works, or the artist's social background, traditions, economic position, etc. On the other hand, we know that each factor greatly shapes the artwork and gives it a kind of identity. So it is with spirituality. To call these "factors" does not make them irreducible elements, since each is a function of all the others, but the idea may help in understanding how the great range of spiritualities takes shape. To choose two illustrative examples, it is obvious that the spiritual life of a peasant in El Salvador will be different from that of a systems analyst who works for an aerospace company in Southern California. It might be helpful to spell this out hypothetically in the two cases.

A Spirituality of El Salvador

Let us think of the Salvadoran peasant as a man who ekes out a bare subsistence living on a tiny plot and is forced to sell his labor to support his family on land which has been expropriated by the coffee baron. For him, the "world" is centered about the direct production of the means of existence, and distorted by brutal and overt oppression and domination. Thus he does not own enough land for the immediate production of life, and is forced to labor under cruel and inhuman conditions for months of the year for the man who does own the land. The world to be rejected, then, is the world of exploitation and hunger—of immense violence, both physical and to his human spirit.

But it is also rejected in the name of something—that is, of a kind of plentitude which is violated. This is represented in an organic village community, stemming from deep Mayan roots, in which the peasant and his large and close-knit family share; and it also appears through a contact with nature which is, relatively speaking, direct and unmediated. On this foundation the world of exploitation becomes rejectable through common understanding that the social order is not only unjust, but also, and crucially, not the only possible one. For this, however, there has to have been an active tradition of revolt and struggle against the conditions of exploitation. Absent such a revolutionizing tradition, spiritual life tends to remain organized by the religion of the master class, which traditionally steers spirit toward an otherworld radically split from this one, a heaven and hell in which the social relations of earth are reproduced strictly according to the terms of the masters: punishment for the "sins" of rebelliousness, reward for humility and self-abasement. This rejecting tradition appears as a coherent set of alternative narratives. These narratives might stem from a number of sources, including pre-Columbian native legends, which preserve a moment outside the social order put in place by the Spanish conquest—a space within which resistance can grow; the many passages in the Bible which commemorate and inspire the struggles of the oppressed; the modern revolutionary traditions, especially Marxism, which ground this spirit in a material analysis of the society that is exploiting the peasantry; and for the Salvadoran peasant, all of these themes are drawn together in the more than half-century history of his people's struggle, under the aegis of Farabundo Marti's Communist Party, and now the FDR-FMLN (Democratic Revolutionary Front-Farabundo Marti National Liberation Front).

Praxis weaves these various strands into a strong fabric which sustains the revolutionary project of the peasantry. By any coherent definition of spirituality, this is a very spiritual thing to do, because it breaks with the given and redefines the self in relation to the world. In addition, a revolutionary struggle involves inspiration, a surge of spirit-power. For this power to be completely realized, a genuine spiritualization may take place as well. Spirituality in this context may or may not be religious, depending in large measure on which side religion takes in the struggle. If religion, in this case Roman Catholicism, succeeds in aligning itself through liberation theology with the peasant's aspirations for a better life, then he tends to accept it without a sense of contradiction. The interweaving of religious and political threads of logos makes the product that much stronger.[6]

One notable example of this interweaving was the great Nicaraguan liberator, Cesar Augusto Sandino, who has inspired the revolutionary struggles of an entire subcontinent. Sandino's background—his father a well-to-do landowner, his mother a poor prostitute—put into his life the contradictions of his people's collective history, allowing personal and collective transformation to occupy common ground. After some years drifting about and accumulating both a little nest egg and experience of the world, Sandino returned to Nicaragua to struggle against the United States' occupation of his country. His refusal to yield or compromise; his taking to the mountains of northern Nicaragua where for years he and his irregular band of guerrillas so harassed the United States Marines that they finally withdrew from the country in 1933; his subsequent martyrdom and resurrection many years later—all this is the stuff of legend. Less well known has been the actual content of Sandino's thinking, which, as the following example shows, was explicitly spiritual in an apocalyptic and utopian vein. Heavily influenced by Zoroastrianism and theosophy, and in many respects anti-Christian as well as anti-Marxist (the latter a conflict which estranged Sandino from Farabundo Marti), Sandino wove his revolutionizing spirit in such a way that both Christians and Marxists could eventually find space under his banner.[7] "By the Final Judgment of the World should be understood the destruction of unjustice on earth and the reign of the Spirit of Light and Truth, i.e., Love. You must also have heard that this twentieth century, the century of Light, is the epoch in which was prophesied the Final Judgment of the World. What will happen is the following. The oppressed peoples will break the chains of humiliation with which the imperialists of the earth have tried to keep us subjugated. The trumpets that will be heard will be the bugles of war intoning the hymn of liberty of the oppressed peoples against the injustice of the oppressors. The only thing that will be submerged forever is injustice; what will remain is the kingdom of perfection or Love with Divine Justice, her favorite daughter." [8]

To the sophisticated urban reader Sandino's manifesto may seem like gnostic ranting, or mere rhetoric. However, it has a resonance with the lived history of the colonized and dominated indigenous people of Latin America. More, it stands outside of the traditional mythologies by means of which that experience had been safely canalized. Thus Sandino mobilizes desire—as rage, as utopian longing— and through his radical reformulation of myth, orients desire transcendentally and opens the self to a new way of being. This would remain rhetoric were it not backed up by a willingness to give one's life in the cause, by military shrewdness, by egalitarianism; in short, by all that constitutes a practical grasp on reality. Combined with these, the manifesto comprises a synthesis—entirely new and entirely derivative at the same time. It becomes the spiritual arm of a coherent, embodied praxis. This should be contrasted, on the one hand, with a purely materialistic creed, and on the other, with the logos of the traditional religions of other-worldly submission. Each of these alternatives splits history from spirit, and can therefore allow neither to advance. An exclusively materialistic creed—one focusing, say, exclusively on redistribution of land—simply denies the spiritual dimension. No doubt such a program, if carried through, would transform the basic structures of society. However, this is a very big "if," and the absence of a spiritual dimension more or less ensures that the program will not be carried through: it will remain abstract or become co-optable. From the other side, traditional religion also splits history and spirit by positing an eternal world of spirit, or an afterlife, with no organic connection to this world or life. The split-off world cannot be recognized, or prefigured in the given world. It is beyond the range of soul. Therefore the real aspirations of people—for land, bread, a decent life free from terror, and ultimately for some control over their being and the power to express this—are set aside, or turned over to charities. The logos of Sandino, by contrast, became the model for an actual revolutionary movement.

It is important to face up to the fact that spirituality in this instance entailed violence, but did not cease to be spiritual for that. This does not make the violence exercised by Sandino in his campaign—or the Sandinistas thirty years later, or the FMLN today—good. Similarly, the violence exercised by the black soldiers in the Civil War, as represented in the recent film, *Glory,* was not good, although anyone who saw the film would have trouble denying that a spiritual process was taking place according to the criteria we have outlined here. Nonviolence is always more spiritual than violence, but all spiritualities are incomplete, and consist in a form of motion. The question is, what is the concrete relation of violence to that motion? Within the situation which spirituality addresses, so much violence may have sedimented— as was surely the case for our slave system, and has been the case for the regimes installed in Central America—that no motion at all may be possible without the expenditure of violence. And no motion means death—spiritual before corporeal, though for oppressed peoples the two go together. Practically speaking, the issue is whether one prefers life to death. If the answer is life, then one may have to risk violence in the aspiration for a less violent order. The violence risked is never good, but its evil may be either tragic or nihilistic, depending upon its opening to further being, as against its closure of being. Indeed, if the violence of struggle opens to further being and a less violent order, then it becomes a movement away from the existing violence, hence a kind of nonviolence, imperfect and tragic as this may be. I do not think this is playing with words.

For this kind of inspiration to occur, however, its message must fall upon ears capable of hearing and responding. That is, soul must be awaiting its call. Sometimes such people—to return to the instance of the peasant—may seem to us simple and even superstitious, believing in "spirits" and the occult. One such Salvadoran—a worker rather than a peasant, but very much in contact with the peasantry—is Miguel Mármol,[9] a living (as of 1989) reminder of the revolutionary tenacity of the Salvadoran people. A founder of the Salvadoran Communist Party, shot by a firing squad and left for dead in the infamous *matanza* ("massacre") of 1932 in which 30,000 peasants and workers were slaughtered, and a main force in the revolutionary movement of his people for sixty years, Mármol succeeds in being both an extremely tough-minded communist and a deeply spiritual man who combines Mayan roots and the Christian ideal of love. Mármol rejects God, but believes in spirits, and recognizes the revolutionary struggle as the fulfillment of spirit. His life is a reminder that spiritual greatness has nothing to do with the absence of contradictions, but with the direction in which contradictions are overcome.

There is no word other than *soul* to convey the openness to being evinced by the peoples engaged in these struggles. We in the "advanced" centers of the world may squirm at this word as a romantic anachronism—but as we do, we should look to our own distorting despiritualization. In any case, the tremendous tenacity of the resistance in the face of a cruel repression backed by the United States, the eternal upwelling of hope, the remarkable cheerfulness, the faithfulness to the goal, the lack of a crippling vengefulness—all these matters of record about the Central American revolutionary movements (and other peasant revolutions) [10] speak to the point. Such qualities of soul emerge from a communal family-cultural-religious matrix, and are annealed by a history of suffering, poverty, and the dignity which comes from fidelity to spirit. On this basis revolutionary struggle becomes an unfolding of spirit, and people become willing to die in order to be free.

A Spirituality of Southern California as Practiced by a Systems Analyst

Although it does not recognize itself as such, the affluent technocrats comprise a recognizable class. Though we often derisively refer to them as "yuppies," it would be better for our purposes to think of them as the *New Class*, that is, the class defined by an allegiance to modernity made possible by control of technical means of power. Hence our imaginary subject becomes a member of the central industrial force of late capitalism, that devoted to information. There is no pejorative implication in the term *New Class* as there is in the term *yuppie*. Like everyone else, members of the New Class have been thrown into history, and are free to transcend it or not. [11] The New Class is not the whole of the United States, to say the least. [12] It is, however, on the cutting edge of the New Age spiritual movements, and home to a spiritually restless fraction of the population.

The term *New Age spirituality* is an extraordinarily vague one, but it conveys well enough the mélange of spiritual-therapeutic movements widely influential in modern American life and adopted by the New Class. One does not see inner city blacks taking up the New Age banner, nor coal miners, nor wheat farmers in Kansas—nor, to be sure, peasants in El Salvador. For here all the elements of spirituality are radically different from those obtaining in El Salvador; and so our hypothetical systems analyst will have a radically different spirituality.

Let's assume the subject here is a thirty-year-old woman, a graduate of the University of California, highly gifted, skilled, and conscientious, and the well-recompensed employee of a large aerospace corporation, just as University of California graduates are supposed to be. She is remarkably trim and fit—the kind of attractive yet no-nonsense person depicted in the computer ads which appear in airline seat-back magazines. Thus we can say readily that the analyst is in a very different place from the Salvadoran peasant. Her self is quite of another type, and so is her world. While the latter lives in a tightly articulated extended family and community, the systems analyst lives alone. She has, and enjoys, relationships, but having been bruised in love, deliberately stays clear of entangling attachments. This essential solitude is accepted as the best lot available, given a fear of the devouring possessiveness characteristic of "serious" relationships in our society; but it leaves her with an abiding inner sense of aloneness. For such a person, "psychology" will be "ego psychology," as Egoic being is the grain of life.

These tendencies are rooted in a whole way of being. To say that it is urban, as opposed to rural, only begins to suggest the distinction with the life of the peasant. This is no mere "lifestyle," but an entire way of appropriating reality—including, decisively, work. The hypothetical systems analyst may be working for the company that makes helicopters for the Salvadoran military; but even if she is a dentist, or an accountant, or a schoolteacher, or a psychoanalyst, she is working within and helping to reproduce a system which itself stands to the Salvadoran peasant as the Hegelian Master to Slave. Our society is an immense machine constructed to extract wealth from the earth through unlimited economic penetration. Its raw materials extend to nature (viewed as "resources"), other societies, culture, and critically, the selves of individual persons. The machine works by controlling, through various kinds of ideology, the consciousness of those who comprise its cogs. And one singular feature of the ideology of advanced capitalism is to deny that the system has any ideology. Thus American people are indoctrinated to believe that American society imposes no systematic structuring of belief. Such is said to be the nefarious operation of communist, totalitarian, and "unfree" societies; while our side has a "free" press, "open" institutions, etc. Thus everyone is "free" also to choose her or his own being. The only thing one is not free to do is to challenge the basic order of society. For this is freedom itself and to challenge it would destroy freedom, the freedom of free markets, free enterprise, and the free choice of being. In reality, as opposed to in ideology, this means, in the phrase of Noam Chomsky, that the United States claims for itself the freedom to rob anywhere on earth as a basic ontological privilege.[13] The resulting global plunder has pauperized most of the world into the status of the Salvadoran peasant—while as a result of the penetration of mental and cultural space and the denial of ideology, the reality of this relationship is virtually absent from the consciousness of the systems analyst and others of her class. This does not make her evil—indeed, for the purposes of this discussion I want it established that the systems analyst is a thoroughly decent person. It simply means that insofar as she lifts up her eyes past the perimeter of the self, she does not see or otherwise experience the Otherness of the Salvadoran peasant as at all integral to her own projected being. She has been so shaped as to not encompass the possibility.

Nor does she experience nature as what has been expropriated by our civilization. Oh, she experiences nature, all right. As an outdoors-oriented Californian, she enjoys running on the beach or looking off into the vast Pacific Ocean from the cliffs at La Jolla. In such a moment she will have an undeniably spiritual experience, as the self, ordinarily held within the densely Egoic bonds of the workplace or strapped into the mechanical space of her Honda and the freeway, expands soulward toward the great Other of the sea. Consistent with this spirituality, the systems analyst joins the Sierra Club, and protests against the desecration of her beautiful coast by offshore oil drilling. She might even join a campaign against the use of pesticides on her table grapes. What will likely elude her, however, is the sum set of the transformations of nature, mediated by crushing labor of billions of others, which puts food on her table or clothes on her back. And this is because the world she inhabits is configured to keep awareness of this kind away from consciousness, and hence from any progression through Otherness and spirit-being. We scoff at state-free people for living in a magically contrived world; yet what could be more magical than a visit of the systems analyst to the supermarket? Here all she has to do is pass a magnetized credit card through a slot and a brilliant array of glossy commodities, including perhaps some coffee from El Salvador, will be hers. Since her company deposits her check directly into the bank whose credit card she uses, the gesture with the credit card is the only physical link between compensation for reproducing the system and her participation in its bounty. In sum, there is essentially no connection between life activity and the transformation of nature which is the material root of life. With no lived connection, consciousness cannot apprehend the humanity of nature, that is to say, the dominated labor which has in fact built the world. Nature remains wilderness, scenery: a surpassing Otherness toward which all spiritual ambitions are submerged into pseudo-universality without any recognition of the human form embedded within.

Because the self in modern society is unmoored and must bear, in solitude, the burdens of life, people of the New Class typically have personal crises, in the course of which a spiritual restlessness arises. Let us assume that the systems analyst is such a person and feels a tug toward the transcendence of her lot. The assumption is certainly a plausible one, for while her material needs have been met, little has been done to adequately feed her soul. In addition, as a woman she feels a persistent contradiction between her inner being and the world. Partly this is a result of persistent discrimination and sexual harassment despite her considerable financial reward. But there is another level of alienation, too, a sense that the reward itself, the Egoic system it represents and its immense and ultimate meaninglessness, denies her emergent desire for wholeness of being. All these distresses converge to produce a detachment of a certain quantum of desire from her world and its deployment toward being. This produces a shudder within the self, a stirring of Otherness and the potentiation of spirit-being. To realize spiritual motion in practice requires, as has been observed, a rejection of the world. And this she now finds herself disposed to do. She is perceptive enough to realize how bogus and spiritually dead the mainstream culture has become, and honest enough with herself to recognize that neither work nor established political channels can provide a larger home for the stirrings of her soul. Neither opportunistic nor servile, she is seized, therefore, with a real spiritual need to make a break with things as they are.

However, the only parts of the world capable of rejection are those which have already been grasped. As we have seen, the analyst does not conceive of, and therefore cannot represent, her world as anything which can be politically changed, or as a place in which nature has been transformed through the domination of labor. The prevailing system of ideological indoctrination has mystified this. The reality of society and nature cannot be presented; and what cannot be presented in the first place cannot be, therefore, re-presented in a spiritual dialectic. For her, therefore, a spiritual break is not drawn into the dialectic of emancipation and class struggle as it would for the Salvadoran; it does not engage such aspects of Otherness as are deployed in representations of classes, social interests, and ideologies; indeed, it does not enter the body of society at all. Society itself is renounced, not any position in its class structure; and society is regarded as an abstract Other which intrudes upon the integrity of the self. In her spiritual path therefore she essentially continues along the plane of cleavage experienced on her runs on the beach: a sense of unmediated communion with the universe. Though she remains determined at every point by social forces, these stay beyond the practical consciousness. That is, she cannot feel the things which activate the Salvadoran peasant, not because she is an unfeeling person, but because much of social reality has not been allowed to become intelligible.

But still the systems analyst wants to do something. Given the New Age, there is no shortage of spiritual choices for the path through Otherness and spirit-being. Most likely she has been raised in one of the liberalized Judeo-Christian religions; yet it is unlikely that she can find a surcease for her restlessness within any of these faiths, whose very liberality is predicated upon an integration with despiritualized society. One cannot reject the world and remain a Reformed Jew or a mainstream Presbyterian. Other passages to rejection remain within Judeo-Christianity, to be sure, including a large portion of Roman Catholicism, Orthodox Judaism, and the vast sweep of Pentecostal and Fundamentalist Protestantism. All of these, however (and we simplify here to draw a basic point), are defined through their opposition to modernity. At times this rejection extends to the fundamentalist assault on the scientific consensus about the world itself (for example, creationism replacing evolution). More often the assault is harmonized with an acceptance of science, while it is only the cultural aspects of modernity which are rejected—moral relativism, sexual permissiveness, lack of respect for tradition, and so forth.

The antimodern perspective is at least as unthinkable for our systems analyst as that of social revolution. Like revolution, the attack on modernity literally makes no sense to her: it is not something which can be drawn into a spiritual praxis, because it is not an object for consciousness. The cries of fundamentalism are experienced as wholly irrational, without any resonance in her being. Indeed, insofar as she can bring herself to think about the antimodernist approach to spirituality, she simply and flatly denies it, rightly so, as having no place in her worldview.

It is in this context that New Age spirituality arises. It arises, and turns inward, to the only frontier left open—to the self itself. That is, it becomes subjective. Subjectivity is like a black hole in contemporary culture, pulling everything into itself; thus when the modern American thinks in spiritual terms, the frame of reference is first of all in terms of personal fulfillment, and spirituality means "getting in touch with the self." Here nature becomes yet another means—another kind of resource. The systems analyst, in search of spirit, discovers a mountaintop or, if she can still find one, a lonely stretch of beach, on which to meditate and "get away from it all." The world of society, that abstract weight, is left far behind, as spirit-being and spirit-power begin to rise in the self; this is felt as a tugging toward Ultimate Being. It is a genuine oceanic experience. There is no question that a soul-like movement is fostered by such conditions, especially in relation to the brutal pace of the synthetic society. Sprung loose from the chains of workaday life, the systems analyst experiences a moment of release, of immediacy and timelessness, and of the connectedness of all beings.

Some such encounter with the universe, and the stillness of nonbeing, is perhaps the quintessential opening onto a spiritual path. I am sure it motivated ancient Sumerians, and modern Salvadoran rebels, for even those under bombardment can pause now and then to admire the heavens and the beauty of the mountains. The main spiritual difference between the Salvadoran and the systems analyst, however, is that in the former instance, the encounter with the universe is defined by the overcoming of domination, while in the latter, staring up at the heavens or off into the sea tends to become an end in itself. And in so doing, it comes under the aegis of the isolated, Egoic self.

There is an irony in this which frequently builds to a contradiction. The self-preoccupation of modern Americans (amply documented in works such as the recent *Habits of the Heart*)[14] is now legendary. It is not an intellectual gesture, but a way of social being which reflects the dominion of consumer capitalism and the breakdown of community which accompanies this.[15] That is to say, the structure of our whole society entails self-preoccupation, and the more so as society is unchallenged. Since New Age thinking does not challenge fundamental social structures, its spirituality remains self-preoccupied, even as it attempts to get beyond the self: thus soul, whose essence is self-abandonment, is cultivated as a project of self-fulfillment. This paradox expresses a kind of spiritual pride intrinsic to the spirituality of the New Age. As the spiritually proud person congratulates him- or herself for humility, so does the aficionado of New Age spirituality congratulate him- or herself for self-abandonment. New Age zealots are forever flexing spiritual muscles, admiring their spiritual transcendence as much as their physical fitness and smart clothing. But how can the self forget or escape itself this way, when spirituality is pursued as if in a gymnasium? The self thus produced is in reality Ego in soul's clothing.

In the New Age, spirituality is determined most of all by self-preoccupation and loneliness. As little as they were originally intended to heal these ills of modern spirit, Eastern religions have proven adaptable for these contemporary needs. Thus the systems analyst might be led from casual meditation in the out-of-doors to a more or less rigorous encounter with a spiritual discipline shaped along Eastern lines. She is likely to find a Zen monastery nearby, or perhaps one devoted to Tibetan Buddhism, or some similar path open for a rigorous meditative practice which enhances selflessness through self-concentration, which seeks the direct grounding of the self in the natural universe, and which treats society as an abstract Other to be set aside. Now meditative practice can be grounded in a reconstruction of community itself, organized around the collective pursuit of self-detachment or abandonment.

However, we should not be surprised to find that as she proceeds further, giving herself over to an Eastern spirituality to the extent that it becomes an embracing religion, many of the problems from society—hierarchies, sexual domination, rivalries, economic pressures, etc.—are carried over into the faith, and compromise the quest for detachment. It says nothing about the essence of Buddhism, Hinduism, or any Eastern discipline to observe that it can be perverted—just as Christianity can be perverted. What must be said, though, is that the essence of any spiritual movement, religious or otherwise, does not exist outside the social relations it puts forward. And since the social relations of spirituality are those of the dialectic between Ego and soul, we can say that the essence of any spiritual movement lies in its practical ability to advance soul as against Ego. The self-centered and uncritical terms of New Age spirituality, however, militate against this.

Let us imagine, in this vein, that the systems analyst were undergoing her crisis in the early 1980's. In that case, she could well have encountered and been enthralled by the late Bhagwan Shree Rajneesh, could even have decided to give up the world and join his spiritual community, Rajneeshpuram, in what was once the small town of Antelope, Oregon. Rajneesh provides a spectacular and disastrous example of a guru who was able to hoodwink a whole subsection of the New

Class by blurring the distinction between Ego and soul. He offered the former in the guise of the latter, employing a truly formidable hypnotic capacity by means of which he could radiate a love approaching agape in its quality. Perhaps the key to the Rajneeshian swindle lay in his ability to erase the spiritual critique of possessiveness. His sayings were full of all the traditional jargon of Eastern spirituality, coupled with a deliberate effort to bring spirit up to date by accommodating it to advanced capitalism. No, the Bhagwan told his adoring *sinnyasin* (the name given to his disciples), it was good to be rich and give vent to desire, whether for things or unlimited sexual gratification.[16] No basic critique of social relations was to contaminate this spirituality. Rather, the existing capitalist order, greed and all, was simply taken to extremes, as if this would ensure its transcendence. Somehow the string of Rolls Royces which the faithful gave their leader were supposed to signify such an abandonment to desire that desire itself would be transcended and turn toward being. But desire reigned nevertheless. Despite a great deal of razzle-dazzle, the entire structure degenerated and became concentrated, as Frances Fitzgerald has documented,[17] into a fully paranoid Egoic society whose inevitable collapse involved a near miss with murder.

Rajneeshism is an extreme example of a New Age spirituality which became corrupted because of Egoism. Yet it would be wrong to dismiss a powerful and recurring hope just because it has been abused. The tragedy of Rajneeshpuram is certainly not the last chapter in the ongoing saga of utopian spiritual communities. Deeply ingrained in the American experience, these spring up continually; indeed, the conditions for creating them grow ever stronger. We may find among the numerous communities which spring up in response to alienated spirituality the germ of a real transformation of our society. A concrete discussion lies beyond our present scope, though our reflections so far offer a perspective on how that discussion might be continued. For a spiritual community, if it is to be really transformative, has to overcome an interlocked set of material problems arising from the persistent power of capitalism and patriarchy. It must decide how it will sustain unalienated production and reproduction, avoid gurus and other remnants of patriarchal domination, advance internal democracy and self government, and relate to the larger society, the increasingly devastated earth, and the oppressed upon it. In a word, the task is to develop communalism. This is a fantastically difficult challenge, but one of the few really worth taking today.

It is also a spiritual challenge—a challenge to develop practically the life of soul. Freud said that where id was, there ego shall be. We continue: where Ego was, there soul shall be, created in collective practice.

The Transcended Self

A rational person will recognize that everyone has to be saved in their own fashion. Dogmatism, fundamentalism, the tyranny of logos—the whole apparatus of spiritual pride—are inadmissible in the critique of spirituality, though of course they are inevitable as well (no doubt, in these pages as elsewhere), given the "fallen" condition of the human species. Having said this, I would add that I do not think it dogmatic to critically reject certain forms of spirituality as unworthy. After all, a facile relativism in which anything goes is just as sterile as dogmatic fundamentalism. Rajneeshism mobilized spirit in an unworthy path. Similarly, it can be "spiritual" to establish a whites-only church, or to relegate women to the "holy" role of illiterate breeding animals. The late Ayatollah Khomeini definitely aroused spiritual fervor, even though—and more significantly, because—he also brutally persecuted dissidents, proclaimed the death sentence on blasphemers like Salman Rushdie, and crushed women's rights. Similarly, the ecstatic transports of the crowds at the Ayatollah's funeral (estimated at two million), which led to the deaths by trampling of at least eight people and culminated in an orgy of manipulating the corpse, cannot be readily divorced from spiritual phenomena.

The ultimate case is Nazism with its profound spiritual appeal to the German "soul," "Volk," and "blood." As George Mosse has written,

> While it is true that the anti-Semitism of the Nazis had a practical intent . . . it also rested its case on purely spiritual, ideological and cultural grounds. The anti-Jewish dynamic that made itself felt in the streets, in political meetings, and in legal decrees, also made great headway through various spiritualist beliefs, theosophical religions which had a Volkish tradition, and within the body of a Germanic Christianity. . . . The party itself sheltered a notorious believer in spiritualistic forces. Heinrich Himmler believed in *karma* and was convinced that he was the reincarnation of Henry the Fowler. Indeed, his whole thought was saturated with . . . nature mysticism. . . . Nor was Hitler himself free from it. Rauschning tells how Hitler occupied himself passionately with works such as those of the nature mystic Edgar Dacque. Dacque wrote of a nature somnambulism. He believed that the magical forces of nature break through in man's dreams though his culture has wrongly sublimated them. This contact with a life force, springing from nature, is the only valid introduction to the cosmos.[18]

Others have argued that the mythic core of the Third Reich, played out, for example, in the rage for Wagnerian opera, was a revival of archaic Christian legends such as the search for the grail.[19] Wilhelm Reich, in *The Mass Psychology of Fascism*,[20] held that Hitler triumphed because he appealed to the repressed sexuality of the German masses. I think it is more accurate to say that Nazism appealed to the spirituality of the German people (with its sexual component), just as Rajneeshism appealed to the spirituality of the New Class and Khomeini appealed to the spirituality of Iranians. But because the spiritualities of Hitler, Rajneesh, and Khomeini were false, they mobilized Egoic rather than soul desire, and in doing so, led to a "return of the repressed," of which the undoubtedly erotized desire for a strong father-god (with projections of hatred to Jews, etc.) was a definite component in the German situation—just as the sinnyasin's idolization of Rajneesh and his Rolls Royces was a manifestation of repressed desire in the context of the New Class of late capitalism; and the persecution of women and dissenters was a manifestation of repressed desire in the Iranian context. It is the malignancy of repressed desire, that violence of the heart, which can cause spirituality to be a dance on the edge of the abyss.

But if certain spiritualities are bad, then others are good, and there must be a way of telling the good from the bad—the genuine, if partial, transcendence from the destructive, violent kind. There is, then, a kind of spiritual virtue to be determined in any concrete instance. This must be done, moreover, without reference to the *telos*, or goal of spirituality—because we can never, logically, say that one goal is more spiritual than another if both are but points on lines that converge asymptotically toward Ultimate Being. A partiality to the Salvadoran peasant's revolutionary spirituality over the systems analyst's New Age spirituality cannot be sustained simply because the revolutionary goals of the former are preferred to the social accommodation of the latter. One cannot argue from ends and ignore means in the spiritual dimension. To the contrary, judging an action spiritually good just because it is revolutionary would be morally monstrous—and profoundly antispiritual. Indeed, Stalinism could be defined by its justification of any crime for the sake of the revolution.[21] The very power of the revolutionary ideal became a prison—both figuratively and literally—for those caught in the trap of Stalinism, for it blinded and overrode any critical inquiry into the means by which the revolution was to be advanced. This discrepancy led to an unimaginably grotesque web of falsification within which any crime could be committed and rationalized.[22]

A Stalin or Pol Pot represents that extreme point of revolutionary opportunism, at which the revolution is reduced to a slogan at the disposal of an authoritarian state. Yet any social revolution is profoundly ambivalent from a spiritual perspective. At its foundation, revolution is spiritual, because it is animated by a wish to be free which, as we have seen, cannot be reduced to any psychological or economic calculus. As oppressed people rise they transform self and Other and bring new spirit into being. Spirit-power is the great fuel of revolution, appearing as *soul-force,* the irresistible drive of mobilized human spirit. But at the same time, the actual revolutionary struggle often comes down to war, and war brings out the worst in people. The warfare of a revolution is more complex and deeper, moreover, than that of ordinary war. In the conventional kind of warfare, two nation-states turn on each other with organized violence. This is terrible, but the violence is *between* two societies. Revolution, however, is a violence *within* a social body; it always involves civil war—between social factions, within families, across genders and generations, and not least, within the selves of individuals, for each human being has multiple points of attachment to history. In reality, revolution without counter-revolution is unthinkable.

Any struggle to gain or hold power is disruptive to spirit, precisely because it is in the service of Egoic desire, and rewards cunning and violence. Moreover, revolutionary struggle, no matter how nobly idealized, is fought out by individuals who have been socialized in the old society, and have internalized its ways. The revolutionary commands an objective justice due to oppression, and may be inspired by the finest and most spiritual ideals—Che Guevara's "great love," in the quotation offered above—but the rest of the revolutionary's being need be no better than the society in which he or she has been formed. The eventual realization of spirit requires emancipation, and this implies not only political and economic revolution but a total revolution in all spheres of domination.[23] But in the here and now, and no doubt, the foreseeable future, this process cannot happen except by going backwards and forwards—and by no means always two steps forward and one back.

In sum, the virtue of a spirituality must be inherent and immediately present. It is in the Way, not the end. This Way is the actual motion of soul. Therefore if we want to sum up all that we can say on the subject of an emancipated spirituality we have to find a way of talking about this at the level of soul itself.

We think of soul as a basic ontological position—an attitude toward being which orients all aspects of existence in its field. But how do we know the presence of soul in human action? We recognize it by the appropriation of the Other, according to our understanding; which is to say, by an overcoming of Egoic relations of being. But what does this mean in practice? Let us consider some of the main Egoic relations:

- attachment to possessions
- non-recognition of the Other, leading to being-over, appropriating the being of the Other, and ultimately, domination
- spiritual pride, leading to the insular and fortified self
- estrangement from nature, leading to the split between mind and body
- attachment to logos

It would seem that soul would be a kind of negation of these. Bearing in mind the clumsiness in enumerating such a subtle and interrelated set as this, let us concede the above list to logos, and proceed.

Soul as Detachment from Possessions

To reach satisfaction in all
    desire its possession in nothing.
To come to possess all
    desire the possession of nothing.
To arrive at being all
    desire to be nothing.
To come to the knowledge of all
    desire the knowledge of nothing.[24]

The "spiritual poverty" espoused by the great Christian mystics was linked, as we have observed,[25] to the profound threat to spirit posed by the coming economic order of capital. This point was driven home by every significant medieval thinker and has not lost its validity. Despite centuries of hegemony by the gospel of possessiveness, material acquisition remains a mortal enemy of spirit. Our language installs the duality in its two most fundamental, irreducible verbs: *to have* and *to be*. The world of having and the world of being are mutually exclusive; for having begins where being ends and vice versa. This ontological divide becomes the basis for the economic realm itself.

> The mysterious nature of commodities consists simply in the fact . . .
> that they reflect back to men the social character of *their own work as*
> *the objective character of the products of the work themselves,* . . .

and therefore present the social relationship between producers and their labor as a whole as a social relationship of objects existing outside themselves. Through this *quid pro quo* the products of labor become commodities . . . It is only the specific social relationship between men themselves which assumes here the phantasmagorical form of a relationship between things. To find . . . an analogy, we must therefore fall back upon the *nebulous region of the religious world*. Here the products of the human brain seem to be independent beings endowed with a life of their own, and related to each other as well as to men. So it is with the products of human hands in the world of commodities. This I call the *fetishism* which attaches to the products of work as soon as they are produced as commodities; this fetishism is therefore inseparable from commodity production.   Karl Marx, *Capital*

The notion of alienation reflects the degree to which being is split from having, and its end stage is the order of capitalism, where the power to work itself becomes a commodity and the whole world is transformed into alienable goods. In capitalism, having masters being: you "are" nothing unless you "have" something, and if you have everything, like Donald Trump, you can be (and do) anything. The craving for "things to own" is a certain sign of nonrecognition of the Other and the flight from being. It also embodies the self's perception that it is unrecognized. Thus material possession is Otherness made into a substantive. Appropriation, denied a pathway through recognition, can be gained only through cash. Radical separateness becomes the precondition for ownership, and a frenzy of possessiveness seizes the society of alienation. The ascension of having over being is paralleled by that of pleasure—viewed as the quantity of stimulation—over happiness. Ultimately, a society defined in its deepest nature by the destruction of spirit finds its last, indeed only, refuge of the sacred in what has been alienated: private property; and so, the almighty dollar.

Soul represents a differentiation between being and having, and this provides an opening for pleasure to become happiness rather than stimulation. This does not mean that a soulful person abandons all possessions. A person without possessions is a person without individuality, and no human being at all. Possessions represent the actual position of human being, both separated and attached from being. They are the objectification of being—the projection of lack into the world and the alteration of the world to reflect the presence of the human. Possessions are the "me-ness" imposed on reality by human being, which changes blank things into meaningful objects. Even the humblest monk has his or her bowl, gown, and sandals. These possessions—clothing in particular—are what gives individuality to the body; they are, we might say, the inscription of being on flesh.

But possessions, being true objects and not mere things, are themselves part of a dialectical flow. They are necessary for human being, but necessarily illusory as well. The object owned provides an essential illusion of permanency. By claiming a part of the object world we establish our being over against the flux of time, where all things change and pass into each other, including most decisively, our own organism and those beings we love. Soul has insight into this dilemma and accordingly wears its possessions lightly. It knows that nothing really belongs to the self because the self does not belong to itself but to being. The religions of the East saw truly that the self is an illusion. Ego is the form of this illusion that does not know it is an illusion. Moreover, Ego sustains the illusion through fixation—and idolization—of property relations. Soul, on the other hand, is the form taken by the illusion that knows the self to be an illusion, albeit a necessary one. Hence it treats property relations as necessary illusions as well, and regards them no more—or less—seriously than it does its own individuality. This means that soul is never mystified by possessions, nor makes property relations into a sacred idol.

The same reasoning tells us there is nothing spiritual about theft, which is always violent. Soul differentiates between possessions which are actually personal and those which are used to squeeze more profit out of the earth. The distinction is simply a question of respect for the Other, recognizing what would be violent, and acting so as to move away from violence. The individual's personal property may be an illusion, but it remains as what necessarily constitutes one's being and cannot be expropriated without expropriating that being. The widow's pension and the small farmer's farm are essential props of being. They are necessary in any case, but all the more so in an antagonistic society which is always stacked against the poor. On the other hand, the property of agribusiness corporations or real estate developers need not be treated with any such reverence, any more than military hardware. For they are fruits of expropriation and the violation of being. Proudhon's maxim, "property is theft," should be seen in this light.

Obviously such an attitude is utterly incompatible with the healthy expansion of the capitalist market. Therefore soul will be crucified just as surely as Jesus unless it establishes a communitarian socialist framework within which it can be protected.

Giving and Compassion

The soul form of the self is a movement toward being and away from the estrangement of Ego. That is why it at times has a conservative character—a conserving of being. In fact, the ideology of modernization and the new belongs strictly to capitalism and Ego, which, in constant flight from being, endlessly piles up new kinds of diversion to distract itself and keep the wheels of accumulation greased.[26] Ego, like the capitalist firm, must expand or die, which it does through its accumulation of possession and diversion. This is another side of the addiction to stimulation as an end in itself, and it leads to the plague of addictions which characterizes capitalist society.

Soul, by contrast, has a more complex, subtle, and dialectical motion. From one side it appears as a contraction and even ablation of the self. The emptiness of mind of Eastern religion, and the humility of the true Christian bear witness to this motion away from Egoic being, as does the characteristic selflessness of the communist revolutionary.[27]

What appears as contraction from one side is expansion from another. For as Ego weakens Otherness flows inward. This countermotion (though the two sides should not be placed in any relation of priority, as one is part of the other) describes well the state of being found in various forms of mental disturbance, religious ecstasy, falling in love, or indeed, going to sleep. Whether or not these relations deserve to be called soul is not an easy matter to decide. One would not want to call going to sleep, for example, a state of soul, although it is surely an ablation of Ego and an inrush of Otherness (which leads to dreaming). What is missing, however, are two conditions which have to be present if soul is to arise from Ego, namely, a heightened consciousness and a coherent practice (though in fact the second of these conditions implies the first). That is, soul is never a passive state of being, but includes a way of being through action.

Mental disturbance is essentially a kind of passivity which precludes the emergence of soul.[28] In madness—whether neurotic or psychotic is not to the point here—Ego is broken down, or invaded. An influx of malignant Otherness appears, split-off and hateful, forcing further compromises: rigidity of Ego, inhibitions, resort to drugs and alcohol, delusions, paranoid attitudes, and so forth. Although these manifestations may each and every one mimic states of soul, they are not identical to it, precisely because soul arises through real praxis.

A paranoid person, for example, aware of an omnipresent threat, may have a greatly sharpened and vigilant consciousness. But paranoid consciousness is by the same token narrowed. It is like a focused beam in the darkness which leaves the rest of darkness all the more dark. In contrast, the consciousness of soul is expansive, open, and modulated. The distinction is related to different attitudes toward being. The paranoid focuses on one loved and hated other, to the exclusion of all others, which are effectively split off. Soul, rather, is open to Otherness as such, and to all others, allowing contact and interpenetration with the whole.

How best to describe a praxis which opens toward soul? Perhaps by the following: that the motion of a person which leads away from Egoic self toward soul is contained in a simple, indeed, elementary gesture, that of *giving*. Giving of self is felt as taking from Ego, hence the sense of diminution and humility. This also helps account for a powerful aspect of spiritual experience which seems to contradict the fact that soul is based on activity. For the experience of soul does seem to be passive: the individual feels seized by a higher power, gives the self over to God or the Holy Spirit, lets the Zen arrow fly "unconsciously," or to be more exact, un-Ego-consciously. That is, soul activity is experienced as an inrush of being.

But this requires real, actual giving. It does not happen in the imagination, but through a conscious change in the relatedness of self to world, whether by giving away objects or giving of oneself in relation to another or to a cause. Not all giving, however, is of soul. Soul-giving is *giving-over*, giving to overcome Ego. It means yielding, but actively, a yielding which does not destroy the center of activity, and whose soulfulness is shown in heightened consciousness. Unless we bear this in mind, the motion toward soul will dissolve into going off to sleep[29]—or, more significantly yet, into those powerful and disastrous pseudospiritualities where individuality is lost through merging with the all-powerful group or mass (from cult, to Volk, to totalized Party, to "my country, right or wrong"). Soul is loss of Ego and transformation of the self. It is not, however, the loss of the self, which cannot be lost so long as the organism exists. It is only because the ideologies of Egoic being have conflated Ego with the self, that we fail to recognize soul as the transformation of the self, and indeed the realization and fulfillment of the self once Ego is overcome. Only dissolution into Ultimate Being constitutes the real loss of the self, and since this is not given to organismic being while life continues, we do not have to worry about achieving it, except as a point of orientation from the given place of being. In any case, the giving-over which realizes soul is in fact the enrichment of the self through the accession of Otherness.

The fully differentiated person is the richest person, the most individualized, and the least a member of the mass. We may say this also of the fully developed holy person, each of whom, from Zen Master to Christian saint, strike us as very sharply defined and fully realized practical individuals for all their humility.[30] And we may say it equally of the fully defined citizen, or political agent, whose individuality is by no means sacrificed through being open to all Others. We can love our country without succumbing to murderous patriotism or loyalty to the state apparatus. It is all a matter of differentiation—a differentiation, it may be added, which imposes different limits to selflessness, and hence different kinds of soulfulness, according to context. Just as the god of nonattachment and the god of love posed different points along the asymptote to Ultimate Being, so is the humility of the Zen monk organized about a relation to meditatively transformed consciousness, while that of the political agent is organized about real empowerment of the Other.

By contrast, the merging of the self into the crowd—or the cult, or the Party led by the maximum leader—is an expansion of Ego from the self to Other. Here Freud's formulation of group psychology as a loss of individuality is accurate. Its accuracy comes from Freud's insight that in the formation of a group, one identifies one's ego with the other members of the group and chooses the leader of the group as the ego-ideal.[31] At this point Freud's usually ambiguous usage of the term "ego" is sharp. In describing those forms of irrational group behavior—mobs, the army, the authoritarian church—in which people lose both individuality and intelligence, Freud calls attention to the profound vulnerability of Egoic being to its own split-off relation to the Other. That is, id and superego are indeed monstrous to the ego, which cannot recognize itself in them. But this usage also defines the limits of Freud's group psychology, which cannot account for rational, self-actuated, spontaneous, and creative group activity, i.e., genuine collectivity. In these non-Egoic kinds of groups, the activity which predominates is a restructuring of the self along collective lines in which Otherness is admitted. That is, the individual does not identify as Ego but as soul, and correspondingly is radically less prone to submit to irrational authority. The situation may be usefully compared with our brief discussion above of paranoia as the quintessential Egoic disturbance. Egoic group behavior and individual paranoia reveal a more than superficial resemblance. The paranoid person is forced, through terror of Otherness, to focus on one object (which only worsens the terror), and thus to narrow and intensify consciousness. The same terror of Otherness leads the member of the Egoic group (whether mob, mass, or cult) to focus on the leader, submitting to him and losing individuality.[32] Thus we have the familiar and deadly paradox which has haunted an age dominated by Egoic being—that the quest for a strong, rationalized Ego leads to mass irrationality and loss of moral as well as intellectual power.[33]

The same critique applies to those individuals who seek spirituality through discipleship, where the maximum leader returns in the guise of the guru. Rajneeshism provided an extreme case, but by no means an isolated one, of a spiritual endeavor which foundered on Egoic group relations and domination. We may generalize: whenever a spirituality becomes fixated on discipleship and a relation to a Master or seer, it betrays the marks of Ego and not of soul. There is obviously a fine line here, between the rational authority of a leader somewhat further along the path of spirit, who can therefore teach or guide soul, and the one who sets him- or herself up as a god over the spiritually faithful.

The Rajneeshian experience also enables us to look more critically at spiritual giving. Certainly the sinnyasin gave all sorts of things, from Rolls Royces on down, to their spiritual Master. But the giving was Egoic, because the material act did not escape the framework of social relations in which it was encased. The same applies to the psychology of many people who enter the "helping professions," from the ministry to psychotherapy. Often such individuals are characterized by a deep need to help others, and to give of themselves in the process. The impulse is good in itself, but no impulse can exist in itself. We are all poised between one degree or another of Ego and soul, and must expect the concrete act of giving, whether of the self or its possessions, to be complex and full of ambiguities.

We might say that Egoic giving exhausts the self (because Ego is defined by what it has, which giving depletes), while soul-giving inspires the self and fills it with spirit-power (because the soul is defined by openness to the Other, which is empowered by giving).[34] Or from the other end: such giving as exhausts the self is Egoic giving and should be critically explored and overcome; while such giving as expands the self is soul-giving and provides the real basis for the actual expansion of spirit.

The active giving-over by which soul is constituted is giving to the Other. From the position of Egoic being this is always risky, and indeed soul always involves a real risk, both inner and outer. The inner risk occurs because of the defenses provided by Ego against our own

violence—the "dark night of the soul." And the outer risk arises because as this relationship is applied to the real world, giving means
transferring from rich to poor, from haves to have-nots, from the empowered to the disempowered. In other words it means going beyond
the safety of charity to the risk of confrontation with class power.

Society establishes charities as a kind of safety valve for some of the
contradictions of the social order—a safety valve whose real purpose
is the maintenance of the status quo by drawing off some distress from
below and some guilt from above. In short, charity provides a short-
term outlet for soul while frustrating its full motion and indeed driving
it backward into the arms of Ego. It follows that any consistent approach to soul must concentrate its efforts on the empowerment of the
disempowered and not in giving them handouts. Even divesting oneself of all one's possessions would not accomplish one-millionth of the
needed transfer of power to those who have been excluded. To take
this position seriously would, needless to say, bring down upon one's
head all the repressive power of the state. Yet this spiritual path is integral to all the world's great spiritual traditions and is only suppressed
insofar as these traditions have allowed themselves to become captive
to the order of things. When the Buddha talks of the necessity for compassion towards all beings he refers, it seems to me, to the same attitude of active giving—of the release from Ego which can only come by
freeing all beings. And when Eckhart talks of "justice" he means the
same:

> Recently I had this thought: If God did not wish as I do, then I would
> still wish as he does. There are some people who want to have their
> own will in everything; that is bad and there is much harm in it. Those
> are a little better who do want what God wants, and want nothing
> contrary to his will; if they were sick, what they would wish would be
> for God's will to be for them to be well. So these people want God to
> want according to their will, not for themselves to want according to
> his will. One has to endure this, but still it is wrong. The just have no
> will at all; what God wills is all the same to them, however great dis-
> tress that may be.
>
> For just men, the pursuit of justice is so imperative that if God were
> not just, they would not give a fig for God; and they stand fast by jus-
> tice, and they have gone out of themselves so completely that they have
> no regard for the pains of hell or the joys of heaven or for any other
> thing. . . . Whoever loves justice stands so fast by it that whatever he
> loves, that is his being; nothing can deflect him from this, nor does
> he esteem anything differently. Saint Augustine says: "When the soul
> loves, it is more properly itself than when it gives life" [the quote is ac-

tually from Bernard of Clairvaux, *Of Precept and Dispensation* 20.60].
This sounds simple and commonplace, and yet few understand what
it means, and still it is true. Anyone who has discernment in justice
and in just men, he understands everything I am saying.[35]

Justice is a function of love, or rather, of *soul-love*. If a person cannot love or feel loved, then life loses its value. Yet love itself can be of
Ego or of soul. Egoic love is the common human lot, defined by the
desire to expand the self by possessing the other. Gratified, it leads to
evanescent rapture; frustrated, to those two emotions at the root of
malevolence; envy and jealousy. Its common feature, with which a
good portion of the woes of the world can be associated, is the need to
control the object, who, as a human being, may be expected to have a
mind of his or her own. In any case, such love gives in order to get.

Eckhart indicates the path of soul-love, secured by a justice which
validates the independent existence of the Other and protects the
Other from Egoic possessiveness. Justice equals love equals soul: the
three relations mutually imply each other. Justice is defined by Eckhart
as, "That man is just who *gives* everyone what belongs to him" (italics
added);[36] and it is an absolute imperative, even superseding God. By
this we understand: from beyond our understanding of God—the
names logos gives to God. Hence justice comes from the place of Ultimate Being, and the absolute character it gives to soul-love is derived
from the infinite comprehended by Ultimate Being. The impersonality
of the imperative may be read as the voice heard through soul, a voice
experienced from the Other, with no Egoic component. Thus the tension of the ideal, the sense of absolute Otherness of Holy Spirit, and
even of the superego—because we all are to some degree Ego, yet also
are given the spiritual capacity to experience a pull from beyond. And
justice, then, is the negation of Ego, which arises as the barrier to Otherness comes down—for then the Other is recognized as not truly separate but a fellow being deserving of his or her share of worldly goods.

The implication is that love, which everyone is ready to admit as a
paramount virtue of spirituality, is not true love unless combined with
a just praxis of giving that empowers the Other. We touch again here
on the puzzle of agape, the disinterested, spontaneous love of God for
beings. A further insight is provided by the great mystic whom Eckhart
confuses with Augustine, Bernard of Clairvaux: "But to love one's
neighbour with perfect justice it is necessary to be prompted by God.
How can you love your neighbour with purity if you do not love him
in God? But he who does not love God cannot love in God. You must
first love God, so that in him you may love your neighbour too. . . ."[37]

Love, or soul-giving, has as its object the concrete living person. But it cannot be wholly grounded in the other person. Rather, the act of loving-giving exists also in reference to a third force, beyond the self and Other: God, or Ultimate Being. Love is triangulated. Yet the third point, which pulls the other two toward itself, is not a creature; it is the universe of being as experienced by human being becoming soul.

Justice as a value reflects a human world that is unjust and built on violent expropriation. To give everyone what is theirs implies an undoing of established power. This cannot be reconciled with any facile sense of love. Soul in this light is like Prince Myshkin in Dostoevsky's tragedy *The Idiot,* the perfectly good man in an evil world, whose goodness brings about new dimensions of evil. There is no resting point; there is only the clearing away of new pathways of spirit.

Soul Is Embodied

We have already discussed something of the relation between spirit and nature, and our estrangement from flesh. This was done mostly from the standpoint of a critique of Cartesian dualism in Chapter Two, and the individual's relation to desire in Chapter Four. But there is a larger, civilizational issue as well. Indeed, our species' survival, and not just the revitalization of soul, hangs upon the restoration of an organic relation to nature. There is no need to review here the hideous predicament which exists by virtue of the attitude that nature exists "out there," as a mere resource for all-conquering Ego. No threat presently looms larger than the violation of the earth—and there can be no doubt that this menace will grow greater as each passing year witnesses more and more devastation of the environment.

Those Egoic attitudes toward nature which undergird the system of capitalism are profoundly implicated in this growing disaster. So is the capitalist economy itself, for any programs which aim to reduce pollution, waste, resource devastation and/or reckless energy inputs also reduce the profits which are capital's lifeblood.[38] Ultimately capital must grow or die, i.e., must destroy the earth to live. An ecological program which does not include a resolution to overcome the devastation of capitalism, therefore, is an exercise in self-deception.

Yet socialism, the traditional alternative to capitalism, has offered little or no ecological hope. Notwithstanding either the gains[39] or the world-historical defeats suffered by socialism in recent years, socialism as it has been actually implemented has largely not improved upon the environmental record of capitalism. Indeed it has in many instances worsened it.[40] These are times to rethink the socialist project as a whole and in every particular, to build on what went well and learn from what went wrong. And this should include a spiritual critique, for it may be said that both the political and economic defeat of socialism and its woeful environmental record are manifestations of a spiritual deformity.

The fatal flaw of socialism has been its tendency toward centralization. It is this which led to the party-state with its economic irrationality and political authoritarianism, and ultimately undermined the socialist ideal itself. Yet this tendency cannot be entirely explained in political, economic, or psychological terms—for it includes a drive toward totality which has resulted in party-worship, state-worship, and the cult of the godlike leader. To use the terms *worship, cult,* and *godlike,* calls attention to the fact that the well-known hostility of socialist societies to religion went along with the building of an alternative religion: an antireligious spirituality. This fact has been strenuously denied, indeed mystified, by appealing to the scientific character of socialism—a maneuver which settles nothing, since there is no inherent antagonism between science and spirituality. More importantly, socialism cannot do without spirit, since its actual historical dynamic, as we have seen, is fueled by the wish to be free and the giving-over of the self to the victims of historical oppression. However, the denial of spirituality, like any form of denial, tends to distort spirit. Undoubtedly this played a role in turning spirit backward, to those very forms of totalization and god-building which the Marxist critique of religion had tried to overcome. And once the spiritual core of socialism decays, it will seek to compensate by aping capitalism's drive to dominate nature.

Marx is usually discredited along with Lenin and Stalin in these matters, but there is a deep difference between them. In fact, the perversion of spirituality into state worship is a chapter from Bolshevism and its successors in the Soviet bloc and Maoist China. On the other hand, the deepest spiritual distortions in the tradition do go back to Marx, where they are played out in relation to nature—and hence reverberate into the ecological crisis.

In his *Economic and Philosophical Manuscripts,* Marx tackled the question of being in history. The result provided a foundation for what would be called historical materialism.[41] The problem of nature figures prominently in the *Manuscripts*—indeed, one of the main lines of argument establishing Marx's materialism is his insistence that human beings are part of nature, albeit that part of nature which transforms nature. With this realization, Marx shares an ontological view which

places his entire work at least potentially in the camp of spirit. By proclaiming the fundamental unity of the human and natural worlds,
Marx was able to address the fragmentation of science. Moreover, he
vitalized the whole notion of what it is to be human by rooting humanity in nature, without sacrificing the essentially historical nature of human being. "The making of the five senses is the work of the whole
history of humanity," wrote Marx, recognizing that the body is really
flesh: self-sentient nature, nature that consciously acts upon itself and
transforms itself.[42]

And yet this stroke of genius stops at the threshold, from which
point it has remained liable to regress and accommodate the domination of nature which characterizes existing socialism. Why? The reason lies in Marx's conception of nature itself. Marx sees "man" as part
of nature, but as one might see the overseer as part of a plantation. He
sees humanity as the active component in nature, and the remainder of
nature as brute matter, passively awaiting the master's hand to bring it
into full being. Thus, for Marx, nature is "man's inorganic body," and
essentially no more. For all his critique of a fragmenting science, Marx
still ends by splitting the world along Cartesian lines, and seeing nature as inert matter and humanity as empty consciousness.

This is wrong. Setting aside the sexism inherent in the attitude
(which arises from the identification of nature as the eternal Female),
it is wrong because it denies true vitality to nature. If nature is "inorganic," then it remains a mere resource for the human project, to be
played with as the will dictates. And if "man" is activity and nature is
inert, then nature is irretrievably Other. Marx cannot escape the Egoic
attitude unless he recognizes the inherent power of nature, and its reciprocity in the emergence of human being.[43] Rather than calling nature
"man's inorganic body," we would be on better ground if we called
humanity "nature's wandering spirit," self-generating until it becomes
capable of forgetting its attachment to the original ground of being
and fancies itself the lord of creation.

An organic rather than an inorganic relation is needed between humanity and nature: one of soul rather than Ego. It is inherent for soul
to recognize nature—not simply as scenery or resources but as the
ground of being itself. This is a common enough idea, having been
conceived independently by countless generations from the beginning
of human habitation, but it relentlessly eludes the modern consciousness, whether capitalist or socialist. Nature seen as the ground of being
is also nature seen as sacred. When the state-free person, then, transforms nature, as for example by cultivating the earth or hunting game,

he or she recognizes the violence inherent to praxis (inscribed in the saying, "one can't make an omelet without breaking eggs") and undertakes restitution, usually through some form of sacrifice or other act of sacralization. The modern technical attitude looks down upon such practices as archaic: at best quaint and generally irrational. However, never have the limits of reason been more sharply displayed than here. For it is the state-free person working on the basis of soul who is clearly the more rational, by building into praxis an intrinsic limit of the violation of nature, while the Egoic technical attitude, by deadening nature, prepares the way for doom.[44]

In any case, if a realization of nature as sacred could in some way be built into the manipulations which go under the name of progress, we would be on the road to ecological survival. Only at the beginning of the road, to be sure, but proper beginnings are necessary. I frankly cannot see capitalism ever turning down that road. A socialist organization of production, on the other hand, provides an essential precondition, by freeing society from the tyranny of profit and the market-driven assault on the environment. What would happen to such a socialism, and whether or how it would incorporate soul once started down the road, is not for us to predict now. It would suffice to join in the building.

Needless to say, the ecological consciousness has not sat around waiting for socialism to mature. It has kept on going, along those spiritual pathways which have been identified with the Otherness of nature. Here one of the most important political movements of recent years has been the fusion of ecology with feminism—that is, the conscious intervention in ecological politics from a feminist perspective.[45] The logic is "elementary." Logos identified the female with dumb nature, which was either deadened or wild. Therefore women transcend this incorporated identity by speaking for nature. Ecofeminism struggles for the earth, and struggles at the same time to empower women. The politics is truly spiritual,[46] because it transforms the self, gives justice to the earth, changes the relation of the self to nature, of men to women, of women to themselves, and of everyone to possessions (since no serious ecological politics can avoid a critique of both production and consumption). And all these are changed in relation to each other, and enrich each other. Contrast this soulfulness to the unmediated withdrawal of our imagined systems analyst, who bypassed the relation of humanity to nature, and indeed of her own history as a woman. The difference is between a full, expanding spirituality, and one which reproduces existing social relations.

Nature is empty for us except as lived through the body, which is that part of nature we inhabit. Yet we are never fully one with the body, either as Ego or soul. We always encounter nature, whether as body or external world, as "second nature"—as nature already impressed with human activity, with the stamp of human being upon it. Consider what our way of being does to the body—how our posture shapes it, how we make the body speak for us, how the body expresses ills that consciousness refuses to register . . . and how the body becomes a medium through which spirit encounters nature. The beginning of spirituality for many, perhaps most, people is a sensory encounter with the realm of nature: a starry night, the roar of the sea, or gazing at fireflies flashing over a darkened field. Meditation draws spirituality inward; it consists of so altering consciousness that the body-organism becomes an infinitesimally diminishing screen between soul and the universe. Second and original nature now approach one another in the hope of an unmediated encounter with the same nature: the flash of pure being dissolving the separateness of human being by merging it with the universe: the mystical moment. We would expect there to be no limit to the degree an individual could strip away the concretions of being human to arrive at the suchness of nature. But we insist that one will never get there, except to find the asymptote of being. And everything encountered on that line, from experiencing the ocean from the boardwalk to the deepest raptures of the mystical consciousness, remains nature modified by the word-presentations of consciousness. It is nature re-presented, hence still lost, still the object of desire. The soul, then, would be measured, if such a word can be used in this case, by the degree to which it approaches the nature-end of the spectrum, the degree to which it approximates second nature to first, original nature.

We have argued that Ego and soul are states of being with various deployments: across societies, within a given society, and within individuals. A person's state of being may be characterized as Egoic or soulful, but this is only a way of referring to the main tendency, or the identifying one. In actuality, the self is a dialectic of the modes, played out in various contexts. Now it strikes us also that there is a dynamic *between* the modes, since the Egoic aspects of being will repel the soul aspects, while the soul aspects will seek union with the Other, which now becomes Ego itself. The main site of this dynamic is the body, especially in relation to sexuality. Because sex is phylogenetically organized for species as opposed to individual preservation, the self can be more readily abandoned in the sphere of sex, and this weakens Ego's grip. Soul, on the other hand, may flourish in the abandonment of sexual rapture, with its more direct relation to nature.

It follows that the life of soul and the erotic are closely linked. The pleasures of flesh are also the pleasures of soul—just as the material care of flesh is the work of soul. Of course it need not appear this way—and why should it?—since what "appears" is the prerogative of the gatekeeper of consciousness, Ego. There is an erotism of Ego in which sex becomes an end in itself and for the self—an end in which the Other is reduced to mere means, a body-place for desire. Under such circumstances, second nature, the residence of soul, becomes also the demonic place Freud called the id, and the chamber in which Saint John of the Cross recognized the dark night of the soul. It is not merely a matter of distorting the perception of the erotic: the erotic itself is distorted by Ego.

We would not see Ego, then, in the rosy light afforded by ego psychology, as the good cop who keeps the local toughs under control; we see Ego as a law enforcer, all right, but regard the law as having a major role in the production of crime. Once a category of the Other is established, then something must be made to fill the bill. And now Ego finishes the job by stigmatization of the excluded. By not recognizing the Other, Ego demonizes the other. This is played out in the war between the sexes, especially in the demonizing hatred of the female by the male, since it is the latter who, having power, takes Ego for his predominant identity, and therefore repels not simply the Other, but, more critically, whatever accepts Otherness.

Not only is the true affinity between soul and the erotic masked in Egoic functioning: it is actually reversed, so that the erotic becomes the realm of the devil and witches. The struggle between Ego and soul internal to the individual extends outward to culture. On this larger scale, nature, especially in regard to erotic life, becomes the "outside" wilderness with respect to which civilization is the "inside," or the zone where Ego recognizes itself. Soul, which takes both Ego and nature for an Other to be reclaimed, seeks to reconcile this opposition by wandering across the boundary between civil society and wilderness. That is, soul cannot be inside and outside at once; so it is now inside and civilized, and now outside and natural, or wild. Thus soul accepts the fact that full human being cannot be internally consistent. This task can be carried out reasonably well in functioning precapitalist societies, all of whom develop a richly elaborate set of taboos, transgressions, rites of passage, bacchanalias, witchery, shamanisms, and other voyages into the realm beyond Egoic apperception.[47]

In modern society, on the other hand, the greater grip of Ego squeezes all but a few remnants out of tradition. We have our atavistic witch cults, our pornographic excesses, our Mardi Gras, our professional wrestlers, our weekends given over to the day at the beach and the escape from toil. But these are adornments and diversions, while the dead hand of Egoic rationalization and the logic of production descends over the whole. Three major possibilities remain by which soul can hope to resume its odyssey across the boundaries into the wilderness. One is madness—the internal overthrow of Ego; another is revolution—the external overthrow of Ego's world system; and the third is art—the imaginative restructuring of reality through a projection of soul.

The Break with Logos

There is an immense space between reality and what we think or say about reality. Ego, which does not recognize the Other, cannot appreciate this space, nor can it appropriate the understanding of it. Wisdom begins with an appreciation that mind only re-presents reality, that it works with word-images and not the real, and that no human being can know the real. Since logos identifies the word and reality, wisdom begins with the criticism of logos.

Beginning with Nietzsche's denial of metaphysical claims for knowledge, modern philosophy has staked its ground on the realization of both the limits and the power of language. A powerful tendency of modern philosophy dismantles logos itself. And yet this philosophy, notably in the deconstruction of Jacques Derrida, does not undertake its attack on logos on behalf of soul. Rather it consumes and discards spirit in the process, leaving no sense of sense of justice, nor any possibility of systematic resistance to a murderous society.[48]

Between annihilating logos and enshrining it lies a third, critical path: the restoration of spirit-power to language, and with it, the restoration of language to being. To be critical means the commitment to demolish Egoic claims to an apodictic truth outside history. For the assertion of absolute knowledge is evidence of domination, not a merely intellectual point. These claims are also those of patriarchy, for the father, in expropriating his right to women and children, does so through a monopoly on the word. The ensemble is tied together at the level of unconscious desire by the signification of the phallus as the word: the thrusting, piercing, truth of the world. Hence logos, the pretender who assumes the mantle of absolute, transcendental knowledge, signifies a structure composed of Ego, patriarchy, fundamentalism, phallocentrism, and domination.

What, by contrast, are the ways of speech open to soul? One hesitates to enumerate, but the following come to mind.

1. *Critique:* Soul confronts logos through a critique which does not deconstruct the text so much as reveal the hidden history of Otherness contained within it—the lost desire, the repressed speech, the hidden transformative capacity. "History" here signifies the mark domination has made upon thought through the splitting-off of class, race, and gender. Hence critique regathers and differentiates what had been split, becoming the work of soul in the realm of language. If texts lie, it is not as a code that reveals yet another text, but in reference to a historical truth whose existence the deconstructionists do not recognize. Critique is emancipatory in spirit, because it releases spirit-power thwarted by domination. It is the "truth that will make you free."

2. *Poesis:* If critical thought expresses soul in its effort to grasp reality objectively, *poesis* expresses the soul's power to project the language of its own being. *Poesis* includes poetry and other kinds of aesthetic expression, but also prayer. For prayer is essentially a form of soul-speech whose power comes from the same place as that of poetry: it is the word restored to its original status as thing, to its original place at the boundary of being emerging from its plasma. There are words that do more than evoke—they stand before being and allow being to flow into them. The giving-over of soul flows through the channels of poesis.

From another angle, poesis is the form of thought corresponding to intuitive, direct, and empathic knowledge.[49] This is not the only way of knowing, to be sure, but without it, knowing and speaking are incomplete. More specifically, dialogue is impossible. Language turned strictly toward the purposes of representing objects and stripped of any connection to being is fine for the conveyance of information, and necessary in its place—but it cannot be the dialogical basis of a human relationship or society. I would not want the computer at which I am working to make any more of the words I am putting into it than I do. But this is because the computer is a being at a very low level of differentiation; and despite all the hoopla, is not capable of dialogue.[50] For a full being, on the other hand, words are both the indicators of something else and the elemental particles of being itself. Dialogue is the transmission of this combined function between beings. Soul restores language to this function—without losing the representative power of language. It is the unity of meaning and being in words. Ego arrogates this spirit-power for logos, where spirit-power and truth become identified. And soul restores by differentiating spirit-power from truth. This allows truth to be shared dialogically, through mutual recognition.[51]

We have been indoctrinated into a belief that science, the source of power in the world, is also the domain of Ego. But this is sheer ideology. Science should refer to the collective pursuit of truth; it depends, therefore, on the adequacy of the notion of truth. This is necessarily inadequate for Ego, because it excludes the Other. Ego may see through cracks in reality, and see clearly, because its field of vision is so narrow. But it sees only a tiny portion of the real, and distorts it, because relationships within reality are lost.

Both critique and poesis, on the other hand, are essential ancillae to a full science. I say ancillae because they cannot replace patient investigation, validation, etc. But these rational faculties are not denied to soul, either. Rather they are put into a framework by critique and oriented by the intuitive knowing characteristic of poesis. Because it reclaims a full notion of truth, soul does not uncritically accept all propositions. If there is a "soul-science," it is a science that weighs evidence, respects logic, and abides by consensual validation. All science is a social project; however, sciences differ from one another according to the kinds of society they represent. The key distinction between soul-science and Egoic science is openness to the "more things in heaven and earth . . . than are dreamt of in your philosophy."[52] This would apply to whether the object of investigation is the normal scientific domain of the objective world, or the phenomena of soul itself.

There is an important distinction, very rarely made, between what is *nonrational* and what is *irrational*. The *nonrational* comprises the "more things in heaven and earth." It is that part of the universe which is real but beyond the power of the human intellect to grasp, including those regions of the inner self Freud unearthed as the unconscious. The *irrational*, by contrast, comprises that which is made violent and incoherent by human agency, i.e., what is actually destructive. There is nothing in nature as such which is irrational, except it be made so by the human mind, or Ego. For Ego, in its pride, makes unreal what the intellect cannot grasp, and so deprives it of being.[53] Rejection by Ego is what makes the unconscious seem irrational rather than nonrational. Of course this same rejection parades itself as reason. We have to learn to recognize such Egoic rationality as rationalization, that is, as the conversion of the nonrational into the irrational—and of itself into the pseudorational. A full rationality, on the other hand, differentiates, accepting the nonrational and working to understand it.

Differentiation is not a technique; it *is* the principle of soul-praxis itself, and the work of a full being. But "differentiation" is also only a word, which should not be elevated, no more than the words, "soul," "spirit," or "being," to the dimensions of godhead. Among the world religions, Judaism has a spiritually sensible practice of not representing God, either in images or words (the signifier being G-d, which does not solve the problem so much as remind us that the representation of Ultimate Being is indeed a problem). By the same token, "Ego," or even "capitalism" should not be made into the Devil, as much as we would wish to overthrow the unholy pair of scoundrels. Splitting is splitting, whether carried out in the name of soul or not—indeed, the holy righteousness of religious and political fundamentalism offers a terrifying perspective on human cruelty. To differentiate well means to differentiate as well between differentiation and splitting, between soul and Ego, and so forth.

In truth, it must be said that soul, being differentiated from Ego, recognizes Ego as its Other, indeed its principal Other. Thus Egoic activities—including capitalism, logos, and the writing of books—cannot be simply abandoned, but need to be resolved into new dialectical syntheses. This point has implications for revolutionary politics, for it mandates nonviolence as both the goal and the means toward the goal, however difficult this may be to fulfill in practice in the heat of action.

Differentiation from logos is experienced as risk-taking and spontaneity. It is jumping into the waves, a letting go. Soul, after all, is a way of passion. To listen to "soul music," to join in the fervor of the religious moment, is to not hold back, but to let go of one's self. It is giving up of Egoic restrictions on emotion. The same applies to the intellect, where soul gives up logos but neither logic nor spirit-power. One plays with language until it does the work of critique and poesis, and inspires being to change the world.

The Soul Seeks the Universal

The value of suffering is downgraded these days, in the feel-good culture of late capitalism. In fact, a general anaesthesia and indifference seem to be the order of things. But just as soul is the passionate site of spontaneity and play, so is it the seat of suffering. Opening to the Other means feeling the pain of the world. There is a place for vacations to scenic islands where one "gets away from it all," but that place is not a spiritual one.

Unhappily, the wicked do flourish, in our own time as much as in that of the Bible. Soul feels this wrongness, embodied in injustice and violence. It suffers also the anguish of Ego and its unfulfillable desire. Soul feels Ego's anguish, it may be added, because it is differentiated and not split from Ego, hence includes Ego even as it transcends Ego. But soul-suffering also implies the hope of a radical happiness. To suffer and remain open to being means to anticipate the possibilities of a full being, to recognize the ground of being in a realm beyond any state apparatus or human law, to recognize the basis of freedom in that ground of being, and to recognize the indissolubility of freedom in each individual person—in short, it means the soul's appreciation of a universal realm of being as the birthright of every being. This birthright is the basis of rights themselves—of human rights, animal rights, the rights of every being. The human rights to which the states of the world pay lip service (for even the fascist government of El Salvador has a "Human Rights Commission") would, if fulfilled, abolish the state itself. That is why all states are forced to lie, and to assume for themselves a false universality. Of course, they don't all lie equally. This is to say that states have within themselves, like individuals, Ego and soul potentialities. I think it fair to call the former authoritarianism, and the latter a democracy open to Otherness—again bearing in mind that every state calls itself democratic, and none comes close to this goal, nor will until class domination is abolished.

Only by recognizing the full ground of universal being can the value of each particular being be asserted. This is not as paradoxical as it appears, since the uniqueness of each individual can only be seen in a light that frees him or her from the mass. From another angle, soul's opening to Otherness allows the particularity of each individual to come to the fore, highlighted against the backdrop of universality.

Hegel was right—the truth resides in the whole—even if he imposed upon this whole the chauvinism of the German bourgeois. Adorno was right, too: the whole is false—since the sense of the whole is imposed by an antagonistic society which tries to deny its internal splits by imposing a false unity. Only when the whole is seen beyond the perimeter of any state propaganda apparatus can it be seen as a true unity.

To direct oneself toward the whole is to become oriented toward Ultimate Being, now as the lodestar of development under the aegis of soul. This happily cuts societies to size and reveals that they all fall short of their goal. There can be no perfect society, since human being can never attain Ultimate Being. There will, in short, always be Ego, with its jealousy, envy, greed, and unfulfillable desire. We should not regard this as bad news, only realism. In fact, it should come as something of a relief, sparing us of the need to moan over the imperfections of society, which is rather like complaining that one's chickens cannot be toilet trained.

However, griping is one thing, and criticizing another. If no society can be perfect, all can be improved, nor are all of equal value. Nothing can make a chicken control its excrements; such is simply not within the perimeter of chicken being. However, human being has been given potentials which have scarcely been understood, much less tapped. This is the real test of the politics of spirit: whether it so empowers and feeds beings as to bring them closer to Ultimate Being. And as we have seen, this is a matter of justice.

We now see at a glance how to tell a pseudospirituality from the real thing. The spirituality of Oliver North, for example, who prays regularly, is bogus because, like the pious imperialists in whose footsteps he stands, his politics are in the service of global plunder and greed. The spirituality of a Bhagwan Shree Rajneesh was bogus, too, because it reproduced cultlike patterns of domination and crawled into bed with capitalist accumulation. And the spirituality of Ayatollah Khomeini was bogus because, like Hitler and Stalin, it fueled itself by murderous splitting and drove its adherents into an Egoic loss of individuality. No spirituality, in sum, transcends its politics, just as no politics can evade its spiritual core . . . or its utopian aspiration, necessary and unrealizable. *U-topia* means "no place," which is to say, the place of Ultimate Being.

Despite the infinitude of our potential an infinite gap remains between us and Ultimate Being.[54] The endless path of development which unwinds before us has therefore no fixed, set line, no correct line to hew. The "correct line," in other words, is false; it loses the asymptote toward Ultimate Being. The path of soul is rather more discontinuous, as soul makes accession over Ego, becomes new Ego, then yields again to soul, and so on. There can be no continuous development of soul, then, but rather bursts, irruptions, stallings, wandering loops, and odd concatenations of spirit. The universal is too big, after all, to be translated into any kind of package or formula. We are all fragments of nothing against the infinite unity of Ultimate Being. Yet despite this unsurpassable truth, the soul's destiny is to be a warrior—for justice, for truth, for nonviolence, for love, for solidarity, for all the manifestations of being—to be a warrior, moreover, whose struggle need have no victory.

Soul Recognizes Death

> *There's a little black train a'coming,*
> *Coming down the track.*
> *You got to ride that little black train,*
> *But it ain't a'going to bring you back.*
>
> Woody Guthrie, *Little Black Train**

> *Fear of death is the most telling sign of a wrong, that is, a bad life.*
>
> Ludwig Wittgenstein, quoted in Duerr, *Dreamtime*

And death shall have dominion over all. Death strikes Ego with special violence, since Ego's pet illusion is its uniqueness over everything, while death levels all beings. Thus the march of Egoic civilization can be measured in its increasingly widespread denial of death and fear of death. Soul, on the other hand, accepts death as the renewing as well as the leveling of being, for it knows that new being emerges out of old and that nothing really dies except as Ego. Soul knows, too, that it lives forever in its projections, which become Otherness accepted by other souls. But if soul accepts death and does not fear death, and even as it realizes its immortality and resurrection and knows that death shall have no dominion, it still does not want to die until its time has come. Before then, soul rides being as on a great wave, and feels life with all the pain and joy of which being is capable. It must be said, too, that soul shares in Ego's dread of death. For though Ego hates soul, soul loves Ego, and is open to Ego as its Other. Even, then, after soul achieves a full differentiation, it still feels the pain and terror of Ego. Then when its time comes to rejoin the being of the universe, soul suffers, as all beings must.

I have tried to find the right words to express the life of soul, or at least their best approximation within the limits of my being, confined by time, place, gender, a narrow range of experience, various preju-

* *Little Black Train* adapted by Woody Guthrie, © 1965 by Stormking Music, Inc. All rights reserved. Used by permission.

dices, and who knows what else. It would have been better, perhaps, had I felt the sure grounding of one of the world's great religions as I undertook the task. But I am as unable to accept established religion at the end of this work as I was at the beginning. However, I am more convinced than before—for the labor was a way of wrestling with my own questioning into spirit—that spirit and soul are valid, and indeed necessary categories of human existence, and that we abandon them at our doom. Necessary but not sufficient, and so much more is required to firmly understand the many points on which soul alights, that I have at times despaired of placing this text before a public already overburdened with inspirational literature. Yet I have persisted, for reasons of Ego if not of soul. If the result may appear antiquated and too much the revival of old saws for the modern spirit, I can only say in reply that the ancient voices of soul struck notes of perennial wisdom. What seems new is too often said in defense of the ancien régime, while to realize the old truths of spirit requires that we win a new world.

Notes

Introduction

1. Herbert Marcuse, *Eros and Civilization* (Boston: Beacon Press, 1966); Norman O. Brown, *Life Against Death* (New York: Random House, 1959).

2. The key distinction lies in their attitudes toward Marx, or rather, toward the question Marx highlighted, namely, between materialist and idealist interpretations of history. Marcuse remains the historical materialist, even if he chooses a different revolutionary agent—students—than the proletariat; thus his emphasis is always political. Brown, on the other hand, is an extreme idealist, one who takes Freud to a point the father of psychoanalysis never intended—where history itself is to be explained by the "slow return of the repressed." Thus for Brown, political engagement becomes a more or less empty category. Marcuse represents the student radicals of the sixties, and Brown the hippies.

3. For an extensive treatment of this theme, see Morris Berman, *The Reenchantment of the World* (Toronto: Bantam Books, 1984).

4. I was raised in a fairly traditional Jewish setting, and underwent the expected religious training, including bar mitzvah. I cannot ever recall a time, however, when the Hebrew religion appealed to me as a coherent faith. In my adult years I undertook some mild exposure to Zen Buddhism, turning away for reasons which are suggested in Chapters Five and Six. At times I have felt drawn to Catholicism—until I considered the Vatican hierarchy, or what Christians have done to Jews, as well as numerous articles of faith which I could not accept.

5. I offer below and in Chapter Six a highly critical view of one Islamic leader, the late Ayatollah Khomeini of Iran. It seems to me, though, that Kho-

meini represents a perversion of the spiritual potentialities inherent to Islam, and that he is no more representative of its tradition than Meir Kahane is of Judaism or Pat Robertson of Christianity. However, I am not competent to say more of the true Islamic tradition.

6. In this chapter I also deal most extensively with the critique of psychoanalysis. One might say that there is a subtext, of the "ontoanalysis of psychoanalysis," going on throughout *History and Spirit,* which reaches a crescendo in Chapter Four with discussions of consciousness, the ego, and the unconscious, and then falls away.

7. See Paul Ricoeur, *Freud and Philosophy* (New Haven: Yale University Press, 1970), for an important demonstration of this thesis.

8. For a description of this signification and its many ramifications, see Stanley Diamond, *In Search of the Primitive* (New Brunswick, N.J. and London: Transaction Books, 1974); also Pierre Clastres, *Society Against the State,* trans. Robert Hurley and Abe Stein (New York: Zone Books, 1987). Obviously these developments were conditioned by many things, including the difference between oral and literate culture. See also Walter J. Ong, *The Presence of the Word* (New Haven: Yale University Press, 1967); Joel Kovel, "Mind and State in Ancient Greece," in *The Radical Spirit* (London: Free Association Books, 1988), 208–25.

9. An outstanding discussion of the many possibilities open to the "religious field" is that of Otto Maduro, *Religion and Social Conflicts,* trans. Robert K. Barr (Maryknoll, N.Y.: Orbis, 1982).

10. The argument here follows Max Weber, *The Protestant Ethic and the Spirit of Capitalism,* trans. Talcott Parsons (New York: Scribners, 1958), who most forcefully pointed out capitalism's initial dependence on and ultimate rejection of spirituality. Obviously, the argument of my work differs radically from Weber in trying to establish a basis for spirituality itself. This was a task he bracketed but believed impossible.

11. Karl Marx, *Capital,* vol. 1, trans. Samuel Moore and Edward Aveling (New York: International Publishers, 1967), 71ff. Marx claimed that to understand this mysterious property of the commodity in capitalist society, "we must have recourse to the mist-enveloped regions of the religious world." See Chapter Six for further discussion.

12. Whereas in precapitalist society spirituality, despite being otherworldly, remained attached to work and social power. Because of this essential shift in the location of power, a bitter conflict developed between traditional religion and the emerging capitalist order. R. H. Tawney, *Religion and the Rise of Capitalism* (New York: Harcourt Brace, 1926), has a classic description of this protracted struggle, lost by the Church. Saint Thomas Aquinas, for example, was quite insistent that economic activity for its own sake, i.e., without a genuine spirituality, was dangerous and destructive. See Joseph Ferraro, "St. Thomas Aquinas and Modern Catholic Doctrine," *Monthly Review* 38 (June 1986): 13–19, who concludes that "St. Thomas would hold that modern capitalist labor relations are intrinsically evil and therefore incapable of reform." On the other hand, this is an "if pigs had wings" kind of proposition, since the actual man, Aquinas, was no rebel, and would have probably found a way to apologize for whatever ruling class was in power. Indeed, the whole resistance by

the Catholic hierarchy to bourgeois society was tinged with a need to protect its class privilege under feudalism.

13. The case of John D. Rockefeller is instructive. The archetypical capitalist felt no contradiction between utter rapacity in the business world and exaggerated piety outside it. Indeed, he became the most celebrated avatar of the gospel of wealth: "I believe the power to make money is a gift from God . . . to be developed and used to the best of our ability for the good of mankind. Having been endowed with the gift I possess, I believe it my duty to make money and still more money and to use the money I make for the good of my fellow man according to the dictates of my conscience." A confirmed Baptist, Rockefeller taught Sunday School, believed in tithing, and endowed many religious and educational institutions, including those from which later emerged Martin Luther King, Jr. The key point here is less the manifested spiritual attitude than the capacity to detach it from the practical activity which was its basis. Peter Collier and David Horowitz, *The Rockefellers: A Family Dynasty* (New York and London: Summit Books, 1976), 48; and Taylor Branch, *Parting the Waters: America in the King Years, 1956–1963* (New York: Simon and Schuster, 1988).

14. Two other prominent factors have been the motion of many ethnic groups across a vast and expanding frontier; and the original Puritan impulse, which constituted the United States as a fundamentally religious society. See Mary Douglas and Steven M. Tipton, eds., *Religion and America: Spirituality in a Secular Age* (Boston: Beacon Press, 1983) for a wide-ranging discussion.

15. Louis Dupré, *Transcendent Selfhood* (New York: Seabury Press, 1978).

16. Gregor Samsa of *The Metamorphosis* is thrown out with the garbage; Joseph K. of *The Trial* is killed and thrown into a ravine; the lieutenant of *In the Penal Colony* is similarly dumped after his killing machine gets through with him; and the hunger artist is swept out of his cage.

17. It is striking how people of earlier times would permit themselves passion that the citizen of today only dreams about or sees in horror movies. We have, for example, the evidence from the late Middle Ages of Johan Huizinga, *The Waning of the Middle Ages* (Garden City, N.Y.: Doubleday Anchor, 1954). Closer to home, I recall hearing that only a little more than a century ago, fistfights and tears were common sights on the floor of the United States Congress.

18. Quoted in Hans Peter Duerr, *Dreamtime,* trans. Felicitas Goodman (Oxford and New York: Basil Blackwell, 1985), 353.

19. Ong, *Presence of the Word.* See also Walter J. Ong, *Orality and Literacy* (London and New York: Methuen, 1982).

20. Where it was mediated by the invention of the printing press and the need to find a locus of authority anterior to Rome. The tendency also manifested the growing importance of abstraction in the emerging capitalist world system.

Prelude

1. The pace of toil continues to mount. I recall recently hearing a chilling statistic over the radio, that whereas twenty years ago the average adult worked forty hours a week and had twenty-six hours of leisure, today (this

broadcast was in 1988) the figures have shifted to forty-six hours of work and but seventeen hours of leisure. The primary forces behind this shift are no doubt economic, but there is a spiritual aspect as well. We might say that the attenuation of the spiritual dimension weakens resistance to the domination of toil. Further, where there is no spirit, leisure is easily industrialized and replaced by frantic activity.

2. Diamond, *In Search of the Primitive;* Duerr, *Dreamtime.* Marshall Sahlins, *Stone Age Economics* (Chicago: University of Chicago Press, 1972) has an interesting discussion in which he estimates that hunter-gatherers work about four hours a day to maintain life, the rest of the time being spent in play, personal activities and—though the word would mean nothing to them— spirituality.

3. See Joel Kovel, "On the Notion of Human Nature," in *Hermeneutics and Psychological Theory,* Stanley B. Messer, Louis A. Sass, and Robert Woolfolk, eds. (New Brunswick, N.J.: Rutgers University Press, 1988), 370–99, for a discussion of the problems surrounding this trampled term, and the reasons for putting it at the center of my work.

4. As should be no surprise, many quotations are drawn from the Bible. Here I have used both the King James version (KJ) and the Revised Standard Version (RSV), according to suitability. Obviously it is important to get back to the exact Aramaic or Greek—but not for the purposes at hand. Since all words are at best relative approximations of spiritual meaning, I have tried to find those combinations of words that best express the meaning I have in mind. That this happens to be a translation of a translation of an oral text matters not. For a discussion of the language of the Bible, see Northrop Frye, *The Great Code: The Bible and Literature* (San Diego: Harcourt, Brace Jovanovich, 1982).

5. This should not be confused with the "archaeology of knowledge" of Michel Foucault, who is, it may be added, a decidedly antispiritual thinker. Foucault's work is based on a series of brilliant investigations into the historical forms taken by thinking and perception. He sees these as ways in which knowledge is constituted as power and used repressively. In his view, however, the successive stages through which knowledge is constituted are essentially sui generis and discontinuous. That is, there is no superordinate principle of which the forms of knowing are manifestations. He forcefully rejects any notion of the whole, or of truth beyond instrumentality. For Foucault, human activity was essentially technical, in the narrow sense, and without any transcendent aspect. As he said with respect to his method of "genealogy": "Once the historical sense is mastered by a suprahistorical perspective, metaphysics can bend it to its own purpose, and, by aligning it to the demands of objective science, it can impose its own 'Egyptianism.' On the other hand, the historical sense can evade metaphysics and become a privileged instrument of genealogy if it refuses the certainty of absolutes. Given this, it corresponds to the acuity of a glance that distinguishes, separates, and disperses; that is capable of liberating divergence and marginal elements—the kind of dissociating view that is capable of decomposing itself, capable of shattering the unity of man's being through which it was thought he could extend his sovereignty to the events of the past." Michel Foucault, "Nietzsche, Genealogy, History," in *The Foucault*

Reader, ed. Paul Rabinow (New York: Pantheon, 1984), 87. It seems to me, however, that the fate of being decomposed, dissociated, and shattered—all of which belong to the very "spirit" of late capitalism—is not one to be very much valued, and that it is not so much a liberation as a kind of nihilism. If so, then we do need to find a larger unifying principle—one which is nonabsolute and nonsovereign, however, and faithful to the particular needs of liberation. It would seem, too, that this principle should not be so much "suprahistorical" as dialectically related to history. The reader must decide if the present work succeeds in developing such a view.

Chapter 1. Spirit as Vital Force

1. Robert Farris Thompson, *Flash of the Spirit* (New York: Vintage, 1984), 5.

2. Quoted in Mircea Eliade, *From Primitives to Zen* (New York: Harper and Row, 1967), 11–12.

3. Gerardus van der Leeuw, *Religion in Essence and Manifestation* (1933; reprint, Princeton: Princeton University Press, 1986), 26.

4. Ibid., 24.

5. Ibid., 25.

6. Rudolph Otto, *The Idea of the Holy,* trans. John W. Harvey (London: Oxford, 1950), 10.

7. Ibid., 12–13, 25.

8. Ibid., 114.

9. W. T. Stace, *Mysticism and Philosophy* (Los Angeles: Jeremy P. Tarcher, 1960). This is a very careful dissection of the phenomenon by a positivist philosopher, whose fascination with yet refusal to share mystical experience lends his work considerable tension.

10. Quoted in ibid., 65.

11. It is worth noting that Stace's rejection of Hegelian logic is principally responsible for his refusal to understand mysticism.

12. Stace, *Mysticism,* 63.

13. See Charles Tart, ed., *Altered States of Consciousness* (Garden City, N.Y.: Doubleday, 1972) for numerous aspects of this.

14. Evelyn Underhill, *Mysticism* (New York: New American Library, 1974) contains an extensive discussion of these phenomena, as does the classic by William James, *The Varieties of Religious Experience* (New York: New American Library, 1958).

15. Richard Maurice Bucke, *Cosmic Consciousness* (Secaucus, N.J.: The Citadel Press, 1961), 8; also quoted in James, *Varieties,* 390, and Stace, *Mysticism,* 78. Bucke was originally published in 1901.

16. Aside from works by Heidegger himself, which will be cited from time to time in this study, my understanding of the philosopher is indebted to Theodor Adorno, *The Jargon of Authenticity,* trans. Knut Tarnowski and Frederic Will (London: Routledge and Kegan Paul, 1973); John D. Caputo, *The Mystical Element in Heidegger's Thought* (Athens, Ohio: The Ohio University Press, 1978); David Michael Levin, *The Body's Recollection of Being* (London, Routledge and Kegan Paul, 1985); Allan Megill, *Prophets of Extremity* (Berkeley: University of California Press, 1985); and Michael Zimmerman, *Eclipse of the Self* (Athens, Ohio: The Ohio University Press, 1981). For Heidegger's politics, see n. 32.

17. Marcuse studied with Heidegger as well as with Husserl; and the initial, and in some ways deepest, current of his thought derives from Heidegger's ontology. He broke with the master in 1932, probably for political reasons, as Heidegger had by that time already revealed deep affinities for Nazism, while Marcuse was a resolute Marxist. Marcuse's Heideggerian side remained in eclipse during his most active period with the Frankfurt Institute of Social Research, but may be said to have reemerged, albeit displaced onto Freud, with *Eros and Civilization.* For a discussion of the entire School, see Martin Jay, *The Dialectical Imagination* (Boston: Little, Brown, 1973).

18. Northrop Frye, *The Great Code,* 29, considers *kerygma* the essential linguistic idiom of the entire Bible, although the term is usually used in relation to the Gospels. Rudolph Bultmann, *Faith and Understanding* (New York: Harper and Row, 1969) places *kerygma* at the center of his theology—a logical step for Protestantism, which seeks an ever-more unmediated relationship between the divine and the human.

19. Spiritual phenomena of this kind can be seen from both sides—the "beyond" and the "earthly." We emphasize here mainly the effects of the beyond on the earthly, but the opposite perspective is equally possible. Thus Mircea Eliade has written about the experiencing of sacred spirit as force: "The great mystery consists in *the very fact that the sacred is made manifest;* for . . . in making itself manifest, the sacred *limits* and 'historicizes' itself. We realize how greatly the sacred limits itself by taking the form of a stone: but we are prone to forget that God himself was accepting limitation and historicisation by incarnating as Jesus Christ." *Myths, Dreams and Mysteries,* trans. Philip Mairet (New York: Harper, 1961), 125.

20. Friedrich Nietzsche, *Ecce Homo,* trans. Clifton P. Fadiman, in *The Philosophy of Nietzsche* (New York: Modern Library, 1927), 896.

21. Eugen Herrigel, *Zen in the Art of Archery* (New York: Vintage, 1971).

22. Daisetz T. Suzuki, *Zen and Japanese Culture* (Princeton: Bollingen-Princeton University Press, 1970), 152–53, 159.

23. Artistic virtuosity undoubtedly reveals the same features. Suzuki makes this point for a number of the oriental arts, but it would apply equally well, I should think, to painting or the performance of music.

24. From the Brihad-āranyaka Upanishad. Quoted in Eliade, *From Primitives to Zen,* 588.

25. Robert C. Zaehner, *Hindu and Muslim Mysticism* (New York: Schocken, 1969), 30. Observe that Zaehner regards the identity of spirit with breath as merely symbolic.

26. As an example of the ambiguities of language here, and to anticipate a later discussion, Buddhist doctrine holds that the enlightened one has no self; i.e., that which we take to be the self is an illusion. It would seem therefore that the fully spiritual person would have no soul, either. I would say, though (for at this level we all are *saying* things), that "no-self" conveys the sense of "soul," and that this soul is an infinitesimal relation to the self. Thus there is no limit to the ablation of the self, yet the self is never completely ablated short of physical death. See Chapter Five for a discussion of the infinitesimal nature of spirit, and Chapter Six for a discussion of the notion of "soul."

27. John McKenzie, *Dictionary of the Bible* (Milwaukee: Bruce, 1965).

28. William Shakespeare, *The First Part of King Henry IV,* in *The Complete Works of William Shakespeare,* ed. William Aldin Wright (Garden City, N.J.: Garden City Books, 1936), 504.

29. "The Marriage of Heaven and Hell," in *The Complete Poetry and Prose of William Blake,* ed. David Erdman (Garden City, N.Y.: Doubleday, 1982), 34–39.

30. The problem with Foucault is that he remains single-visioned, merely substituting one eye for another. That is, he refuses to see that there is something definite and material which is produced, and that the relations of production make a difference. In a word, he fatally relativizes the notion of truth. For further discussion, see n. 5, Prelude, as well as Perry Anderson, *In the Tracks of Historical Materialism* (London: Verso, 1983); Peter Dews, *Logics of Disintegration* (London: Verso, 1987); and Megill, *Prophets.*

31. See Ivan Morris, *The Nobility of Failure: Tragic Heroes in the History of Japan* (Rutland, Vt. and Tokyo: Charles Tuttle, 1982), for a discussion of these issues in the light of Japanese history and culture. Morris emphasizes that the hero acts from a need for "purity of motive." He has a "longing for absolute meaning out of time and . . . a realization that the social, political world is essentially a place of corruption whose materiality is incompatible with the demands of pure spirit and truth" (23). Hence the logic of ritual suicide, as an act of spirit-power turned against the organism. This is only a short step from the ideal of the Zen warrior; or rather, it is that warrior when the times are too far out of joint.

32. Such being the principle interpretation of Zimmerman, *Eclipse.*

33. For certain aspects of the German crisis, see George Mosse, *The Crisis of German Ideology: Intellectual Origins of the Third Reich* (New York: Grosset and Dunlap, 1964).

34. Heidegger's formal adoption of Nazism came in 1933, and at a crucial place, for he had recently assumed the position of rector of Freiburg University. According to self-serving accounts made by him late in life, he did so only in order to save the University and the Jews within it. He left the Party in less than a year and eventually fell out of favor with the regime. However at no time did he ever renounce his fascism or adequately denounce Nazism. Moreover, later research strongly supports the hypothesis that his fascist politics were all too authentic. See Karl A. Moehling, "Martin Heidegger and the Nazi Party: an Examination" (Ph.D. diss., Northern Illinois University, 1972) and Victor Farías, *Heidegger and Nazism,* ed. Joseph Margolis and Tom Rockmore (Philadelphia: Temple University Press, 1989). The latter has much definitive material, including a revealing correspondence between Heidegger and Marcuse in 1947–48 on responsibility for the Holocaust. In it Heidegger says "I expected from National Socialism a spiritual rejuvenation of all life, a reconciliation of social antagonisms [!], and the rescue of Western existence from the dangers of communism. . . . to the severe and justified reproach that you [Marcuse] express over a regime that has exterminated millions of Jews, that has made terror a norm and that transformed everything connected to the concepts of spirit, freedom and truth into its opposite, I can only add that instead of the 'Jews' one should put the 'East Germans,' and that is even more the case for one of the Allied Powers. . . ." To which Marcuse replied: "Do you not

situate yourself with this proposition outside the dimension in which a discussion is possible between people—outside of reason [logos]?" (283–87).

35. Martin Heidegger, *An Introduction to Metaphysics,* trans. Ralph Manheim (New Haven: Yale University Press, 1959), 133–34.

36. Quoted in Zimmerman, *Eclipse,* 9.

Chapter 2. Spirit as Occult Being

1. Mircea Eliade, *Shamanism,* trans. Willard Trask (Princeton: Bollingen-Princeton University Press, 1972), 5.

2. Ludwig Wittgenstein, *Philosophical Investigations,* trans. G. E. M. Ancombe (New York: Macmillan, 1953), 18.

3. Descartes was a very decent sort of person, according to Frederick Copleston, *A History of Philosophy,* Book Two (New York: Doubleday Image, 1985), 66.

4. For an outstanding discussion of this development from a feminist viewpoint, see Carolyn Merchant, *The Death of Nature* (San Francisco: Harper and Row, 1980).

5. Copleston, *History,* 70.

6. René Descartes, "Discourse on Method," quoted in Merchant, *Death of Nature,* 231.

7. Ibid., 188.

8. Ibid., 205. Merchant points out that Descartes's reduction of nature to inert substance was even more thoroughgoing than Newton's.

9. Copleston makes no mention of her in his stupendously thorough (over 4,000 pages) history of philosophy—a shocking omission yet characteristic of the traditionally masculine world of logos.

10. Quoted in Merchant, *Death of Nature,* 258.

11. Alfred North Whitehead, *Science and the Modern World* (New York: Free Press, 1925), 194–96.

12. René Descartes, "Discourse on Method," trans. John Veitch, in *The Rationalists* (Garden City, N.Y.: Doubleday Anchor, 1960), 46, 48. See also Perry Anderson, *Lineages of the Absolutist State* (London: NLB, 1974).

13. Letter to Mersenne, quoted in Merchant, *Death of Nature,* 205.

14. Marcel Mauss, "A Category of the Human Spirit," *The Psychoanalytic Review* 55, no. 3 (1968): 457–81.

15. Paul Radin, *Primitive Man as Philosopher* (New York: Dover, 1957), 259. In the point of view developed in the present work, the term *Ego* will be employed as the antispiritual form of the self characteristic of capitalist modernity.

16. Ibid., 258.

17. Marx almost certainly would have been quite hostile to the assertion that anything as nonrational as a spirit-being could be truly constitutive of human beings. In my opinion, this attitude is a remnant of Cartesianism in Marx and the Marxist tradition, and has been both theoretically and practically costly.

18. See Chapter One, n. 10.

19. See, in addition to *Science and the Modern World,* Whitehead's metaphysical masterpiece, *Process and Reality: An Essay in Cosmology,* ed. David R. Griffin and Donald W. Sherburne (New York: Free Press, 1978), in which

he develops the notion of the "prehension" as the basic unit of a unified reality. Whitehead's overarching concern was to develop a notion of the physical world which would allow us to see the interconnected unity of all things while remaining capable of speaking of discrete bodies.

20. Roderick Nash, *Wilderness and the American Mind,* 3d ed. (New Haven: Yale University Press, 1982).

21. This being the terminology advanced by Heinz Kohut, whose revision of ego psychology along the lines of narcissism was an attempt to break loose from the rigid confines of mainstream psychoanalysis. Kohut recognized that Hartmannian ego psychology severely limited our ability to speak of the range of self-experience, and he attempted to get around this—how successful he was is another matter. See Heinz Kohut, *The Analysis of the Self* (New York: International Universities Press, 1971); and his *The Restoration of the Self* (New York: International Universities Press, 1977); also the discussion in Joel Kovel, *The Age of Desire* (New York: Pantheon, 1981). One cannot cover everything at once, and for practical reasons I have elected to greatly limit discussion of the many variations in psychoanalytic theory in which the various issues raised by this work are treated. One would particularly want to do greater justice to the British schools of object relations and Kleinian analysis as well as the work of Margaret Mahler and colleagues on separation and individuation. My contention is that all these schools of psychoanalysis remain within the spiritual limits first staked out by Freud. See D. W. Winnicott, *The Maturational Process and the Facilitating Environment* (New York: International Universities Press, 1988)—perhaps the most spiritual of major modern psychoanalytic thinkers; Juliet Mitchell, ed., *The Selected Melanie Klein* (New York: Free Press, 1987); Hanna Segal, *Introduction to the Work of Melanie Klein* (London: Hogarth, 1973); Margaret Mahler in collaboration with Manuel Furer, *On Human Symbiosis and the Vicissitudes of Individuation* (New York: International Universities Press, 1968); and Margaret Mahler, Fred Pine, and Annit Bergmann, *The Psychological Birth of the Human Infant* (New York: Basic Books, 1975).

22. For an extended discussion of Saul and madness in the Bible, see George Rosen, *Madness in Society* (Chicago: University of Chicago Press, 1968), chap. 2.

23. Blake, *Complete Poetry and Prose,* 474–75.

24. G. W. F. Hegel, *The Phenomenology of Mind,* trans. J. B. Baillie (New York: Harper and Row, 1967). See Alexandre Kojève, *Introduction to the Reading of Hegel,* trans. James Nichols, Jr. (Ithaca, N.Y.: Cornell University Press, 1969) for a classic exposition of the theme, particularly influential here. The discussion is amplified in Chapter Four.

25. Merchant, *Death of Nature.* See also Evelyn Fox Keller, *Reflections on Gender and Science* (New Haven: Yale University Press, 1985).

26. Nancy Chodorow, *The Reproduction of Mothering* (Berkeley: University of California Press, 1980), develops the theme from the standpoint of psychoanalytic object relations theory. Blake touches the core of male terror in his "Mental Traveller" (*Complete Poetry,* 484):

And if the Babe is born a Boy
He's given to a Woman Old

Who nails him down upon a rock
Catches his Shrieks in Cups of gold

27. Thus establishing the ontological equivalence of homoerotic desire with the socially prescribed heterosexual position. We are not able to explore this theme here, though it must be said that any full theory of the Other would have to account for the extreme intensity of hatred against the image of the homosexual—especially male—in our society.

28. Freud's main discussion of the superego takes place in "The Ego and the Id," in James Strachey, ed. and trans., *The Standard Edition of the Complete Psychological Works of Sigmund Freud* (London: Hogarth Press, 1959; henceforth *Standard Edition*) 19 (1923), 1–59; and "Civilization and Its Discontents," *Standard Edition*, 21 (1930), 57–146.

29. See Joel Kovel, *White Racism* (New York: Columbia University Press, 1984) for further discussion.

30. The theory of alienation enters into the foundation of Marx's work, and is indispensible for the radical understanding of society. See "The Economic and Philosophical Manuscripts," in T. B. Bottomore, ed. and trans., *Karl Marx: Early Writings* (New York: McGraw Hill, 1964), 61–279. Ultimately, if we are alienated, it is from what we could become in a society free of domination. Because we are not yet ourselves, we live a life of Otherness. There is a very sharp issue concerning the relation of Marx's view of alienation to spirituality, which hinges on the following: is alienation a product of the "human condition" (in other words, is it ontological, inherent in human being as such), or is it a function of an external social domination which can be overcome through political action? Or are ontological and political alienation two sides of the same thing? In this latter case, to which I subscribe, domination remains key, yet there can be no purely external domination. See István Mészáros, *Marx's Theory of Alienation*, 4th ed. (London: Merlin Press, 1975); Erich Fromm, ed., *Socialist Humanism* (Garden City, N.J.: Doubleday Anchor, 1968); Adam Schaff, *Marxism and the Human Individual* (New York: McGraw-Hill, 1970); and further discussion in Chapter Six.

31. See Joel Kovel, "The Victims of Anticommunism," *Zeta* 1 (January 1988): 84–89.

32. John Clark, personal communication. For a fuller discussion of nuclear weaponry, including its Otherness and its manipulation for ideological ends, see Joel Kovel, *Against the State of Nuclear Terror* (Boston: South End Press, 1984). It might be added that some of the impetus for the present study grew out of the unfinished ends of that one.

33. Black Elk, *Black Elk Speaks,* ed. John G. Neihardt (Lincoln: University of Nebraska Press, 1961), 2–3, 43.

34. The intellectual basis of the abortion controversy depends in good measure on how much of an independent existence the fetus is considered to have within the womb. Of course, the passions which animate the controversy cannot be reduced to this ontological problem. Yet the question of just how attached one being is to another draws upon real emotional fire; indeed, it is the source of emotion as an archaic, preverbal mode of communication.

35. Merchant, *Death of Nature,* has the definitive discussion of this trans-

formation, in which both nature and women suffered world-historical defeats. I am not implying that woman-as-nature was an emancipated position in traditional society, which was generally a scene of harsh sexist oppression, to say the least. Nonetheless, in premodern or precapitalist society, women had considerably more access to production and social power than was to become their lot in early modernity—and this opened a space for them which certain modern feminist movements have sought to reopen.

36. See Chapter Six for a discussion of ecofeminism.

37. Starhawk, *Dreaming the Dark: Magic, Sex and Politics* (Boston: Beacon Press, 1988), 58.

38. This quintessential saint, shaman, and holy man was certainly disturbed. Imagine if the mental health industry had existed in fourteenth-century Assisi and had gotten its claws into the rebellious young Giovanni Francesco Bernadone, who actually stripped naked and ran from the courtroom at a hearing called by his protobourgeois father to deal with his behavior! Some electroconvulsive therapy, plus a good dose of corrective psychotherapy, might have brought Francesco into line and cured him of his spiritual obsessions. He could even have gone to work in his father's store. See G. K. Chesterton, *St. Francis of Assisi,* (Garden City, N.Y.: Doubleday Image, 1957); and Leonardo Boff, *Saint Francis,* trans. John Diercksmeier (New York: Crossroad, 1984).

39. Saint John of the Cross, *Dark Night of the Soul,* ed. and trans. E. Allison Peers (Garden City, N.J.: Image Books, 1959), 61.

40. Jerome Rothenberg, ed., *Technicians of the Sacred,* 2d ed. (Berkeley: University of California Press, 1985), 135–37. Reprinted by permission of the estate of Knud Rasmussen.

41. Duerr, *Dreamtime,* 65, has a very thorough discussion of the kind of reality lived by shamans, witches, and the like, all who "voyage" through the night. "What actually takes place is not that the shaman *turns into* an animal, but rather that he has now experienced his 'wild,' his 'animal aspect.' Not until that happens will he be a true shaman. For he cannot *know* his human side until he also becomes aware of what it is *not.* To put it differently, he needs to become estranged from it, to have *seen* it, that is, to have seen it from the *outside.* After experiencing that, he is no longer what he once was. In pictorial representations, he now appears as a human bird or a human with bird's legs." In our terms, the differentiation must be lived.

42. Paulo Freire, *Pedagogy of the Oppressed,* trans. Myra Bergman Ramos (New York: Seabury Press, 1970).

43. Here, though it is not the proper place to enter into an adequate discussion of the theme, we would include neurotic as well as psychotic forms of trouble.

44. Some variant of this notion has been the basis of every worthwhile notion of psychotherapy. Unless the therapist recognizes the "method in madness," its thwarted creative impulse, no real help can be given.

45. See Edward Conze, *Buddhism, Its Essence and Development* (Harmondsworth: Penguin, 1975). The role of Buddhists in the Indochinese wars is well known, but their activism did not stop there. In "Thai Cliffhanger: Case of the Puritannical Buddhist," *New York Times,* 12 July 1989, we read of Phra Bodhirak, a Thai monk and former television announcer, entertainer, com-

poser, and public relations expert, who is embroiled with authorities of this nation with three to four hundred thousand monks, over his demands for austerity and asceticism, and the hierarchy's demand that he stay out of politics. This latter-day Luther is presently about to be defrocked but is defying authority. See Max Weber, "Religious Rejections of the World and their Directions," in H. H. Gerth and C. Wright Mills, eds., *From Max Weber* (New York: Oxford University Press, 1946), 323–59.

46. Paul Ricoeur, *The Symbolism of Evil* (Boston: Beacon Press, 1967), 8.

47. For the ontological necessity of the notion of transgression, see Georges Bataille, *Erotism: Death and Sensuality,* trans. Mary Dalwood (San Francisco: City Lights, 1986).

48. Freud, "Beyond the Pleasure Principle," *Standard Edition,* 18 (1920), 1–64.

49. J. Sprenger and H. Krämer, *Malleus Maleficarum,* trans. and ed. Montague Summers (London: Pushkin Press, 1951; New York: Dover, 1971).

50. For a discussion of this theme, see Thomas Szasz, *The Manufacture of Madness* (New York: Harper and Row, 1970); Joel Kovel, "A Critique of DSM-III," *Research in Law, Deviance and Social Control* vol. 9 (1988), 125–44. Szasz's discussion of the subject, while indefatigable, is marred by a marked degree of splitting in which the demon is displaced from witches and other victims of the persecutory system onto psychiatry. See Chapter Four for a further discussion of witches.

Chapter 3. Authentic Spirit

1. Pyrelal, *Mahatma Gandhi: The Last Phase,* vol. 2 (Navjivan Publishing House, 1958), 789, quoted in James W. Douglass, *Lightning East and West* (New York: Crossroad, 1986), 1.

2. One must recognize the impossibility of representing a figure of Gandhi's scope in anything less than a full-scale work. No one in this century has pushed back the boundaries of spiritual experience further, nor seen more deeply into the relations between political action and spiritual development. Yet we should not turn Gandhi into a god, as many tend to do. His inability to come to grips with the class struggle in India worked against his success as an emancipator of his people; and his extreme sexual repressiveness must also be weighed in the balance. Taken all in all, these problems militate against literally following Gandhi's spiritual path. See Ramashray Roy, *Self and Society: A Study in Gandhian Thought* (New Delhi: Sage Publications, 1985); Erik Erikson, *Gandhi's Truth* (New York: W. W. Norton, 1969); and my review of the latter, "Erik Erikson's Psychohistory," in Joel Kovel, *The Radical Spirit: Essays in Psychoanalysis and Society* (London: Free Association Books, 1988), 68–79.

3. Adolf Grünebaum, *The Foundations of Psychoanalysis: A Philosophical Critique* (Berkeley: University of California Press, 1984) has the most penetrating discussion of the problems surrounding the logical validation of Freud's theories; however, Grünebaum does not consider himself a positivist. Significantly, the one area in which Grünebaum most approves of Freud is the latter's interpretation of religion. See "Psychoanalysis and Theism," *The Monist* 70 (1987): 152–92. For a particularly provocative reading of Freud,

see Samuel Weber, *The Legend of Freud* (Minneapolis: University of Minnesota Press, 1982), who takes an approach along Derridean lines.

4. Freud is careful to state that psychoanalysis is about "psychic reality," that is, what is inwardly real for persons. And since what is inwardly real is the kind of self-experience which leads people to use the language of spirit when they are trying to describe what life is like, Freud does not hesitate to use the term *Seele*, or "soul," in referring to the self. Nor, as representatives of a more technical discourse, did James Strachey and Freud's other English translators hesitate to erase the term *soul* and all spiritualized reference when they prepared the magisterial *Standard Edition* of Freud's psychological writings.

This is the essence of the argument recently put forward by Bruno Bettelheim in his *Freud and Man's Soul* (New York: Alfred A. Knopf, 1983). Bettelheim goes on to conclude that the bowdlerization of Freud by his English translators has played no small part in a loss of the humanistic impact of Freudian thought and its reduction to a narrow technical jargon. Freud's intention is humanistic, not scientistic, argues Bettelheim. Therefore psychoanalysis is for man. And for the discourse of "man," terms such as *soul* are essential. Quoting a letter of Freud to Oskar Pfister, the admiring pastor who challenged Freud's hostility to religion, Bettelheim notes that Freud refers to the psychoanalyst as a *Seelsorger*—a secular minister of souls. Along the same lines, Bettelheim emphasizes that the technical-sounding terms of *ego, id,* and *superego* look much less forbidding when translated directly from Freud's German of *Ich, Es,* and *Überich,* as *I, it,* and *over-I.* Even if the terms have to be treated as substantives, as "the I," and so forth, they have a much more recognizably humanistic sound. Finally, there is the notorious case of Freud's marvelously ambiguous term for the dynamic force of the psyche, *Trieb.* Although *Trieb* can be most legitimately translated as "drive," Strachey somehow renders it as "instinct." This is a considerable violation of Freud's intention. Where the German connotes something conceptually mysterious but recognizably human, the English connotes something conceptually familiar and recognizably infrahuman.

Bettelheim has raised an important issue, which is obviously resonant with the theme of this essay. We, too, think that Freud's use of *Seele* and other related terms to describe human beings is not accidental; and that it reveals some fundamental sense on Freud's part of what human 'being' is about. Similarly, the erasure of and substitution for these terms betrays a technicist, if not antihumanist, impulse on the part of the English-speaking psychoanalytic establishment—which, it should be added, became the dominant center of world psychoanalysis in the years after Hitler came to power and drove the Freudian tradition (Bettelheim included) out of the German-speaking world. There are, however, a number of problems with Bettelheim's reasoning.

First, Freud is a writer who disdains orthodox usages—witness his cavalier disregard for the distinction between "civilization" and "culture." Freud takes a certain delight in using old words in new ways, and in confounding labels. As a German-speaking writer, he can scarcely be expected to avoid terminology having a spiritual ring, since the German language is suffused with such terms. Though this may be related in some important way to the preeminence of German philosophy, the mere usage of a terminology does not entitle one to share in what the terminology signifies. Bettelheim's point would be sounder if Freud had written in English and used the term *soul* to describe the psyche—and if German translators had bowdlerized this back in a technicist direction. As it stands, it has a vaguely chauvinist ring: the soulful German *Geist* confronting heartlessly technological Anglo culture. We have heard this sort of thing too many times before (for example, from Heidegger and exponents of *völkish* thinking) to accept the argument at face value.

Second, as we have glimpsed already, Freud himself is more than a little enamored of despiritualized discourse himself. He does not need Strachey to teach him any lessons in scientism. There is no possible way of eliding the immense influence on Freud of "bio-logical" thinking, as Frank Sulloway has made quite clear in *Freud, Biologist of the Mind* (New York: Basic Books, 1979). Of course it may be argued—and perhaps should be argued—that Freud transcends this in the psychoanalytic project. Fair enough. However, this is a point that has to be dialectically demonstrated, as the outcome of a complex process of negation. But Bettelheim fails to convey any sense of Freud's own ambivalence, making him out instead to be a thoroughgoing and immutable humanist who was simply victimized by an Anglo technocracy which wanted to distort his meaning. No room is allowed for distortions—or at least, profound ambiguities—within Freud's meaning itself.

Further, if Freud is a humanist, he is not a very humane or universal one. His idea of humanity is that of a narrow European elite confronting a wretched and dangerous working class and worldwide savagery. It is Freud who writes, "the masses are lazy and unintelligent" ("Future of an Illusion," *Standard Edition* 21 (1927), 7). For him, common people have to be coerced into civilization. Meanwhile, "savages" are like children, complete victims of instinct. As for women, space does not permit detailing of the insults meted out to them by the father of psychoanalysis. To call this "humanism" is to stretch the term to the breaking point. A mere belief in "civilization" does not make one a humanist. The least we can expect of humanism is some incorporation of the ideal of a universal brotherhood/sisterhood of human beings (whence we should not talk of "man," either). Freud pays the ideal no more than lip service, and shows his disdain for it at every opportunity.

Our point, however, is not to criticize Freud. For even if Freud could be called a full-fledged humanist, Bettelheim's thesis would be dubious, precisely because humanism itself is dubious, at least in the present moment. And no one showed this more forcefully than Freud. It sounds fine to say one is for human beings—until you realize that "human being" is an open category. As an abstraction it is a useful conceptual device. But an abstraction of human nature is not something on which to build a value system. What counts are real, concrete human beings, historically situated and determined. The ideals of humanism are superb, but also empty until we talk about which human beings in which circumstances are to realize them. This Freud does—and what he finds, namely, the decentering of the ego and the dissolution of the identified state of being, is not reassuring to humanism. Given the inwardly and externally torn condition of human beings, we can neither project the current mode of being forward into the future, nor take refuge in nostalgia. Freud shows very plainly why this has to be so, because the historically given state of human being is too chaotic to bear the utopian dreams of the species.

5. In my opinion there is considerable truth in the Freudian critique of Jung, even if the motives behind the attack are dubious. Mysticism is not in itself irrational, but neither is it necessarily rational. And the case of Jung reveals a mysticism which was irrational. Jung's central concept, that of the collective unconscious and its archetypes, is specifically not grounded. It comes from beyond the world, and the world is to fall in line with it. This kind of reasoning is unacceptable because it bypasses real life and history. Furthermore, it is conducive to malignant ends such as racism and fascism, because its dissociation from real life allows reactionary impulses to proceed unchecked. Anyone who doubts the justice of such a harsh assessment of the widely revered Jung may turn to Farhad Dalal's "The Racism of Jung," *Race and Class* 29 (Winter 1988): 1–22, which documents an outrageous number of floridly racist remarks, which are in no sense peripheral to Jung's thought. It is amazing what culture heroes are allowed to get away with; e.g., "Racial infection is a most serious mental and moral problem where the primitive outnumbers the white man. America has this problem only in a relative degree, because the whites far outnumber the coloured. Apparently he [sic] can assimilate the primitive influence with little risk to himself. What would happen if there were a considerable increase in the coloured population is another matter" (Dalal, 19). If an ideologue of apartheid were to write this, he would be roundly excoriated—yet what is this if not an argument for apartheid?

As for fascism, we should also recall that like Heidegger, Jung unconscionably allowed himself to be used by the Nazis—although he was a much less active supporter of the Hitler regime. In 1934, after taking over a-psychotherapy journal at the request of the Nazis, Jung wrote in it: "The Aryan unconscious has a higher potential than the Jewish; this is the advantage and the disadvantage of a youthfulness not yet fully escaped from barbarism. In my opinion it has been a great mistake of all previous medical psychology to apply Jewish categories which are not even binding for all Jews, indiscriminately to Christians, Germans or Slavs. In so doing medical psychology has declared the most precious secret of the Germanic peoples—the creatively prophetic depths of *soul*—to be a childishly banal mass, while for decades my voice has been suspected of anti-semitism. The source of this suspicion is Freud. He did not know the Germanic soul any more than did all his Germanic imitators. . . . Has the mighty apparition of National Socialism which the whole world watches with astonished eyes taught them something better?" (quoted in Vincent Brome, *Jung* (New York: Atheneum, 1978), 217, italics added). Jung spent a lot of time denying statements like this with arguments along the lines of "some of my best friends are Jewish." Meanwhile the mass of his worshippers has looked the other way. We should attend especially to the usage of "soul" as a way of mystifying Jung's racial attitude.

6. See W. W. Meissner, *Psychoanalysis and Religious Experience* (New Haven: Yale University Press, 1984) for a thorough discussion. Meissner is a Jesuit as well as a medically trained Freudian analyst.

7. Freud, "Future of an Illusion," 53, 54.

8. Catherine Keller, *From a Broken Web: Separation, Sexism, and Self* (Boston: Beacon Press, 1986), 98.

9. Notably, the most celebrated woman in the annals of psychoanalysis, Anna Freud, resisted this insight, perhaps out of a profound loyalty to her father.

10. Dorothée Sölle, *The Strength of the Weak: Toward a Christian Feminist Identity,* trans. Robert and Rita Kimber (Philadelphia: Westminister Press, 1984); Rosemary Radford Reuther, *Sexism and God-Talk: Toward a Feminist Theology* (Boston: Beacon Press, 1983); and Elisabeth Schüssler-Fiorenza, *Bread Not Stone: The Challenge of Feminist Biblical Interpretation* (Boston: Beacon Press, 1984).

11. David Michael Levin, *The Opening of Vision* (New York and London: Routledge, 1988), 219.

12. Freud, "Civilization and Its Discontents," 75.

13. Ricoeur, *Freud and Philosophy.*

14. Freud, *Standard Edition,* 1 (1895), 281–397. The "Project" remained unpublished. Despite its relatively speculative manner and the fact of being written before the discovery of basic neurological structures such as the synapse, it was able to anticipate many later neurophysiological findings. It was focused on the human organism, however, and not the being of that organism. The organismic mode of thinking was carried forward most famously in the seventh chapter of "The Interpretation of Dreams." Here the notion of a "mental apparatus" was used to describe the psyche as functioning along the model of a reflex arc, and with "mental energy." See, for example, *Standard Edition,* 5,536.

15. Except in trivial cases of more or less reflexive awareness. I say "trivial" because these cases, whatever their scientific complexities, can be safely referred to the level of organism. There is nothing wrong with "bracketing" the level of being for the purpose, say, of a neurophysiological experiment. After all, the organism has its own ways. The distinction, as before, lies between a differentiated bracketing and a remorseless splitting which denies the bond between being and organism.

16. Freud, "The Unconscious," *Standard Edition,* 14 (1915), 159–204. This essay represents, along with the seventh chapter of the "Interpretation of Dreams," *Standard Edition,* 4, 5 (1900), 1–628, Freud's deepest venture into psychological theory as such.

17. The famous *Pensée* 477, in Blaise Pascal, *The Pensées,* trans. G. M. Cohen (Baltimore: Penguin, 1961), 164. He goes on to say that "I say that the heart has a natural love for the Universal Being or for itself, according as it surrenders to the love of one or the other; and it hardens against either at its own will. . . ." These are lines Freud would have done well to heed.

18. For example, the son of a person of my acquaintance was suddenly taken ill and rushed to the hospital where he underwent an emergency appendectomy at dawn. When his grandmother, who lived 1700 miles away, was informed of the operation two hours later, she reported that at dawn she had been awakened by a dream in which one of her grandchildren was clutching his abdomen in great distress. I believe many other examples of the kind could be told.

19. I commend to the reader Wendy Doniger O'Flaherty, *Dreams, Illusions and Other Realities* (Chicago: University of Chicago Press, 1984). Through primarily a study of the Hindu view of such matters, this enchanting work opens the whole question of just how limited our Cartesian worldview is. At the level of hard science, I would also recommend Robert Jahn and Brenda Duane's *Margins of Reality* (San Diego: Harcourt Brace Jovanovich, 1987). Through painstaking experimentation, Jahn and Duane demonstrate conclusively (that is, by all the statistical standards known to normal science) that consciousness as such is active within reality—i.e., is not a mere registration of reality. We cannot go further here with the important implications of this and other work, except to say that our expanded notion of consciousness has been developed to reflect it.

20. Freud, "Group Psychology and the Analysis of the Ego," *Standard Edition*, 18 (1921), 65–144.

21. An accurate reading of similar events which we habitually think of as "mob action" will show a similar process—for example, the Paris Commune. See George Rudé, *The Crowd in the French Revolution* (Oxford: Oxford University Press, 1959). The current tide of conservative scholarship has been busy in reducing the French Revolution itself to a reign of terror; yet Rudé demonstrates that a great deal of the activity was along the lines of just such self-regulated collective action. This does not deny the latent tendency for degeneration into terror which is ever-present where there is a history of domination. Similar self-regulatory processes took place during the overthrow of the Stalinist governments of Eastern Europe in 1989.

22. The *Sixth Thesis on Feuerbach,* in *Writings of the Young Marx on Philosophy and Society,* ed. and trans. Loyd D. Easton and Kurt H. Guddat (Garden City, N.Y.: Doubleday Anchor, 1967), 402. Norman Geras, *Marx and Human Nature: Refutation of a Legend* (London: Verso, 1983) has a very thorough discussion of this *Thesis,* in which he demonstrates that Marx retained a very definite conception of a "human nature;" i.e., that he does not reduce human being to its relations with others, as strict social constructionists would hold.

23. "The Ego and the Id," 29; "Mourning and Melancholia," *Standard Edition*, 14 (1917), 249.

24. See Mahler, *On Human Symbiosis,* and D. W. Winnicott, *The Maturational Process,* for major psychoanalytic contributions in this area.

25. For example, Dorothy Dinnerstein, *The Mermaid and the Minotaur: Sexual Arrangements and Human Malaise* (New York: Harper, 1976); Juliet Mitchell, *Psychoanalysis and Feminism* (New York: Pantheon, 1974); and Chodorow, *Reproduction of Mothering.*

26. Gilles Deleuze and Felix Guattari, *Anti-Oedipus: Capitalism and Schizophrenia,* trans. Robert Hurley, Mark Steem, and Helen R. Lane (Minneapolis: University of Minnesota Press, 1983), definitely smashed the bias of the "family-ar." However, they did so in the "spirit" of nihilism. Immersion in their world of "schizoculture" and desiring machines is enough to make a person yearn for the secure madness of the nuclear family. See n. 73, Chap. 4.

27. Freud, *Standard Edition,* 18 (1920), 1–64. There is a fascinating commentary, full of dithering insight, in Jacques Derrida, *The Post Card,* trans.

Alan Bass (Chicago: University of Chicago Press, 1987). David Bakan, *Sigmund Freud and the Mystical Jewish Tradition* (Princeton: Van Nostrand, 1958) has a good discussion of Freud's roots in Jewish mysticism and the kabbalah. See also Gerschom Scholem, *Kabbalah* (New York: New American Library, 1978).

28. This was also the point at which Norman O. Brown sought the spiritualization of psychoanalysis.

29. The view of Ego presented here may be briefly compared with that of Freud and the mainstream psychoanalytic tradition, as well as that of Lacan. In Freudian thought, the ego refers principally to a means of adapting to reality through the mastery—and especially the frustration—of the instinctual drives of sexuality and aggression. Hence the ego is related essentially to nature, since despite the plasticity of instinctual drive, its essence is rooted in biological givens. There are many complications to this, expressed in the theories of narcissism and identification, but the essential point is the fundamental *rationality* of the ego, and its adherence to the reality principle (where the real is considered rational). The main difference between Freud and the dominant school of ego psychology which followed him in mainstream psychoanalysis may be regarded in terms of the triumphalism of the ego. Freud sees the ego in a relatively tragic light, dependent on superior dark forces of a harsh external reality, an indifferent nature, and a punitive superego. For ego psychology, on the other hand, the ego rules like a prosperous bourgeois in a well-ordered state, with nature tamed, the lesser classes docile, and the laws just and temperate. See Heinz Hartmann, *Ego Psychology and the Problem of Adaptation*, trans. David Rapaport (New York: International Universities Press, 1958); and Heinz Hartmann, *Essays in Ego Psychology* (New York: International Universities Press, 1964).

In Lacan's view, the ego loses its fundamental rationality, and has no essential relation to the material world. It is, rather, the basic illusion by means of which the developing psyche achieves a spurious integrity through identification with its own reflected image. Thus the autonomy of the ego so desired by ego psychology is for Lacan only a greater estrangement. The more we think we know ourselves, the further from the self we become. Lacan's basic difference from the orthodox Freudians is, then, a critique of rationality— grounded, it must be added, in a radically different notion of language as constitutive of human being. Jacques Lacan, *The Language of the Self*, ed. and trans. Anthony Wilden (Baltimore: Johns Hopkins Press, 1968); *Écrits*, trans. Alan Sheridan (New York: W. W. Norton, 1977); see also the discussion in Dews, *Logics of Disintegration*.

The view developed here combines certain features of Freud and Lacan in a context which places psychological and linguistic development in a materialist and ontological framework. With Lacan, we deny the essential rationality of the ego, and see it as a flight from the terror of being, a fundamental alienation in the original Hegelian sense chosen by Lacan. But with Freud, we see Ego in a fundamental relation to material nature, which surpasses Lacan's view of language as primary. That is, we see language as an attempt to reconstitute separateness, and recognize modes of knowing and being, e.g., intuition and empathy, which stem from being-organism without the use of language. As being-organism, the emerging self denies and flees from Otherness. We reject the crude materialism of the traditional psychoanalytic theory of instinctual drive; but, being Marxist as well as Hegelian, insist on a materialist framework for mental development which Lacan regards as no more than epiphenomenal. We emphasize also the splitting tendencies of the ego: the ego is not split just from nature or other humans, but also from—and within—itself, so that multiple egoic forms can appear, to provide a pseudoharmony between the individual and social expectations. Finally, this notion of the ego creates space for the restoration of a concept of soul as a mode of being, which is antithetical to the thinking of Freud and Lacan alike.

30. "Splitting of the Ego in the Process of Defense," *Standard Edition*, 23 (1940 [1938]), 271–78.

31. This notion appears as the sexual perversion of fetishism in which an isolated part or appendage of the (female) body—e.g., hair or shoes—becomes the condition for sexual arousal. See Freud, "Three Essays on the Theory of Sexuality," *Standard Edition*, 7 (1905), 125–243, "Leonardo Da Vinci and a Memory of His Childhood," *Standard Edition*, 11 (1910) 59–137, and "Fetishism," *Standard Edition*, 31 (1927), 152–57. For Marx's concept of fetishism, in which the commodity takes into itself the power of the whole, see Chap. 6.

32. This line of reasoning evidently abuts on the whole question of "left-brain" and "right-brain," the former obviously associated with Egoic, the latter with soullike states of being. See here the arguments of Julian Jaynes, *The Origins of Consciousness in the Breakdown of the Bicameral Mind* (Boston: Houghton Mifflin, 1976). Certainly the bicameral nature of the central nervous system is implicated in forms taken by consciousness, at least as their organismic substrate. It seems to me, though, that to take the matter much beyond this level, and make the two halves of the cerebrum somehow responsible for a basic division between states of being, is the rankest reduction of being to the level of organism. It is Egoic, "left-brain" thinking at its most literal and linear, and violates the ontological givens of the human situation in separation and attachment.

33. Marx's famous dictum, "life (or 'social existence') determines consciousness," is true, therefore, in more than the economic sense. The first usage is from *The German Ideology*, the second from the "Introduction" to the *Critique of Political Economy* (quoted in Howard Selsam and Harry Martel, *Reader in Marxist Philosophy* (New York: International Publishers, 1963), 190, 186). This would tend to imply that "false consciousness" is consciousness that may be factually correct, yet has lost its orientation to being.

34. A task facilitated by the German language: *Geist* can be translated as either "mind" or "spirit."

35. Hegel's time was not serene, but he was enabled by its culture (in the construction of which his own philosophy played such a large role) to set aside certain contradictions, or to absorb them ideologically. If we read, for example, his *The Philosophy of History*, trans. J. Sibree (New York: Dover, 1956), we encounter the most atrocious racism directed at the darker "Others" who had already been consumed by the West's expansion (by Spain in the Western Hemisphere, and through the African slave trade), and whose subjugation and

uprising was to preoccupy the coming times, and render any ordered calculus of it impossible. To the great German idealist, these people were outside of History, and therefore not human:

> The peculiarly African character is difficult to comprehend, for the very reason that in reference to it we must quite give up the principle which naturally governs all *our* ideas—the category of Universality. . . . We must lay aside all thought of reverence and morality—all that we call feeling—if we would rightly comprehend him; there is nothing harmonious with humanity to be found in this type of character. . . . Another characteristic fact in reference to the Negroes is slavery. Negroes are enslaved by Europeans and sold to America. Bad as this may be, their lot in their own land is even worse, since there a slavery quite as absolute exists; for it is the essential principle of slavery that man has not yet attained a consciousness of his freedom, and consequently sinks down to a mere Thing—an object of no value. Among the Negroes moral sentiments are quite weak, or more strictly speaking, non-existent. (93,96)

Note again how the universal becomes false through abstraction—and how this is both cause and effect of Hegel's racism. Abstraction and invisibility are two sides of the same coin. Then there were the growing numbers of proletarian outsiders within his own society whom he also did not allow himself to see. Marx did see them, however, and transformed Hegel's doctrine. On the other hand, we should recognize that Hegel was theoretically assimilable by Marx, because the dialectic itself is emancipatory. See Charles Taylor, *Hegel* (Cambridge: Cambridge University Press, 1975); and, for a reading which develops the emancipatory potential in Hegel, Herbert Marcuse, *Reason and Revolution* (Boston: Beacon Press, 1960).

36. See Karl Löwith, *From Hegel to Nietzsche,* trans. David E. Green (New York: Holt, Rinehart and Winston, 1967).

37. See, for example, Soren Kierkegaard, *Fear and Trembling,* trans. Alastair Hannay, (Harmondsworth: Penguin, 1985); and Friedrich Nietzsche, *The Will to Power,* trans. Walter Kaufmann and R. J. Hollingdale (New York: Random House, 1968), 544–50.

38. To do further justice to this theme, we would have to pursue the question of postmodernism, which is that contemporary cultural condition marked by the absence of real struggle over tradition. In postmodernism, all boundedness evaporates and a promiscuity of cultural form results, including a promiscuity of philosophy and spirituality. As Fredric Jameson has best expounded, this is the logic of advanced capital itself. "Post-modernism, or the Cultural Logic of Late Capitalism," *New Left Review* 146 (July-August 1984): 53–93.

39. Some principal works wherein these ideas were advanced are Soren Kierkegaard, *Concluding Unscientific Postscript,* trans. David F. Swenson and Walter Lowrie (Princeton: Princeton University Press, 1941); *Attack Upon 'Christendom,'* trans. Walter Lowrie (Boston: Beacon Press, 1956); *Fear and Trembling;* Friedrich Nietzsche, *The Will to Power;* Martin Heidegger, *Being and Time,* trans. John Macquarrie and Edward Robinson (New York: Harper and Row, 1962); Jean-Paul Sartre, *Being and Nothingness,* trans. Hazel Barnes (New York: Philosophical Library, 1956); and *Critique of Dialectical Reason,*

trans. Alan Sheridan-Smith (London: NLB, 1976). See also Löwith, *From Hegel to Nietzsche;* Josiah Thompson, *Kierkegaard* (New York: Alfred A. Knopf, 1973); Ronald Hayman, *Nietzsche* (London: Wiedenfeld and Nicolson, 1980); Allan Megill, *Prophets of Extremity,* Levin, *The Body's Recollection of Being;* Zimmerman, *Eclipse of the Self;* Mark Poster, *Sartre's Marxism* (London: Pluto, 1979); and Ronald Aronson, *Jean-Paul Sartre: Philosophy in the World* (London: NLB, 1980).

40. *Los Angeles Times,* 8 February 1990.

41. See Joel Kovel, *The Age of Desire* for further discussion.

42. "Contribution to the Critique of Hegel's Philosophy of Right," in Karl Marx and Frederick Engels, *On Religion,* (New York: Schocken, 1964), 42.

43. Jose Porfirio Miranda, *Marx Against the Marxists,* trans. John Drury (Maryknoll, N.Y.: Orbis, 1980).

44. A great deal has been written about Marx and religion, especially with reference to Christianity. For a study of the man, see Trevor Ling, *Karl Marx and Religion* (London: Macmillan Press, 1980). For a study of the movement, see Alasdair MacIntyre, *Marxism and Christianity* (New York: Schocken, 1968). Obviously, the man and his ideas are two different, though related, matters.

45. Marcuse, *Reason and Revolution.*

46. The collapse of the communist regimes of the Soviet bloc may seem to add force to this statement, but really changes nothing. It had been apparent for decades that these experiments had gone astray and bore little resemblance to Marxism except in the writings of anticommunists; their final disintegration, as tumultuous as it has been, ultimately clears the air.

47. Historical amnesia sets in so rapidly that it may already be too hard to remember that up until only two decades ago capitalism was looking forward to an ever-rising curve of prosperity. Such was in fact the context which defined the optimistic views of Marcuse (who counted on the conquest of scarcity as a main condition for the social revolution which would release Eros) and Brown (who could more or less assume that the economic system would work on automatic pilot while people got in touch with their repressed side). Today we have a steady decline in living standards for all but the wealthy. Though the leadership of the "free world" and its captive press are drunk with exultation over the breakdown of Soviet communism, and though they continue to beat the drums of progress, the generation currently coming of age in America is the first in modern times to face a lower standard of living than its elders, not to mention the long-term implications.

48. See Leszek Kolakowski, "Marxist Roots of Stalinism," in *Stalinism: Essays in Historical Interpretation,* ed. Robert Tucker (New York: W. W. Norton, 1977), 283–98, for a discussion of this with respect to Stalinism. Kolakowski's claim—fueled by personal experience—is that all Marxisms are tainted with the same pathogen. To me, this is splitting, however brilliantly done.

49. Maynard Solomon, "Marx and Bloch: Reflections on Utopia and Art," *Telos* 13 (Fall 1972): 68–85.

50. Ernst Bloch, *The Principle of Hope,* trans. Neville Plaice, Stephen Plaice, and Paul Knight (Cambridge: MIT Press, 1986), 146.

51. See Chapter Six for a discussion of the difficulties in Marx's philosophy of nature.

52. Obviously, trade union consciousness is a long way from class consciousness, a fact well recognized in the Marxist tradition, especially by Lenin. But it is also a major jumping-off point on the way to class consciousness.

53. This determination extends far beyond the workplace. If one regards the systematic nature of indoctrination through schools, mass culture, the church, medical institutions, not to mention the corruption of existing trade unions—all that Gramsci meant by the term "hegemony"—then it becomes no mystery why workers so often fail in their efforts at self-determination. Recent trends in U.S. history have only worsened this decline, which reached its low point when workers at a Nissan plant in Tennessee voted to reject the United Auto Workers union. I happened to watch coverage of the event on television, and was startled to see workers actually cheering the victory tally of the company over the union.

54. It is worth noting that the much-maligned Communist Party–USA has had an exemplary record with respect to white-black racism. Whatever the failings of the Party, this achievement can only be explained on the basis of the power of communism to recognize the concrete reality of people of color, as well as to subsume racial Otherness into a more universal vision. In South Africa, the viability of the Communist Party derives from the same accomplishment.

55. In the *New York Times* of 17 February 1990, 10, Michael deCourcy Hinds writes in an article titled "Miners Cheered by Contract Terms" that the walkout against Pittston was "a strike that will be remembered for its bitterness as well as the surprising degree of solidarity that it brought to the troubled labor movement. A *thousand* (italics added) unions, churches and community groups rallied to the miners' cause, and some provided picketers at the offices of Pittston Company, the parent organization in Greenwich, Conn."

56. Luther's populist adversary in the Reformation, and leader of the great peasant rebellions of the early sixteenth century. Marx and Engels were great admirers of Münzer, and considered him a forerunner of communism. See Frederick Engels, *The Peasant War in Germany* (New York: International Publishers, 1966).

57. Ernst Bloch, *On Karl Marx,* trans. John Maxwell (New York: Herder and Herder, 1971), 20.

58. The subject is vast, and requires a separate study. As I write, liberation theology has come under a cloud, thanks to the withering fire of the current pontiff and reactionary elements of the Vatican. Liberation theologians such as Gustavo Gutierrez have tended to adroitly sidestep the Marxist implications of their doctrine. The reasons are understandable, since Marxism equals commitment to class struggle, which implies a major confrontation with church as well as state. John Paul II has never been persuaded to downplay the threat. For a sociologically astute study, see Maduro, *Religion and Social Conflicts;* and Gustavo Gutierrez, *A Theology of Liberation* (Maryknoll, N.Y.: Orbis, 1973).

59. Bill Devall and George Sessions, *Deep Ecology* (Salt Lake City: Gibbs M. Smith, 1985). Deep ecology reflects an important trend within the ecological movement, whose essential postulate is the critique of anthropocentrism—

the view which makes man the measure of all things. Instead, deep ecology sees things biocentrically: "that all things in the biosphere have an equal right to live and blossom and to reach their own individual forms of unfolding and self-realization within the larger Self-realization" (67). This is an excellent idea; however, it remains empty without a deeper insight into human nature. For suppose that the "self-realization" of human being is to be in a state of tension with nature. What then? It seems to me that deep ecologists fail to come to grips with this problem, and as a result end up preaching about "vital needs" like the New Age gurus they criticize. Related to this is a shallow grasp of social structure and political and economic reality, which can make their pronouncements vapid. For example, consider the following, on the principles of resource conservation: "Our first principle is to encourage agencies, legislators, property owners and managers to consider flowing with rather than forcing natural processes" (145). As the saying goes, "don't hold your breath."

I do not think the movement as a whole should be saddled with the more outrageous pronouncements of some representatives, to the effect that the AIDS pandemic and mass starvation might be a good thing since they would take pressure off the environment. (See "Ecology's Family Feud," *Los Angeles Times*, 27 March 1989). However, if deep ecology is to make a political difference, it will have to come up with more than vague moral slogans and New Age inspiration to address the problems of society. Without a critique of capitalism or domination, it will remain captive to a misty escapism. This does not deny, however, that the movement has "inspired"—as it should—some important direct-action politics such as the Earth First! movement. (This latter has made crucial alliances with labor.) For another major line of reasoning which is "social-ecological," and strongly opposed to deep ecology, see Murray Bookchin, *The Ecology of Freedom* (Palo Alto: Cheshire Books, 1982).

60. For example, by Phillipe Ariès, *The Hour of Our Death*, trans. Helen Weaver (New York: Vintage, 1982).

61. All of which is reinforced by and plays into the youth cult of capitalism and modernity.

62. "Death is an abstract concept for which no unconscious correlative can be found. . . . the fear of death [is] a development of the fear of castration." "The Ego and the Id," 57–58.

63. Morris, *The Nobility of Failure*.

64. All of which share the property of elevating nature over history, so that things are made to seem impossible to change.

65. See Kojève, *Introduction*, for a discussion of Hegel's dialectic, especially of the *Phenomenology of Mind*. See also Hegel, *Logic*, trans. William Wallace (Oxford: Oxford University Press, 1975). A wide-ranging discussion of dialectics as it has been rendered by orthodox Marxism (designated "dialectical materialism" though the term was foreign to Marx) may be found in Ira Gollobin, *Dialectical Materialism: Its Laws, Categories and Practice* (New York: Petras Press, 1986). For a point of view which has been particularly influential on the present author, see Theodor Adorno, *Negative Dialectics*, trans. E. B. Ashton (New York: Seabury Press, 1973).

66. Notably by Klaus Riegel, who was a right-wing Hegelian. See *Foundations of Dialectical Psychology* (New York: Academic Press, 1979). A system-

atic attempt to develop a dialectical-materialist psychoanalysis was made by the Marxist psychologist Lucien Sève, *Man in Marxist Theory and the Psychology of Personality,* trans. John McGreal (Atlantic Highlands, N.J.: Humanities Press, 1978). The problem with all these efforts, as I see it, has been an inability to incorporate deep subjectivity to the degree done by Freud, Lacan, and the psychoanalytic tradition in its better moments. For a discussion of the problems besetting the Marx-Freud synthesis, see Joel Kovel, *The Radical Spirit.* One might say that a hypothesis of the present work is that such a synthesis cannot be found unless both Marx and Freud are regarded spiritually.

67. Norman Gottwald, *The Tribes of Yahweh* (Maryknoll, N.Y.: Orbis, 1978).

Chapter 4. Spirit and Desire

1. James, *Varieties,* 28.

2. Max Weber: "The relationship of religion to sexuality is extraordinarily intimate, though it is partly conscious and partly unconscious, and though it may be indirect as well as direct." *The Sociology of Religion,* trans. Ephraim Fischoff (Boston: Beacon Press, 1963), 236.

3. Jerome Rothenberg, ed., *Technicians of the Sacred,* 2d ed. (Berkeley: University of California Press, 1985), 322. Copyright 1968, 1985 by Jerome Rothenberg. Reprinted by permission.

4. Rothenberg, *Technicians,* 583. Mircea Eliade, *A History of Religious Ideas,* vol. 1, trans. Willard Trask, Alf Hiltebeitel, and Diane Apostolos-Cappadona (Chicago: University of Chicago Press, 1978), 64.

5. Ronald M. Berndt, *Djanggawal: An Aboriginal Religious Cult of North-Eastern Arnhem Land* (New York: Philosophical Library, 1953), 256. Reprinted by permission.

6. Maurice Merleau-Ponty, *The Visible and the Invisible,* ed. Claude Lefort, trans. Alfonso Lingis (Evanston, Ill.: Northwestern University Press, 1968). See especially the chapter "The Intertwining—the Chiasm." In his last works the phenomenologist broke radically with the Cartesian mind-body duality. See also Levin, *The Body's Recollection of Being:* and *The Opening of Vision* (London and New York: Routledge, 1988).

7. Sandor Ferenczi, *Thalassa: A Theory of Genitality,* trans. Henry Alden Bunker (New York: W. W. Norton, 1968). Perhaps the most freely speculative and imaginative mind in the history of psychoanalysis, Ferenczi argued that at the individual level genitality, considered the highest stage of sexual development, was at the same time an opportunity to experience the deepest regression, back to the fluid environment of the womb. This in turn was phylogenetically related to the origins of life in the waters. There are considerable elements of male fantasy embedded in Ferenczi's argument, which claims, for example, that the vaginal "incorporation of the penis [is] certainly an intended castration as well" (26). However these, as well as other unwarranted speculations, are in principle correctable, and we do not need to reject the core of his insight. I have tried to incorporate this in the notion of the "plasma of being" (see below).

8. According to Walter Burkert, *Greek Religion,* trans. John Raffan (Oxford: Basil Blackwell, 1985), 110, "In the Dionysos [sic] cult ecstasy plays a quite unique role, with the result that Dionysos almost acquires a monopoly

over enthusiasm and ecstasy. . . ." See n. 39.

9. Otto, *Idea of the Holy,* 12–13.

10. We tend to exaggerate the uniqueness of Christianity in its anti-eroticism. As Max Weber wrote, "Despite the widespread belief that hostility toward sexuality is an idiosyncrasy of Christianity, it must be emphasized that no authentic religion of salvation had in principle any other point of view." *Sociology of Religion,* 241. The point is that once religion reaches a certain scale sufficient to spiritualize statist society, it must also engage in repression.

11. For a general survey of ancient Judaism's attitude toward sex, see G. Rattray Taylor, *Sex in History* (New York: Vanguard Press, 1970). With the Diaspora and the subsequent process of assimilation, the attitudes of the Jewish people underwent a very divergent and complex development which we can no more than suggest here. In brief, those elements which remain attached to the centuries of ghettoization—in a word, the Orthodox—adopt a reactionary sexual repressiveness worthy of the most radical Christian fundamentalists (with whose unlikely hands they have often joined in causes such as opposing gay rights). On the other hand, those elements of Judaism which embrace the paths of modernization also have the possibility, which many have exercised, of viewing sex without the weight of Christian hostility to the body. Hence the role of Jews like Freud and Reich in opening up new ways of seeing sexuality. (Note by way of contrast how Jung, the son of a Protestant minister, tried to close this path in his theory, if not his life.) It has even been observed that a disproportionate percentage of porn movie stars are Jewish (see *Shmate Magazine,* June 1989, for a survey). As might be expected, the state of Israel embodies this contradiction acutely. We read in the "And When Is a Dancer Not Kosher?," *New York Times* of 22 July 1989, of the travails of Ilana Raskin, an immigrant from Philadelphia and a social worker, whose passionate avocation is belly dancing. It seems, however, that belly dancing so enrages the powerful Orthodox rabbinate as to have led them to deny kosher certificates to any place which permits the diabolical practice. This has effectively squelched Ms. Raskin, who is suing.

12. As if "party-spirit" could be blamed on merely bodily impulses. This is diabolism, pure and simple, where the body is made the bad Other. Who can say whether it could have turned out differently for Christianity? Certainly there were other, more liberal tendencies in the early Church, as Elaine Pagels, *The Gnostic Gospels* (New York: Random House, 1979) has pointed out. See also Robin Lane Fox, *Pagans and Christians* (New York: Knopf, 1987). History is written by the winners, hence the triumph of repressiveness is made to seem the inevitable march of God's Word. Still, one cannot avoid the impression that the repressiveness of early Christianity, lasting as it did for well more than a millennium, was syntonic with the overall state of Western civilization. To paraphrase Freud's aphorism about Jews, Europe got the Christianity it deserved.

13. Quoted in Sprenger and Krämer, *Malleus,* xix–xx. For a discussion of these persecutions, see also Thomas Szasz, *The Manufacture of Madness;* and Barbara Ehrenreich and Deirdre English, *Witches, Midwives and Nurses* (New York: Feminist Press, 1963).

14. Sprenger and Krämer, *Malleus,* 115.

15. Duerr, *Dreamtime,* has a discussion of the erotic phenomena of witchcraft, especially the various salves used to induce altered consciousness. Paral-

lel phenomena can be traced back to the cults of Dionysius which spread from Asia Minor to Greece in the fifth century B.C. See Burkert, *Greek Religion,* for a discussion. The essential feature was a rite whereby women could retreat from the male-dominated world of the state and its logos. All of these rituals were ecstatic, though some were chaste and others orgastic. The key, in any case, is the threat to logos. The contemporary revival of witchcraft and other pagan religions deserves more attention than I can give here. Despite hovering on the brink of irrationalism, it represents an important spiritual confluence of feminism, paganism, and an ecological consciousness. See Starhawk, *Dreaming the Dark;* and Margot Adler, *Drawing Down the Moon* (Boston: Beacon Press, 1986).

16. 1 Cor. 14 is devoted to a harangue against speaking in tongues, in the interests of fostering rational conduct viewed as necessary for building the church: "if you in a tongue utter speech that is not intelligible, how will anyone know what is said?" (9).

17. Elaine Pagels, *Adam, Eve and the Serpent* (New York: Random House, 1988).

18. For some further comments on Swaggart, see Joel Kovel, "Jimmy Swaggart's Crystal Palace," *Zeta* 1 (April 1988): 76–80.

19. Quoted in Taylor, *Sex in History,* 254.

20. Edward Gibbon, *The Decline and Fall of the Roman Empire,* vol. 1 (London: J. M. Dent and Sons, 1960), 466. See especially the famous Chapter Fifteen, "On the Progress of the Christian Religion . . ." One is tempted to quote the whole chapter; nothing matching it has ever been written on the folly of splitting spirit and flesh. Of course, Gibbon was guilty of some fissioning himself, being unable to grasp the rational aspect of Christian spirituality.

21. *The Collected Works of St. Teresa of Avila,* trans. Kieran Kavanaugh and Otilio Rodriguez, vol. 1 (Washington: Institute of Carmelite Studies, 1976), 192–93.

22. She was instrumental in getting the aged Freud out of Vienna, just ahead of the Gestapo.

23. This distinction is related to gender as well, as is the condescending attitude often taken toward Saint Teresa by the male theological establishment, despite Teresa's impressive combination of practical, literary, and mystical skills. She was a figure of controversy during her lifetime as well, many of the church fathers regarding her profuse spells as visitations from the Devil. That is, the saint and the witch were ever so close. Antoine Vergote, *Guilt and Desire,* trans. M. H. Wood (New Haven: Yale University Press, 1988), concludes with respect to the same text: "There is no trace here of pathology. . . . This vision . . . can be taken as a sign of the psychic health and lucid judgment of this woman. She indeed mortified her body, not out of a horror of sexuality but because of her project to grow into a love that might be worthy of him whom she believed herself destined to love in the depths of her identity, an identity she shared universally with all men and women" (163).

24. *Erotism,* 223–24. Bataille, the prophet of excess and evil, is spiritual because he recognizes that the principle of transgression is inherent in erotic life. He sees sexuality as a passage of the soul through nonbeing. This is anathema—if the term could be used—to the prevailing climate in which sex is commodified and subjected to health ethics.

25. It would be tedious to recount all the translations, but in essence the various entities of psychoanalytic theory become ways of signifying the properties of desire. Thus Freud's notion of the libido and his theory of instinctual drive become the attempt to grasp the fact that desire is primarily erotic; the structural division of psyche into ego, id, and superego recognizes that the subject must constitute itself over and against desire; the theory of narcissism represents the turning of desire towards the subject; the primary and secondary process represent a way of grasping the effects of desire upon thought; and so forth.

26. When Freud speaks of Eros, as in "Beyond the Pleasure Principle," he enters ontological ground, and explains desire, and *pari passu,* instinctual drives, without primary reference to psychology or biology. We have already pointed out the subversive character of this within the history of psychoanalysis. Notably, Herbert Marcuse opts for the same stance in *Eros and Civilization.*

27. Emily Brontë, *Wuthering Heights* (New York: Bantam, 1981), 74–75, 153.

28. Of all the schools of psychoanalysis, that associated with Melanie Klein has developed this insight most fully. Klein's description of the passage from the paranoid to the depressive positions of being essentially describes development from a being who cannot tolerate separateness into one who recognizes—painfully—the individuality of others.

29. See Chapter Five; and Anders Nygren, *Agape and Eros* (Chicago: University of Chicago Press, 1982). The superego behaves like the Holy Spirit in that its commands appear unmediated by any objective influence, even though external action is also regulated objectively. In *Civilization and Its Discontents,* Freud has a full discussion of this puzzling phenomenon. The reason is the law of desire, for which the real is secondary. On the other hand, the superego never achieves the bounteous love experienced by the Christian in agape. For a general survey of the relation of desire and guilt to religious experience, see Vergote, *Guilt and Desire.*

30. Pope John XXIII, *Journal of a Soul,* trans. Dorothy White (New York: McGraw-Hill, Signet Edition, 1966). All references to the *Journal* of Roncalli are from this edition.

31. There is no surer way to get a blank stare than to introduce the subject of social class to a gathering of psychoanalysts—none of whom, it may be observed, belong to the lower echelons of society, and all of whom are invincibly armed against thinking about this aspect of reality by their technology of the unconscious. Because psychoanalysis accepts the given reality principle as rational, it can offer no critique of the desire sedimented into the pursuit of wealth and power. For them, it's just the normal thing to do.

32. Although the Church never fully lost this moment, either, which was set going in the primitive communism of early Christianity and persisted through the darkest days of reaction. The literature is vast, as it frames the historical and theological justification of liberation theology. See Jose Porfirio Miranda, *Marx and the Bible,* trans. John Eagleson (Maryknoll: Orbis, 1974); and *Communism in the Bible,* trans. Robert Barr (Maryknoll, N.Y.: Orbis, 1982) for presentation of the thesis that the original root of Christianity is primitive communism (a basis being the famous passage in Acts 2:44–45:

"All whose faith had drawn them together held everything in common . . ."). See also George Pixley, *God's Kingdom: A Guide for Biblical Study*, trans. Donald D. Walsh (Maryknoll, N.Y.: Orbis, 1981); and Roger Garaudy, *The Alternative Future: A Vision of Christian Marxism*, trans. Leonard Mayhew (New York: Simon and Schuster, 1974). For a rejection of this thesis see Jacques Ellul, *Jesus and Marx: From Gospel to Ideology*, trans. Joyce Main Hanks (Grand Rapids, Mich.: Eerdmans, 1988). For general discussion, see MacIntyre, *Marxism and Christianity*, Peter Hebblethwaite, *The Christian-Marxist Dialogue and Beyond* (London: Darton, Longman and Todd, 1977), and René Coste, *Marxist Analysis and Christian Faith*, trans. Roger Couture and John Cort (Maryknoll, N.Y.: Orbis, 1985). An extraordinary memoir testifying to the immediacy of the identification between Christianity and Marxism (which ends in the murder of its author by Honduran state security forces) is James Carney, *To Be a Christian Is to Be a Revolutionary* (San Francisco: Harper and Row, 1987). It seems to me that the linkage between Christianity and communism is authentic, yet always shadowed by its dialectical opposite at both poles; i.e., both Christianity and communism may turn into instruments of domination. The balance of these dialectical forces suppressed the emancipatory side of Catholicism until post–World War II developments having to do with the breakup of the Western empires (i.e., the rise of the Third World and of communism) created the space for a Roncalli. Even then, John XXIII was something of a fluke. The hierarchy thought they were getting an aged simpleton who would do nothing while they regrouped following the death of Pius XII. For further discussion, see Joel Kovel, "The Theocracy of John Paul II," *Socialist Register* (1987): 428–79.

33. Paulo Freire, *Pedagogy of the Oppressed;* and *Education for Critical Consciousness* (New York: Seabury Press, 1973).

34. Bataille, *Erotism*, has a fine discussion of Sade, who may be said to have defined the paradigmatic end point of capitalist relations based on pure exchange. See also Michel Foucault, *Madness and Civilization*, trans. Richard Howard (New York: Vintage, 1988), who emphasizes the threat to order posed by Sade's regime of pure desire.

35. Freud, *Civilization and Its Discontents*, 111–12.

36. Freud introduced the concept of the aggressive instinct in *Beyond the Pleasure Principle*. The idea is particularly firmly installed in the Kleinian school, for which an innate oral rage is a cardinal defining trait of human nature. It constitutes, in my opinion, the greatest drawback in the Kleinians' otherwise important insights into the dialectic of separateness. See n. 28.

37. My attention has recently been drawn to a book by a Japanese farmer, Masanobu Fukuoka, *The Natural Way of Farming*, trans. Frederic P. Metreaud (Tokyo: Japan Publications, 1985), which seems to specifically deny these assertions. According to Fukuoka, the true farmer moves entirely with nature, and does not even turn over the ground. He may be right (though I cannot imagine the method working in my garden, given its harsh growing conditions)—but if so, it is by setting the limits nearer to differentiation than I am able. For even here the totally organic farmer—and I doubt there is a position more extreme than Fukuoka's—promotes some beings over others, and resorts to means that are at least in principle relatively violent, e.g., pruning.

38. Significantly, it is only those who stand outside modernity who have such experiences today. This is, however, no insignificant fraction. The most rapidly growing religion in the United States and through much of the developing world is Pentecostal Protestantism (also called Evangelical, or Charismatic, the distinctions being immaterial for present purposes), which is based on exactly these kind of transformative moments. The social base for such movements is comprised variously of relatively unassimilated migrants, disenfranchised masses, and certain elements of the political right, including the anti-choice movement. See Kilian McDonnell, *Charismatic Renewal and the Churches* (New York: Seabury Press, 1983); Richard Quebedeaux, *The New Charismatics* (Garden City, N.Y.: Doubleday, 1976); and, for a study of right-wing movements, Sara Diamond, *Spiritual Warfare* (Boston: South End Press, 1989). Similar considerations can be applied to the African-American churches, although here charismatic religion has served as a sustained institution of cultural survival. This dates back to the era of slavery, when religion, though force-fed by the whites, became virtually the only space in which African-Americans could elaborate and transmit conceptions of culture and politics. Deriving partly from persistent African currents, and partly from conscious political resistance, the African-American church, although predominantly conservative, still retains a core of political radicalism. The phenomena of Martin Luther King, Jr., Malcolm X, and Jesse Jackson, indeed, the whole spirituality of the civil rights movement, would be unthinkable without this cultural foundation. See Gayraud Wilmore, *Black Religion and Black Radicalism* (Maryknoll, N.Y.: Orbis, 1983); and Branch, *Parting the Waters*.

39. Euripedes' masterwork, *The Bacchae,* concerns an exceedingly violent episode in the course of Dionysian rituals occurring in ancient Greece: the bacchantes, "out of their minds," turn on, kill, and devour King Pentheus. Of course this is mythic; yet it expresses something real. The horror is magnified by the fact that the celebrants are led by the king's mother. However, Euripedes makes clear that this violence, though always latent, becomes activated only by the king's Egoic interference in the event, and his subsequent voyeurism which sharply polarizes the sexual tension. For a discussion of Dionysian rites that calls attention to their widespread occurrence and at times violent character (which could include, as in the play, the dismemberment of a sacrificial animal and the eating of its raw flesh), see E. R. Dodds, *The Greeks and the Irrational* (Berkeley: University of California Press, 1951), 270–82.

40. Contemporary evangelical Protestants are sharply divided on the question of speaking in tongues, and on ecstatic elements in general. On one side are the fundamentalist modernizers such as Jerry Falwell, who reject these nonrational components of religion; on the other are a large and diverse group ranging from the Pentecostals to populist evangelists such as Jimmy Swaggart, who accept them. Evidently Pat Robertson was given to speaking in tongues on television until this was deemed imprudent for a man with Presidential ambitions. (Diamond, *Spiritual Warfare*, 143). Glossolalia has been studied in detail by modern social science, which has been unable to find anything psychopathological about it. For references, see Diamond, 264, n. 76.

41. Meanwhile people stay up all night outside the walls of the penitentiary to await the killing and express their desire for revenge; while politicians use capital punishment as an instrument to mobilize this desire on a mass scale, thereby distracting attention from poverty and powerlessness. Thus capital punishment becomes yet another spectacle of mass culture. See Guy DeBord, *Society of the Spectacle* (Detroit: Black & Red, 1977).

42. Quoted in Joachim Fest, *The Mind of the Third Reich* (New York: Pantheon, 1970), 115.

43. Freud, "On Narcissism, an Introduction," *Standard Edition,* 14 (1914), 67–104.

44. This is not the place to enter into a substantial critique of Zionist politics. However, with respect to the present point, it might be recalled that the Israeli invasion of Lebanon in 1982 followed evidence that the Palestine Liberation Organization was embarking on a more peaceful course. For a discussion of this and related matters, see Noam Chomsky's *The Fateful Triangle* (Boston: South End Press, 1983). There can be no fully satisfactory answer to the question of whether Zionism necessarily leads to this kind of violence, and certainly none that would leave everybody happy. However it seems to me that a professedly democratic state identified with but one ("Chosen") people cannot escape deep and terrible contradictions, which are redoubled when the society in question is a settler society displacing prior inhabitants. No amount of rationalization, justification by reference to the Holocaust, or historical manipulation can paper this one over, though it must be said that apologists for Israel have tried hard enough.

45. See Norman Gottwald, *The Tribes of Yahweh;* and Hyam Maccoby, *Revolution in Judaea: Jesus and the Jewish Resistance* (New York: Taplinger, 1980), for discussion of these periods.

46. Less in its actual body count, which is grimly matched by other genocides such as that of the Spaniards in Mexico or the Belgians in the Congo, than in the total subsumption of carnage to the logic of the bureaucracy and the factory. That is, the Nazis developed genocide as a mode of production.

47. And is at the theoretical core of "Beyond the Pleasure Principle." The return is to the organic condition which comes before individual history—in our terms, a flight from separateness and consciousness into the oblivion before differentiation into being-organism.

48. Most fully expressed in the *Will to Power.* One can interpret Nietzsche's eternal return, however, either as the recycling of a wheel which always returns to the same place, or as a kind of expanding spiral. This is consistent with the remarkable range of political possibilities which can be drawn from Nietzsche. (As might be expected, Heidegger, who prepared a very extensive commentary on Nietzsche, took the former view.)

49. Does this mean that Jews have to suffer and be persecuted in order to be authentic, so that what is ordinary human comfort for others is a moral disaster for them? Nobody who takes Jewishness seriously should flinch from such an idea. There is a resolution—of sorts—which many Jews have elected, which is to transfer their particularity as Chosen People to the victims of history. Such a position implies a stance of universalism. This, however, means a vitiation of Jewishness, the mark of whose identity has been the notion of being chosen by God. But then, Jewishness has always meant living dangerously, and by the dialectic. For a particularly transcendent and ecstatic affir-

mation of Jewishness, see Franz Rosenzweig, *The Star of Redemption*, trans. William Hallo (Boston: Beacon Press, 1972).

This dialectic does not take the Palestinians out of history, either. Palestinians have to be judged by the violence expressed in response to their oppression, and by how creatively and intelligently they make use of their spiritual and political openings. There is no automatic virtue in being a victim. At best it wipes the slate clean of the sins of being Master; at worst, it catches one up in an endless and ultimately nihilistic spiral of revenge for its own sake. At times, liberation movements of the oppressed—one thinks here of the IRA—appear hopelessly trapped in the logic of victimization and revenge.

50. Heraclitus, frag. 130b, from Milton C. Nahm, ed., *Selections from Early Greek Philosophy* (New York: Appleton Century Crofts, 1947), 96.

51. An apparent exception is the recent demobilization of Eastern European governments. Here, however, the collapse was preceded by a long period of decay resulting in a virtually total loss of legitimacy. Coupled with the decision of the Soviet Union to withdraw support, this left the rulers of Eastern Europe in fact without power, and so they fell like so many houses of cards. I think, too, that many had simply ceased to believe in themselves, because they had for so long violated socialist principles. The Chinese elites in 1989 also lost a great deal of legitimacy, but they retained enough of the instruments of state power to engage in a violent defense.

52. Communist societies tend to call those who challenge state power "counterrevolutionaries." When the Masters of China recently decided to slaughter the people of Beijing, such was the label chosen. It should be added that only vestiges of socialism remain in China. See William Hinton, *The Great Reversal* (New York: Monthly Review Press, 1990). Interestingly, when the regime was under pressure from its people, our propaganda apparatus called it "reformist" and "modernizing;" Henry Kissinger even stated on television that it would be a "tragedy" if "our great friend Deng" were deposed. Once the tanks rolled out and started firing, then Deng became a true "communist" once again, though his rehabilitation began soon after the blood was wiped off the square.

53. Given the decisive effect of concrete variations in each instance, it is hazardous to generalize as to which side tends to commit the most violence. In the instance of Cambodia, for example, the horrors of the Khmer Rouge are inextricably linked to the cynical and brutal policy of Nixon and Kissinger, which laid waste the country, creating the chaos that prepared the way for Pol Pot. See William Shawcross, *Sideshow: Kissinger, Nixon and the Destruction of Cambodia* (New York: Simon and Schuster, 1979); and Michael Vickery, *Cambodia 1975–1982* (Boston: South End Press, 1982).

54. The United States security elites, from the comfort of their air-conditioned offices, launched a "low-intensity" war of hellish proportions on Nicaragua, one of the poorest nations in the hemisphere. Per capita deaths would have translated to over 2,000,000 in the United States, while the economic damages were indescribable. All this against what was arguably the least violent and most spiritual revolution in modern history. See Joel Kovel, *In Nicaragua* (London: Free Association Books, 1988).

55. A somewhat technicist, but still valuable survey is Gene Sharp, *The*

Politics of Nonviolent Action (Boston: Porter Sargent, 1973). I have presented some views in *Against the State of Nuclear Terror* (Boston: South End Press, 1984), and, responding to a critique of that book, in "Reply to Caffentzis," *Social Text* (Spring 1989): 142–46.

56. I rather prefer a variation I have seen: "Visualize Impeachment."

57. Freud, "Totem and Taboo," *Standard Edition*, 13 (1913), 1–162. The appellation was Freud's own, in response to criticism—though it didn't stop him from clinging to his fantastic account of prehistory.

58. Van der Leeuw, *Religion in Essence and Manifestation*, 350.

59. Mircea Eliade, *The Myth of the Eternal Return*, trans. Willard Trask (Princeton: Bollingen-Princeton University Press, 1971), 108–10.

60. Christ is also in the long line of the dying god, who was originally sacrificed as a fertility rite. This theme was made famous around the turn of the century by James Frazer's *The Golden Bough* (New York: Macmillan, 1971), and led through that route into Freud's meditations about totemism and the Oedipus complex.

61. The notion of Merleau-Ponty. See n. 7.

62. For a discussion which explores the representation of female nakedness in Christianity, see Margaret Miles, *Carnal Knowing* (Boston: Beacon Press, 1989). The supposed "naturality" of women is grounded in the sex-specific realities of menstruation and childbirth; its ontological core is the knowledge all males bear of having been contained in the body of a creature of a different gender; and its social scaffolding is the set of rules according to which a man is not allowed to identify himself with the (m)Other. See also Susan Griffin, *Woman and Nature: The Roaring Inside Her* (New York: Harper and Row, 1978).

63. John Paul II has claimed, for example, that a man sins if he even imagines sexual gratification with his wife. See Kovel, "The Theocracy of John Paul II," for further discussion.

64. Karl Rahner, *Theological Dictionary*, trans. Richard Strachan (New York: Herder and Herder, 1965), 53. See also his *Foundations of Christian Faith* (New York: Seabury Press, 1978).

65. Reich's *The Function of the Orgasm*, trans. Vincent Carfagno (New York: Farrar, Straus and Giroux, 1973), written in 1927, was his main break with Freudian orthodoxy. By insisting on what he called "orgastic potency," Reich refused any purely psychological cure, and thereby set his sights on what he would later call "orgone energy." His error lay in a need to treat this insight in a scientistic and crudely materialistic framework, that is, in not differentiating clearly enough between organism and being—or, what comes to the same thing, not recognizing the importance of desire in human existence. By giving the orgone the same kind of substantive nature as the objects of normal scientific research, Reich was led to postulate a kind of crude materiality to his discoveries which left him wide open to criticism and even satire. This only accentuated his isolation, intensified his grandiosity, and played a role in his shameful death. Thus when the U.S. government came down on him in the 1950s for promoting his orgone therapy, Reich refused to submit to the court's authority. For this his books were burned and Reich himself was convicted of contempt of court and imprisoned, where he died. Reich's errors or mental

disturbances should not blind us to the profundity and prescience of his contribution—or to its spiritual character. There was no more "holistic" thinker than Reich, and his therapeutic emphasis upon the breath was positively Hindu in its evocation of spirit-power. See Myron Sharaf, *Fury on Earth* (New York: St. Martin's Press, 1983); and Joel Kovel, "Why Freud or Reich," in *The Radical Spirit*, 251–69.

66. In line with the work of David Michael Levin, who, following Merleau-Ponty, has argued (see n. 7) for a "prosocial" character to the body. That is, we are innately open to the Other, i.e., endowed with soul-potential which is only repressed under radically Egoic conditions.

67. Meister Eckhart, "Counsel 23," in *The Essential Sermons, Commentaries, Treatises and Defense,* trans. Edmund Colledge and Bernard McGinn (New York: Paulist, 1981), 281. All excerpts reprinted by permission.

68. The argument follows Marx's "Economic and Philosophical Manuscripts of 1844." See István Mészáros, *Marx's Theory of Alienation* (London: Merlin Press, 1970).

69. Thus the proposition "we are at one with nature" is and must remain an illusion simply because it is a proposition. And as a proposition, it belongs to a logos which necessarily stands over and against nature. The claim of truth for this proposition is made, therefore, in the light of a sense of falsehood. It sets up a dichotomy between the true and the false, and tells "nature" that we belong to it. All of this is entirely foreign to nature, which simply *is*, without having to be told anything; nor does nature worry itself over who belongs to it or not. Thus any proposition spoken in words constitutes a signified realm which by its very "nature" is no longer at one with the rest of nature.

70. As Laplanche and Pontalis have put it, "If Freud's discovery had to be summed up in a single word, that word would without doubt have to be 'unconscious.'" J. Laplanche and J. B. Pontalis, *The Language of Psychoanalysis,* trans. Donald Nicolson-Smith (New York: W. W. Norton, 1973), 474. The term admits of a number of different senses within Freudian thought. First of all, "unconscious" is descriptive of whatever exists in the psyche without the property of consciousness, as measured by the capacity to put something into words. There are some things one would talk about, some things one could talk about but which are not immediately present in consciousness (that which is "preconscious"), and some things that simply couldn't be talked about at all (that which is truly unconscious). This adjectival usage was amplified and made into a substantive in the early, so-called topographic stages of Freud's thinking, as "unconscious" became the "system-*unconscious,*" or "*Ucs.*" Later, with the development of the structural division of the mind into ego, id, and superego, "unconscious" retreated again to the status of an adjective describing all of the id and large parts of the ego and superego. Nonetheless, usage as "the unconscious" continued informally, to indicate the abiding sense that this was the true psychic reality.

71. Freud, "The Unconscious." Certain implications are developed in my "Things and Words," in Joel Kovel, *The Radical Spirit,* 80–115.

72. The only point worth noting is a connection Freud drew between schizophrenia and unconscious thinking, where he claimed that the schizophrenic used words like things.

73. Within the psychoanalytic tradition (or antitradition), this idea bears a resemblance to the reasoning of Gilles Deleuze and Felix Guattari's *Anti-Oedipus*. Deleuze and Guattari argue that the coding organized around the Oedipus complex—which is an internalization, along libidinal lines, of familial relations—could not encompass what people were all about. In other words, we are more than what mommy, daddy, and the surrounding culture tells us we are. I have severe disagreements with these authors, who ground their notion of human being in a reheated and *gauchiste* Nietzschean ontology. However, the basic notion remains true, in my opinion, because it is grounded in the reality of a plasma of being which is prepsychological and presocial. Deleuze and Guattari called their particular ontology of the unconscious a "desiring-machine." As the name suggests, this is inherently asocial. Their rejection of the elementary dialectic of human sociality led to the silly conclusion that schizophrenia is the essential personal condition. However, this does not deny the point that human being surpasses any possible social coding, even as it is prosocial. See Chapter Three, n. 29.

74. Heidegger studied to be a Jesuit as a youth.

75. Barnaby B. Barratt, *Psychic Reality and Psychoanalytic Knowing* (Hillsdale, N.J.: Analytic Press, 1984) has a good discussion of this point.

76. See Chapter Six, n. 49, for further discussion of Derrida.

77. Meister Eckhart, quoted in Evelyn Underhill, *Mysticism*, 319.

Chapter 5. Divine Spirit

1. As a proposition, that is. It makes a great deal of sense, however, as an ideological principle suitable to the peculiar history of the Jewish people, who needed some such idea for cultural survival in a very hostile world. See Gottwald, *Tribes of Yahweh;* Salo Baron, *A Social and Religious History of the Jews,* 2d ed. (New York: Columbia University Press, 1952); Erich Kahler, *The Jews Among the Nations* (New York: Frederick Ungar, 1967).

2. I draw this phrase from Rosemary Radford Reuther's *Sexism and God-Talk,* in which the critique is applied with elan and rigor to the ubiquitous designation of god within the terms of patriarchy.

3. See Wittgenstein, *Philosophical Investigations*.

4. Ludwig Feuerbach, *Essence of Christianity,* trans. George Eliot (New York: Harper and Row, 1957).

5. Pseudo-Dionysius, "The Mystical Theology," in *The Complete Works,* trans. Colm Luibheid with Paul Rorem, The Classics of Western Spirituality (New York: Paulist Press, 1987), 141. Reprinted by permission.

6. With respect to Heidegger, it would seem that his conception of Being did not attend enough to the strictures of Pseudo-Dionysius. Thus there remained a lingering positive ground in Heidegger's being which was inflated to the level of an ultimate, while retaining the projections of his very specific German being. This conflation provided a matrix for the rapport with National Socialism. See the discussion in Chapter Two.

7. See Max Weber's discussion in "Religious Rejections of the World."

8. We are assuming that both *a* and *b* are equally logical.

9. "[The Pythagoreans] said the universe was produced by the First Unit (the Heaven) inhaling the Infinite (or Void), so as to form groups of units or

numbers . . . and that all things (even, e.g., opinion, opportunity, injustice . . .) were numbers and had position." "Pythagoras," *The Oxford Classical Dictionary* (Oxford: Clarendon Press, 1949). Probably no other school of thought is so basic to the Western mathematical tradition as this mystical movement. It may be added that Pythagoras founded a religious community based on his theory of numbers as well as on the shamanistic doctrine of the transmigration of souls. The community was highly ascetic and ritualized, resembling many of our own spiritual movements in this respect. It was crushed by the expanding Greek state in the fifth century. See Walter Burkert, *Lore and Science in Ancient Pythagoreanism* (Cambridge: Harvard University Press, 1972).

10. Observe how, as soon as we add an article to the term, calling it *an* Ultimate Being, or, worse, *the* Ultimate Being, we have given the game away. I am indebted to David Michael Levin for this suggestion.

11. In the early years of the cold war F. S. C. Northrop argued for the cross-fertilization of the great world cultures in *The Meeting of East and West* (New York: Macmillan, 1946). Obviously Asia took this message more to heart than the Occident, and is now given over to capital. With the results evident in Tokyo, Bangkok, Singapore, and Shanghai, it appears that the survival of the Eastern perspective now depends at least as much on its Western transplants as on its strength in the Oriental heartland.

12. Taoism emerged in fourth-century B.C. China as a critical alternative to the reigning Confucianism. It has survived in two streams: an attitude identified with the early sages, and an organized and highly ritualized faith. The latter plays a major role in Chinese society; see John Lagerway, *Taoist Ritual in Chinese Society and History* (New York: Macmillan, 1987). However, it is the former attitude, associated with the *Tao Teh Ching* and Chuang-Tzu, which has become eponymous for the "Eastern attitude." To be sure, Confucianism, the religion of the state and bureaucracy, has played a larger role in Eastern society than either form of Taoism. See also Max Weber, *The Religion of China*, trans. and ed. Hans H. Gerth (Glencoe, Ill.: Free Press, 1951).

Buddhism, it should be recalled, was an earlier religious innovation than Taoism; indeed, the Buddhists have criticized the Taoist lack of compassion and moral intensity. In that branch of Buddhism known as Zen, however, the Taoist stress on spontaneity found the fullest explication and embodiment in ritual and institution. The Taoist attitude in one degree of adulturation or another also suffuses a great many other spiritual disciplines, from certain strands of Tibetan Buddhism to the faddish variant of Hinduism developed by the recently deceased Bhagwan Shree Rajneesh. The mode of its transmission across doctrines so diverse in time, place, and orientation is complex, but rests fundamentally on the resistance of the Taoism of the sages to become encapsulated in any established religion. This has been associated with its virtually complete freedom from dogmatism.

13. See Heinrich Zimmer, *The Philosophies of India,* ed. Joseph Campbell (Princeton: Princeton University Press, 1969).

14. This rather understates the case for Chuang-Tzu. Graham justifiably places him on the same level as William Blake, as one with "an absolutely fearless eye . . . he gives that slightly hair-raising sensation of the man so much himself that, rather than rebelling against conventional modes of thinking, he

seems free of them by birthright." *Chuang-Tzu: The Seven Inner Chapters and Other Writings from the Book "Chung-Tzu,"* trans. A. C. Graham (London: George Allen and Unwin, 1981), 3–4. A problem is the ferocious difficulty of translation, nay, of even assembling the texts. See p. 27ff. for an excellent discussion of this.

15. John Clark has argued well for Taoism as the first and in many ways unsurpassed critique of domination, as well as a precursor of philosophical anarchism, in "On Taoism and Politics," *Journal of Chinese Philosophy* 10 (1983): 65–88. As Max Kaltenmark has written, "[The early Taoists] felt that any abrogation of their freedom or any compromise with the ruling powers would defile them." *Lao-Tzu and Taoism,* trans. Roger Greaves (Stanford: Stanford University Press, 1969).

16. Chap. 4, from *Tao Teh Ching,* trans. John H. C. Wu (Boston and Shaftesbury: Shambala, 1989).

17. Thomas Merton, *The Way of Chuang-Tzu* (New York: New Directions, 1965), 11.

18. It would be distracting to pursue the point here, but what is being described can also apply to psychoanalytic praxis at its deepest, the difference being that psychotherapy continues holding onto logos with one hand while releasing it from the other. This is only another way of stating that the plasma of being is at the end of psychoanalytic work just as Tao is at the end of Eastern meditative practice. After many years of practice and meditating on the essence of psychoanalytic work, it finally seemed to me that its truth was in the simplest, most elemental kind of "being there" with another person.

19. *Tao Teh Ching,* Chap. 39.

20. It must be said that the Buddhist and Hindu monasteries of today tend to be light-years from the ideals of the Tao. True, they provide a meditative space; but along with this, and in some ways as a condition for it, they also tend to embody the most arrant sexism and exploitation. This is tied up with the virtually inevitable guru system, according to which an authoritarian figure, usually but not necessarily male, exploits the nonspiritual desire which is necessarily released in the abandonment of the self to an influx of spirit. This may also be seen as a perpetuation of the feudal relations from which the religions sprang in an era where such relations have lost all rational content and can only serve reactionary ends.

21. This fact did not remove ancient religion from politics; quite the contrary, it raised the stakes. As sublime as they could be, the practitioners of the original Eastern faiths were just as ambivalently embroiled in the world as is the Vatican of today. Thus they could oppose emperors, but also prescribe foot-binding for women.

22. *Paradiso,* chap. 33, lines 142–45, trans. Philip Henry Wicksteed, quoted in Huntington Cairns, *The Limits of Art* (Princeton: Bollingen, 1948), 391.

23. Nygren, *Agape and Eros.*

24. The only unconditional love which Freud posited was that of a mother for her son—surely one of the odder notions the great "master of suspicion" ever put to paper. It undoubtedly reflected Freud's deep attachment to his own mother. See Peter Gay, *Freud: A Life for Our Times* (New York: Doubleday Anchor, 1989).

25. Freud's trifiguration of the psyche into ego, id, and superego is paralleled in the Christian Trinity, where God the Father, the source of all power, speaks in the place of the id, while the ego becomes the figure of Jesus which the self incorporates, and the Holy Spirit, the voice of God, is the superego. Freud emphasized that the superego drew from both id and ego, just as the Holy Spirit combines Father and Son. The root of this tripartite thinking is Plato, as discussed in Bennett Simon, *Mind and Madness in Ancient Greece* (Ithaca, N.Y.: Cornell University Press, 1978).

26. Peter Brock, *The Roots of War Resistance: Pacifism from the Early Church to Tolstoy* (Nyack, N.Y.: Fellowship of Reconciliation, 1981).

27. See Sara Diamond, *Spiritual Warfare*. In the case of Rios Montt, it is worth observing that he was "inspired" by Gospel Outreach, a California-based cult of "Jesus Freaks," themselves an offshoot of the sixties counterculture. For the nightmare of Guatemalan repression and its connection with the U.S. security apparatus, see Michael McClintock, *State Terror and Popular Resistance in Guatemala* vol. 2 of *The American Connection* (London: Zed, 1985). (Volume One, equally impressive, is about El Salvador.)

28. For a moving account of the growth and tribulation of the people's church, see Penny Lernoux, *Cry of the People* (New York: Penguin, 1982).

29. For details, see Colledge and McGinn, *The Complete Sermons*. The church has recently forgiven Eckhart for his radical temerity, though it was quite correct, in my opinion, to recognize him as a threat to its dogmatic authority.

30. *Che Guevara Speaks,* ed. George Lavan (New York: Grove Press, 1967), 136.

Chapter 6. Paths of Soul

1. And conversely, become less true as they stray from spirit. Thus a fragmented psychology, without consciousness, without organic filiations, without associations to class and the economy—in short, a positivistic, instrumental, behaviorist psychology—is false in the very narrowness of its truth. Similarly, we can call psychoanalysis a potentially truer kind of psychology because of its appropriation of desire and the plasma of being, but still criticize it for its greater or lesser fidelity to spirit.

2. I have been forced to set aside the spiritual associations of art for reasons of economy. A separate volume would be required to analyze the different art forms, the aesthetic state of being, and many fascinating matters such as "soul" music, liturgical art, and so forth, all in relation to history. If such an account were to be written according to the line of thought developed here, it would be centered, I think, about the notion of the *work* of art, as a created being outside of the constraints of everyday life. Since the work of art is not figured against the ground of actual others, it affords desire a free field, unlimited by the traps of Egoism. Thus art is the realm of exuberance and plenitude, irrespective of questions of medium, genre, and subject matter. But this only begins to state the problem.

3. Erik Erikson, *Young Man Luther* (New York: W. W. Norton, 1956), Norman O. Brown's *Life Against Death* also deals extensively with the theme.

4. Max Weber, "Religious Rejections," describes this for traditional religions, but the same would hold true for secular spirituality.

5. The Greek root of technique, *techne*, means "art" or "craft," a notion which in itself is not cut off from spirituality. But in the age of despiritualization, "technique" has come to signify all those purely instrumental measures in which the notion of being has been obliterated. A great deal of New Age spirituality and pop psychology comes under this heading; indeed, so does much of psychotherapy.

6. The insight that a synthesis between modern political and traditional cultural forms of spirit would be a more potent revolutionizing force than either could be separately has arisen at several points, most notably in Europe in the work of Antonio Gramsci, and in Latin America from Jose Carlos Mariátegui. See Antonio Gramsci, *Selections from the Prison Notebooks,* ed. and trans. Quinton Hoare and Geoffrey Newell Smith (New York: International Publishers, 1971); Alastair Davidson, *Antonio Gramsci: Toward an Intellectual Biography* (London: Merlin, 1977); Jose Carlos Mariátegui, *Seven Interpretative Essays on Peruvian Reality,* trans. Marjory Urquidi (Austin: University of Texas Press, 1971); Jesus Chavarria, *Jose Carlos Mariátegui and the Rise of Modern Peru, 1890–1930* (Albuquerque: University of New Mexico Press, 1979). It is not accidental that these figures, unlike most other great Marxists, arose from the ranks of the lower classes. Liberation theology is very definitely one of the fruits of such an insight. We tend to forget how much liberation theology is shaped, in a kind of "reverse mission," by the organic precolumbian spiritualities of Latin America. It is certainly not a simple Eurocentric development. See Paul Buhle and Thomas Fierher, "Liberation Theology and Latin America: Dispensations Old and New," *The Year Left* 1 (London: Verso, 1985): 203–38.

7. Giulio Girardi, *Sandinismo, Marxismo, Cristianismo en la Nueva Nicaragua: La Confluencia* (Managua: Centro Antonio Valdivieso, 1987); Donald C. Hodges, *Intellectual Foundations of the Nicaraguan Revolution* (Austin: University of Texas Press, 1986). Hodges quotes a contemporary observer: "I realized the strange profound soul of Sandino had created in his army a religious sect imbued with the fire of a new revelation," and himself adds, "His soldiers recognized the spirituality of this remarkable man who became their teacher as well as general," 15, 16.

8. The "Light and Truth Manifesto," quoted in Hodges, *Intellectual Foundations,* 59.

9. Roque Dalton, *Miguel Mármol,* trans. Kathleen Ross and Richard Schaaf (Willimantic, Conn.: Curbstone Press, 1987). See also Joel Kovel, "Two Spiritual Revolutionaries," *Monthly Review* 40 (January 1989): 22–34. This deals also with the North American Jesuit, Father James "Guadelupe" Carney, another legendary figure among Central American revolutionaries. See Carney's memoir, *To Be a Christian Is to Be a Revolutionary.*

10. See Eric Wolf, *Peasant Wars of the Twentieth Century* (New York: Harper, 1969). I have witnessed similar qualities among the South Africans struggling against apartheid.

11. One might say that the "yuppie" represents a subset of the New Class defined by its lack of interest in transcendence, its utter materialism. The derisiveness attached to the term reflects, I think, a lingering desire for spiritual fulfillment.

12. In fact, the class of technocrats is becoming rapidly distanced from a vast, growing, and increasingly pauperized underclass. The American economy has long prided itself on its ability to paper over class differences. Those days are gone, probably for good. See Benjamin DeMott, *The Imperial Middle* (New York: William Morrow, 1990).

13. Chomsky has written voluminously on this theme. For a study of Central America, see *Turning the Tide* (Boston: South End Press, 1985), especially chap. 2, "The Fifth Freedom," i.e., the freedom to rob.

14. Robert Bellah, et al., *Habits of the Heart* (New York: Harper and Row, 1986).

15. I say "reflects," because there is no sharp distinction between cause and effect in this system. Self-preoccupation and breakdown of community are each cause and effect of the other. The economy has a relatively greater degree of autonomy, because of its iron laws of accumulation; yet it, too, is partly determined by self-centeredness (which creates the psychological type for capitalist production and consumption) as well as loss of community (for an organic community would have no place for either the capitalist workplace or its shopping malls).

16. This imperative was later scrapped, largely because of AIDS.

17. Frances Fitzgerald, *Cities on a Hill* (New York: Simon and Schuster, 1986). Rajneesh's clientele was concentrated among the highly educated and sophisticated elements of the New Class. Given the concentration of talent and resources these devotees who numbered over 100,000 could mobilize, it is not surprising that Rajneeshpuram, the "City on a Hill" which the faithful built in the wilds of Oregon, went as far as it did before the spiritual and political bills came due. The Bhagwan was deported for illegally performing weddings, and a number of his disciples were jailed for attempted murder and other crimes, which were related to a ruthless struggle for power at the top. After his deportation in 1985, Rajneesh went back to India, reconstituted something of his ashram, and died in 1990.

18. Mosse, *The Crisis of German Ideology*, 305–6. See also Fest, *Face of the Third Reich*.

19. Jean Michel Angeberg, *The Occult and the Third Reich: The Mystical Origins of Nazism and the Search for the Holy Grail* (New York: McGraw-Hill, 1974), a very peculiar work. Much of this line of reasoning—which we do not have the space to examine further—is a dubious effort to depoliticize Nazism and avoid looking at its actual nightmare. Nonetheless the theme of the grail was undoubtedly present in Nazism.

20. Wilhelm Reich, *The Mass Psychology of Fascism*, trans. Vincent Carfagno (New York: Simon and Schuster, 1970).

21. See Isaac Deutscher, *Stalin* (New York: Oxford, 1967). Updated studies exist on this malignant figure, but none have Deutscher's depth or perspective.

22. The most famous literary account of the Stalinist trap remains Arthur Koestler's *Darkness at Noon*, trans. Daphne Hardy (New York: Bantam, 1981).

23. See Raya Dunayevskaya, *Philosophy and Revolution* (New York: Dell, 1973), for a similar line of reasoning based on Hegelian Marxism.

24. Saint John of the Cross, "The Ascent of Mount Carmel," bk. 1, chap. 1: 11, in John of the Cross, *Selected Writings,* trans. Kieran Kavanaugh (New York: Paulist Press, 1987), 78. Reprinted by permission.

25. See n. 12, Introduction.

26. Even though capitalism is the actual ancien régime, it is striking how this order captures the lingo of the new. Thus China's diversion from the path of socialist construction onto the capitalist road is called its "modernization," as is the revamping of the West's nuclear arsenal at the behest of the military-industrial complex. The notion is most deeply anchored in the industries of fashion and mass culture, especially in their capacity to redefine the notion of femininity. See Michèle Mattelart, *Women, Media and Crisis* (London: Comedia, 1986).

27. As contrasted to the "cult of the leader" which arises in negation to this, and from the frustration of hopes for transcendence. See Dalton, *Miguel Mármol,* for a portrait of revolutionary selflessness.

28. We must be careful not to oversimplify here. The line between religious insight and real madness is not a clearly drawn one. In actual life, where splitting of Ego occurs constantly, many people have both states of being simultaneously, much to the confusion of the reductive mind of the psychiatrist. My point is only that spirituality and madness are two distinct states which may occur separately or combined. That is, some people are soul-ful and not mad, others are mad and not soul-ful, and others still are both soul-ful and mad. A wider canvas would be necessary to do justice to this theme.

29. One of the bugbears of meditative practice. In the Zen service, monitors are often assigned to rap with sticks on the shoulders of those who doze.

30. Saint Francis (chap. 2, n. 38) combined cleverness with sublimity to a unique degree. He often had to take it upon himself to correct or rein in some of his more foolish disciples. Pope John XXIII, the holiest of modern pontiffs, was also a man of farsighted and subtle judgment. In short, the highest degree of soul is fully compatible with shrewdness. Nobody ever said that being a saint meant being stupid. Moreover, the domain enclosed by psychology remains whether one develops soul or not. Certain spheres may be enhanced by soul; to be more exact, they may be charged by spirit-power, while others may play a lesser role in the mental economy. However, the person remains recognizable whether the direction of soul or Ego is pursued.

31. Freud, *Group Psychology.*

32. We should not sentimentalize. All groups are vulnerable to infusions of irrationality. A rationally constituted soul group is still one in which individuals put themselves at risk of malignant Otherness. The "dark night of the soul," that is, the influx of madness once Ego barriers are down, is always a possibility. It is important to realize, too, that this possibility increases as the group is itself marginalized, which is necessarily the case when society as a whole is irrational. The more rational the soul group in such circumstances, the further out and the more at risk it is from its own violence.

33. Victor Wolfenstein, *The Victims of Democracy* (Berkeley: University of California Press, 1981), has a fine discussion—in the context of the life of Malcolm X—of the convergence of paranoia with normal capitalist group life. The common ground is the Hobbesian jungle of each against all.

34. This point is relevant to the training and counseling of mental health workers and members of the ministry, many of whom find themselves exhausted and "burnt out" by their constant giving. In my years of training mental health workers, we encountered the problem very frequently. Usually it was ascribed to an unresolved infantile conflict leading to a "rescue fantasy," or "unsatisfied dependency needs." But I think that these were only the psychological correlates of a fuller and more complex state of being.

35. Meister Eckhart, Sermon 6, in *The Essential Sermons* (1981), 186.

36. Ibid., 185.

37. Bernard of Clairvaux, "On Loving God," in *Selected Works,* trans. G. R. Evans, The Classics of Western Spirituality (New York: Paulist Press, 1987). Reprinted by permission.

38. For discussion of the capitalist roots of the environmental crisis, see Harry Magdoff and Paul Sweezy, "Capitalism and the Environment," *Monthly Review* 41 (June 1989): 1–10; James O'Connor, "Capitalism, Nature, Socialism: A Theoretical Introduction," *Capitalism, Nature, Socialism* 1 (Fall 1988): 11–38.

39. In these days when socialism is being written out of the books, we might remind ourselves that socialist societies have been able to provide for the well-being of great masses of people much better than capitalist societies at a comparable level of development. Thus China did better than India before its system went haywire; while Cuba, that bête noire of the U.S. establishment, is for all its troubles a veritable paradise compared to the showcases of Latin American capitalism—for the poor that is. Indeed, standard of living indices in Cuba—literacy, life expectancy, infant mortality, and so forth—are superior to those of inner city blacks in Chicago and other metropolises of capitalist wealth.

40. One instance among the countless: in the USSR, the Aral Sea, one of the world's largest freshwater bodies, is about to disappear, owing to the diversion of the rivers which fed it. Fishing towns which used to be on the coast are now thirty miles or so from the water. This is leading to regional climatic changes, among other calamities. To be sure, these changes, massive as they are, remain in some degree local. Socialism never mustered the global power to bring about the kinds of worldwide transformations we can lay at the doorstep of capital, e.g., fuel consumption with carbon dioxide release, ozone destruction, deforestation. This of course is nothing to congratulate the Soviet bloc and China about. I may add, however, that the Sandinistas in Nicaragua remained remarkably open to ecological innovation during their stay in power—although there was a considerable degree of struggle with those who wanted, understandably, in view of the country's horrendous poverty, to rush pell-mell toward the maximization of productive forces. There can be no easy answers to the ecological crisis, especially in the context of the near-starvation brought about by centuries of brutal exploitation. Of course the whole was shadowed by Washington's remorseless cruelty to the Nicaraguan revolution—in the face of which Sandinista openness becomes all the more remarkable.

41. In Bottomore, ed., *Early Writings*. There is a well-worn controversy in Marxism over the degree to which the "Manuscripts" are continuous with

Marx's later political and economic doctrines, as against a youthful diversion. There is no need to enter this debate here. I would say only that the "Manuscripts" expressed the philosophical core of a project with many potential outcomes. A number have been tried and found wanting—and would likely have been rejected by Marx himself. Others have yet to be explored, whatever the historical Marx may have meant.

42. See Mészáros, *Marx's Theory of Alienation*, 1975, for a discussion.

43. See also Frederick Engels, *Dialectics of Nature* (New York: International Publishers, 1940). Lest we be too harsh on Marx (and Engels) here, mention should be made of a fascinating footnote to the history of Marxist thought, the notion of "Qual." I know of two passages in the massive corpus of Marx and Engels in which this mystical notion, drawn from no less a figure than Jacob Boehme, is introduced: The first is from "The Holy Family," 1844, quoted in Marx and Engels, *On Religion,* 64: "The first and most important of the inherent qualities of matter is motion, not only mechanical and mathematical movement, but still more, impulse, vital life-spirit, tension, or, to use Jacob Böhme's expression, the throes [*Qual*] of matter. The primary forms of matter are the living, individualizing forces of being inherent in it and producing the distinctions between the species." The second mention of "Qual" appears in a note by Engels to the English edition of *Socialism: Utopian and Scientific,* 1892, Ibid., 291. "'Qual'" is a philosophical play on words. Qual literally means torture, a pain which drives to action of some kind; at the same time the mystic Böhme puts into the German word something of the meaning of the Latin *qualitas;* his "qual" was the activating principle arising from, and prompting in its turn, the spontaneous development of the thing, relation, or person subject to it, in contradistinction to a pain inflicted from without." The problem is that these remarkable insights, which express a subterranean tradition in the philosophy of nature, remain a footnote. They still await their realization in a philosophy of praxis.

44. I do not wish to glamorize actually existing tribal peoples. As we know, many preindustrial societies have depleted their resource bases, and in general behaved unwisely toward nature; while the sacralization of nature is constantly being rediscovered in the midst of technologically advanced society. However, it is important to realize that the insight that nature is the ground of being and therefore sacred is one which derives from the beginning of society, before the growth of the state and technocracy. We should understand, therefore, that in working toward an ecological society we are also trying to reclaim something from the origins of society.

45. See Ynestra King, "Healing the Wound: Feminism and the Nature/ Culture Dualism," in Alison Jaggar and Susan Bordo, eds., *Gender/Body/ Knowledge* (New Brunswick, N.J.: Rutgers University Press, 1989), 115–41; Ynestra King, *Ecofeminism and the Reenchantment of Nature* (Boston: Beacon Press, forthcoming); and Judith Plant, ed., *Healing the Wounds* (Philadelphia: New Society, 1989). Of similar origin is the association of feminism with antimilitarism. See Pam McAllister, ed., *Reweaving the Web of Life* (Philadelphia: New Society, 1987); Sara Ruddick, *Maternal Thinking* (Boston: Beacon Press, 1988); and Adrienne Haris and Ynestra King, eds., *Rocking the Ship of State: Toward a Feminist Peace Politics* (Boulder: Westview Press, 1989). Note how recent these publications are—the movement is both rapidly growing and one of the few survivors of recent political disasters.

46. A more complete discussion would require attending to the tension between "social ecological" and "deep ecological" perspectives. This has generated much controversy, particularly along the spiritual dimension. The social ecological approach (for which see Murray Bookchin, *The Ecology of Freedom*) stands within the anarchist and post-Enlightenment tradition, and is more democratic in outlook but tends to have less of a spiritual orientation. This weakens its appeal relative to the deep ecological perspective, which engages the spiritual relation to nature but tends to be uncritical and politically obtuse. We await a true synthesis of these perspectives, though ecofeminism is clearly moving in this direction.

47. Duerr, *Dreamtime,* is a vast and panoramic compendium, arranged with verve. I would give this work higher praise were it not for Duerr's unrelenting hatred of Marx, which leads him to ignore the one Marxist principle essential for the understanding of these phenomena: the role played by production in society. There is therefore no historical grounding to the soul-passages Duerr outlines; they just seem to happen out of the air. Also, there is no way to distinguish between Duerr's values and those of nature-fascism, which I assume he does not share.

48. See Jacques Derrida, *Of Grammatology,* trans. Gyatry Spivak (Baltimore: Johns Hopkins Press, 1976); and *Writing and Difference,* trans. Alan Bass (Chicago: University of Chicago Press, 1978). For a penetrating critique, see Dews, *Logics of Disintegration.* Derrida can seem a contemporary version of Chuang-Tzu, with his endless insistence on the inadequacies of logos and the vanity of all received ideas. Like the ancient sage, Derrida is also a master at poking fun. At times, indeed, he seems to have broken loose from the prison of language into a hitherto unentered space of nondiscursive writing. And yet one would never read Derrida as a Taoist: the "spirit" of emancipation which renders Taoist texts an eternal delight is absent from his obsessive attack on signification—as is the entire category of spirit. In fact, Derrida's thought may be read as the definitive philosophical effort to read spirituality out of thought. Where Chuang-Tzu and Lao-Tzu seek to shake the mind free of its chains so that Ultimate Being can be confronted through the Way, Derrida flees into another cage—that of the text. There is nothing to be said within language—yet nothing but language: surely one of the bleakest perspectives ever advanced on the human condition. The Chinese masters defeat logocentrism through aphorism; their texts remain as brief poetic signposts indicating Ultimate Being, Derrida, however, writes endlessly within a labyrinth of the deepest philosophical abstraction—the most metaphysical attempt to overcome metaphysics there ever was. There is nothing signified by this abstraction, because for him there is nothing beyond or within. Yet while Derrida tells us that nothing can mean anything, he tries to rivet our attention, thus indicating that *he* means something, even if he doesn't. In this respect, Derrida behaves like the Irishman in the logical puzzle who informs us that "all Irishmen are liars," in which case he is not an Irishman, hence truthful, etc. Of course Derrida needn't mind this, since truth cannot exist and he can claim to have escaped from this trap in his language. On the other hand, Irishmen do exist, and

liars—and unless thought is mediated to a real signified, it chases its own tail. Finally, Derrida bypasses the problem of production, even though he is one of the most productive of modern thinkers. His claim is that being exists only in the interstices of the fracture-points of language—its *différance,* to advert to a Derridean neologism. This, however, is little more than a solipsism in its "in-difference" to the world, whether to the world of the organism or to the social world. It is a claim, essentially, that nothing like production ever takes place or even matters in human affairs. This is the classic elevation of the intellectual over the common herd, an illusion much favored by the ruling classes. Thus Derrida shows that the paradoxical effect of trying to think free of any meta-physical assumptions is to lose reality itself. Abandoning the transcendent is also abandoning the real.

49. See Chapter Three, 98ff.

50. Because information is considered the very life-plasma of advanced capitalism, it has been subjected to a great deal of fetishization. Nowhere is this more apparent than in the idolization of the computer as a kind of super-mind. Yet the limits of the computer are inscribed precisely in its undifferenti-ated being. No matter how many billions of calculations the computer can un-dertake in a second, it will never have a soul, despite all the yearnings projected onto it.

51. This observation touches on the massive philosophical project of Jurgen Habermas. See his *Theory of Communicative Action,* trans. Thomas McCarthy (Boston: Beacon Press, 1984, 1989). To present Habermas ade-quately would greatly exceed present limits. The considerations presented here raise the issue of an ontological dimension within the communicative action which Habermas rightly considers the foundation of society.

52. William Shakespeare, *Hamlet,* I, v. 166–67. In *The Complete Works,* 743.

53. To be exact, Ego thinks of nonrational objects as without being. This makes them unreal and chaotic, hence irrational. Then they are treated as such in their actuality, which only confirms them in this irrationality. An important example is the genesis of so-called mental illness, with its progressive stig-matization of the deviant, until the deviant has to take upon him- or herself the way of being of madness. All of this also interdigitates with the institutions of rationalization which are supposed to convert madness into sanity. For further discussion, see Kovel, *The Age of Desire.*

54. There are orders of infinity. The set of whole numbers is infinite, as is the number of points on a line. But the latter is infinitely greater than the for-mer. Just so, the infinity of Ultimate Being is infinitely greater than the infinite potential of human being.

Index

Adorno, Theodor, 12–13, 234
Agape [love], 127, 183, 190–92, 194–96, 211, 223
Aggression, 82–83, 136–40. *See also* Violence
Alienation/aloneness, 8, 18–19, 24, 52, 55, 93, 166, 204–12, 215–17
Annihilation, 12, 65, 122, 125, 126, 144, 149, 157
Appropriation, 91–92, 94–96, 100, 215, 216
Arnhem Land [Australia], 113–14, 117, 122, 132
Art, 30–31, 98–99, 230
Asceticism, 120–21, 128–33, 160–61
Attachment, 81, 105, 172, 226. *See also* Detachment; Nonattachment
Augustine, 131, 222–23
Authentic spirit. *See* Spirit-meaning

Bataille, Georges, 122–23
Becoming, 108, 166, 182
Being: and divine spirit, 177, 180, 184–89, 191, 192–93, 195; and history, 88, 89, 172, 187; junctures of, 87–91; limitations of the discussion of, 13–14; and "no-thing," 170–72; and ontogeny, 169–72; and the Other, 90–91, 133–34, 149, 162–63, 167, 169, 170–71, 172, 215; plasma of, 161–72, 184–86, 187, 189, 192; and praxis, 162–72; quest for, 70–72; and spirit-meaning, 65, 70–91, 94–96, 100, 102, 104, 105–6, 109; and spirit-power, 28–29, 35, 37, 102; and "thing," 170–72; and

violence/nonviolence, 138–40, 148, 149, 152, 153, 168. *See also* Being—and desire; Being—and ego; Being—and the self; Being—and spirituality; Infantile being; Is-ness; Soul; Spirit-being; Ultimate Being/Universal Being; *name of specific topic*
Being—and desire: and the body, 155, 156, 158–59, 160, 161; and divine spirit, 189; and ego, 135, 144, 148, 166; and the plasma of being, 161–72; and sacred sex, 114, 116; and the self, 161, 162–63, 166–67, 169, 170–71; and sin, 135–36, 138–40; and spirituality, 124, 126, 130–31, 133–35, 202; and spiritual pride, 140–41, 144, 147; and violence/nonviolence, 148, 149, 152, 153
Being—and ego: and desire, 135, 144, 148, 166; and self, 166; and spirit-meaning, 83–87, 105–6; and spirituality, 205, 215, 220–22, 228–29
Being—and the self: and desire, 130–31, 133–34, 144, 161, 162–63, 166–67, 169, 170–71; and ego, 166; and spirit-meaning, 76–77, 87–91; and spirituality, 197–98, 214–15, 221
Being—and spirituality: and being spiritual, 197–98, 199; and death, 236; and desire, 124, 126, 130–31, 133–35, 202; and ego, 205, 215, 220–22, 228–29; and the embodiment of soul, 225–30; and giving, 218, 219, 221–22; and logos, 230–33; in modern

Heidegger, Martin: and being/non-being, 28–29, 37, 89, 90–91, 167–68, 170; contributions of, 28–29; and desire, 145–46, 167–68, 170; and divine spirit, 177, 180; and existentialism, 89, 91; and God/godhead, 168; as a model for the study of spirituality, 5–6; and nature, 104; and politics, 37–39, 90–91, 104; and religion, 4, 28–29; and spirit-meaning, 89, 90–91, 104; and spirit-power, 28–29, 37–39; and spiritual pride, 145–46; and the unconscious, 167–68, 170; and utopianism, 90–91
Heraclitus, 147–48
Himmler, Heinrich, 141–42, 146, 212
Hinduism, 3, 7, 32, 42, 106, 184, 210
Historical dialectic, 132
Historical materialism, 94–96, 225–26
History: and being, 88, 89, 172, 187; denial of, 145–46; and desire, 145–46, 172; and divine spirit, 187, 190, 193–94; and nature, 137, 147; and the Other, 48, 94–96; recycling of, 146–47; and soul, 109; and spirit, 2, 4, 5–6; and spirit-meaning, 88, 89, 109; and spirituality, 197, 198, 202, 225–26, 231. *See also name of specific topic*
Hitler, Adolf, 62, 213, 235
Holocaust, 12–13, 63, 141–42, 146
Holy Spirit, 30, 51–52, 62, 127, 140, 191, 223
Homosexuality, 118
Human nature/spirit, 107–10
Hume, David, 48
Husserl, Edmund, 26

Id, 2, 85, 156, 165–66, 212, 220, 229
Ideology, 143–44, 205–6, 207

Individual: and being, 166–67; and desire, 166–67; and guilt, 135; and meaningfulness, 92; mind of the, 88; and the Other, 234; and social relations/society, 78–80, 88, 135, 166–67, 234; and spirit-meaning, 88, 92; and spirituality, 11–12, 198, 199, 234; and Universal Being, 234
Individualism/individuality, 9, 11, 81, 92, 161, 166–67, 216–17, 219, 220, 235
Infantile being [Freud], 66–70, 71, 79, 86, 106, 130
Innocent VIII, 118–19
Inspiration, 25, 29–36, 201, 203. *See also* Charisma
Instincts, 82–83, 123, 126, 129, 136–37, 138, 146–47, 149, 159, 163, 167
Irrationality. *See* Rationality/reason
Islam, 3, 32, 33, 173, 175, 180, 190
Is-ness, 73, 176–77, 178
Israel, 144–46

James, William, 86, 112, 122
Jerome, Saint, 121
Jesus Christ: and desire, 118, 120, 139, 152, 153, 190; and divine spirit, 180–81, 183, 190, 191, 192, 196; and the godhead, 62; and inspiration, 29–30; and the Living God, 180–81; and logos, 62; and love, 190, 191; as the Redeemer, 153, 183, 191; and sacred sex, 118, 120; and shamanism, 59; and sin, 139, 153; and spirit-being, 59, 62; and spirit-power, 29–30; sword of, 139, 152, 190
Jews, 47, 62–63, 109–10, 141–42, 144–46, 147, 173–74, 177, 198, 212
John the Baptist, 139
John of the Cross, 57–58, 59, 229
John Paul II, 118, 122, 156, 193
John XXIII [Angelo Roncalli], 128–33, 160–61, 193

189–90, 194, 195, 213, 220, 228, 235; as concrete, 4; and consciousness, 78–79; and death, 105; and ego, 234–35; and groups, 78–79, 100; and individual, 234; and logos, 233; and loss, 219; search for the, 173–78; and soul, 233–36

Ultimate Being/Universal Being: and spirit-meaning, 78–79, 100, 105

Ultimate Being/Universal Being: and spirituality, 197, 209, 213, 219, 223–24, 233, 234–36; as unpredicate-able, 176, 179, 181, 186. *See also* Divine spirit; God/godhead

Unconscious, 28, 106, 163–72, 184, 230–31, 232

Unity: and being, 87, 172; and consciousness, 87; and desire, 115, 126–27, 134, 172; and love, 126–27; and mysticism, 27; and the self, 41; and spirit-being, 41, 44; and spirit-meaning, 67, 68–69, 87; in tribal societies, 7; and Ultimate Being, 234

Upanishads, 32–33

Utopianism, 91, 97–99, 153–54, 201, 202, 211, 235

Van der Leeuw, Gerardus, 23, 24, 86, 116, 152–53

Violence: and being/nonbeing, 138–40, 148, 149, 168; and capitalism, 149; and class, 148–49; and death, 149, 236; definition of, 138; and desire, 138–40, 145, 147, 148–49, 168; and differentiation/splitting, 145–46, 148, 149, 150; and domination, 148–49; as ecstatic, 139–40; and ego, 148, 150; and hatred,

148; and the Holocaust, 146; and instincts, 149; and logos, 148, 232; and the master-slave relationship, 147–50; and morality, 149; and the Other, 149, 150; and politics, 150; and religion, 139–40; and repetition, 149; and the self, 139–40, 150; and sin, 138–39, 140–41; and soul, 150; and spirit-being, 139–40; and spirit-power, 139–40; and spirituality, 199, 200, 203, 214, 217, 221–22, 224, 226–27, 232, 234, 236; and spiritual pride, 140–41, 145, 147, 149. *See also* Aggression; Nonviolence; Revolutionary movements

"The Vulva Song of Inana" [Sumer civilization], 112–13

War, 145, 150, 154, 214
Way, the, 184, 185, 188, 189, 214
Weber, Max, 2
West Bank/Gaza Strip, 144–46
Whitehead, Alfred North, 43–44, 47
Witches, 7, 30, 43, 55–56, 63, 118–20, 141, 229–30
Wittgenstein, Ludwig, 40, 236
Women, 55–56, 63, 68, 155, 207, 226, 227. *See also* Gender
Work, 18–19, 169
Worldview, 11–13

Yahweh, 173–74, 175, 177
Yoruba people, 22
Young Hegelians, 90

Zaehner, R. C., 33
Zen Buddhism, 31–32, 36–37, 38–39, 183, 189, 194, 210
Zionism, 146, 147, 180